The Preacher
and
His Preaching

The Preacher
and His Preaching

or, "Thyself, and the Doctrine" (I Tim. 4:16).

Helpful Information to Christians who are interested in
the preparation and presentation of the
gospel and teaching
message.

By

ALFRED P. GIBBS

Author of "Through the Scriptures," "A Dreamer and His Dream,"
"The Marvelous City of Mansoul," "Worship," "Gospel Hymns and
Choruses for Young and Old," Numbers 1, 2, 3, 4, 5, 6, and 7;
"God's Good News," "Scriptural Principles of Gathering," "The
Christian's Guide," "Ye Must Be Born Again," "The Uplifted Christ,"
"The Lord's Supper," etc.

WITH A FOREWORD BY

H. G. LOCKETT, M. A., B. Paed

SIXTH EDITION

Box 2216 Kansas City
Kansas

Printed in U.S.A.

OUTLINE OF CONTENTS

Chapter 1. *The Qualifications of the Preacher*

I. *He must be regenerated.*
1. The possibility of self deception.
2. The description of such mere professors.
3. The necessity for the preacher's own assurance of salvation.

II. *He must love the Lord Jesus.*
1. The love of Christ, the constraining motive.
2. The example of Christ in love.
3. The commission to His disciples.

III. *He must love souls.*
1. Possible to love to preach, and not love souls.
2. Christ's passion for souls.
3. Need for a right estimate of the value of a soul.

Chapter 2. *The Qualifications of the Preacher*

IV. *He must be a student of the Bible.*
1. He must know it by reading it.
2. Must quote it from memory.
3. Must study it by diligent application.
He must be a D.D.D.D.

V. *He must be a man of prayer.*
1. Our example in prayer.
2. Our encouragement in prayer.
   (1) Regarding each detail of his life.
   (2) Each aspect of his service.
3. Prayer in the life of Paul.

VI. *He must be clean in his life.*

3

2. Born in a spiritual atmosphere.
3. Comes in midst of Christian activity.
II. *It is definite.*
III. *It is varied in circumstances.* Some examples.
IV. *It does not necessarily involve full time service.*
   1. No distinction, in New Testament, between "clergy," and "laity."
   2. The evils of professionalism in the Lord's work.
V. *The elements that combine to constitute a Divine Call.*
   1. The inward urge of the Holy Spirit.
   2. Some definite word from the Scriptures to deepen conviction.
   3. The compassions of the heart.
   4. The advice of godly Christians.
   5. The word and action of some Spirit-led servant of God.
   6. The Divine ordering of God's providences.
   7. The commendation of one's home assembly.

I. *The God-ordained means of spreading the gospel.*
   1. The Divine order outlined. (Rom. 10:9-17).
   2. The Divine commission given. (Matt. 28:18-20).
   3. The Divine program being carried out.
   4. The Divine terms examined.
II. *Preaching is a witness to the facts of the gospel.*
   1. The definition of a witness.
   2. The purpose of a witness.
   3. The gospel is a manifestation of the truth of God.
   4. Witness illustrated in the Acts.
III. *Preaching is the means of generating faith in the hearer.*

4. The danger of appealing to one part of the personality at the expense of the others.
5. The Intellect.
   (1) An endowment of God.
   (2) Enlightened through the Word.
   (3) Appealed to in the Scriptures.
6. The Emotions.
7. The Will.
   (1) God respects it and never coerces it.
   (2) God demands unconditional surrender of it.
   (3) The preacher must demand a decision from it.
8. A study of the word "heart," in Scripture.

I. *Scripture contemplates full-time preachers,* called, equipped, commended, and sent forth.
II. *These should be supported by the saints.*
   I Cor. 9:1-23.
   1. Paul's authority stated. The four questions. vs. 1-3.
   2. Paul's right to maintenance declared. vs. 4-6.
   3. Paul's proof of his right to maintenance. vs. 7-14. The four appeals.
   4. The inevitable conclusion. v. 14.
III. *Paul's right to support waived by grace.* vs. 15-23.
   1. The preacher must be independent of man.
   2. The preacher is responsible alone to the Lord for
      (1) His field.
      (2) Nature of work.
      (3) Methods he uses.
   3. The preacher's determination.
      (1) To preach the gospel freely.
      (2) To seek by all means to win souls.

I. *The peril of undue familiarity with Divine things.*

5. *The Conclusion.*
   (1) The definition of it.
   (2) Some suggestions regarding it.
       It should be
       (a) Short.
       (b) Varied.
       (c) Real.
       (d) Personal.
       (e) Pointed.
       (f) Conclude.
       (g) Elements of a good address.

   I. *Reading.*
      1. The advantages.
      2. The disadvantages.
  II. *Recitation.*
      1. The advantages.
      2. The disadvantages.
 III. *Extemporaneous.*
      1. The advantages.
      2. The disadvantages.

      Introduction.
      1. The example of Christ.
      2. The example of Paul.
   I. *The Personal Testimony.*
      1. The definition of it.
      2. The value of it.
      3. The importance of it.
      4. Hints on the telling of it.
      5. The dangers of it.

  II. *The Expository Sermon.*
      1. The definition of it.
      2. The advantages of it.

13

14

  (5) He should be careful in his use of Divine titles.

 4. The language used should be correctly pronounced.
  (1) A good dictionary essential.
  (2) A pronouncing Bible is useful.
  (3) Be a discriminating reader.
  (4) "The well dressed message."
    (Dr. Norman Bartlett).

III. *He should watch his voice.*
 1. The possibilities of the voice.
 2. The four powers of the voice.
 3. The three pitches of the voice.
 4. The purpose of the voice.
 5. Some poor examples of the voice.
  (1) The Mumbler.
  (2) The Yeller.
  (3) The Sing-song.
  (4) The Monotone.
  (5) The Voice-dropper.
  (6) The Repeater.
  (7) The Throat-clearer.
  (8) The Meanderer.
 6. Some hints on voice cultivation.
  (1) Each individual is a distinct personality.
  (2) The value of voice cultivation.
    Note by J. H. Manins.

IV. *He should watch his audience.*
 1. It commands the respect of the audience.
 2. It enables the speaker to watch the reaction of the audience.
 3. Enables him to see if audience is comfortable.

V. *He should watch his time.*
    1. He should find out the length of the service.
       (1) Plan it within limits of the time appointed.
       (2) Start on time.
       (3) End on time.
    2. When sharing a meeting with another, keep to his time.
    3. Better to leave an audience longing rather than loathing.
    4. He should keep his promise to his audience.

VI. *He should watch his theme.*
    1. The characteristics of this present age.
    2. The necessity for Scriptural preaching and teaching.
    3. The qualities of an effective sermon.
    4. The distinction between an evangelist and a teacher.
    5. The seven cardinal truths of the gospel.
       (1) The Need of the Gospel, or Ruin by the Fall.
       (2) The Provision of the Gospel, or Redemption through the Blood.
       (3) The Command of the Gospel, or Repentance towards God.
       (4) The Condition of the gospel, or Reception of Christ as Savior and Lord.
       (5) The Result of the Gospel, or Regeneration by the Holy Spirit.
       (6) The Solemnity of the Gospel, or The Responsibility of the Hearer.
       (7) The Penalty of rejecting the Gospel, or Eternal Retribution on the Christ rejecter.

18

4. Strict attention to the punctuation marks.
5. The passage to be announced clearly and at least twice.
6. The passage to be read clearly, deliberately, reverently and feelingly.
7. The Bible is a literary masterpiece.

VI. *Some suggested passages of Scripture for practice reading.*

    1. It must be intelligent.
    2. It must be intelligible.
    3. It must be edifying.
III. *Some causes for unedifying prayers.*
    1. Uttered in too low a tone.
    2. It was too long.
    3. It was too involved.
    4. The prayer was, in reality, a little sermon.
    5. It contained too much repetition.
    6. Contained an over use of the Divine titles.

*   *   *

*   *   *

19

FOREWORD

I have read with interest and appreciation the proofs of this book: "The Preacher and His Preaching." For some years it was my privilege to conduct Homiletic classes at the Guelph Summer Bible School and at Hamilton, and I consider this book would make an excellent text-book for such classes, which are now being held in an increasing number of centers.

As in the case with all of Mr. Gibbs' books, much material is packed into small space, and each chapter contains a wealth of helpful suggestion. The illustrations of the various types of sermons are invaluable.

Needless to say, this book will be a boon not only to Homiletic classes, but to the many exercised young people who are not fortunate enough to have such opportunities. It is a real pleasure to write the foreword and to send it on its way with the earnest wish that it may fall into the hands of all young men who have a heart stirred to sound forth the Word of Life.

H. G. LOCKETT

Hamilton, Ontario, Canada
March, 1939

PREFACE TO THIRD EDITION

A third edition has become necessary, and is sent forth, still further revised, and with more material added.

This includes a very fine article by the late Dr. Norman Bartlett, of the staff of the Moody Bible Institute, Chicago. It originally appeared in "The Moody Monthly," and is here reproduced, in its entirety, with his most kind permission. It is indeed a valuable contribution to the subject of this volume.

While this edition was being prepared for publication, my good friend, Albert E. Horton, missionary for many years in Portuguese West Africa, wrote an excellent series of articles on: "The Teaching, Interpretation and Application of Scripture." These appeared in "The Witness," of London, England. With Mr. Horton's very kind permission, these splendid articles have been added, as an appendix, to this volume. They should be read in connection with Chapter twelve.

I am also indebteded to my good friend, J. H. Manins, of New Zealand, for the extracts from his articles on: "The Delivery of the Sermon," found in chapter thirty-five.

The title of this book has been changed from "A Primer on Preaching" to: "The Preacher and His Preaching." It goes forth with the same desire as the previous editions —the glory of the Lord, and the edification of His people.

Chicago, 1951   A. P. G.

PREFACE TO FIFTH EDITION

Again it is our privilege to issue another Edition of this book. The commendation of such valued magazines as "Light and Liberty," "The Sunday School Times," "The Witness" (England) and "The Moody Monthly," has been most encouraging.

This fifth Edition, is published to the glory of the One whose incarnation, life, words, substitutionary death, resurrection and glorification has made both the salvation of the preacher, and the preaching of the gospel of the grace of God possible.

Waynesboro, Georgia, 1964.   A. P. G.

INTRODUCTION
(Please read it)

THERE can surely be no question as to the tremendous importance, and the paramount need for the prayerful preparation and the effective presentation of the gospel message. This is a matter of concern, not only to the Church of God in general, but to each Christian in particular.

We are faced with the painful fact that the ranks of the older preachers are being thinned by the hand of death. One by one their nerveless hands have relinquished the gospel torch they carried so faithfully during their lifetime. Who is to take the place of these tried and trusty veterans, and bring "the light of the glorious gospel of Christ" to those who sit in the darkness of sin, ignorance, indifference, superstition and unbelief? There is obviously only one answer to this question. The younger believers must fill up the gaps in the ranks of this gallant army.

To each believer comes the unmistakably clear command of his Lord and Master: "Go ye into all the world and preach the gospel to every creature" (Mark 16:15). With the object of aiding young Christians to fulfil this Divinely given task, this book has been written. It is intended primarily for beginners, and has purposely been made simple, so that the elementary principles governing the preparation and presentation of the gospel message may be readily understood by the young believer. Should a fuller treatment of the subject be desired, there are many good books available. Broadus, on "The Preparation and Delivery of Sermons," will prove invaluable.

All the Scripture references indicated should be looked up and carefully noted, for they are essential to the understanding of the subject. It is of vital importance that we know what the word of God actually *says* and be able to

quote it correctly. It is this alone that will give assurance
to the preacher and authority to his message. One well
quoted: "Thus saith the Lord," is better than ten thousand repetitions of that hackneyed expression: "I may
state without any fear of successful contradiction"! The
first is based on a Divine revelation, while the other rests
on a human and fallible assumption.

It is hardly necessary to say that the writer makes no
claim, either for originality in the statement of these
principles governing the necessary preparation for preaching, or to an exemplification of them in his own ministry.
Should these pages prove to be the means of better fitting
Christians for the high and holy service committed to
them by their Lord and Master, the author will feel more
than amply repaid.

It should be obvious to all that the reading and study
of this book will not *impart* to any believer the *gift* of
preaching, or of teaching the word of God. Nor will a
course at any Bible School or Theological Seminary accomplish it. All the reading of books, or listening to lectures *can never create* the ability to preach or teach. Only
God can impart this gift of public utterance to His people.
The purpose of this book is merely to aid the Christian in
developing whatever gift he has in this direction. A scrip-
turally sound Bible School, excellent though it is, must not
be thought as a "preacher factory"; where ungifted and
uncalled men and women, are mysteriously and mechanic-
ally transformed into spiritually-gifted and God-called
preachers and teachers, by merely listening to a series of
lectures, or by passing certain examinations.

A spiritual gift, like life itself, cannot be humanly imparted. It must be given by God Himself. Once it has been
imparted, it can and should be developed by right training
along those lines best calculated to make for future usefulness to God, and blessing to others.

Three words should be clearly understood and kept distinct in our thoughts: *gift, knowledge* and *ability*. *Gift,* or talent, comes from God. *Knowledge* stems from prayerful, concentrated and conscientious study of the word of God. *Ability* is developed as the gift is exercised in an atmosphere of spirituality. (Eph. 4:11-12; II Tim. 1:6; I Pet. 4:10).

The principal subject of this book is Homiletics. By this is meant the science and art governing the preparation and delivery of sermons. The word probably comes from "homily," a discourse. Others think the term comes from a combination of two words: "homos" a saying; and "illa," a company.

Note the distinction between the words: *"science"* and *"art."* By "science" is meant classified knowledge. By "art" is meant the application and use of that knowledge. It is one thing to have a theoretical knowledge of a subject and another to be able to utilize that knowledge, to the best advantage, in passing it on to others. This art, of course, comes largely through *practice.* Thus each preacher, to use a military term, is on "K. P..": the "K." standing for knowledge, and the "P" for practice. Theory has been defined as *thinking,* while practice consists of *doing.* A boy, asked to define agriculture, replied: "Agriculture is something like farming, only farming is *doing* it." So we may say: "Homiletics is something like preaching, only preaching is doing it."

The subject of Homiletics involves, amongst other things, a consideration of the essential qualifications of a preacher; the urgent necessity for preaching; the importance of the proper preparation of the preaching material, including its discovery and arrangement; and the best means of securing the effective presentation and reception of the message. Thus the importance of the subject can easily be appreciated.

Inasmuch as preaching is the God-ordained means of spreading the gospel amongst the unsaved, and also of teaching the word of God to believers, any attempt to increase the effectiveness of both preaching and teaching deserves the serious consideration of every believer. It will surely be admitted there is much room for improvement in the *quality* of preaching and teaching today. Many a sermon has been lost on an audience because of a lack of order in it. Many good things were said, but these were so jumbled up that only a discerning mind could discover them. Scrambled addresses, like scrambled eggs, soon become a very monotonous diet. The paramount need in preaching is for a more thoughtful preparation of the sermon, a better logical arrangement of the material, an improved, clear and forceful presentation of the truth, plus, and above all, a greater cultivation of those spiritual qualities that are fundamental to all preaching.

These basic principles governing Homiletics may appear to be somewhat dry and uninteresting and, perhaps to some, even unnecessary; but it is essential that they be grasped if they are to be of any lasting benefit. The fundamental principles of music, art, mathematics, science and teaching do not have much appeal for the beginner; but they must be painstakingly learned, step by step, if ever the subject is to be mastered. Though the elementary processes may be looked upon as an irksome drudgery and become exceedingly monotonous to the pupil, yet the resultant proficiency more than repays for the labor expended. There is no royal road to success. It comes through *hard work* and the goal must ever be kept in view.

These homiletical hints, while appearing new and strange to a beginner, will be perfectly self-evident to a person with years of experience in preaching. The purpose of this book is merely to *speed up* the process of learning for the beginner, and thus save some years of

his very valuable time! The multiplication table can undoubtedly be learned through experience, but it is more
quickly grasped by rote.

The value of developing what has been aptly termed,
"the homiletic habit", in one's early years cannot be
overestimated. Once the fundamental principles of homiletics have been mastered, it will become second nature
to arrange one's sermon material in logical order. This,
in turn, will make for its orderly presentation and consequent effectiveness.

It will be realized, of course, that only as these guiding
principles are closely studied, individually applied and
consistently practiced, shall the student be really helped
in his task. To merely memorize these principles, with
a view to passing an examination, is to fail.

These suggestions have already been used as the basis
for a series of lectures on Homiletics at the Emmaus Bible
School, of Oak Park, Illinois. It is to be hoped it will not
be true of these lectures, as was once said of lecturing in
general that: "It is often the means by which the notes of
the lecturer are transferred into the notebook of the student, without passing through the heads of either!"

One of the basic laws governing teaching is: "There can
be no *impression* without a corresponding *expression*." It
is the personal and persistent application of these principles in one's own work that will determine their value
to the student as he prepares and presents the gospel and
teaching message.

We shall seek to discuss at least seven main topics regarding the preacher and his preaching.
  1. The qualifications of the preacher.
  2. The call of the preacher.
  3. The necessity for preaching.
  4. The sermon itself; its definition, structure and types.
  5. The preparation for the sermon.

6. The gathering of the material.

7. The delivery of the sermon.

Our Lord Jesus Christ made His Father's business the supreme object of His life on earth. His first recorded utterance was: "Wist ye not that I must be about My Father's business?" (Luke 2:49). He rested not until He could triumphantly testify: "I have glorified Thee on the earth: I have finished the work which Thou gavest me to do" (John 17:4).

Before Christ left the earth to ascend to the right hand of the Majesty on high, He said to His disciples: "As My Father hath sent Me, even so send I you" (John 20:21). Thus each Christian is a sent one; chosen, called, commissioned and equipped by his Lord to do business for Him in a world that despised and rejected Him and which, in turn, will despise and reject those who name His name. The words which Queen Elizabeth addressed to Sir Walter Raleigh are not without signifance to us. As the intrepid explorer was about to set sail on one of his voyages, she said: "You make *my* business *your* business, and I will make *your* business *my* business.

The biggest business on this earth is God's business. The ambition of each Christian should be to "serve his own generation by the will of God" (Acts 13:36). May "the Lord of the harvest" stir the hearts of each reader to a greater realization of his wonderful privileges, and a more faithful discharge of his solemn responsibilities in respect to the proclamation of the good news of God's salvation! In this way each shall become better fitted to do business for the One who has saved him by His grace, and who has now become the supreme Lord of his life and the absolute Master of his service. (John 13:13-15).

CHAPTER ONE

The Qualifications of the Preacher

The Scriptures clearly teach that it is through the word of God, applied by the Spirit of God, that souls are awakened to a sense of their need as guilty sinners, led to rest in the substitutionary sacrifice of Christ on their behalf, trust Him as their Savior and confess Him as Lord.

This is usually, though not always, accomplished by the oral presentation of the gospel on the part of a Christian. The person who proclaims the gospel is called a "preacher," and the presentation of the gospel message is described as "preaching the gospel." (Romans 10:14; II Cor. 10:14; cp. I Cor. 1:17).

We cannot divorce the preacher from his preaching. In a very real way the *man* is his *message*: the *preacher* is his *proclamation*: the *speaker* is his *sermon*. It is the man behind the message that determines its weight for in this, as in everything else, *quality* is to be preferred to *quantity*.

It was this fact that Paul had in mind when he wrote to Timothy: "Take heed unto *thyself,* and unto the *doctrine;* continue in them; for in doing this thou shalt both save thyself, and them that hear thee" (I Tim. 4:16). It was this scripture that suggested the title of the book: "The Preacher and His Preaching." Emerson once remarked: "What you *are,* speaks so loud the world cannot hear what you say!" The Stony Brook School has, as its excellent motto: "Character before career." Perhaps the best definition of preaching was that given by Henry Ward Beecher, who declared it was: "Truth through personality."

Paul, writing to the believers at Thessalonica, whom he had been used to lead to Christ could say: "Ye are witnesses, and God also, how holily and justly and unblame-

ably we behaved ourselves among you that believe" (I
Thess. 2: 3-10). Our Lord, when asked by the Pharisees:
"Who art Thou?" answered: "Even the same that I said
unto you at the beginning" (John 8: 25). In other words,
Christ declared: "I *am* what I *said.*" He was the living
exemplification of His doctrine. Before a word of the sermon on the mount was preached, it had been demonstrated
by Him in His life during the thirty years of His obscurity of Nazareth. Thus He *exemplified* in His life what
He *expounded* by His lips.

With these things in view, let us ask ourselves the question: What are the essential qualifications of a preacher?
We shall devote some time to a consideration of the pre-
requisites which are necessary to one who seeks to preach,
or teach the word of God.

I. He must be regenerated. (John 3:3-7).

1. *The possibility of self deception.*

To many, the statement that a preacher should be born
from above may seem self evident. The fact remains,
however, that there are literally hundreds of preachers
who have never experienced the regenerating power of the
Spirit of God. They know nothing of what it means to be
saved by the grace of God, through personal faith in
Christ. It was the Son of God Himself Who solemnly announced to one of the most religious, moral and sincere
men of his day: "Verily, Verily, I say unto thee, except a
man be born again, (or from above) he cannot see the
kingdom of God" (John 3:3).

To these unregenerated ministers, preaching is merely
a profession, or means of livelihood. It is viewed by them
as being in the same class as medicine, law, accountancy,
teaching, business, army, navy or the Civil Service, etc.
They have been "theologically educated," "ordained,"
"taken holy orders," "entered the ministry," and assumed

the title of "reverend"; but all the while have never been born from above. Consequently they are but lost and guilty sinners, dead in their trespasses and sins, and on their way to an eternity of blackness and darkness for ever! How terribly tragic this is! In many instances, these men are naturally intelligent, moral, religiously inclined, cultured, eloquent, and often possessed of charming personalities; yet they are absolutely in the dark as to spiritual realities, and abysmally ignorant of God's way of salvation.

Dr. Thomas Chalmers, one of Scotland's greatest preachers of a hundred years ago, confessed he had been preaching for ten years before he was regenerated. A preacher named Haslam, contemporary of Billy Bray, the Cornish miner, was saved in his own pulpit as he preached! In recent years, a young minister complained to the Ministerial Association of his city concerning a sign he had seen on a tent where gospel services were being held. He indignantly protested the propagation of such heresy which, according to the sign, announced: "To him that worketh not, but believeth on Him that justifieth the ungodly, his faith is counted unto him for righteousness." He appealed to the Ministerial Association to take official action against those who were advertising such "blasphemous teaching"! An old preacher, a true Christian, arose and informed the young minister, to his great embarrassment, that his quarrel was not with the preachers in that tent, but with the word of God, for the words on the sign were a direct quotation from the Bible! Murray McCheyne declared the saddest sight on earth was to see a *dead* preacher, preaching to *dead* sinners the *living* word of the living God!

2. *The description of such mere professors.*

Christ likened the Jewish leaders of His day to "Blind leaders of the blind" (Matt. 15:14). We read in Ps. 50:16: "But to the wicked, God saith, What hast thou to do to

declare My statutes, or that thou shouldst take My covenant in thy mouth?" Peter refers to the false prophets of
his day as: "wells without water." These appear inviting
to the weary and parched traveller, but provide nothing
with which to slake his thirst. (II Peter 2:17). God declares that: "The natural man receiveth not the things of
the Spirit of God: for they are foolishness unto him;
neither can he know them, because they are spiritually
discerned" (I Cor. 2:14). From conversations with returned Christian soldiers, it appears that saved and evangelistic chaplains were the exception, rather than the rule.

3. *The necessity for the preacher's own assurance of
salvation.*

Each one who seeks to present the word of God to others
should be certain he has experienced the new birth for
himself. He should be able to truthfully testify: "Behold,
God is *my* Salvation; I will trust and not be afraid: for the
Lord Jehovah is *my* Strength and *my* Song; He also is become *my* Salvation!" (Isa. 12:2). Paul could quote: "I believed, and therefore have I spoken," and then confidently added: "We also believe, and therefore speak" (II Cor.
4:13). He could refer to his fellow laborers in the gospel
as those: "Whose names are in the book of life" (Phil.
4:3. cp. Luke 10:20; Rev. 20:15).

We could paraphrase, to advantage, the words of a well
known hymn:

> "Ye teachers and preachers, attend to the word
> So solemnly uttered by Jesus, the Lord;
> And let not this message to you be in vain:
> 'Ye must be born again!'"

It is only as the preacher is fully assured, in his own
heart, from the word of God, that he is "accepted in the
beloved," and "justified freely by His grace through the
redemption that is in Christ Jesus," that he can confidently
and powerfully appeal to his hearers to be "reconciled
unto God" (Eph. 1:6; Rom. 3:24; II Cor. 5:20).

The last we read of the apostle Paul, he is described as "preaching the kingdom of God, and teaching those things which concern the Lord Jesus with all confidence, no man forbidding him" (Acts 28:31). The assurance and the confidence of the preacher, concerning his own salvation, conveys itself to the audience and carries conviction of its reality. The person who can humbly but boldly say: "I *know* Whom I have believed, and am persuaded that He is able to keep that which I have committed unto Him against that day;" may be assured that the audience will be impressed with his own confidence in his Savior, and the salvation he has experienced. (II Tim. 1:12).

II.   He must love the Lord Jesus.

1.   *The love of Christ must be the constraining motive of all his service.*

Paul wrote: "For the love of Christ constraineth us, because we thus judge, that if One died for all, then were all dead: and that He died for all, that they which live should not henceforth live unto themselves, but unto Him which died for them and rose again" (II Cor. 5:14-15). To preach from a sense of duty, while necessary, is not enough. Only as the love of Christ is the impelling motive, shall one's preaching be worth anything. Hence the imperative need for personal heart devotion to Christ.

The expression, "the love of Christ," occurs three times in Scripture. In Eph. 3:19, it is spoken of as something that we must be brought to *know* in ever increasing degree. Thus it is to be our *supreme study.* In II Cor. 5:14-15, it is described as the essential and constraining motive in all our *sacrificial service* for Him. In Rom. 8:35-39, it is set forth as that from which no power, visible or invisible, can separate us. Thus it becomes, amid all the vicissitudes of life, the believer's *sustaining strength.*

2. *The example of Christ.*

The Son of God declared: "But that the world may know that I love the Father; and as the Father gave Me commandment, even so I do" (John 14: 31). Long before His incarnation, He said through the lips of David: "Sacrifice and offering Thou didst not desire . . . Then said I: Lo, I come, in the volume of the book it is written of Me, I delight to do Thy will, O My God: yea, Thy law is within My heart" (Ps. 40: 6-8, cp. Heb. 10: 5-10).

Christ's love for His Father brought Him down to earth in voluntary subjection to His will and word. This constraining love led Him all the way to Gethsemane where He prayed: "Not My will, but Thine be done." It guided Him to Gabbatha, where "He gave His back to the smiters, and His cheek to them that plucked off the hair." It moved Him to go to Golgotha, where He willingly allowed God "to lay on Him the iniquity of us all." Alone, upon that cross, He suffered all the judgment of a holy God against our sins, and died to secure our eternal redemption (Luke 22: 42; Isa. 50: 6; 53: 6). The Lord does not ask His people to do what He has not done Himself. In constraining love, as in everything else, He is the believer's supreme Example. See I Peter 2: 21.

3. *The commission to His disciples.*

This constraining love of Christ was also emphasized by our Lord, after His resurrection, in His charge to Peter. By the side of the lake of Galilee, and near the pile of fish that had been miraculously caught, our Lord said to Peter: "Simon, son of Jonas, lovest thou Me more than these?" (Doubtless He referred to the fish.) Notice Peter's answer: "Yea, Lord, Thou knowest that I love Thee." Upon this confession of his love for Christ, the Lord said to him, "Feed My lambs." This question was repeated twice more, as though to drive home the great necessity for this essential love for Christ as the impelling dynamic for all service for Him. (John 21:1-19).

Peter seems to have laid the lesson well to heart, for he writes in his epistle: "Christ . . . Whom having not seen, ye love; in Whom, though now ye see Him not, yet believing, ye rejoice with joy unspeakable and full of glory" (I Pet. 1:7-8). John, by the Spirit declared: "We love Him, because He first loved us" (I John 4:19). Paul delighted in the blessed fact that "The love of God is shed abroad in our hearts by the Holy Ghost, which is given unto us" (Rom. 5:5).

Seeing that love *for* Christ is so essential to the preaching *of* Christ, it is fitting for each believer to pray:

> "More love to Thee, O Christ,
> More love to Thee;
> Hear Thou the prayer I make
> On bended knee;
> This is my earnest plea—
> More love, O Christ to Thee,
> More love to Thee!"

III. He must love souls.

1. *It is possible to love to preach, without loving those to whom we preach.*

A lawyer may develop great ability in his profession without necessarily loving his clients. A physician may enjoy great success without loving his patients. A business man can rise to great heights of prosperity without loving his customers. But a preacher can never be a real worker for Christ without a deep passion for the lost souls to whom he preaches the gospel of God's grace.

It is a thrilling experience to be able to sway an audience with one's eloquence, and this can easily become a snare, if divorced from a love for souls. A preacher once remarked to Dr. Bonar: "I love preaching." The good doctor replied: "Do you love the people to whom you preach?" There is a certain prominence that preaching gives the preacher, which is not without its appeal to the flesh. The love of publicity, of basking in the limelight, of hearing the praises of men and of courting popularity has ruined many a preacher. His heart, "being lifted up with pride," has caused him to "fall into the condemnation of the Devil" (I Tim. 3:6).

The following story, culled from a current magazine, will serve to illustrate the menace of this subtle temptation to which all preachers are susceptible. It is entitled, *"A Worker's Dream."*

"I sat down in an arm-chair, wearied with my work. My toil had been severe and protracted. Many were seeking Christ, and many had found Him. As for myself, I was joyous in my work. My brethren were united. My sermons and exhortations were evidently telling on my hearers. My church was crowded.

Tired with my work, I soon lost myself in a sort of half-forgetful state.

Suddenly a stranger entered the room, without any preliminary "tap" or "Come in." He carried about his person measures, chemical agents and implements, which gave him a very strange appearance.

The stranger came toward me and, extending his hand said: "How is your zeal?" I supposed that the query was to be for my health, but was pleased to hear his final words; for I was quite well pleased with my zeal, and doubted not the stranger would smile when he should know its proportions.

Instantly I conceived of it as *physical quantity* and putting my hand into my bosom, brought it forth and presented it to him for inspection.

He took it and, placing it in his scale, weighed it carefully. I heard him say, "One hundred pounds!" I could scarcely suppress an audible note of satisfaction; but I caught his *earnest* look as he noted down the weight, and I saw at once that he had drawn no final conclusion, but was intent on pushing his investigation. He broke the mass to atoms, put it into his crucible, and put the crucible into the fire. When the mass was fused he took it out, and set it to cool. It congealed in cooling, and when turned out on the hearth exhibited a series of layers or strata, which all, at the touch of the hammer, fell apart, and were *severally tested and weighed,* the stranger making minute notes as the process went on.

When he had finished, he presented the notes to me, and gave me a look of mingled *sorrow and compassion,* as without a word, except: "May God save you!" he left the room.

The "notes" read as follows:

Analysis of the Zeal of Junius, a Candidate for a Crown of Glory

Weight in mass ....100 lbs.

On this, on analysis, there proves to be—

Bigotry ....10 parts		"Wood,
Personal ambition ....23 "		Hay,
Love of praise ....19 "		and
Pride of denomination ....15 "		Stubble .."
Pride of talent ....14 "		
Love of authority ....12 "		
Love to God .... 4 "		Pure
Love to man .... 3 "		Zeal

100

I had become troubled at the peculiar manner of the stranger, and especially at his parting look and words; but when I looked at the figures, *my heart sank as lead* within me.

I made a mental effort to dispute the *correctness* of the record. But I was startled into a more honest mood by an audible sigh from the stranger (who had paused in the hall). I cried out, "Lord save me!" and knelt down at my chair, with the paper in my hand and my eyes fixed upon it. At once it became a mirror, and I saw my heart reflected in it. *The record was true!* . . . I saw it, I felt it, I confessed it, I deplored it, and I besought God to save me from myself with many tears. Then, with a loud cry of anguish I awoke.

I had once prayed to be saved from hell, but prayer to be saved from *myself* now was immeasurably more fervent and distressful. Nor did I rest until I had judged, confessed and turned from the shameful thing, and knew His restoring grace.

When the toils of my pilgrimage shall be at an end I shall kneel in heaven at the foot of the Divine Alchemist and bless Him for the *revelations of that day.*"

Let us not wait until the judgment seat of Christ to have our zeal analyzed. "If we would judge ourselves, we should not be judged" (I Cor. 3:9-15, Rom. 14:10, I Cor. 11:31). The scriptural injunction is: "Let every man prove, (or scrutinize) his *own work*" (Gal. 6:4).

2. *Consider Christ's passion for souls.*

The earthly life of our Lord Jesus Christ, as "Jehovah's Servant," is again the preacher's example of what it means to love souls. His gracious, solicitous, tender and loving compassion is everywhere evident in the four Gospels, which contain the brief record of His ministry. It is instructive to mark the many times when it is stated that: "He had compassion." His heart went out in love to the lost and guilty sinners He had come to "seek and to save" (Luke 19:10).

We are told He had compassion on the blind in their darkness (Matt. 20:34); on the lepers in their uncleanness (Mark 1:4); on the sick in their weakness (Matt. 14:14); on the hungry in their need (Matt. 15:32); on the friendless in their loneliness (Mark 6:34) and on the bereaved in their sorrow (Luke 7:13). Compassion has been defined as: "feeling the pain in another person's heart." Love is ever measured by the sacrifice made on behalf of the one loved. We are told that "Christ *loved* the Church and *gave* Himself for it" (Eph. 5:25). The preacher, who really loves souls, will give himself unstintingly and wholeheartedly to the task of winning them for Christ.

I Cor. 13 contains Paul's great poem on the superexcellence of love. In it we discover that love is more than we can *say* (v. 1); more than we *have* (v. 2); and more than we can *give* (v. 3). Without it, all other gifts are worse than useless and, indeed, degenerate into a spiritual menace. This love must not be confounded with mere sentiment, of the soft, sugary and sickly type. Love can rebuke, chasten and warn. It was Paul's love for the Corinthian believers that led him to write as he did, and so faithfully expose their shortcomings, and sternly rebuke them for their inconsistencies. He had to complain: "The more abundantly I love you, the less I be loved" (II Cor. 12:15).

3. *The need for a right estimate of the soul's value.*

We must ever see men as *souls* having *bodies*, rather than *bodies* having *souls*. Christ's words must grip our hearts: "What shall it profit a man, if he gain the whole world and lose his own soul?" (Mark 8:36). This should impress us, as nothing else, with the tremendous value of a soul. Someone has said: "There is nothing great in this world, but man; and there is nothing great about man, but his soul." We must estimate the value of the soul by the price Christ paid to secure its redemption, even His most precious blood. We must therefore view man and estimate his worth, not by the size of his bank account, his position in the world, his family connections, his education, his clothes, his color, race, or tongue; but we must view and value him as one for whom Christ died.

Paul, as he contemplated the spiritual blindness and the hardness of heart of Israel, actually exclaimed: "I could wish that myself were accursed from Christ for my brethren, my kinsmen according to the flesh" (Rom. 9:3). Is it any wonder that God so mightily used him in his preaching and teaching ministry? Moses, the great leader of Israel, also rose to great heights when he interceded for his sinful nation and said: "Yet now, if Thou

wilt forgive their sin—and if not, blot me, I pray Thee
out of Thy book which Thou hast written" (Exod. 32:32).
These instances should be sufficient to drive home to our
hearts this essential requirement of a love for souls, if our
ministry is to be what it should.

CHAPTER TWO

The Qualifications of the Preacher

(Continued)

IV.   He must be a student of the Bible.

A preacher must be a man of the Book.

1.   *He must know it by reading it.*

It is essential that a preacher should be well acquainted with the book from which he preaches. In order to teach mathematics, one must *know* mathematics. What would you think of a "music teacher" who did not know music; or of an "English teacher" who did not know English? He who is called to preach the Bible, is also called to study the Bible, for there cannot be one without the other: the first necessitates the last. Like David, each preacher should be able to testify: "Oh, how love I Thy law!" (Ps. 119:97).

The preacher should be acquainted with the Bible as a *whole,* and this can only be accomplished by reading the Bible from cover to cover. The entire Bible can be read in fifty-four hours, reading at the rate of two hundred and fifty words a minute. By reading three chapters of the Old Testament in the morning, and two chapters of the New Testament each night, the Old Testament can be read once a year, and the New Testament twice a year. Surely this is not too big a price to pay for a working knowledge of this Book of books.

He must both *make* and *take* time for the devotional reading of the Bible for his own soul's profit. It is possible to be so busy cultivating other people's gardens that one's own is apt to be neglected. One can be so occupied

40

in feeding others that he becomes undernourished himself. It has been pointed out that there are two kinds of readers: those who go through a book, and those who allow a book to go through them.

The humble cow can provide us with a valuable lesson in this connection. She feeds upon the rich pasture without any thought whatsoever of providing someone else with her milk. She eats the grass to satisfy her own appetite. When she has eaten all she wants, she lies down contentedly, brings back what she has been feeding on and chews the cud. The resultant rich milk and cream which she gives is purely incidental to her. It was simply the inevitable result of satisfying her own desire. Likewise as the Christian reads the Bible to refresh his own soul and gratify his own spiritual appetite, and then seeks to meditate upon what he has read, he will be enabled to give to others the rich and "sincere milk of the Word" that they need (I Pet. 2:2).

2. *He must be able to quote it from memory.*

This necessitates that he commit to memory certain verses and passages of the Bible. This will stand him in good stead as he faces his audience, for the Bible is his authority and final court of appeal. It is God's ultimation to humanity. See Heb. 1:1-3. To be able to quote a passage correctly and impressively from the Scriptures will engrave it upon the mind of the hearer, for it will leave the audience in no doubt as to the Divine authority of the message.

Perhaps the best method of memorizing texts from the Bible is to take a number of large blank visiting cards of a *good quality* cardboard. Write on one side of the card, the Scripture location, such as Romans 6:23. On the other side write out, in full, the whole of the verse, and thoroughly memorize the actual words of the text. Add one card a day to this list and review as often as possible. In the course of a year there will be a pile of 365 cards, and the memory will have become a treasure house of priceless value. A number of these cards can be taken on a street car, or train, and constantly reviewed until all can be repeated correctly, either by stating the location of the verse, or by quoting the verse from the location given. The more often one can use them by quoting them. the more proficient he will become in this valuable and most useful art.

3. *He must study it by diligent application.*

There is no royal or easy road to knowledge. It comes through persistent and painstaking study. Someone has said that "study consists of the application of the seat of the trousers to the seat of the chair, until such time as the subject has been mastered!" It is the maintenance of this point of contact that calls for earnest and self denying determination. It is one thing to read, or to hear, or to talk about study; but an entirely different thing to *do* it and, more difficult still, to *keep on* doing it, but this is the only way a subject can be mastered.

An Irishman was seeing his son off on a ship that was to take him to the U. S. A. As the ship left the dock he shouted: "Remember, my boy, make good use of the three bones!" A bystander inquired of the father: "What did you mean by that expression: "Remember the three bones?" The man replied: "Why, the proper use of these three bones is the secret of all success. The first bone is the *wish bone.* By using it a man is kept aspiring after success. The second bone is the *jawbone.* By using it well, he can learn from wise men the best way to become successful. The third bone is the *back bone.* By using this, he can keep on constantly striving until he has gained the success he seeks."

Genius has been aptly defined as "an infinite capacity for taking pains." Study is the price that must be paid for knowledge, and every preacher must be prepared to pay the price, or he will never become a worthwhile preacher of the gospel, or a teacher of the Word. He must make the Bible the "man of his counsel" and, by diligently comparing Scripture with Scripture, and "spiritual things with spiritual," come to an all round knowledge of the Book of books as a whole (I Cor. 2:13).

Each preacher should become a D. D. D. D. D. That is to say, he should study the Bible:

(a) *Diligently.* This calls for heroic measures and a holy determination to allow nothing to hinder. It may necessitate getting up a half an hour earlier in the morning, but the time will be well invested.

(b) *Devotionally.* He must allow the Bible to speak to his own heart and minister to his own spiritual needs, before he can minister to the needs of others.

(c) *Discerningly.* He must learn to "distinguish between things that differ" (Phil. 1:10, Marg.). He must study so as to "rightly divide the word of truth" (II Tim. 2:15). All the scriptures relating to a subject need to be consulted before one can come to a right conclusion regarding it. Hence the need for comparing what this scripture says, with what that other scripture affirms.

(d) *Doctrinally.* He must get a grasp of the great doctrines of the Bible. *Sound* words, plus *sound* doctrine, makes a *sound* believer, and a *sound* preacher, whose *sound* preaching should leave the audience "*sound* in the faith." Read II Tim. 1:10, 1:13; II Tim. 4:3; Tit. 1:9, 13; Col. 2:7.

(e) *Dispensationally.* He must find out where he is in relation to God's present program, or he may discover he is at cross purposes with God and His plan for this age.

Should the reader come to the conclusion that this is hard work, let him be assured that he has certainly arrived at a right understanding of the matter! It *is* hard work, but a *grand* work, and for the best Master that man could ever have. David's words may be pondered in this connection "Neither will I offer to the Lord . . . that which cost me nothing" (II Sam. 24:24).

A lady once remarked to Lord Northcliffe: "Thackeray awoke one morning and found himself famous." Lord Northcliffe answered: "When that morning dawned, Thackeray had been writing eight hours a day for fifteen years. The man who wakes up and finds himself famous *hasn't been asleep!*"

V.   He must be a man of prayer.

It has well been said that "He who would speak much *to* man *for* God, must speak much *to* God *for* man." A prayerless ministry is both powerless and profitless. *The*ology must ever be accompanied by *knee*ology. Much prayer equals much power; little prayer equals little power; no prayer equals no power. God places at each believer's disposal a force that can "move the hand which moves the world, and brings deliverance down." Wise indeed is he who rightly values and consistently utilizes this tremendous force. It is still true that "They that wait upon the Lord shall renew (exchange) their strength; they shall mount up with wings as eagles, they shall run and not be weary: and they shall walk and not faint" (Isa. 40:31).

Alex. Whyte's splendid definition of prayer is worth memorizing: "Prayer is the exercise of a will that is free within a will that is sovereign." In other words: prayer does not change the will of God, but brings the believer into alignment with the will of God, so that he now asks for that which God desires to give him in answer to believing prayer. It was this that John had in mind when he wrote: "If we ask anything according to His will, He

heareth us: and if we know that He hear us, whatsoever
we ask, we know that we have the petitions that we desired of Him." (I John 5:14-15). Thus, while the believer
is free to ask God for whatever he desires, God does not
promise to grant the request unless it is in accordance with
His sovereign will. Therefore the need for each Christian
to pray: "Thy will be done."

We will think of two things regarding prayer: our example and our encouragement.

1. *Our example in prayer.*

Once more, let us "look off unto Jesus" and learn, from
His life on earth, as God's perfect Servant, the place and
value of prayer. We need ever to remember that, as the
Son of Man, He lived His life in voluntary subjection to
the Father's will, under the absolute control of the Holy
Spirit, and in perfect obedience to the word of God. In
other words, our Lord lived His life on earth, as the incarnate Son of God and Son of Man; by the same means
that Christians must live their lives on earth: in dependence on the Father, led and empowered by the Spirit, and
obedient to the Scriptures. This life of dependence upon
His Father was evidenced in two ways.

(1) *By His own testimony*: "The Son can do nothing
of Himself, but what He seeth the Father do" . . . "I can
of Mine own self do nothing: as I hear I judge: and My
judgment is just because I seek not Mine own will, but the
will of My Father which hath sent Me" (John 5:19, 30).

(2) *By a life of prayer.* He affirmed: "Men ought always to pray and not to faint," and then illustrated its
value by the parable of the importunate woman (Luke 18:
1-8).

In Luke's gospel, which sets forth Christ particularly as
the Son of Man, we read of many instances of His life of
prayer. He is described as praying at His baptism (Luke
3:21). He withdrew from the multitudes to be alone with

God in prayer (Luke 5:16). He "continued all night in prayer" on the mountain top, and afterwards chose His disciples (Luke 6:12). He prayed before the great confession of Peter (Luke 9:18). It was "as He prayed" that "the fashion of His countenance was altered" on the Mount of transfiguration (Luke 9:29). It was while "He was praying" that one of His disciples, moved by His example, said to Him: "Lord, teach us to pray." In response to this plea, He taught them the beautiful prayer generally called "the Lord's prayer" but which, in reality, is the disciple's prayer. He prayed for Peter that His faith would not fail (Luke 22:32). He prayed in Gethsemane: "Not My will but Thine be done" (Luke 22:42). He prayed for His enemies as they nailed Him to the cross (Luke 22:34). After He had uttered the triumphant cry: "It is finished!" we are told He prayed: "Father, into Thy hands I commend My Spirit." Having thus said, He bowed His head and dismissed His spirit (Luke 23:46).

Thus our Lord's life is seen to have been lived in the atmosphere of prayer. In the closing hours of His earthly ministry He spoke much about prayer. Read John, chapters fourteen to sixteen. No believer can remain unmoved as he reads the wonderful prayer recorded in John 17, where Christ interceded for the disciples He was soon to leave. He prayed for their Preservation (vs. 9-12); Separation (vs. 13-19); Unification (vs. 20-21); and Glorification (vs. 22-26). The deduction from all this is surely obvious: Since our Lord placed such an emphasis on prayer in His own life, how much more should we who profess to follow His steps? (I Pet. 2:21).

2. *Our encouragement in prayer.*

The word of God is united in its testimony to the necessity for and the great value of prayer. Every believer is both urged and encouraged to pray. Read Matt. 6:5-13. Each Christian should therefore be prayerful:

(1) *Regarding every detail of his life.* Nothing is too insignificant as a subject for prayer. Our heavenly Father "knoweth that we have need of all these things," and has promised to supply them according to His riches in glory by Christ Jesus" (Matt. 6:32-33; Phil. 4:19).

In fact we are told to "Be careful (over anxious) for nothing, but in everything by prayer and supplication, with thanksgiving, let your requests be made known unto God. And the peace of God, that passeth all understanding, shall keep your hearts and minds through Christ Jesus" (Phil. 4:6, 7). An old saying has it that "prayer changes things;" but it does more than this: it changes Christians!

(2) *Regarding every aspect of his service for the Lord.*

Christ said to His disciples: "The harvest truly is plenteous, but the laborers are few; pray ye therefore the Lord of the harvest, that He will send forth laborers into His harvest" (Matt. 9:37, 38). All service is to be sanctified by prayer. The Christian needs to pray for guidance in his service. He will do well to plead with David: "For Thy name's sake, lead me and guide me" (Ps. 31:3). He needs to pray for wisdom, and this God is willing to give in answer to earnest and believing prayer (James 1:5, 7). He needs to pray for courage, strength and power, as he seeks to serve the Lord, and he shall not ask in vain. See Acts 4:23-31; Isa. 40:28-31. To a congregation who were seeking a preacher, the question was put: "How big a preacher do you want?" They answered: "One who is big enough to reach heaven on his knees!"

(3) *The prominence of prayer in the life of Paul.*

Chrysostom said of Paul: "Three cubits high, he touched the sky." Though small physically, he was a giant spiritually, and prayer played no small part in his attainment to such spiritual height. One has only to read some of his prayers, which are recorded in his epistles, to realize the value he placed on prayer. See Eph. 1:16-23; 3:14-19; Phil. 1:4; Col. 1:12; I Thess. 1:2. Not only did he pray for the believers, but he requested their prayers on his behalf (Rom. 15:30; II Cor. 1:11; Phil. 1:19; I Thess. 5:25; Col. 4:3). The great need today is for more of the Epaphras' type, whom Paul said was: "always laboring fervently for you in prayers" (Col. 4:12, cp. I Tim. 2:14).

In view of the importance of prayer, Tennyson's words should come home, with peculiar force, to every believer:

"More things are wrought by prayer
Than this world dreams of. Wherefore let thy voice
Rise like a fountain for me night and day.
For what are men better than sheep or goats
That nourish a blind life within the brain,
If, knowing God, they lift not hands of prayer,
Both for themselves, and those who call them friends."

VI.   He must be clean in life.

The world's adage: "Cleanliness is next to godliness," should be altered to read: "Cleanliness is godliness," as far as the believer is concerned.

1.   *The absolute necessity for it.*

The Divine dictum is: "Be ye clean, that bear the vessels of the Lord" (Isa. 52:11). A preacher of the gospel, of all people, should be above reproach in his life. It is essential that he have "a good report of them that are without:" that is, of those who make no profession of being Christians (I Tim. 3:6, 7). Thus, every herald of the gospel, or teacher of the Word, should be "well reported" from the domestic, commercial, social and ecclesiastical spheres in which he moves. He must not only *preach* the doctrines of the word of God, but he should also *"adorn the doctrine of God our Savior in all things"* (Tit. 2:10). This "adornment" consists of honesty in business, truthfulness of speech, morality of life, wholesomeness of mind, evenness of temper, righteousness of acts and godliness of character. These are the qualities which speak louder than words. It has been well said that Christianity does not come into the world tariff free; but there is always a *duty* associated with it. See Titus 2:11-14.

This essential balance of lip and life is summed up in Phil. 2:15-16. Paul's desire for the Philippian believers was: "That ye may be blameless and harmless, the sons of God, without rebuke, in the midst of a crooked and perverse nation, among whom ye shine as lights in the world, holding forth the word of life." Here is the *consistent* life backing up the *persistent* testimony; the shining forth of the *life*, and the holding forth of the *light* of the word of life: an ideal combination indeed!

Someone has said: "Unless there is *within* us that which is *above* us, we shall soon yield to that which is *around* us." A young preacher once received this good advice from an old believer: "Take care of your *character* and the Lord will take care of *your reputation*." Character is what a person is, reputation is what others think of him. God is far more concerned with what we *are* than what we *do*; for what we *are* determines the value of what we say and do. The beatitudes of Matt. 5:1-11 are really "*be-attitudes*," for they are attitudes of *being*. Christ describes the blessedness of the person that "*is*" something: such as "poor in spirit," or one who "mourns," etc. Thus, it is a description of a person's character.

2. *The menace of inconsistency.*

More damage has been brought to the cause of Christ through the inconsistent lives of those who profess His name and preach His word than anything else. Paul, by the Spirit, asks some searching questions: "Thou therefore which teachest another, teachest thou not thyself? Thou that preachest a man should not steal, doest thou steal? . . . Thou that abhorest idols, dost thou commit

sacrilege? Thou that makest thy boast of the law, through
breaking the law dishonorest thou God? For the name of
God is blasphemed among the Gentiles through you, as it
is written" (Rom. 2: 21-24).

Note also that inconsistency of life causes both God's
doctrine and His word to be blasphemed. See I Tim. 6: 1;
Tit. 2: 5. It is recorded that Nathan said to David, concerning his double sin of adultery and murder: "Because
of this deed, thou has given great occasion to the enemies
of the Lord to blaspheme" (II Sam. 12: 14). Time has
proved how true this statement was. A man once said of
a loose-living, but eloquent preacher: "When he is in the
pulpit, I wish he'd never get out; but when he's out, I
wish he'd never go back again"!

Years ago, a good chorus was sung, the words of which
were as follows:

> "What you are, speaks so loud
> The world can't hear what you say!
> They're looking at your walk,
> Not listening to your talk,
> They're judging by your actions every day.
> Don't believe you'll deceive
> By claiming what you've never known,
> For they know you to be
> By what they can see—
> They'll judge by your life alone!"

Someone once said in a defence of a certain preacher
who was being accused of living an immoral life: "But he
is sound on the atonement." The reply he got was:
"What's the use of his being sound on the atonement if
the atonement doesn't make him sound?"

Worldlings chuckle with unholy glee when some
preacher is discovered to be living a life of duplicity, and
his shame is published abroad. How gladly they take advantage of the occasion and use it as an excuse to remain
in their sins. Thus they hide behind his inconsistency and
say scornfully: "If *he* is a sample of what a Christian is,

then I certainly don't want to become one"! The person who takes the place of a preacher of the word of God, must be prepared to pay the price that such a position rightly demands. He will need to avoid the very "appearance of evil," lest the name of the Lord and the work of the Lord be brought into disrepute (I Thess. 5:22). Someone once said of a preacher whose ministry, though not spectacular, was greatly used of God: "I can't understand your preacher's power; I don't see much in him." The other answered: "The reason for his power is that there are thirty years of holy living behind each sermon!"

3. The peril of prominence.

A preacher occupies a far more prominent place in the public eye than those who take no part in preaching; therefore the need for a correspondingly circumspect walk before men (Eph. 5:15-16). A pocket watch and a public clock both serve the same purpose: to tell the time. If a watch gets out of order, only the owner is affected; but if a public clock goes wrong, hundreds of people are misled. Thus a prominent position carries with it a far greater necessity and responsibility for a consistent life. This will involve merciless self-judgment, separation from all known sin and, in some cases, even the denying of the legitimate things of life, that the testimony of Christ and "the ministry be not blamed" (I Cor. 6:12; II Cor. 6:3).

Mountain climbers, who seek to scale the high peaks, do so because of its *delights*, but they are not unaware of its *dangers*. Accordingly, they take every precaution in the way of securing proper equipment. They also see to it that they keep themselves in good physical shape, so that they may be enabled to maintain their poise. With every thrill there is the risk of a spill, and this keeps them perpetually on the alert. Apply this to one who seeks to be a mouthpiece for God, and the need for vigilant spiritual precaution will easily be seen. It is one thing to start off well, and another to continue and end in the same manner. See Gal. 5: 7.

Perhaps one of the most common faults of a preacher is that of exaggeration. Sometimes the incidents he describes are so highly colored by his gifted imagination that the principals, who originally figured in the story, would never recognize it! When describing an actual incident, the *facts of the case* should be rigidly adhered to and the truth, the whole truth and nothing but the truth declared. This baneful habit of exaggeration causes an audience of a hundred to become two hundred and fifty. It also looms large in the preacher's experiences. As another has said: "Everything he sees or owns, or comes in contact with, is the best, the brightest and the most beautiful. His joys are the greatest, his sorrows the keenest and there is nothing ordinary about him." While the imagination is a great boon, it can also become a bane when linked with exaggeration. Let us beware of this bad habit, for it brings much discredit on the work of the Lord.

While discussing the subject of exaggeration, it may not be amiss to draw attention to the present tendency, in some circles, to indulge in wild flights of imagination—or worse —in advertising the abilities of certain preachers, teachers and singers, etc. Superlatives are piled on superlatives in the attempt to assure the reader, or hearer, that all who come to hear this marvelous person will be both greatly honored and highly privileged. The public is invited to listen to: "The most gifted, the most eloquent, the most dynamic speaker that has ever graced the town with his illustrious presence."

It is to be feared that sometimes the preacher himself becomes a party to this form of self-advertising, which savors greatly of a circus billboard, or the midway of a fair, with its ballyhoo merchants who loudly cry their wares, and invite the public to come and see "the most stupendous exhibition on earth." Such adjectives as "wonderful," "marvelous," "tremendous," "thrilling," "awe inspiring" and "colossal" are common place terms with these men. The servant of the Lord, however, who has been gifted by the Lord to preach, should ever remember that he is an "ambassador of Christ," and only a servant of the One who "made Himself of no reputation" (Phil. 2: 7; cp. Prov. 27: 2).

While advertising is a real asset, it should never be allowed to degenerate into a *"lie-ability"*! Though it certainly should be made as attractive as possible, it should not be allowed to go beyond the bounds of good taste. It should be characterized by the truth, and couched in terms compatible with Christian humility. How good it would be if it could be said of each born-again preacher, what was affirmed, so beautifully and simply, of one long ago: "There was a man sent from God whose name was John" (John 1: 6). Who could wish for a higher commendation than this?

Luke's description of John the Baptist's call and commission is significant. See Luke 3: 1-3. Note how he first calls attention to the great of this world, the high and mighty of the land such as: Tiberius Caesar, Pontius Pilate, Herod, Philip, Annas and Caiaphas. Then he comes to the climax of his description. Against the background of these men of worldly fame, he says: "The word of the Lord came unto John, the son of Zacharias in the wilderness; and he came into all the country about Jordan, preaching." Thus God by-passed the so called wise and mighty and noble, and laid His hand on and gave His power to a humble and godly man from the wilderness. See also I Cor. 1: 26-29.

CHAPTER THREE

The Qualifications of the Preacher
(Continued)

VII. He must be fit for the work.

When God calls a person to His service He also fits
and equips him for it, for "God's commands are His en-
ablings." When God wishes one of His creatures to fly,
He gives it wings to fit it for the sphere in which it is to
live and move and have its being. We shall think of the
fitness of the preacher in a four fold sense; spiritually,
physically, mentally and educationally.

1. He should be spiritually fit.

We have deliberately placed this first in the list, for it
is the most important.

(1) *He must be gifted of the Lord to preach or teach
publicly.*

Not all Christians are spiritually gifted to preach or
teach in public. We have already pointed out, in the introduction to this book, that all the education in the
world will never succeed in imparting this gift to anyone.
Eph. 4:7-16 makes this fact perfectly clear: "When He
(Christ) ascended on high, He gave gifts unto men . . .
and He gave some apostles, and some prophets, and some
evangelists, and some pastors and teachers, for the perfecting (maturing) of the saints, for the work of the ministry, for the edifying of the body of Christ." The first two
gifts "apostles and prophets" belong to the foundation, and
are no longer needed (Eph. 2:20-22). The evangelist's
sphere is chiefly in the quarry of sin where, by the "dynamite" of the gospel preached, souls are delivered from

their condition and position by nature. (Rom. 1:16). Pastors, by their godly care of these "living stones," seek to shape them. Then, by a skillful use of the word of God, teachers are used to edify, or build them up in their most holy faith.

While every believer does not possess the gift of an evangelist, pastor or teacher; yet each Christian is an ordained witness for Christ. As such he is both privileged by, and responsible to the Lord to testify to others of Christ's saving, keeping and satisfying power. The Lord said to His disciples: "Ye shall be witnesses unto Me" (Acts 1:8). In John 15:16, the Savior is recorded as saying to His followers: "Ye have not chosen Me, but I have chosen you and ordained you, that ye should go and bring forth fruit, and that your fruit should remain." This is "the mighty ordination of the pierced hands," which is *the portion of every believer*. There is no such thing in the New Testament as human ordination for evangelists, pastors and teachers. The only ordination that is described therein is for *elders*, or those who by reason of age, experience and godliness of character are thus fitted to take the oversight in an assembly of believers. See Acts 14:23, Titus 1:5.

The fact that a Christian is gifted by the Lord to evangelize or teach publicly, does not place this person in a superior caste, or in a professional class, or elevate him above his fellow saints. When he preaches or teaches the word of God, he is simply exercising this particular gift, given to him, as unto the Lord. There is therefore no cause for him to adopt a superior air, as though he were better than, or distinct from the other Christians. Each believer has his own gift and, as each exercises that gift in the spirit of humble dependence upon the Lord, the whole assembly is edified, or built up. See I Cor. 12:1 to 14:21.

The New Testament knows nothing whatever about that unholy distinction, seen in Christendom today, between the so-called "clergy" and "laity." Such a distinction is most emphatically not of God, but of man. It was introduced early in the second century, and has resulted in untold mischief through the years that have followed.

We may assuredly gather, from what has gone before, that the believer who is to preach or teach publicly, must be the recipient of a distinct gift, which has been given him by the ascended Lord for this particular purpose.

(2) *He must seek, by all the means in his power,* to *develop this gift.* It is not enough for a Christian *to possess* this gift of public utterance: he must also *develop* it.

(a) *This gift should first be earnestly coveted.* The believer is exhorted to "covet earnestly the best gifts" (I Cor. 12:3). He is told to: "follow after charity (love), and desire spiritual gifts, but rather that ye may prophesy" (I Cor. 14:1).

"Prophecy" here has the force of *forth*telling, and not of *fore*telling. It refers to the ability to set forth the word of God to the edification of the hearer. A prophet, in this sense, is one who is able to communicate the mind of the Lord to others. Once again Paul enjoins the believer and says: "Wherefore brethren, covet to prophesy" (I Cor. 14:39). From these Scriptures it is clear that the preacher must, first of all, have a deep and holy desire to be a mouthpiece for the Lord. This desire, implanted by the Lord in the believer, must then be allowed to develop unhindered in the atmosphere of prayer, Bible study, godly living and active participation in the Lord's work.

(b) *This gift, when received, must be "stirred up."* Paul wrote to Timothy: "Wherefore I put thee in remembrance that thou stir up the gift of God, which is in thee" (II Tim. 1:6). Gift must be treated in the same manner as the sugar we put in tea or coffee. Unless it is stirred, it will sink to the bottom and be of no use. All the *stirring* of a cup will never sweeten its contents, unless the *sugar* has been placed within. Likewise, all the sugar that has been placed in the cup will be of no avail unless it is *stirred*. Both the sugar and the stirring are necessary. To attempt to stir up a gift that is *not* within us, will soon stir up trouble *around* us from those who have to *listen to us!* We need to heed Solomon's words: "Whoso boasteth himself of a false gift is like clouds and winds without rain" (Prov. 25:14). These windy preachers bring no refreshing showers of blessing as they say nothing at extreme length! The audience is the best judge as to whether or not we have this gift to preach or teach the word of God publicly. The scriptural test is: "Let the prophets speak . . . and let the others judge" (I Cor. 14:29).

This stirring up of a gift is accomplished by earnest application to the task, much fervent prayer, diligent Bible study, and the *constant use* of what we already possess in the way of material. To "stir" suggests *effort* on the part of the stirrer, and this word has an unwelcome sound to some. Thus there are two sides to this question of gift: the divine and the human. It is God's prerogative to *give* the gift, or talent; it is ours to *stir* it up by assiduous study, faithful application and constant use.

(c)   *This gift must be developed by exercise.*

Gift improves with use and becomes brighter by constant polishing. Just as proficiency in music, or in art, or in any other profession can only be achieved through constant practice; so the gift of preaching and teaching must be developed by constant exercise. We are all inclined to envy the expert pianist, or the gifted preacher, and perhaps little appreciate how much concentrated effort lies behind the finished product. It has been well said that: "nine-tenths of inspiration consists of perspiration!" The Bible puts it thus: "As every man hath received the gift, even so minister the same one to another, as good stewards of the manifold grace of God. If any man minister, let him

do it as of the ability which God giveth, that God in all
things, may be glorified through Jesus Christ, to Whom be
praise and dominion for ever and ever. Amen" (I Pet. 4:
10, 11).

It will be observed that this gift is said to be a *stewardship*. The Christian has only been entrusted with it in
order that he might invest it to the best advantage on
behalf of his Lord. Christ used two parables to illustrate
two different aspects of this truth. In the parable of the
pounds, each servant received an *equal amount*, with the
injunction from his master: "Occupy (or do business) till
I come" (Luke 19:12-27). Thus in this parable each servant was *equally responsible* with every other servant. Each
Christian has been given some particular gift, and is therefore directly responsible to his Lord as to how he uses it
during his lifetime. In the parable of the talents, each servant was given a *different* amount: "To each man according
to his several ability." Here the emphasis is not on *responsibility*, but on *ability* (Matt. 25:14-30). All Christ's
servants are therefore equal in *responsibility*, but not in
ability. Responsibility has been well defined as: "Human
response to Divine ability." The pound could illustrate
the gospel, which has been entrusted to each believer, and
with which he must seek to gain souls for his Master. The
talents illustrate the varying measures of gift which Christ
has given to His people.

(d) *This gift may be lost through neglect.*

Paul exhorted Timothy: "Neglect not the gift that is
within thee." He wrote concerning another: "Say unto
Archippus: 'Take heed unto the ministry which thou hast
received in the Lord, that thou fulfil it' " (or fill it full)
(I Tim. 4:4; Col. 4:17). It is sadly possible for a Christian,
through neglect, to fail to fill full the ministry which the
Lord has given to him. The Lord deliver us from an unfulfilled ministry! It is not without significance that the

napkin, in which the unfaithful servant wrapped the pound and the talent, was his sweat cloth, which the servants of that time used to tie around their waists so as to be handy as occasion demanded. This man argued, in effect: "Seeing I do not intend to do any labor for my master, or put myself to any inconvenience on his behalf, there will be no need for my sweat cloth with which to wipe my brow. I shall therefore turn it into a shroud in which to bury my gift, take my ease and let others do the work." (Luke 19:20-21).

There is a principle which obtains in nature that is called "the law of atrophy." This decrees that any function of a member of the body which is *wilfully* discontinued, causes that member to lose its ability to function. For instance, the person who refuses to use his legs, will lose his ability to walk. The muscles which control these members, through disuse, will atrophy, or waste away. There are the so called "holy men" of India who have held up their arms so long they can no longer put them down. There is a case on record of a woman who, because she was jilted, took a vow of silence for fifty years. After this period had expired she attempted to speak, but found she could not: her vocal chords had atrophied through their long disuse.

If God has gifted and called a person to preach, and he neglects or refuses to exercise this gift, he will lose this ability, and discover that he *cannot* preach. Let us lay to heart the solemn fact that what we do not *use* we shall *lose!* The poet has expressed it thus:

> "A talent bright was mine long years ago,
> 'Use it,' the Giver said: ' 'twill brighter grow.'
> I used it: how it shone! And then, one day,
> For just a whim I laid my gift away.
> Untouched I left it while the years rolled on;
> Today I seek it, but my gift is gone!"

When a God-given gift is allowed to pass out of circulation because of the effort required to keep it going, the moth and the rust will combine to do their deadly work. Both are silent in their operation, but what havoc they play with hoarded and unused treasure! (Matt. 6:19-20). There are literally thousands of Christians in our midst who might have been honored preachers and teachers of the Word; but who neglected to develop their gift because of the effort and self sacrifice involved. Over their lives, which may appear to some to be successful, the sad word *"failure"* must be written. The judgment seat of Christ, at which every Christian must appear, will rightly appraise the true value of all our service. On this occasion, reward or loss shall be meted out by our Lord and Master (I Cor. 3:10-17). May it be ours to hear from His lips the commendation: "Well done, thou good and faithful servant ... enter thou into the joy of thy Lord!" (Matt. 25:21).

(3) *This gift must be developed in the atmosphere of spirituality.*

Spiritual gifts require spiritual power for their operation. This demands that the preacher himself must be spiritual. We cannot do better than quote the weighty words of an honored servant of Christ, the late Henry Groves. Speaking of the early disciples he said: "It was a spiritual work they had to do, therefore He *spiritualized* the men who were to do it. It was faith they had to plant, therefore He made His missionaries men of faith. They had to deliver the nations from the idolatry of gold and silver, therefore He took care His messengers should have none. They had to deliver people from the idolatry of wisdom, therefore He took care they should be looked on as foolish. They had to deliver the world from the idolatry of power and might, therefore He took care they should be weak. They had to deliver from the idolatry of fame and reputation, therefore He took care they should be despised; making them in all respects models of the doctrine which they were sent forth to preach."

"Truly, this is what the Church needs, and this must be the aim of any who would stand in the counsel of God and act for Him, whether in ministry in the Church, or in evangelizing those who are outside and afar off. They must themselves *live* the truths they teach and be *examples* of those divine principles they are sent to inculcate."

To maintain this spiritual robustness of character, the preacher must obey the laws of spiritual hygiene. He must feed himself regularly with the word of God. He must know what it means to spend much time in fellowship with God in prayer and thus breathe deep of the celestial atmosphere. He must seek to convert the bread of divine truth into the blood, bone, muscle and fiber of his character, by a prompt and obedient response to the opportunities of service for his Lord and Master. This is the spiritual environment in which alone he can do effective work in the vineyard of the Lord.

2. He should be physically fit.

Public speaking exacts a tremendous strain on one's supply of nervous energy. In fact, one hour of preaching is the equivalent of eight hours of physical labor, in terms of the expenditure of nervous energy. The physical is more closely linked to the spiritual than we imagine. The ideal, so far as preaching is concerned, is to have a healthy soul in a healthy body. The apostle John realized this and wrote to his beloved friend, Gaius: "I wish above all things that thou mayest prosper and be in health, even as thy soul prospereth" (III John 2).

(1) *The value of the body.*

A Christian father wrote to his son, who was also a believer, and gave him the following terse but good advice: "Your body is the divinely ordained vehicle, through which the Holy Spirit expresses Himself: therefore take good care of it." The bodies in which we live are ours only for the duration of our life on earth. At death, the spirit of the believer goes to be "with Christ" which is "far better." At the second coming of Christ each believer's body, whether raised or raptured, shall be made like unto the body of Christ's glory. (Phil. 3:21). While it is now called "the body of our humiliation," it must neither be despised, nor should it be allowed to occupy too much of our time or attention. It must neither be neglected, nor molly-coddled. We must be neither careless, nor over-anxious about it. In this, as in many other things, the balance of the divine and the human sides of the question must be taken into consideration. God gave us our bodies at birth, but we must take care of that which He has entrusted to us. Remember, it is impossible for the disembodied spirit of a believer to function on earth at peak efficiency! It is only while "in the body" that he can serve as he should. Therefore, the necessity to take good care of the body!

Each Christian should therefore take good care as to what he puts *into his body* in the way of food. He should avoid what he knows, by experience, to be detrimental to his physical health, or what he realizes unfits him for his most efficient service for the Lord. He should abstain from either over-eating or under-eating, and only take the kind and quantity of food necessary to keep him physically at his best for God. Any habit that is harmful to clear thinking or pure living should be shunned. Such habits as the drinking of alcoholic liquors, or smoking, should be avoided like a plague; lest they hinder the effectiveness of the preaching of the word of God. While it is true that temperance, and not total abstinence, is the teaching of Scripture yet, for the sake of example, it is far better to leave all questionable things severely alone.

A careful reading of Romans 14 will show that even that which is quite legitimate must be refrained from if it will cause a weaker brother to be spiritually stumbled. As Paul puts it: "It is good neither to eat flesh, nor to drink wine, nor anything whereby thy brother stumbleth, or is offended, or is made weak" (Rom. 14:21).

The believer should also be careful what he puts *on his body*. Each should see to it that the clothing worn should be proper to the occasion and consistent with the demands of decent society. Here again the extremes should be avoided, either of sartorial splendor on the one hand, or untidy carelessness on the other. Many a Christian worker has been laid aside by sickness which he or she contracted because of insufficient clothing. A little use of that somewhat uncommon commodity, called "common sense," would have warned him of the danger of subjecting his body to a chill without proper protection. God does not usually suspend the laws of nature in favor of His people. The preacher often has to learn, by painful and costly experience, that he must be careful how he clothes his body so as to keep it fit for the Master's use.

Then again, the servant of the Lord should exercise reasonable precaution as to *where he takes his body*. It is hardly necessary to say that he should avoid questionable places of amusement, where his presence would bring reproach on the testimony of the gospel. One sometimes hears a Christian use the expression: "I can take Christ with me everywhere I go." Such a statement utterly fails to take into account our Lord's own words: "When He putteth forth His own sheep, He goeth before them, and the sheep *follow Him*, for they know His voice" (John 10:4). A Christian cannot take his Lord *anywhere*: but he can safely follow Christ *everywhere* He leads.

Sound common sense demands that undue risks of one's life should not be undertaken. What shall be said of a believer who puts his head into the mouth of a lion and then fervently prays: "O Lord, please keep this lion from biting my head off?" If he had prayed about putting his head into the lion's mouth, he never would have put it there! Many a most useful Christian life has been, humanly speaking, cut short by death through his own recklessness and carelessness. He might have lived for many more years to preach the gospel if he had exercised reasonable care. The huge toll of automobile fatalities, in which discourtesy, carelessness and excessive speed plays a no small part, should speak with a loud voice to every preacher of the Word who drives an automobile. Some time ago there appeared in "The Sunday School Times" an article entitled: "The Sin We Brag About." This sin was that of a Christian breaking the laws of the land by excessive speeding, and thus endangering not only his own life, but the lives of those travelling with him.

Lastly, the believer must take care of what he *does to his body*. He must avoid the two extremes of *rusting* out through sloth, or of *tearing* out through over-work. By a judicious use of food, exercise and rest, he should seek to keep his body at its best for God. In other words, he should *wear* out in his Master's service. We read in Psalm 103:14 that: "The Lord . . . knoweth our frame, He remembereth that we are *dust*." Mark well the last word. Many a preacher seems to imagine he is made of *cast iron*, instead of "dust," and consequently strains himself beyond the limits of his endurance and has to be laid aside, through "nervous prostration," from any further active participation in the work of the Lord.

On every railroad car there is marked, in clear letters, its load capacity. To load that car beyond its limit is to risk a breakdown. Wise and happy is that preacher who recognizes his own labor capacity and then keeps within that limit. Someone has said: "When Satan can't keep a

Christian from working, he jumps on his back and rides him to death." The story is told of D. L. Moody and a fellow preacher who were waiting for a night train. As the train pulled in, Moody walked towards the Pullman sleeping coach. The other preacher, as he walked towards the day coach said: "I'm saving the Lord's money." Moody retorted: "I'm saving the Lord's servant."

(2) *Our bodies are the Lord's.*

The Bible puts it thus: "Now the body is not for fornication, but for the Lord and the Lord for the body" (I Cor. 6:13). The Christian's body, as does everything else pertaining to him, belongs to the Lord. Nothing could be plainer than this: "Know ye not that your body is the temple of the Holy Ghost, which is in you, which ye have of God and ye are *not your own?* For ye are bought with a price: therefore glorify God in your body and in your spirit, which are God's" (I Cor. 6:19-20).

Seeing that our bodies do not belong to us, but that we are merely tenants in them for the duration of our lifetime on earth, what should our attitude be in regard to our bodies? The word of God leaves us in no doubt as to the answer. We are urged, first of all, to *yield our bodies* for a *righteous* life: "Yield yourselves unto God, as those that are alive from the dead, and your members (i. e.: hands, feet, tongue, etc.) as instruments of righteousness unto God" (Rom. 6:13).

The believer is next urged to present his body to God for a *useful life.* "I beseech you therefore brethren, by the mercies of God, that ye present your bodies a living sacrifice, holy, acceptable unto God, which is your reasonable (or intelligent) service" (Rom. 12:12). The verses which follow indicate that this presentation of our bodies will fit us for a life of devoted, useful and joyous service for Him.

Our bodies, which have been yielded to Him, must now be *kept for Him.* Paul testified: "I keep under my body, and bring it unto subjection, lest that by any means, when I have preached to others, I myself should be a castaway" (I Cor. 9:27). The flesh, or that principle of enmity against God which each of us received through his physical birth, is still within the believer. This corrupt nature will seek, by all its arts and wiles, to use the body as a vehicle by which to express itself. These "lusts of the flesh" must therefore be resolutely denied and the believer must determine to rule his body, and not allow it to become his master. To keep the body *under,* the believer needs constantly to keep the spirit on *top.*

Lastly, our bodies *can be used,* by God, for His glory. David spoke of this in Psalm 92:1, 3. Note the words: "It is a good thing to give thanks unto the Lord, and to sing praises unto Thy name, O most High. To show forth Thy loving kindness in the morning, and Thy faithfulness every night, upon an instrument of ten strings, and upon the psaltery; upon the harp with a solemn sound." The body could be likened to this ten stringed instrument which, when placed unreservedly in the hands of the Divine Musician, is capable of producing exquisite melody to the glory of God. These ten strings could represent our two eyes to read His word; two ears to hear His voice; two feet to walk in ways well pleasing to Him; two hands to gladly do His bidding in useful service; a mouth to testify for Him, and a heart in which He reigns supreme. When these ten members of the body are thus yielded to the Lord, He can produce wondrous melody and harmony as His fingers sweep over the responsive chords. No wonder Frances Ridley Havergal wrote:

> "Take my life and let it be
> Consecrated, Lord, to Thee;
> Take my moments and my days,
> Let them flow in ceaseless praise."

(3) *The value of good health.*

This is often not realized until it is lost for a season and then, unfortunately, it is too late. Dr. A. T. Scofield, a distinguished nerve specialist and a most intelligent and devoted Christian, has written several good books which every Christian worker would do well to read. "Nerves in Disorder" and "Christian Sanity" are perhaps the best known. They combine a keen spiritual perception, with an equally sound knowledge of the functions of the human body, and the result is good practical advice to all who seek to preach.

He points out that the words: "health," "whole," and "holy," are from the same root, and then likens man to a three story building. The ground floor is the *body* which, as far as possible, should be kept in a *healthy condition.* The second floor is the *soul,* which should be kept whole, or in a *wholesome* state. The third floor is the *spirit,* which should be kept *holy.* Spiritual health consists in the proper care and functioning of each story of this wonderful house.

Many Christians, who used to be active and useful servants of the Lord, have now been laid on the shelf because of their failure to observe the simple rules governing good health. Each preacher should make it his business, as far as it lies in his power, to keep his body in the best possible condition for effective service on behalf of Him, "Whose he is, and Whom he serves" (Acts 27:23).

CHAPTER FOUR

The Qualifications of the Preacher
(Continued)

3. He should be mentally fit.

Or, to put it in Scriptural language, he should be possessed of a "sound mind." We read: "God hath not given to us the spirit of fear, but of power, and of love, and of a sound mind" (II Tim. 1:7). There are, of course, varying degrees of mental alertness. Heredity plays a large part in this. Some have a greater capacity than others, yet each should seek to be his best, mentally, for God.

(1) *The danger of fanaticism.*

A fanatic has been well defined as: "one who *majors on a minor*"! That is to say, he takes *one aspect of truth* from the word of God and then pushes it to the extreme, to the entire exclusion of all the other Scriptures which would have given him a correct balance of the truth as a *whole.* Much discredit has been brought on the preaching of the gospel and the teaching of the word of God because of these mental "kinks" on the part of some preachers. These people seem to be mentally incapable of interpreting one verse of Scripture, or one phase of truth in the light of *all the other verses* that bear on that verse or aspect of truth.

Fanaticism has its origin in an unbalanced mind, for it seeks to distort, out of all proportion, one truth to the ignoring of all other truths. We do well to beware of the preacher who "specializes" in one line of teaching and harps on this particular theme every time he speaks. He is blind to all else in Scripture, save this pet subject of his. Someone, speaking on the text: "Hast thou faith? Have it thyself alone," added: "And it might well be said: 'Hast thou a kink? Have it to thyself alone!' " (Rom. 14:22).

The Devil is well satisfied if he can switch a preacher from his God-given task of expounding in "all the Scriptures," to riding a little hobby horse of some peculiar line of teaching that will absorb all his time and energy. The only difference between riding a horse and riding a hobby, is that a person can get off a horse! We need ever to remember that "*All* scripture is given by inspiration of God." Therefore *all the Scriptures,* relative to any truth or doctrine, need to be examined before one can come to any definite conclusion regarding the matter under consideration.

Whenever one particular line of truth is allowed to become an obsession, it produces a lopsidedness in the preacher. This particular line of teaching may be all very well in its place, but when it is magnified out of all proportion to the other truths of Scripture it becomes a mischievous thing, and is calculated to cause confusion and produce division. It may be a certain interpretation of prophecy relative to the second coming of Christ, or it may consist of some aspect of Church truth, or even the *kind* of bread and wine that should be used at the Lord's supper, or some peculiar idea regarding the various dispensations.

It is a sad sight to see a promising preacher who might have been a power for God, leaving his useful sphere of teaching *all* the word of God, and becoming obsessed with some minor truth, or some peculiar theory, or some odd interpretation of Scripture. This idea becomes a fatal fascination to him, and forms a rivulet that runs through his mind, into which all his thinking capacity is drained. This obsession colors all his ministry. It matters not what is the theme of the text he may take: sooner or later he will drag his pet subject into his sermon. It must ever be kept in mind that any truth of Scripture that is held at the *expense* of any other truth is fanaticism. Many a preacher has had to be laid aside from active service because of this very thing.

(2)   *The need for sane and sound thinking.*

In this letter to Titus, Paul emphasizes this necessity for soundness. In it he refers to *"sound doctrine."* He speaks of the need to be *"sound* in the faith." He points out how necessary it is to maintain the things "which become sound doctrine." He advises the use of *"sound speech that cannot be condemned."* See Titus 1: 9, 13; 2: 1, 2, 8. Sound speech comes from sound thinking: hence the necessity for a preacher to be able to think sanely and soberly.

A preacher, of all people, ought to be able to think his way clearly through a proposition and come to a sensible conclusion of what he has read or heard. Mental alertness is surely an essential requisite for a preacher. He is occupied with the loftiest and the most sublime of all truths: the great doctrines of God, Christ, the Holy Spirit, sin, salvation and the eternal weal or woe of humanity. How great, therefore, is the need for this ability to think sanely, soberly and reverently on these subjects. He should also be a man of vigorous imagination, who can see, in nature and history, illustrations of the truth he wishes to apply to the hearer. It must ever be kept in mind that God does not want His people to be either weak-kneed, weak-handed, weak-hearted or, least of all, weak-headed!

4.   He should be educationally fit.

To be found educationally deficient at conversion is no disgrace, for many have not had the same educational opportunities and advantages as others; but to remain, wilfully and willingly in that condition, is inexcusable. Every Christian should have this text hung on the wall of his

home: "Cursed be he that doeth the work of the Lord
negligently!" (Jer. 48:10, marg.)

(1) *The need for it.*

Surely the Lord's work demands the very best that is
within one's power to give. Each young believer should
be able to truthfully sing:

> "Just as I am, young, strong, and free,
> To be the very best that I can be
> For truth and righteousness and Thee,
> Lord of my life, I come!"

God places no premium, or value on ignorance. The
penalty of wilful ignorance is deeper, darker, grosser and
more abysmal ignorance, until the victim becames so
steeped in it that he becomes complacent, and even proud
of his lack of knowledge. One such person was once heard
to pray: "O, Lord, I thank Thee that I don't know nothing!" Another such individual once remarked to a group
of people: "I am thankful for my ignorance." One of them
replied: "Well, you certainly have a great deal to be
thankful for!"

The Bible puts the matter thus: "If a man (will) be
ignorant, let him be ignorant" (I Cor. 14:38). The idea
that "anything is good enough for the Lord's work," certainly has no support from the word of God. On the contrary, it is soundly condemned. The Christian is enjoined
to show himself "approved unto God, a workman that
needeth not to be ashamed." This demands the very best
he can give, in the way of concentrated study, painstaking preparation and arrangement, and the earnest presentation of the preaching material. The best of our time,
energy and ability should be placed unreservedly at the
disposal of the Lord, for the work of the Lord. As Oswald
Chambers so tersely put it: "My utmost, for His highest!"

The example of the Lord Jesus offers no encouragement to those who belittle special training for Christian

work. He chose and called certain disciples, and the reason for this act is stated thus: "That they should be with Him and that He might send them forth to preach" (Mark 3:14). For the next three years these men companied with the Lord, and were thus under the tuition of the greatest of all Teachers, *before they began to preach* and teach in His name. There was much that Christ said to them that they could not understand, for they were "foolish and slow of heart to believe" (Luke 24:25). There were many things that Christ could have taught them, but would not, for their capacity was limited. He had to say: "I have yet many things to say unto you, but ye cannot bear them now" (John 16:12). After Pentecost the Holy Spirit, as Christ had promised, brought back to their remembrance these words and drove home to their hearts the lessons He had so patiently taught them. These lessons, in turn, became a great power in their lives and gave divine authority to their ministry.

Though the Pharisees, blinded by their religious prejudices, looked upon these disciples as "ignorant and unlearned men;" they were, most emphatically, *nothing of the kind!* (Acts 4:13). They were, in reality, the *best educated* people in the world, for they had been for three years or more in the best school in the world, the school of Christ! Let those who ignorantly criticize a Bible School, which is conducted along Scriptural lines, remember that it exists for the same purpose as the school of Christ; that is, of imparting Bible knowledge and consequently better fitting young believers to know and preach the living word of the living God. Let such criticizers take good heed and seriously, soberly and intelligently consider what they say, in the light of this example set by the Lord Himself.

There is a tendency on the part of some unthinking believers to depreciate "scholarship," but surely the Lord has given brains to His people in order that they might use them for Him! While brains are not everything, most people, including Christians, would find it rather awkward to get along without them! Regeneration does not rob a believer of his intelligence, but enlightens, ennobles and empowers it for the purpose intended in the beginning— the glory of God. Our intellect was not given to us to be *deprecated, or depreciated,* but to be *developed* for Him.

Two Christians were once engaged in a rather warm discussion. The better educated of the two was getting the best of the argument, and the other, thinking to end it exclaimed: "God doesn't want your knowledge, brother." The other calmly replied: "No, that's quite true, but neither does He require your ignorance!"

Of course, there is no such thing as a "finished education." A course of study on any subject is simply designed to place at a student's disposal certain sources of information and methods of study by which he may be better enabled to educate himself. There is no easy road by which a person may lounge through a prescribed course of study in three or four years. Herein lies the difference between *knowledge* and *wisdom.* Knowledge consists in the intellectual accumulation of facts; wisdom in the ability to correlate, hold and use them aright. Mere knowledge, when unaccompanied by wisdom, succeeds only in "puffing up," and is to be deplored. (I Cor. 8:1).

Preaching certainly does not exist for the purpose of enabling a speaker to display his knowledge before an audience, or of impressing it with a sense of his learning. Such a thing is obnoxious in the extreme. It has been rightly said: "Knowledge dwells in the heads of men, replete with thoughts of other men; but wisdom dwells in minds attentive to their own. Knowledge is proud, because it knows so much: wisdom is humble, because it knows no more."

A school teacher who had been passed over in the pro-
motion list and a younger man given the position he imagined should have been his, complained to the principal
and said: "But I have had *twenty years of experience* as
a teacher." "No," replied the principal; "in reality you
have only had one year of experience repeated twenty
times!" The moral is obvious!

The following quotation from the writings of C. F.
Hogg is worth memorizing: "Wisdom comes only with
experience and is gained by adapting knowledge to the
needs and circumstances of life." Knowledge therefore
serves the useful purpose of better knowing, better representing, and better presenting the Lord Jesus Christ to
others.

(2) *The advantage of knowledge.*

Anything that better equips a preacher to proclaim
"the glorious gospel of the blessed God" more effectively
deserves his most earnest consideration (I Tim. 1:11).
Spurgeon said: "If I can be a ram's horn for God, this is
good; but if a silver trumpet, that is far better." All
other things being equal, from a spiritual standpoint, the
educated preacher has a decided advantage over the un-
educated. His knowledge of grammar and his command
of words is greater, as well as his correct use and pronunciation of the words by which the message is conveyed. His range of general knowledge is wider, and all
this store of information will prove to be of great use in illustrating and driving home the points he wishes to make.

We may well thank God that all the men of great learning are not on the side of the Devil. Moses was an intellectual giant. We are told he was "learned in all the
wisdom of the Egyptians and was mighty in words and
deeds" (Acts 7:22). When he made his great choice for
God, and turned his back on Egypt's treasures and pleas-

ures, God used him mightily as a leader of Israel, and inspired him to write the first five books of the Bible. The apostle Paul is in a similar category. Brought up at the feet of Gamaliel, the greatest teacher of his time, he received a splendid education. When he was brought to know Christ, he gladly and unreservedly placed all he was, and all he had at the disposal of his Lord and Master. By Divine inspiration, the greater part of the New Testament has come to us through his pen.

One has only to look at his bookshelf to see the honored names of men who combined a high degree of intellectual attainment with a higher degree of spirituality. Though these men of God are now with Christ, their "works do follow them," and their writings are still used to bless and edify the people of God.

The average audience of today is better educated than that of a generation ago. The consolidated schools in the country districts have given the farm boy the same educational advantages as the city-born. The widespread network of radio has also contributed very largely to the forming of a far more discriminating audience than was possible forty years ago. On the whole, these radio programs are couched in good English, clearly enunciated and correctly pronounced. Surely it is not too much to expect that the gospel preacher, with the greatest and grandest message in all the world, should be able to tell out the good news in equally good forceful English, clearly enunciated and correctly pronounced.

(3) *The provision of it.*

God has both anticipated and supplied the need for the preachers' education; but the student must lay hold upon this provision and make it his own by diligent application. It is one thing for food to be provided, but quite another to appropriate it for one's self. It is possible for a person to starve to death in the midst of plenty, simply by a failure to eat the food that has been supplied. Let us look at this abundant provision for the preacher's education.

(a) *The Bible.*

The preacher will not lack in facilities to improve his education. The Bible comes first and foremost. In fact, the study of the English Bible is a magnificent education in itself, and no one's education is complete without it. Viewed only as literature it is unsurpassed. "It is cast into every form of constructive composition and good writing: history, prophecy, poetry, allegory, emblematic representation, judicious interpretation, literal statement, precept, example, proverbs, disquisition, epistle, sermon and prayer; in short, all the rational shapes of human discourse." (*Maclagan*).

The Bible is a library in itself and, of course, must be the preacher's constant companion, and his "Inquire within about everything." There is no other book in all the world that can, for one moment, compare with it. It dwarfs into utter insignificance, all secular literature. The preacher must saturate himself with the holy Scriptures. This can only be done as he reads and rereads it, and it thus becomes part and parcel of his very being, influencing and governing his thoughts, words and acts. He must be "a man of the Book" and a master of its contents. He should be able to quote from it freely and thus make its beautiful language his own.

(b) *A good library.*

The present-day Christian can also say, with David: "The lines are fallen unto me in pleasant places; yea, I have a goodly heritage" (Ps. 16: 6). Perhaps we little realize the tremendous debt we owe to men of learning, who have devoted their great abilities and vast store of Bible knowledge to the service of Christ and His people. These men have left behind them, in the form of books, the valuable legacy of truth we now possess, and of which we would do well to take every advantage. It can be truthfully said of their sacrificial efforts: "Other men labored, and ye are entered into their labors" (John 4:38).

Let no man despite books, for in so doing *he despises what God has given.* Teachers are a divine gift for the Church's edification, whether their ministry be oral, or written. The person who foolishly refuses to read books written by sound teachers of the Word must, to be consistent, refuse to go and listen to any of them speak! In doing this, he would be taking issue with God who has given it for the specific purpose of his edification. See Eph. 4:11-16. The only difference between oral and written ministry, is that the latter is likely to be more profitable! When a person commits himself to writing for publication, he takes far greater care in expressing himself, lest there should be any misunderstanding of his meaning. Thus these good books only await the opportunity of pouring out their treasures of knowledge at the feet of the diligent seeker. Read Proverbs 2:1-12; 3:13-26. While the Bible must ever have the first place in one's reading, and never allowed to be crowded out; yet these other books will prove to be a very valuable adjunct to it and of much spiritual profit.

Needless to say, it will not be the number of books on one's library shelves which constitute the preacher's possession; but only those he has really made his own by personal reading. It can be truthfully said that many a good library remains unpossessed by its owner! These books should be purchased with great care. The advice of an experienced Christian should be sought in their selection. It is far better to have a few really good books than a large number of the other kind which merely take up valuable space, to say nothing of the expense in acquiring them. We shall devote quite a little space, later on, to a suggestive list of books for a preacher's library.

The preacher should also read fairly widely the best of secular literature, including history, poetry and the classics. In this way, he will widen his horizons, increase his vocabulary, become better acquainted with good English and thus learn to express himself better. It is astonishing how much time is uselessly frittered away during the course of every twenty-four hours, which could have been much better utilized in reading. It is always a good idea to take a book everywhere one goes, and read when the opportunity presents itself.

(c) *Correspondence courses.*

There are a host of courses available and the preacher is faced with a galaxy of subjects from which to meet his own particular need. The Emmaus Bible School, of 156 N. Oak Park Avenue, Oak Park, Illinois, has some splendid courses on the Scriptures that should prove very useful. A postcard sent to this address will bring a catalog of these excellent Bible courses. Then again, a course in English, or in public speaking, or in journalism, will all aid in better fitting the preacher to present the message of the gospel, or to teach the word of God, and surely this is no small matter.

(d) *Writing.*

The preacher would also be well advised to write as much as possible. This will materially aid him in acquiring both clarity of thought and facility of expression. Incidentally, it will do much to correct any mistakes in his grammar. The very effort of writing is an excellent discipline for the mind, for it compels a person to state his facts clearly and concisely. A lot of muddied thinking and ambiguous speaking would have been avoided if the speaker had written down what he would have *liked* to have said, but *didn't!*

(e) *Criticism.*

The preacher should both seek and welcome criticism from others on his subject matter, expressions, pronunciation, grammar, gesticulations, mannerisms and anything else that would hinder the effective presentation of the message through him. We shall refer more fully to this matter, later on.

Jeff. D. Day has finely expressed this thought. He says: "Really trying to preach involves persistent, careful and prayerful preparation of the sermon in all its details, its doctrines, its homiletical order, its vigorous English, its grammatical correctness, its proper pronunciation of the words, its winsome delivery, in modulated vocalization, clear enunciation and correct gesticulation." All this sounds like hard work, and it most certainly is, but it is well worth while, for "pay day" is coming! (Col. 3:24).

May it be ours, not only to pray for "the wisdom that cometh from above" (James 1:5-7; 3:17), but to use every opportunity to develop our capacity for that wisdom, which shall better fit us for the task of being "ambassadors for Christ," and enable us to earn the: "Well done, thou good and faithful servant" of our blessed Lord and Master (II Cor. 5:20; Matt. 25:21).

We have used quite a little space to this matter of the qualifications of the preacher, and for the very good reason that we cannot disassociate the preacher from his preaching. We must remember the Divine order in Paul's injunction: "Take heed unto *thyself* and unto the doctrine," (or teaching) I Tim. 4:16.

CHAPTER FIVE

The Preacher's Call

We have already mentioned that each preacher must be gifted, called and equipped by the Lord for "the work of the ministry." All Christians are "saints by calling," but not all are "preachers by calling." (I Cor. 1:2). Let us therefore consider some things regarding this Divine "call" to preach the Word.

I. It is individual, or personal.

It is purely a matter between each Christian and his Lord and Master. The authority of the call is the prerogative of Christ alone, for He calls whomsoever He wills. He said to His disciples: "Ye have not chosen Me, but I have chosen you, and ordained you that ye should go and bring forth fruit, and that your fruit should remain" (John 15:16). We read that Christ called "unto Him whom He would" (Mark 3:13-14). Of Paul, the Lord said: "He is a chosen vessel unto Me, to bear My name before the Gentiles and kings and the children of Israel" (Acts 9:15). Both secular and theological education are utterly useless, apart from this call of the Lord.

The fact that a person possesses a natural fluency of speech and facility of expression does not, in itself, qualify that person to preach. It is good, but not sufficient, to have natural gifts and possess physical, mental and educational fitness. Alexander MacLaren spoke of a certain preacher who was "fatally fluent in speech." Though these natural gifts are necessary, they are not enough. The fact of their possession does not constitute a call to preach.

1. *It involves personal heart-dealing alone with God.*
God is the God of the individual. There is no such

thing as "mass production" in this matter. Preachers are not turned out by the dozen. The Lord burdens the heart of an individual, impresses him personally with the necessity of preaching the gospel, and gives him that holy urge to be a mouthpiece for Deity. It is not without significance that Isaiah, called of God to preach His word, speaks repeatedly of his message as "a burden" which must be delivered (Isa. 13:1, 14:28, 15:1, 17:1, etc.). Paul spoke of it as a "*necessity*" laid upon him and exclaimed: "Yea, woe is unto me, if I preach not the gospel!" (I Cor. 9:16). Joshua, as he fell upon his face before the Captain of the host of the Lord, asked: "What saith my Lord unto His servant?" There, all alone with his Lord, his shoes removed, for it was holy ground, Joshua bowed his head, received his call and commission and then went forth to do exploits for God. (Josh. 5:13-15).

2. *It is born in the atmosphere of spirituality.* It comes when the soul is enjoying fellowship with God through the reading and meditation of His word and prayer. The carnal believer, or the worldly Christian, will know nothing of "the still small voice" which falls upon the soul under such circumstances. Samuel's word to Saul has a message for each believer: "Stand thou still a while, that I may show thee the word of God" (I Sam. 9:27). This atmosphere of spirituality is made possible as the believer deliberately presents his body as "a living sacrifice, holy, acceptable unto God, which is your reasonable service" (Rom. 12:1-2). It comes through fervent supplication at the throne of grace to know the will of God for one's life. It is maintained by prompt obedience to the known will of God, as found in the holy Scriptures. This, then, is the spiritual atmosphere of the call.

3. *It comes usually in the midst of Christian activity,* not in monastic isolation. It does not come to *lazy* Christians. It was while Barnabas and Saul "ministered to the

Lord" that the divine call came: "Separate me Barnabas and Saul for the work whereto I have called them" (Acts 13:2). It was while Moses tended his flock, that he was commissioned to be a leader of Israel (Exod. 3:1-2). It was while Gideon threshed the wheat, that he was selected to deliver Israel from the oppressors (Judg. 6:11). It was while Elisha was busy plowing, that the mantle of Elijah was thrown on his shoulders and God claimed his life (I Kings 19:19). It was while Peter was busy with his fishing, and Matthew with his business, that the voice came and called each to service for Christ (Matt. 4:18-19; Luke 5:27). It is as the believer is doing *what already lies to his hand,* that the call comes for further service. "If any man will *do* His will, he shall know," said Christ (John 7:17). Prompt, unquestioning obedience to what we know, will lead to further revelations of His will. Hosea's message should have a voice to each believer: "Then shall we know, *if we follow on to know the Lord"* (Hos. 6:3).

II. It is definite.

Though the call may come in various ways and under different circumstances, it is none the less distinct. It leaves the believer with the assurance that God desires him for a certain specific work. This, in turn, gives a joyous confidence and a holy boldness to the preacher, as he realizes the authority that lies behind the message and the messenger. The promise: "My presence shall go with thee and I will give thee rest," nerves the soul to courageously face the opposition that will inevitably show itself. The cheering assurance: "The Lord is with thee!" sustains the servant of the Lord, who now realizes that Omnipotence is on his side (Exod. 33:14; Judges 6:12).

III. It is varied in circumstances.

A study of the ways by which God called some of His servants for the work He had for them should be a profitable exercise of the soul. Let us look at just a few out of many.

1. *Abraham.* We are told: "the God of glory appeared unto him" and a definite call was given him, with the promise of his own blessing and, through him, to all the families of the earth (Acts 7:2; Gen. 12:1-3).

2. *Moses.* Exod. 3-4. This is most instructive, for God had to overcome the reluctance of the one He called. Moses had many objections to offer, but every objection was met with a definite promise, until Moses was convinced that God knew what He was doing in calling him.

3. *Joshua.* To this man, God first gave a commission with a promise and then granted him a vision of the One who had commissioned him (Josh. 1:1-9; 5:13-15).

4. *Gideon.* He was a humble man, who was hailed by God as a "mighty man of valor," and who was sent forth to deliver Israel with these words ringing in his ears: "Go, in this thy might . . . have not I sent thee?" Not until the Lord had wrought two miracles on his behalf was this man convinced of his call and commission (Judg. 6:11-24).

5. *Elisha.* Here was a prosperous and energetic young man, who was suddenly called by God, from the midst of a busy life, to leave all his rosy prospects of worldly success for the comparative obscurity of menial service for Elijah, the prophet of the Lord. For years he was unheard of, until the time that his master was to be translated. Then his years of faithful service, in secret, was "rewarded openly" and his name became a household word in Israel (I Kings 19:19-21; II Kings 3:11).

6. *Isaiah.* The moving description of this great prophet's vision, call and commission has stirred the hearts of the people of God for two and a half milleniums and led

many, like him, to say in response to the call of God: "Here am I, send me" (Isa. 6:1-13).

7. *Peter.* This man, naturally impulsive and energetic, was brought by Andrew to the Savior, thus evidencing the value of personal evangelism. The miracle of the miraculous haul of fish served to provide the circumstances under which his call and commission came (Luke 5:1-11).

While the circumstances of the call were different in each of these cases, for God is a God of infinite variety; yet the purpose and results were the same: the glory of God, the blessing of the one called and the benefit of those to whom he was sent with the message. Each of these people had an experience that was distinctly his own, and from which he emerged with the conscious assurance of God's call to him.

IV. It does not necessarily involve full time service.

The great need today is for Christian preachers or teachers who can support themselves by secular employment, and devote their spare time to the preaching and teaching of the word of God. Thank God for the noble army already thus engaged, but there is plenty of room for more, for the field is large, the need great and the laborers few. William Carey, "the father of modern missions," was once asked what his business was. He replied: "My business is preaching the gospel, and I cobble shoes to pay expenses!"

1. *There is no distinction made, in the New Testament, between so-called "clergy" and "laity."*

Every Christian is viewed as "a minister," which simply means "servant." The terms "clergy" and "laity," are absolutely foreign to New Testament language, which knows nothing of either! The word 'clergy' comes from the word, "cleros," translated "heritage" in I Peter 5:2, 3. It thus refers to *all the people of God* and not to a small section of believers. The present distinction of clergy and laity, as now seen in Christendom, is purely the invention of man, and doubtless at the Devil's instigation. It has wrought untold evil, for it has blinded Christians to the fact of their gift, and of the necessity to use it for the glory of God and the blessing of others. There are literally thousands of Christians, who ought to be teachers and preachers of the Word but, because of this false theory, remain silent. It is to be feared that, in many cases, they are sitting under the ministry of unsaved "clergymen" who are attempting the impossible task of expounding the Scriptures.

2. *The evils of professionalism in the Lord's work.*

This cannot be too strongly condemned. The only difference between the whole-time preacher and the part-time preacher, is merely the amount of time which each spends in preparation and preaching and the matter of his financial support. The Lord deliver us from all thought of professionalism in the Lord's work, or the separation of the Lord's people into two classes! An understanding of I Peter 4:10 should deliver every believer from this travesty of the Scriptural pattern. Mark the words carefully. It will be noted there is not even the remotest suggestion of professionalism implied in it: "As every man hath received the gift, even so minister the same one to another, as good stewards of the manifold grace of God."

The Christian who teaches and preaches, is only discharging the stewardship which God has entrusted to him. "All believers are "ministers," or servants of the same Master, and are engaged in the same service, the work of the Lord.* The New Testament clearly teaches the *priest-hood* of all believers. It knows nothing of the *priest-craft* of a few believers as seen in Christendom today. See I Pet. 2:5-9; Rev. 1:5; 5-10.

*See the author's pamphlets "Scriptural Principles of Gathering," and "An Introduction to a Study of Church Truth."

The story is told of a young Christian who approached an older believer with the remark: "I want to enter the Lord's service." The older brother asked: "How long have you been saved?" He replied: "Three years." At this, the old believer enquired: "Then whose service have you been in for the past three years?" The moral of the story is surely obvious!

V   The elements that combine to constitute a God-given call.

There are many things that enter in and combine to constitute this definite call of God.

1. *There is the inward urge of the Holy Spirit,* who indwells each believer, and who desires to "guide him into all truth" (John 16:13; Rom. 8:14). As this "holy heavenly Guest" dwells ungrieved within us, He can impress our hearts and guide our thoughts into certain definite convictions as to the will of God for the life. (Read Rom. 8:26-27). This leading of the Spirit is difficult to define and describe. The Scotch have a proverb: "It's better felt than telt," or: "it is better *experienced* than *described.*" Each believer, who is called to preach or teach, must experience it for himself and undoubtedly will, if he is walking in fellowship with Christ, in the enjoyment of God's word, in obedience to the known will of God, and in communion with Him by prayer. This urge of the Spirit must not be confused with a passing whim, or a "hunch," or an idea generated by fleshly enthusiasm, which will soon pass away. Many have been carried away by a tide of mere emotionalism and mistakenly imagined it was God's call to full time service.

2. *Some definite word from the Scriptures will serve to deepen this conviction.* The word of God has been given for this very purpose. As we seek to know the will of God, He will leave us in no doubt, for He never leads

contrary to the principles He has laid down in His word. God will not leave His people to flounder in confusion, but will guide them, in His own good time and way. Prompt obedience to what we know, will lead to further knowledge. "Then shall we know, if we follow on to know" . . . "If any man will *do* His will, he shall *know*" (Hosea 6:3; John 7:17). Habbakuk learned the value of this and said: "I will stand upon my watch, and set me upon the tower, and will watch to see what He will say unto me, and what I shall answer when I am reproved" (Hab. 2:1). Samuel also was taught this truth by Eli and, in response to God's fourth call replied: "Speak, for Thy servant heareth" (I Sam. 3:10).

3. *The compassions of the heart.* As one is brought to realize the deep need of the unsaved and views them, in the light of Scripture, as lost and guilty, helpless and undone and thus in danger of eternal ruin; the conviction is borne home to his soul of the dire necessity for them to hear the soul-emancipating message of the gospel. This is what Christ meant when He said to His disciples: "Lift up your eyes and look on the fields, for they are white already to harvest" (John 4:35). Doubtless, as He said these words, the woman of Samaria was returning to the well, bringing with her many of the Samaritans who had heard her glowing words of testimony to Christ. Thus, in this sense, the very need of the sinner becomes part of the call to the saint to meet that need. Both Prov. 24:11, 12 and Ezek. 33:1-6 should be read upon one's knees, alone in the presence of God, and the words allowed to sink deep into the heart. Properly speaking, the need does not in itself constitute the call, but simply provides the opportunity for the believer to respond to the previous call of God.

4. *The advice of godly Christians.* Let no one belittle this. These older believers have seen some evidence of a

gift for preaching in a Christian's life. They will now seek to encourage this person by their advice, which is based on a riper knowledge of God's word, a longer experience in God's work, and a more mature realization of God's dealings both with themselves and others. This counsel, though not in itself conclusive, should be valued as a *contributing factor* in God's call to preach the word. Let no one despise the godly counsel of experienced Christians. Even Paul did not neglect this (Gal. 2:2). Their superior discernment in the things of God will aid them in the giving of this godly counsel.

5. *The word and action of some gifted and Spirit-led servant of the Lord.* Apparently this was one of the contributing elements of Timothy's call to wholetime service. (See Acts 16:1-3). God used Paul to be the deciding factor in his case, for God had gifted Paul with discernment, and he saw in Timothy one who would become "profitable to him in the ministry." How grateful we should be to those older brethren, who will take a younger man with them and allow them a little part in the meeting, and thus encourage them to develop their gift. Many a grand gospel preacher started out this way. (II Tim. 4:11).

6. *The Divine ordering of God's providences,* by which He makes His will clear through the circumstances of one's life. God opens up a door of utterance at the right time, or perhaps closes a door of secular employment (Rev. 3:8; I Cor. 16:9). In the case of some believers, their hands became so full with preaching that they could no longer do justice to their secular work, so had to decide which to give up.

However, we must beware of imagining that all the circumstances of one's life represent the Divine ordering of God's providence. Jonah, as he fled from God's call and commission, found a ship leaving from Joppa on which he took passage. He might have argued that the very fact of the ship being there was proof that God desired him to travel by it! It is important to remember that it is the providences of *God's ordering, combined with these other factors,* that gives the cumulative proof of God's leading.

The late E. J. Pace, for many years the cartoonist for the Sunday School Times, illustrated this matter of guidance in a most striking way. He drew three beams of light which converged on a prism. The name of the first beam was, "The principles of God's word." The second was entitled, "The promptings of God's Spirit." The third was labelled, "The providences of God's ordering." As these three beams of light converged on the prism, they emerged, through it, in one blaze of light which was called, "The will of God." It was thus the sum total of these three factors that indicated it. In our study of it, we are adding four more factors, by which the child of God may come to know the will of God in regard to his path of service.

7. *The commendation of one's brethren in assembly fellowship.* No one should take the step of going into wholetime service for the Lord unless he has secured the warm-hearted approval, fellowship and commendation of the assembly of which he forms a part. No person is qualified to become a competent judge of the worth of his own ministry, for it is obvious that he will be manifestly predisposed in his own favor!

Spiritual pride has blinded the eye and warped the understanding of many on this question. The scriptural principle is: "Let your prophets speak . . . and let the other judge . . . The spirits of the prophets are subject to the prophets" (I Cor. 14: 29, 32). If the spiritually minded elder brethren of an assembly, after due and prayerful consideration, do not feel free to commend the applicant to wholetime service, then that individual would do well to bow to their decision, reconsider the matter and revise his previous estimation as to his call.

We need ever to remember that: "God is not the Author of confusion, but of peace, as in all churches of the saints" (I Cor. 14:33). A willful disregard for this scriptural "decency and order" has resulted in much that is to be greatly regretted. Scripture does not contemplate a "free lance" who, acting in selfwill and in the energy of the flesh, determines on a certain course of action and carries out his own ideas, either in opposition to, or in utter independence of the responsible brethren of his home assembly.

May each believer be led to seek humbly, sincerely, perseveringly, believingly and obediently to know the will of God for his life and then do it! This necessitates prayerful dependence on the power of God, obedience to the leading of the Spirit of God, yieldedness to the will of God, the diligent study of the word of God, and active engagement in the work of God; for, as we have previously noted, it was while Paul "ministered to the Lord," that God's call came to him (Acts 13:2).

The Christian worker, to be spiritually effective in his ministry, should be found doing the *work* of the Lord, in accordance with the *word* of the Lord, in obedience to the *will* of the Lord, while engaged in the *warfare* of the Lord, offering *worship* to the Lord, and walking in the *way* of the Lord. Dr. J. H. Jowett, concluding his famous Yale lectures on preaching said: "Brethren, your calling is very holy. Your work is very difficult. Your Savior is very mighty, and the joy of the Lord is your strength."

CHAPTER SIX

The Necessity For Preaching

Having discussed the qualifications of the preacher and touched on the preacher's call; let us now consider why such emphasis is laid on the necessity for preaching, and for preachers, in the word of God. We shall note a seven-fold necessity.

I. Preaching is the God-ordained means of spreading the Gospel.

1. *The Divine order outlined* (Rom. 10:9-17).

This is the classic passage on this subject: "The word is nigh thee, even in thy mouth and in thy heart: that is the word of faith which we preach; that if thou shall *confess* with thy mouth the Lord Jesus, and shalt believe in thine heart that God hath raised Him from the dead, thou shalt be *saved* . . . For whosoever shall *call* on the name of the Lord shall be saved. How then shall they call on Him in Whom they have not *believed?* And how shall they believe in Him of Whom they have not *heard?* And how shall they hear without a *preacher?* And how shall they preach, except they be *sent?* As it is written: 'How beautiful are the feet of them that preach the gospel of peace, and bring glad tidings of good things'!"

It will be observed, from the italicized words, that there are seven key words in this passage: "confess," "saved," "call," "believed," "heard," "preacher" and "sent." Each of these words has a vital link with each other, and combine to present a logical progression of thought. It will also be noted that these words occur in the chronologically *reverse* order, and proceed from the *effect* to the *cause.* Let us briefly note the steps indicated.

(1) A person *confesses* Christ as his Lord. Why?
(2) Because he is *saved*. How was he saved? (3) By
calling on the name of the Lord. How did he come to
call on the name of the Lord? (4) Because he *believed* a
message. How did he come to believe this message? (5)
Because he *heard* the word of truth. How did he come to
hear? (6) Because a *preacher* proclaimed the gospel. How
did the preacher come to be preaching? (7) Because he
was *sent* by God to preach and was obedient to His command.

Now view the passage the other way around, and trace
the order from *cause to effect*. (1) A preacher is *sent* by
God. (2) He *preaches* the Word. (3) Someone *hears*
the Word. (4) This person *believes* the message. (5) He
then *calls* on the name of the Lord. (6) As a consequence
he is *saved* by the grace of God. (7) This saved person
then *confesses* Christ as the Lord of his life. Thus, viewed
from either direction, the divine cycle of grace is seen to be
complete. The preacher is sent forth *by* God and the sinner is brought *to* God.

2. *The Divine commission given* (Matt. 28: 18-20).

The gospel according to Matthew concludes with these
striking words that fell from the lips of the risen Son of
God. We read: "And Jesus came and spoke unto them
saying: 'All power is given unto Me in heaven and in
earth. Go ye therefore, and teach (make disciples, marg.)
all nations, baptizing them in the name of the Father,
and of the Son, and of the Holy Ghost: teaching them
to observe all things whatsoever I have commanded you:
and, lo, I am with you alway, even unto the end of the
world (age). Amen.' "

Notice the four "alls" in this commission, which combine to outline the Divine program for this age.

(1) *The "all" of His power.* "All power is given unto
Me in heaven and in earth." There will be no lack of pow-

er to guarantee the accomplishment of His commission. Omnipotence is at the back of every preacher! See Eph. 1: 15-23.

(2) *The "all" of His parish.* "Go ye therefore and teach all nations." Here is a field big enough for all. Wesley, on the strength of this verse, said: "The world is my parish." There is plenty of room for every God-sent herald of the gospel.

(3) *The "all" of His program.* This is twofold: "Baptizing them in the name of the Father, and of the Son, and of the Holy Ghost: teaching them to observe all things whatsoever I have commanded you." The commission does not end with the preaching of the gospel. Those who believe and are saved are to be baptized and then taught the word of God, so that they may grow in His grace and knowledge. Thus we are commissioned to give all the truth of God to all the people of God.

(4) *The "all" of His presence.* "And lo, I am with you alway (literally, "all the days"), even unto the end of the age. Amen." Here are our marching orders from the Commander in Chief. It is ours to obey them.

In the closing verses of the gospel according to Mark is the well known commission: "Go ye into all the world, and preach the gospel to every creature. He that believeth and is baptized shall be saved: but he that believeth not shall be damned" (Mark 16:15, 16). There can surely be no doubt in any one's mind as to what Christ meant by these words. Each Christian is to go into his own particular sphere, which constitutes his "world," and there preach the gospel. Christ did not say: "If you cannot go, pray, or pay, or send someone else in your place." He said "Go!" It is therefore the duty of all Christians to obey.

Just before the Lord ascended to heaven to take His place at the right hand of the majesty on high, He gave a further commission to His disciples. In the light of the imminent coming of the Holy Spirit, He said to them: "Ye shall receive power, after that the Holy Ghost is come upon you: and ye shall be witnesses unto Me, both in Jerusalem, and in all Judea, and in Samaria, and unto the uttermost part of the earth" (Acts 1:8). In these words Christ indicated the ever widening sphere of their field of witness. Thus from Jerusalem, the home base, to earth's remotest bound, the gospel was to go forth in the form of witnessing.

3. *The Divine program being carried out.*

One has only to turn to the recorded history of the early church to see how well the disciples understood their Lord's commission and sought, by all the means in their power, to carry it out. It is significant that there is no mention of a special class of Christians called "the clergy," who did all the preaching and teaching, nor was this preaching confined to the apostles.

Acts 8:1 records a great persecution against the Church in Jerusalem, which scattered the believers abroad "throughout the regions of Judea and Samaria, *except the apostles,*" who remained in Jerusalem. In Acts 11:19-21, we read what the rank and file of these believers did when they were scattered. We are told they: "travelled as far as Phenice, Cyprus and Antioch, preaching the word . . . and the hand of the Lord was with them, and a great number believed, and turned to the Lord." This resulted in the forming of an assembly of believers at Antioch.

All this was accomplished without the presence or the permission of a single apostle! Thus the church at Jerusalem was *shattered* that it might be *scattered,* and God wonderfully blessed the witness of these dispersed saints.

There is no mention whatever of these scattered believers receiving a "license to preach," or being "ordained to preach," by the apostles in Jerusalem. The words: "preaching the word," in Acts 11:19 have no reference to a formal discourse and can be literally rendered: "they gossiped the gospel." They simply "talked the good news" whenever the opportunity presented itself, and thus won many for the Lord. We need more of this kind of preacher and preaching today! There are altogether too many "D. D.'s" and not enough G. G.'s! (Gospel Gossipers).

As one reads the Acts, he will be impressed with the *naturalness* and entire absence of formality that marked the spread of this witness to Christ on the part of the early disciples. There was a simplicity, freshness, courage and power in their ministry. They obeyed the Lord's commission implicity and proved His promised presence and power abundantly. We find that Jerusalem, Judea and Samaria were early evangelized. From Acts 10, the gospel began its journey towards "the uttermost part of the earth." Had this rate of progress been allowed to continue uninterruptedly, the world would soon have been evangelized; but alas, this forward march was allowed to bog down; but this is another story, which necessitates the reading of a reliable book on Church history.

4. *The Divine terms examined. A study of the Scripture terms for preaching,* in the original language of the New Testament, will serve to show us how varied are the means of presenting the gospel to others. Let us look at four of these words which are translated "preach" in the Authorized Version:

(1) *"Kerusso,"* to proclaim as a herald. This is used of the public proclamation of the gospel. See Matt. 11:1; Mark 1:4; 3:14; 16:20; Rom. 10:15, etc.

(2) *"Euaggelizo,"* to tell good news. This is the word from which we get our terms, "evangel, evangelist, evan-

gelize." See Matt. 11: 5; Luke 4: 18; 7: 22; I Cor. 1: 17; Gal. 1: 8; Heb. 4: 2, etc.

(3) *"Katangello,"* to tell thoroughly. See Acts 4: 2; 13: 38; 15: 36; Col. 1: 28.

(4) *"Laleo,"* to talk. See Mark 2: 2; Acts 11: 19; 14: 25, etc.

Of the 112 times the word "preach" is found in the New Testament, in only 6 instances does it mean a formal discourse. Thus to preach, in the New Testament sense of the term, is to proclaim as a herald the message of the King of kings and Lord of lords; to tell the good news; to tell thoroughly all the truth of the gospel, holding back nothing, but declaring "the whole counsel of God"; to talk to others, as we meet them on the highways, or in their homes, of the love of God as revealed in the gift of His Son, and of the salvation He has secured for whosoever will believe on Him.

A reading of the New Testament will impress us with the fact that those who knew the Lord sought, both by means of private testimony and public proclamation, to spread the good news of a dying Savior's love, a risen Savior's power and a coming Savior's glory. Well might the word come to each of us: "Go thou and do likewise!"

II. Preaching is a witness to the facts of the Gospel.

Acts 1: 8; 10: 39-42; 22: 15; I John 5: 9; Acts 26: 22; John 15: 27.

1. *Definition of a witness.*

A witness is one who testifies to what he has seen, what he has heard and what he knows to be the facts of the case. He is enjoined to: "Speak the truth, the whole truth and nothing but the truth." God wants people to know what His Son has done. Consequently He has subpoenaed all His people as witnesses to this fact. Christ Himself declared: "Ye shall be witnesses unto Me." In that won-

derful discourse recorded in John 15, He declared that the
Holy Spirit should testify (or witness) of Him and then
added: "And ye also shall bear witness, because ye have
been with Me from the beginning." (John 15:26-27). Thus
the believer is a co-witness with the Holy Spirit. What
an honor, privilege and responsibility!

2. *The purpose of a witness.*

Witness involves a revelation from God to the believer,
and a proclamation by the believer to man. Each Christian should be able to say, like his Lord: "We speak that
we do know and testify that we have seen." (John 3:11).
Christ declared that the gospel should be preached for a
witness (Matt. 14:14). A witness may either testify *for*
or *against* a person. Witnesses are used by both the prose-
cution and the defense. The solemn words of the Son of
God need to be pondered by all: "If any man hear My
words and believe not, I judge him not: for I came not to
judge the world, but to save the world. He that rejecteth
Me and receiveth not My words, hath One that judgeth
him: *the word that I have spoken,* the same shall judge
him in the last day" (John 12:47, 48). Thus the gospel
becomes "a savor of life" to those who believe, and "a
savor of death" to those who refuse its message (II Cor.
2:15-17). It will either be a witness *to* the believer of the
certainty of his eternal blessedness, or it shall be a witness
against the unbeliever, and the Christ rejecter, at the
great judgment bar of God. See Matthew 12:41-42; Rev.
20:15; Acts 17:31.

The Christ-neglecter, rejecter and despiser will have no
excuse in that day when God does His "strange work"
of judgment. The glib excuses, which now come so
readily to his lips, will give place to silence as he faces the
great white throne, upon which sits the Judge, whose eyes
are like "a flame of fire," and to Whom "all things are

naked and open." The gospel witness that he heard, and which might have proved to be the means of his salvation, now only serves to insure his eternal damnation. Note the words of God to Ezekiel, His witness in a past dispensation: "And they, whether they will hear, or whether they forbear . . . yet shall know that there hath been a prophet among them." And again: "Thou shalt speak My words unto them, whether they will hear, or whether they will forbear" (Ezek. 2:5-7).

3. *The gospel witness is the manifestation of the truth of God to men.*

Furthermore, the gospel is the "manifestation of the truth of God" to men, and preaching is the Divinely authorized means by which this truth may be made known unto others. We also read: "God . . . hath in due times manifested His word through preaching" (Titus 1:3; II Cor. 4:2). The gospel is, therefore, not so much an *offer* on the part of God, as a *revelation* from God of the facts of Christ's Person and work. See I Cor. 15:1-4. Hence the necessity for making these truths known to others. The authority of the preacher lies entirely in the Divine origin of his message. It is God who speaks through him. The preacher has no dignity of his own to stand on; it is the word of God alone which gives him this.

Moreover the messenger is provided with the message he is to deliver. He is not left to himself as to its content. It is not something that "comes to him" out of a blue sky, but something that is found written in the scriptures of truth. What would we think of a mother who asked her child to take a message to a neighbor, and when the child asked what the message was, her mother replied: "O the message will come to you as you go!" Haggai is described as "the Lord's messenger in the Lord's message unto the people" (Hag. 1:13). Oh, for more like Haggai!

4. *This gospel witness is abundantly evidenced in the Acts of the Apostles.*

Every preacher would do well to carefully study the sermons recorded in the Acts of the Apostles. Notice how the speaker first states the great facts concerning the life, words, works, death and resurrection of Christ, and then applies the truth to the hearts of his hearers. See Peter's sermons Acts 2: 14-36, note v. 32; also 3: 12-26, note v. 15; 4: 8-12; Stephen's defense 7: 1-54. Peter's address to Cornelius 10: 34-43, note v. 39. Paul's sermon at Antioch in Pisidia, 13: 16-43. Then look at his sermon at Mar's Hill, Acts 17: 22-31. A good exercise would be to outline all these sermons recorded in the Acts and make a close study of their divisions and contents.

Thus, whether men will believe or not, God desires the gospel to be presented to them. If they believe, they will be saved; if they believe not, they will be without excuse in the coming day of judgment. It is for the preacher to present the facts of the gospel in the power of the Holy Spirit, and then leave the results with God.

III.   The preaching of the Word is the means by which faith is awakened in the hearer.

1. *Faith always presupposes a previous revelation.*

"Faith cometh by hearing and hearing by the word of God" (Rom. 10: 17). This can be easily verified: "How shall they believe in Him of whom they have not heard?" (Rom. 10: 14). Compare the case of Abel, Enoch, Noah, Abraham, etc. (Heb. 11: 4, 7, 8, 17). These men acted upon a word from God—this is faith. Saving faith is the soul's confidence in the Person, the word and the work of Christ, which evidences itself by the sinner's reception of Christ as his Savior, belief in the word of Christ, trust in the accomplished redemption of Christ, and confession of the Lordship of Christ. The language of faith is: "I believe God, that it shall be even as it was told me" (Acts 27:25).*

2. *Faith necessitates an Object.*

Faith has no virtue in itself. It must have an *Object* on which to rest in implicit confidence. This object is Christ, as revealed in the Scripture of truth, and presented by means of the preaching of the gospel. We are not saved *by* faith but *through* faith in the Person and work of Another. (Eph. 2:8). Strong faith in a weak bank has led many to invest their life's savings in it only to lose it all. It was the bank and not their faith that determined the safety of their money.

The gospel has been given "for the obedience of faith among all nations" (Rom. 1:5). The writer of the epistle to the Hebrews says of some: "The word preached did not profit them, not being mixed with faith in them that heard it" (Heb. 4:2). Paul could say of the believers in Thessalonica: "When ye received the word of God which ye heard of us, ye received it not as the word of men, but as it is in the truth, the word of God, which effectually worketh also in you that believe" (I Thess. 2:13).

Faith should not be occupied with itself, but with its object. In other words: it is to be *exercised* and not *analyzed.*

> "Faith, mighty faith, the promise sees;
>   And looks to God alone;
> Laughs at impossibilities
>   And cries: 'It shall be done!' "

A godly woman was once approached by a person who asked her: "Are you the woman with a great faith?" She replied: "No, I am the woman who has faith in a great God!"

*See Author's booklet "God's Good News."

3. *Faith is the essential condition of salvation.*

Paul's reply to the jailer's query: "What then must I do
to be saved?" was: "Believe on the Lord Jesus Christ and
thou shalt be saved" (Acts 16: 30-31). The business of the
preacher is to preach the word of God, in dependence on
the Lord, and in the power of His Spirit, and there his
responsibility ends. Only God can save and He will do
this as the sinner fulfills the condition which God has im-
posed: namely, faith in the Person and work of His Son.
"Preach the Word," was Paul's advice to Timothy (II Tim.
4: 2). If the preacher has furnished the hearers with
enough material to awaken faith within their hearts, and
they deliberately refuse to believe, their judgment will
be upon their own head. "Whosoever heareth the sound
of the trumpet, and taketh not warning . . . his blood shall
be upon his own head" (Ezek. 33: 4). Of course the worthwhile preacher will not adopt a "take it or leave it" attitude with his audience, but will endeavour. with godly
sincerity and earnest entreaty, to beseech men to be "reconciled unto God" (II Cor. 5: 20).

CHAPTER SEVEN

The Necessity For Preaching

(Continued)

IV. The preaching of the Word, under God, results in the regeneration of those who believe.

1. *The word of God is a living thing.*

The word of God is a living, a life imparting and a life-sustaining book. "The word of God is quick, (or living) and powerful, and sharper than any twoedged sword" (Heb. 4:12). Peter reminded those to whom he wrote that they were "Born again, not of corruptible seed, but of incorruptible, by the word of God which liveth and abideth for ever . . . And this is the word which by the gospel is preached unto you" (I Peter 1:23-25).

2. *The word of God is life-imparting.*

The Divine order is first, the preaching of the Word; second, the hearing of faith; and third, the regeneration of those who believe. This fact is made clear in Eph. 1:13, where Paul brings to the remembrance of the saints at Ephesus the circumstances of their own salvation: "That we should be to the praise of His glory, who first trusted in Christ. In Whom ye also trusted, after that ye heard the word of truth, the gospel of your salvation: in Whom also, after that ye believed, (or, 'on believing') ye were sealed with that Holy Spirit of promise." The same truth is revealed in James 1:18, where it is affirmed: "Of His own will *begat He us* with the word of truth, that we should be a kind of first-fruits of His creatures." Christ Himself declared: "The words that I speak unto you, they are spirit and they are life." (John 6:63).

The words of Peter should thrill the soul of each preacher of the gospel. Mark his words as he declared: "God made choice among us that the Gentiles, *by my mouth*, should hear the word of the gospel and believe. And God, which knoweth the hearts, bare them witness, giving them the Holy Spirit, even as He did unto us" (Acts 15: 7, 8). What an unspeakable privilege is thus conferred upon the preacher to be the instrument, under God, through whom lost and guilty sinners, hearing and believing the message, shall be eternally saved! It was this thought that gripped the soul of D. L. Moody, whom God so mightily used in the years gone by. He put the thought in these words, which might well become the battle cry of every preacher: "My human lips, filled with the word of God!"

The following words, addressed to preachers many years ago by a godly servant of Christ, should stir the heart of each herald of the gospel:

"We are aiming at a miracle—it is well to settle that at the commencement. We are sent to say to blind eyes, "See"; to deaf ears, "Hear"; to dead hearts "Live"; and even to a Lazarus, rotting in that grave . . . "Lazarus, come forth!" Dare we do this? We shall be wise to begin with the conviction that we are utterly powerless for this unless our Master has sent us and is with us. But if He that sent us is with us, all things are possible to him that believeth.

O preacher, if thou art about to stand up to show what *thou* canst do, it will be thy wisdom to sit down speedily; but if thou standest up to show what thine almighty Lord and Master can do through thee, then infinite possibilities lie about thee. There is no bound to what *God* can accomplish if He is allowed to work by thy heart and voice!"

3. *The word of God is life-developing.*

The very word that imparts spiritual life to the believer also develops the life it has given. Peter urged his hearers: "As newborn babes, *desire* the sincere milk of the word, that ye may grow thereby" (I Peter 2:1-2). Unconsciously to himself, but visibly to his fellow ·Christians, the believer, as he feeds upon the Scriptures, develops spiritually and "grows in grace, and in the knowledge of his Lord and Savior, Jesus Christ" (II Peter 3:18).

V. Preaching is the means by which the hearer is built up in his most holy faith.

1. *Paul's threefold desire.*

The threefold objective of Paul's ministry is described in Col. 1:28, 29. "Whom we preach, *warning* every man, and *teaching* every man in all wisdom; that we may *present* every man perfect in Christ Jesus." It is not enough that a soul has been won for Christ and thus regenerated. That soul must now be led on in ways well pleasing to the Lord and built up in his most holy faith. The preaching and teaching of the word of God is the means by which this is accomplished. This should be the desire of every preacher and teacher.

The yearning of Paul's heart for the upbuilding of the people of God is evidenced in his farewell address to the elders of the church at Ephesus: 'And now, brethren, I commend you to God and to the word of His grace, which is able to build you up and to give you an inheritance among all them which are sanctified" (Acts 20:32). Peter had the same thing in view when he exhorted his fellow elders: "Feed the flock of God which is among you, taking the oversight thereof, not by constraint, but willingly; not for filthy lucre, but of a ready mind; neither as being lords over God's heritage, but being ensamples to the flock" (I Peter 5:1-3).

2. *The sevenfold work of the word of God* (II Tim-3:15-17).

This is found in Paul's letter to a young preacher who needed, like all of us, to have his spiritual backbone strengthened. Let us note the sevenfold purpose for which the Scriptures were given by Divine inspiration.

(1) *To make wise unto salvation* (v. 15). It puts the sinner wise as to his need of God's provision for the salvation He has provided, of the condition by which that salvation is received and of the assurance of its possession.

(2) *For doctrine.* This word indicates the great fundamental teachings, or the foundation truths upon which our faith securely rests. This establishes the believer in his faith.

(3) *For reproof.* The Scriptures not only reveal the truth, but expose all error. The Bible is like a plumbline which shows the crookedness of all that is contrary to it.

(4) *For correction.* It enables the believer to correct any crookedness of thought or deed which it has revealed. It leads him to judge the error and adjust himself to the will of God.

(5) *For instruction in righteousness.* That is, it encourages him to lead a life of moral rectitude, of honesty, truth, soberness and sincerity that will commend the gospel to the unsaved amongst whom he moves. It will fit him to adorn every circle of life: the family, social, business and the assembly of believers of which he forms a part.

(6) *To develop Christian maturity.* Here the word "perfect" carries with it the thought of maturity, or growth in grace and knowledge of the Lord Jesus Christ. Such development involves a personal experience of finding and doing the will of God. This, in turn, will fit the believer to teach others who are younger in the faith.

(7) *To thoroughly furnish unto all good works.* God wants His people to be well furnished. Unfurnished flats are as cold a proposition as unfurnished Christians.

This then, is the effect of the word of God when it is allowed to have its way in a preacher's life. It was men of this caliber that Paul had in mind when he wrote: "The things that thou hast heard of me among many witnesses, the same commit thou to *faithful men,* who shall be able to teach others also" (II Tim. 2:2).

3. *The threefold purpose of the ministry of the word of God.*

All ministry to the people of God is given by the risen Head, through those whom He has gifted, for a threefold purpose: "For the perfecting (or maturing) of the saints, for the work of the ministry and for the edifying (or building up) of the body of Christ" (Eph. 4:12). Let us look at these things for a few moments.

(1) *The maturing of the saints.* We have already touched on this in the previous division. Protracted spiritual childhood is indeed a tragedy. Paul had to bemoan the fact that the Corinthians were but "babies," because of their carnality; and the Galatians were but "little children," because of their legalism (I Cor. 3:1; Gal. 4:19). The fault, in this case, was not with the teacher, but with the pupils. cp. Heb. 5:12-14. The teacher therefore must make it his aim to so study, prepare and present his message that the hearers will be led on to Christian maturity.

(2) *The work of the ministry.* This has a varied application. Sometimes his work may consist of *warning* the believers (I Thess. 5:14). At other times he may have to *rebuke* fearlessly (I Tim. 5:20). Then again he will need to *comfort* (I Thess. 4:18). Whatever the need may be the preacher will find, in the Word, all that is needed for his ministry.

(3) *The edification of the body of Christ.* Here is the grand aim: the building up of the people of God. This is the "profit" of real ministry in the Spirit. See I Cor. 14: 6. From v. 31 we see that the acid test of ministry is the spiritual profit of the hearers. All true, spiritual ministry comes down from God, through Christ, in the power of the Holy Spirit, by means of the human instrument chosen for the purpose. It has been finely said: "Effective preaching is the intelligent, forceful and persuasive presentation of the truth of God."

VI. Preaching is the solemn responsibility of all who have been thus gifted.

We have before noted that it is the responsibility of all Christians to witness. God's word to them is: "Sanctify the Lord God in your hearts, and be ready always to give an answer to every man that asketh you, a reason of the hope that is in you with meekness and fear" (I Peter 3: 15). One of the tragedies of today is that the Church has delegated this task of witness to a comparative few, and thus the truth of individual responsibility has been shelved and, in many cases, lost sight of completely.

Preaching, however, is distinct from witnessing. All Christians have not been gifted with the ability to publicly set forth the truth of the gospel. Those who have received such a gift are under a solemn obligation to be faithful to their trust.

1. *It is a necessity laid upon each preacher.*

No preacher should have any cause for self-congratulation because he has preached the gospel, for he has only done his duty, just as any other servant would at the command of his master. Christ, in His parable of the servant and the master, concluded: "So likewise ye, when ye shall have done all those things which are commanded you, say: 'We are unprofitable servants, we have done that which was our duty to do' " (Luke 17:10).

Jeremiah discovered that preaching was a *burden* laid upon him, and which he was responsible to the Lord to deliver. Because his message caused Israel to deride him, he said on one occasion: "I will not make mention of Him, nor speak any more in His name." Thus he tried to shirk his duty, but he had to confess: "His word was in mine heart as a burning fire, shut up in my bones, and I was weary with forebearing and *I could not stay!*" (Jer. 20:8-9). See also Isa. 13:1; Ezek. 12:10; Hab. 1:1; Zech. 9:1; Mal. 1:1. Paul spoke of a similar urge to preach and said: "Necessity is laid upon me: yea, woe is unto me if I preach not the gospel!" (I Cor. 9:6). Nelson, as he led the British fleet to the battle of Trafalgar, caused this signal to be flown at the masthead: "England expects, this day, that every man will do his duty." From a higher masthead our Lord, the "Captain of our salvation," gives His signal: "Christ expects, this day, that each of His servants will do his duty."

2. *It is a trust committed to each preacher.*

The gospel is a sacred trust given to each of His servants, and we read: "It is required in stewards that a man be found faithful" (I Cor. 4:2). Paul referred to the gospel as something which had been committed to his trust. (I Tim. 1:11). At the end of his life he could write to Timothy and say: "I have fought a good fight, I have finished my course, I have kept the faith" (II Tim. 4:7). He earnestly pled with Timothy and exclaimed: "O Timothy, keep that which is committed to thy trust!" The day will come when each servant must give an account of his stewardship to his Lord and Master. How will our account look in that day when it is estimated in the light of the judgment seat of Christ? (I Tim. 6:20; I Cor. 3:9-15; Rom. 14:10).

3. *It is a debt to be paid by each preacher.*

Paul declared: "I am debtor both to the Greeks and the Barbarians; both to the wise and to the unwise. So, as much as in me is, I am ready to preach the gospel to you that are at Rome also" (Rom. 1:14-15). The socialist assumes that he is a *creditor* and that the world is his *debtor*. He therefore argues that the world is under an obligation to provide him with all the essentials of life, and to do its best to make him comfortable during the period that he graces the earth with his illustrious presence. Christianity, on the contrary, states that the world is the *creditor* and that each Christian owes it the gospel.

Common decency demands that a person should pay his just debts and preaching the gospel is just this. A young man, who left home and country to go to the regions beyond to preach the gospel, said to the senior missionary as he arrived at the mission station: "I've come to pay my debt." He knew what it was to "have *necessity* laid upon him."

How are the unsaved, who lie in the darkness of heathenism, ignorance, superstition and indifference to hear, if we, who have been gifted to proclaim the gospel, fail to take it to them?

> "Shall we whose souls are lighted
>   With wisdom from on high;
> Shall we, to men benighted,
>   The lamp of truth deny?
> Salvation! O, salvation!
>   The joyful sound proclaim,
> 'Till earth's remotest nation
>   Has learned Messiah's name!"

George Muller founder of the famous Ashley Down Orphanage of Bristol, England, was also an able preacher and teacher of the Word. His aim in preaching might well become both a challenge and an example to each preacher. He declared his ambition was: "To preach the gospel in the simplest way possible that persons might understand how the blessing which sinners receive through faith in Christ is to be obtained; to try to impart to the children of God a knowledge of their standing in Christ; to bring Christians back to the Scriptures, to urge them to test everything by the word of God, and to value that only which will stand the test; to aim at the removal of sectarianism, and to promote brotherly love amongst Christians: to strengthen real faith and trust in the living God; to seek to lead Christians to more real separation from the world; and to strive to lead the Church of God to look for the second coming of Christ as her great hope."

William Perkins an old Puritan divine, used to admonish himself on the fly leaf of any book he possessed by writing: "Thou art a minister of the Word: mind thy business!"

4. *The causes and tragedy of an unfulfilled ministry.*
One of the tragic possibilities for a Christian is to fail in fulfilling the purpose for which Christ saved him. This was Paul's great dread. He said: "None of these things move me, neither count I my life dear unto myself, so that I might finish my course with joy, and the ministry, which I have received of the Lord Jesus, to testify the gospel of the grace of God" (Acts 20:24).

How sad it is when God has to write "failure" over a life that once showed great possibilities of fruitful service for Him! One thinks of Samson, Solomon, Demas and others who started well, but failed to run their course and fulfil God's purpose in their lives. Let us briefly notice some of the causes which combine to hinder a servant of the Lord from fulfilling his ministry as a teacher of the Word, or discharging his responsibilities as a preacher of the gospel.

(1) *The fear of man.* "The fear of man bringeth a snare" (Prov. 29:25). Many a person has been hindered

in his ministry by the fear of being considered "odd" by the worldling, or even by worldly minded Christians. The preaching of the truth does not lead to popularity. Many preachers, in seeking to maintain their own reputation, popularity and prestige, have lost the approval of their Lord and Master. A preacher should, most emphatically, not be a *man-pleaser*. It is possible for a speaker to "play to the gallery." That is, to only say those things which he knows will be pleasing to his audience, and deliberately keep back truths that should be stated, but which he fears will make him unpopular with his audience. Even Peter fell into this snare, but Paul courageously and faithfully rebuked him for his inconsistency. See Gal. 2:11-14. Paul could testify: "If I yet pleased men, I should not be the servant of Christ" (Gal. 1:10).

Nor should a preacher be a *self-pleaser,* for he is told definitely that he is "not to please himself." See Rom. 15:1. This was the cause of Samson's failure. When rebuked by his parents for seeking a wife of the Philistines he replied: "Get her for me, for she pleaseth *me* well!" (Judg. 14:3). The fact that the word of God forbade such a union didn't carry any weight with him. He was intent on pleasing himself, cost what it might—and it cost him much. It has been well said that "a self made man is but a horrible example of unskilled labor!"

Each preacher should make it his life's ambition to be a *God-pleaser*. Paul wrote: "We beseech you brethren and exhort you by the Lord Jesus . . . how ye ought to walk and to please God" (I Thess. 4:1; Col. 1:10). Enoch is an example of a God-pleasing walk and a God-honoring life (Heb. 11:5). For a Christian to be disapproved of God is a tragedy for which there is no compensation (I Cor. 9:24-27).

(2) *Slothfulness.* Preaching involves study, and study means *work,* and with many this word has an unwelcome sound. The cost in time, energy and self-denial that preaching imposes, causes many to shirk their responsibility. Many therefore adopt as their life's motto the language of the self-centered parasite who exclaims: "Let George (or the other fellow) do it!" whenever some service for the Lord is proposed. Thus their light, instead of being allowed to shine, is put "under the bed" of laziness (Matt. 5:15). Solomon's description of a lazy bones should be "read, marked and inwardly digested" by all (Prov. 24:30-34).

Our Savior said: "I must work the works of Him that sent Me while it is day: the night cometh when no man can work" (John 9:4). Compare John 4:34; Luke 2:49. "Is the servant greater than his Lord?" (John 15:20). Since the Son of God loved and *gave Himself* for us, is it too much for Him to expect us to give ourselves, our time, our energy and our faithful and devoted service for Him? Hearken to the stirring words of that great warrior for God: "Be ye steadfast, unmovable, *always abounding* in the work of the Lord, forasmuch as ye know that your labor is not in vain in the Lord!" (I Cor. 15:58). Paul's ambition for his life for Christ could be comprehended in three short phrases: "*Forsaking* all that hinders, *forgetting* the past failures and *forging* ahead to the prize that awaits." (Phil. 3:8, 13, 14).

(3) *Selfish ambition.* There are many who do not lack for ambition and energy, but unfortunately devote all these efforts to the furthering of their own interests. They are busy from morning until night feathering their own nests, developing their own businesses and piling up their bank accounts; but allow little or no time for the most important thing in life—the Lord's work. Many a so-called "successful" business man, at the end of his

earthly life, has had to lament: "I have gained worldly prosperity, but my life has been frittered away and lost in the furtherance of my own trivial and selfish interests!" See Mark 8:36.

The parable, told by an unnamed prophet to king Ahab, should serve the purpose of driving this truth home to our hearts (I Kings 20:35-43). He said to the king: "Thy servant went out into the midst of the battle and behold, a man turned aside and brought a man unto me and said: 'Keep this man: if by any means he be missing, then shall thy life be for his, or else thou shalt pay a talent of silver.' And as thy *servant was busy here and there*, he was gone!" The king of Israel replied: "So shall thy judgment be: thyself has decided it." At this the prophet pointed out that Ahab's unseasonable leniency to Benhaded, king of Syria, when he had him in his power, was a similar case.

Let us paraphrase this prophet's words: "While thy servant was busy here and there, my *time* was gone; my *talent* was gone; my *spiritual energy* was gone; my *opportunity* was gone; my *joy* was gone; my *enthusiasm* was gone; my *life* was gone!" This will have to be the sad confession of men who were too busy with selfish ambition to spend time for God. The shores of time are strewn with the wrecks of "might-have-beens." These people were so intent on furthering their own interests, that they lost the life for God that might have been theirs.

The hiding of one's light under a *bushel*, speaks of a testimony obscured by business. Christ must have "the pre-eminence in all things." Only as we put first things first, and *keep them first*, shall we amount to anything for Him. God enjoins us to be "not slothful in business," but to be "fervent in spirit, *serving the Lord*" (Rom. 12: 11). The obvious inference is that we are not to engage in business at the *expense* of the Lord's work. The words of Haggai could be well paraphrased: "Is it time for you to be immersed in your own business when the work of the Lord lieth waste?" (Haggai 1:4-7). It is possible for "the good to become the enemy of the best," and to miss God's best is the *worst!*

(4) *The excuse: "I have no talent for preaching."* It is quite a common thing to hear this plea from people who are asked to engage in some form of Christian service. Often this excuse is due to the following causes:

(a) *A failure to test their possession of a gift.* No one will ever know whether or not he has a gift for preaching or teaching until he honestly and perseveringly *tries.* No one learns to swim by looking at others, or by reading books on the subject. The only way is to get into the water and try. Have we honestly given ourselves a good test of our possession of the gift of preaching or teaching? *One attempt is not enough,* for no one becomes proficient the first dozen or so times. If, after many trials, we are convinced, as also is our audience, that we have no gift in this direction, well and good. At least, we have made an honest endeavor.

(b) *A failure to realize that a gift can only be developed by study and exercise.* The gift of music, art, etc., is developed by *practice.* There are good preachers today who, when they started out, gave little or no indication that they would ever become gifted speakers. Many give up too easily and stop when they should have gone on.

(c) *A failure to be full of one's subject.* Many who profess their inability to preach the gospel are eloquent enough when the subject of automobiles is introduced! It is a case of: "Out of the abundance of the heart, the mouth speaketh" (Matt. 12:34). They have studied up on autos, driven autos and repaired autos and conse-

quently can *talk* autos. Their heart has become a kind
of *garage,* so that every time their mouth opens, out pops
a car! When the heart is filled with Christ, this will be
evidenced by a desire to develop any gift He has given
to proclaim the glorious gospel of His grace. David could
say: "My heart is inditing a good matter: I *speak* of the
things which I have made touching the king: my *tongue*
is the pen of a ready writer" (Psa. 45:1).

A preacher, meeting a young Christian of the "I-have-
no-talent" variety, asked him to explain the mechanism
of his motorcycle. After he had clearly described how it
functioned the preacher said: "Young man, if you would
describe the way of salvation to others as well as you
have described the working of that motorcycle to me,
you would be greatly used of God!" The lesson was not
without result, for the young man saw the point and began
to preach the gospel.

(5) *Unjudged sin and worldliness of life.* Questionable habits and amusements have combined to hinder
many a Christian from fulfilling the ministry he has received of the Lord. Where prayer and Bible study is
neglected, confession of Christ avoided, the meetings for
assembly fellowship unattended, and sin in the life allowed to remain unconfessed and unjudged, there can be
no development of any gift from the Lord.

The only remedy for this backslidden condition of soul
is a frank confession of the sin, a resolute turning away
from it, and a return to that Bible study, prayer, witness
for Christ and attendance at the meetings of the assembly.
Then, restored to the Lord and walking in fellowship
with Him, the neglected gift may be developed and used
for Christ.

Whatever may be the cause of failure to fulfil one's
ministry, it is none the less tragic. There is a *present*
compensation in the way of peace of mind, joy and satis-

faction that comes from fulfilling the work God has given us to do; to say nothing of the promise of future reward at the judgment seat of Christ. Many Christians who have failed, or who are now failing to fulfil their ministry, are haunted by the specter of "the man they might have been." The Lord deliver us from such a depressing vision!

> "Couldst thou in vision see
>   Thyself, the man God *meant:*
> Then nevermore wouldst be
>   The man thou *art*, content!"

CHAPTER EIGHT

The Necessity For Preaching

(Continued)

VII. Preaching, to be effective, must reach the whole personality of the hearer.

1. *The personality defined.*

Personality is a difficult thing to define, as it is a somewhat complex and intangible thing. It might be described as the sum total of those distinctive characteristics of our mental, moral and spiritual qualities by which we impress our fellow men. It is the impression that a person makes upon others because of what he *is*, intellectually, emotionally and volitionally; or because of what he knows, feels and does. The personality represents the sum total of a person's make up, as seen in the impact he or she makes upon the lives of his fellow men or women.

2. *The personality expressed.*

Each individual expresses his personality in a threefold way: by his *intellect*, that enables him to acquire, retain and reproduce knowledge; by his *emotions,* by which he reacts to what he knows; and by his *will,* that enables him to determine and carry out the impulses of the intellect and emotions. In other words, each person is possessed of the ability to know, feel and act. Though these three powers are distinct, yet they form a tri-unity, so that each activity of the intellect, emotions and will, is the action of the *whole man.*

3. *The whole personality must be appealed to and won for Christ.*

If a person is to be reached and won for Christ, three things must take place.

(1) *His intellect must be enlightened.* This is done as the *facts* of the word of God are clearly made known in the message preached. We have before mentioned that the gospel is not so much an offer on the part of God, as a statement of certain facts concerning the Person and work of the Son of God.

(2) *His emotions must be stirred.* This is brought about as he reacts to the facts that have been presented to him in the preached message.

(3) *His will must be brought to the point and act of decision.* This is accomplished as he is intellectually convinced of the facts of the gospel and emotionally stirred in favor of the gospel. He now decides to do something about the matter and carries out his decision by an act.

4. *The danger of overemphasizing the appeal to one part of the personality at the expense of the others.*

This is where many preachers fail. Note carefully what follows.

(1) *To stress the appeal to the intellect,* at the expense of the emotions and the will, results in a formal and cold *intellectualism.* This leaves the hearer as clear as an icicle and just as cold.

(2) *To stress the appeal to the emotions,* at the expense of the intellect and the will, results in a frothy *sentimentalism* and sensationalism, so hot that he burns every one that touches him.

(3) *To stress the appeal to the will,* at the expense of the intellect and emotions, results in a rugged *individualism,* with whom no one can get along.

Each of these classes is lopsided, for only one part of his personality has been reached. This is the explanation of the many thousands of mere empty professions that are left in the wake of a modern "Revival campaign." The preacher was out to get "results" and succeeded only too well. He was more anxious to obtain "decisions," than to let God do the work that only He can do: for "salvation is of the Lord!" (Jonah 2: 9). Only God, who gave to His creature a personality, can reach and win it for Himself. True, He usually does it through a human instrument, divinely led and empowered, but it must be done along Scriptural lines, and reach both the intellect, emotions and will of the hearer. * Now let us look at each of these parts of the human personality which is to be won for Christ if salvation is to be experienced.

5. *The Intellect.*

(1) *It is an endowment of God.* God has endowed man with certain capabilities, of which the intellect is by no means the least. There is a tendency on the part of some preachers to depreciate the intellect, or the reasoning faculties of man, and concentrate on the emotional side of his nature. A reading of the Bible will show the folly of this. It is not for nothing that we are told: "The god of this age hath blinded the minds of them which believe not, lest the light of the glorious gospel . . . should shine unto them" (II Cor. 4: 4). While it is true that mere human reasoning, apart from the Holy Spirit's illuminating and regenerating power, cannot bring salvation; yet it is the Spirit of God who, through the Word, enlightens the intellect of the sinner, and enables him to understand the truths of the gospel that otherwise could not be known. (I Cor. 2: 14).

(2) *It must be enlightened through the preaching of the Word, as applied by the Holy Spirit.* "The entrance

*See author's pamphlet "Child Evangelism. Its Delights, Dangers and Design.

of Thy word giveth light, it giveth understanding to the simple" (Ps. 119:130). Therefore the need to preach the Word clearly, intelligibly, intelligently and powerfully. The Bible speaks of "the eyes of the understanding being enlightened" (Eph. 1:18). David prayed: "Open Thou mine eyes, that I may behold wondrous things out of Thy law" (Ps. 119:18). Only God can give this spiritual insight. It is our work to "preach the Word," and to be "in season and out of season" (II Tim. 4:2). A Paul may plant, an Apollos may water, but only God can "give the increase" (I Cor. 3:6).

(3) *It must be appealed to in preaching.* The apostle Paul, in his preaching, is described as "opening and alleging," and "reasoning and persuading" (Acts 17:3; 18:4). His epistle to the Romans is perhaps the most masterly setting forth of clearly stated and unanswerable logic that we have in the whole realm of literature. From his premise to his conclusion he proceeds, in orderly sequence, to prove his contention. Using well-marshalled arguments close reasoning and forceful illustrations, he proves conclusively the assertion he stated at the beginning of his epistle.

In the Gospels, the Lord Jesus, the greatest of all teachers and preachers, stated clearly and succinctly the great truths He sought to impart to His hearers. In the Sermon on the Mount this is particularly evident, where He sought to reason from the propositions He had made. See Matt. 5:23, 29, 46, etc., etc. A careful reading of the four Gospels will show how often our Lord stated a truth and then, from the propositions He had made, drew simple and logical conclusions.

Thus the preacher must seek, by all the means in His power, to present the truth in as clear, forceful, intelligible and intelligent a manner as possible. He must so seek to reach and enlighten the understanding that the hearer will be left in no doubt as to just exactly what God wants him to know. This will call for orderly arrangement, clear statements, logical arguments, close reasoning, telling illustrations and well-applied conclusions.

6. *The Emotions, or Feelings.*

By the emotions is meant the reactions of an individual to the impressions made upon his intellect. He forms certain conclusions regarding the things that he hears, sees, smells, tastes and touches. There is the sensation of pleasure or of pain; of love or hate; of sympathy or antipathy; of forgiveness or revenge; of generosity or miserliness, etc.

Nothing is so calculated to stir the emotions as the setting forth of the gospel story. As the heinousness of sin is presented, it should cause *hatred* of it to fill the soul. As the dread consequences of dying in one's sins is depicted from the word of God, *fear* of this dreadful fate will be the predominant emotion. As the story of the Savior's love is unfolded, and His awful substitutionary sufferings described, *sympathy, gratitude* and *love* will be the reaction. As the way of salvation is simply and lovingly set forth, surely the emotions of *hope, joy* and *peace* will be evidenced.

No one can hear the story of Calvary and remain wholly unmoved. The challenge to the emotions is surely evident in the appeal: "Is it nothing to you, all ye that pass by? Behold, and see if there be any sorrow like unto My sorrow, which is done unto Me, wherewith the Lord hath afflicted Me in the day of His fierce anger!" (Lam. 1:12). Thus the whole story of the gospel is not only calculated to enlighten the intellect, but also to stir the emotions of the hearer in favor of the message preached.

7. *The Will.*

(1) *God respects man's will and never coerces it.* God appeals to the will, but never forces it. Salvation is for

"whosoever *will*" (Rev. 22:17). Christ's plaint was: *"Ye will not* come unto Me that ye might have life" (John 5:40). He lamented over Jerusalem and said: *"I would* have gathered you . . . but ye *would not"* (Matt. 23:27). He cried: "If any man thirst, let him *come* unto Me and drink" (John 7:37). His invitation to the sinner was: *"Come* unto Me, all ye that labor and are heavy laden, and I will give you rest" (Matt. 11:28). He declared: "If any man *will* do His will, he shall know of the doctrine" (John 7:17). Christ is no burglar. He will not force His way into any life. He said: "If any man hear My voice and open the door, I will come in to him, and sup with him and he with Me" (Rev. 3:20). Christ pleads with and warns the sinner, but does not compel him to trust Him as his Savior. This must be the result of a willing decision on the part of the hearer.

(2) *God demands the unconditional surrender of the will.* The will is the last fort in the city of Mansoul to capitulate to the Son of God. There can be no experience of salvation until the white flag of surrender flies from its masthead. To bring the hearer to a definite decision to receive Christ as Savior and an acknowledgment of Him as Lord of the life, should ever be the ultimate purpose of preaching the gospel. A person may be intellectually convinced and emotionally stirred; but until he consents, by a definite act of his will to commit herself to Christ as Savior and Lord, there can be no realization of deliverance from sin's dread consequences.

It was when the prodigal said: "I *will* arise and go unto my father," that the battle was won, for his once proud and wilful heart was now humbled in the dust. The marriage ceremony furnishes a good illustration of this fact. The question is first put to the groom: "Wilt thou have this woman to be thy lawful wedded wife?" If he answers: "yes," and he usually does, then the question is put to the bride: "*Wilt* thou have this man to be thy lawful wedded husband?" If she replies: "I do," then it's all over—they are man and wife. Each having willed to take each other as husband and wife, these twain are now one flesh. Christ put the question to the helpless cripple: "*Wilt* thou be made whole?" before he said: "Take up thy bed and walk" (John 5:6). See also the case of Bartimaeus (Luke 18:41).

(3) *The preacher must therefore demand, in his Master's name, a decision of the will for Christ.* In this matter, he "speaks as the oracles of God," with all the authority of the word of God behind him (I Pet. 4:11). Against this demand for unconditional surrender, the sinner may rebel and seek to "hedge," or to compromise, and thus attempt to "save his face;" but the issue must be kept squarely before him. It is purely an individual matter between the sinner and the Savior, and no one else can make this decision for him. Only as he cries from his heart:

> "I yield, I yield;
> I can hold out no longer!
> I sink, by dying love compelled,
> *And own Thee conqueror!*"

shall salvation be experienced.

(4) *All "high pressure" methods of forcing results must be resolutely shunned, for they are a deadly plague.*

"Salvation by formula," and "mass production" methods have only succeeded in increasing the already over abundant crop of lifeless professors of Christianity. These have become a spiritual menace. Mass hysteria, produced by an expert use of applied psychology, and all mere emotional appeals should be definitely out in all preaching of the gospel, or teaching of the Word.

Thus, in the presentation and reception of the gospel, the whole personality of man is involved: intellect, emotions and will. Each must be reached and won if real salvation is to be experienced. May it be ours to so prepare ourselves for the task, that we shall be enabled to "make full proof of our ministry!" (II Tim. 4:5).

(5) *The test of true preaching.* Three questions should be asked regarding a sermon preached. First, did it enlighten the intellect? Second, was it calculated to stir the emotions? Third, did it demand a decision of the will? If the answer to each of these questions is in the affirmative, it was true preaching, for it prepared the hearer to *think* rightly, *feel* rightly, and *act* rightly.

The speaker must therefore preach clearly, intelligibly, logically and illustratively, to reach the *intellect.* He must preach sincerely, fervently and feelingly to stir the *emotions.* He must preach boldly, faithfully and authoritatively to capture the *will* for Christ and His word. A Christian is thus a person who has been intellectually convinced, emotionally constrained and volitionally converted. We must emphasize again that only God can bring about this miracle of regeneration.

8. *A study of the word "heart," in Scripture.* From an examination of its many occurrences, it seems clear that the *whole personality* of man is involved by its use. Sometimes the word places the emphasis on the *intellect;* at other times it is the *feelings* that are stressed; while in many other cases the *will* appears to be the dominant factor.

It may be of profit to look at a few of these Scriptures and note where the *emphasis* is placed.

(1) *The Intellect,* or the mind, the seat of our *reasoning* faculties. See Luke 1:51, 66; 2:35; 5:22. "What reason ye in your hearts"? Note also the expression, "wise-hearted," or intelligent. Exod. 28:3; 31:6; 36:1.

(2) *The Emotions,* or the feelings, the seat of our *reactionary* faculties. See Luke 21:26, "hearts failing for

fear"; Luke 24: 32, "Did not our heart *burn"*; II Cor. 2: 4, *"Anguish* of heart"; Rom. 9: 2, *"Sorrow* in my heart"; Rom. 5: 5, *"love* of God shed abroad in our hearts."

(3)   *The Will,* the seat of our *resolving* faculties. Acts 4: 32, "of one heart"; Acts 11: 23, *purpose* of heart"; Rom. 6: 17, *"Obeyed* from the heart"; Eph. 6: 6, *"Doing* the will of God from the heart"; Rom. 10: 1, "My heart's *desire."*

(4)   *Where the intellect, emotions and will* seem to be combined in the word. See II Cor. 4: 6; Matt. 12: 34; Rom. 10: 9, etc.

Thus to "believe in the heart" (Rom. 10: 9), involves the intelligent apprehension of the truth of the gospel with the *mind,* the favorable reaction of the *emotions,* and the full consent of the *will* to a reception of Christ as personal Savior and Lord of the life.   When this has been done, the heart can be said to be reached and won for Christ.

May it be ours to preach from heart to heart!

CHAPTER NINE

The Preacher's Support

Inasmuch as the subject of Homiletics not only concerns itself with the question of preaching, but also with the preacher himself; it may not be amiss to devote a little space to a consideration of the matter of the material, or financial support of those preachers who are devoting all their time to the ministry of the Word.

We have already observed that the only difference between the "full-time" preacher and the "part-time" preacher, is the amount of time devoted to the work of the Lord, and the matter of his financial support. We have also seen that the distinction between "clergy" and "laity," which obtains in Christendom, has *no place whatever* in the New Testament and is entirely foreign to its principles. All believers are described as being "a kingdom of priests," and as constituting "a royal priesthood" (Rev. 1: 6; I Pet. 2: 9). One of the great needs today is for an army of devoted Christians, gifted of God to preach and teach, who will support themselves by secular employment and use their spare time in ministering the word of God.

It is a cause for much thankfulness to God that a goodly number of such have responded to the call and commission of their Lord, and have gone, and are now going "everywhere preaching the word" (Acts 8: 4). These men are just as much "the Lord's servants," as those who devote all their time to this service. We must ever be on our guard lest the thought of *professionalism* be allowed to creep in, and rob us of that "simplicity that is in Christ" (II Cor. 11: 3). Some of the most gifted preachers and teachers are those who "labor, working with

their hands the thing which is good, that they may
have to give to him that needeth" (Eph. 4:28). They
have taken literally the advice of Paul to the Thessalonian believers: "Do your own business, and . . . work
with your own hands" (I Thess. 4:11).

The scriptural plan is not for a select few to be wholly
engaged in the work of the Lord and do all the preaching and teaching while the rest sit idly by; but that
every believer, being a servant of the Lord, is fitted for
some particular service for the Master. Each Christian
is a minister and should be a soul-winner for the Lord.
Each is exhorted: "Sanctify in your heart Christ as Lord,
and be ready always to give an answer to every man
that asketh you, a reason of the hope that is in you with
meekness and fear" (I Pet. 3:15, R. V.). There are no
exhortations addressed to the "clergy" as distinct from
the "laity." Let us get this fact firmly implanted in our
minds, for it will deliver us from much of the confusion
that exists in Christendom at this present time regarding
these things. With this fact firmly in our minds, now let
us note three things regarding those Christians who devote all their time to the ministry of the word of God.

I. Scripture Contemplates Full-time Preachers.

When a dissension arose in the early church regarding
the allocation of funds, the apostles called the disciples
together and advised them to select seven men of good
report to look after these business affairs: "But," said
they, "we will give ourselves continually to prayer and
to the ministry of the Word" (Acts 6:1-4). Here, then,
were at least twelve whose whole time was spent in the
Lord's work. Later on, Barnabas and Paul were called by
the Spirit of God and went out into whole-time service,
and were commended, by the saints, to the grace of God
for the work (Acts 13:1-4). We read still later of the

"Elders who labor in the word and doctrine;" and that these men were "worthy of double honor"; that is, of financial support to supply their physical needs. These full time preachers are described in the word of God as being:

1. *Called of the Lord to do a particular work* (Acts 13:2).

We have already observed that it was while they were busy in the Lord's work that they were called. God does not call slothful Christians into full time service. The scriptural treatment for a person who "will not work" is: "neither let him eat" (II Thess. 3:10). This starvation diet, though very salutary, would certainly prove to be a most efficacious cure in dealing with a lazybones!

2. *Equipped by the Lord.*

These men had been gifted by the Lord for their work. (Eph. 4:11, 12). These gifts, which had been bestowed by the Lord, had also been given liberty for exercise in the assembly of believers with whom they were associated in happy fellowship. The saints, in turn, had recognized their gift, for they had been edified by it. The proof that one really possesses a gift is its recognition, appreciation and commendation by one's fellow believers.

3. *Commended by the brethren* (Acts 13:3).

There was not only exercise of heart on the part of those called into full time service, but the assembly itself was of one mind regarding the matter. This is seen in the fact that, after they had fasted and prayed, they laid their hands upon them as a token of their acquiesence in their call, and their full fellowship with them in the work to which they had been called. Realizing the validity of their call, they gave them their wholehearted identification in this ministry to which the Lord had called them.

It is to be noted that this laying on of hands did not give them "authority to preach and teach," or make them "ministers," for they had been doing this for some considerable time! There is no such thing as the *ordination of preachers* in the New Testament. The only believers whose ordination is described are *elders,* and these only by direct apostolic authority, either in person, or by those delegated by an apostle to do so. (See Acts 14:23; Tit. 1: 5). This act on the part of the assembly at Antioch was simply an expression of their warm hearted fellowship with Barnabas and Paul. The fallacy of so called "Apostolic Succession," upon which Romanism and Episcopalianism rests, has no foundation either in the word of God, or in the facts of history. We need to emphasize the necessity for apostolic *success,* and not of apostolic succession!

Later on, Paul and Barnabas returned to Antioch: "from whence they had been recommended to the grace of God for the work which they had fulfilled" (Acts 14: 26). Still later, Paul chose another companion named Silas and departed on his second missionary journey: "being recommended by the brethren unto the grace of God" (Acts 15:40). How simple all this was, and how unlike the "ordination service" of Christendom apart from which, in many circles, a person cannot preach, or baptize, or "administer the elements" of the Lord's supper! C. H. Spurgeon, who refused human ordination, used to bemoan the oft "laying on of empty hands on empty heads!"

For one to go into full-time service without this hearty commendation of his brethren, has no support in Scripture. No assembly, of course, should commend any believer to full-time service as a preacher unless he has proved himself, over a period of time, to be a godly, consistent, faithful, gifted and acceptable minister of the Word.

4. *Sent forth by the Holy Spirit* (Acts 13:4).

They were not sent forth by a committee or a missionary board; but, having been commended, the brethren "let them go" (v. 3 R. V.). Then the Spirit of God took over and so led and empowered them that great blessing resulted from their ministry. How utterly useless—and worse—it is to go forth into full-time ministry apart from the Holy Spirit's power! All the theological education, missionary training and assembly commendation in the world cannot fit a person for this exacting task. The Divine requirement is stated in Zech. 4:6: "This is the word of the Lord . . . Not by might, nor by power, but by My Spirit saith the Lord of hosts."

II. Scripture clearly indicates that such full time preachers should be supported by the free-will offerings of the saints.

The classic passage on this subject is I Cor. 9:1-23, which should be read and re-read carefully by all believers. Several things seem to stand out clearly as the chapter is analyzed. Let us look at them.

1. *Paul's authority, as the Lord's apostle and servant, is stated as a fact and proved to be true* (vs. 1-3).

Paul's footsteps were dogged by Judaizing teachers, who became the plague of his life. They sought to bring the Gentile believers under the bondage of the law. In fact, they actually affirmed: "Except ye be circumcised, after the manner of Moses, ye cannot be saved" (Acts 15:1). These "false brethren, unawares brought in," also sought to discredit the validity of the apostleship of Paul and, in many cases, succeeded only too well in their evil work (Gal. 2:4). Paul's letter to the Galatians was especially written to combat the wrong teaching of these legalistic men. In his letter to the Corinthians he proceeds to prove his apostolic authority. Note the four opening questions, each of which anticipates an affirmative answer.

(1) *"Am I not an apostle?"* An apostle means, "a sent one." He begins his epistle: "Paul, called an apostle of Jesus Christ, through the will of God" (I Cor. 1:1). He was an apostle by Divine call. Note also II Cor. 1:1; Rom. 1:1; Gal. 1:1; Eph. 1:1; Col. 1:1; I Tim. 1:1; II Tim. 1:1; Tit. 1:1. No man had conferred this honor upon him; it had been given him by the glorified Lord Himself.

(2) *'Am I not free?"* He had been liberated from the bondage of Judaism and thus was "the Lord's freeman" (I Cor. 7:22). He was at perfect liberty to exercise the full rights and powers that were his as an apostle of Christ. He was not in bondage to any man, or under obligation to any committee. He was free to do all the will of God and teach all the word of God.

(3) *"Have not I seen Jesus Christ, our Lord?"* This seems to have been an essential requirement for an apostle; cp. Acts 1:21, 22. He had been a witness, not only to a risen but a glorified Christ in heaven. He says in another place: "And, last of all, He was seen of me also" (I Cor. 15:8). This glorious sight had completely revolutionized his life. It had changed him from a blasphemous and persecuting Pharisee into a humble, devout and loyal bond-slave of the Son of God, Whom he now loved above all others, and for Whose sake he had suffered as few men.

(4) *"Are not ye my work in the Lord?"* The very fact that these Corinthians had become Christians was proof of his apostleship. This is the thought in II Cor. 13:3-5: "Since ye seek a proof of Christ speaking in me . . . Examine yourselves, whether ye be in the faith." The very fact that they were 'in the faith," proved his apostleship and that Christ was "speaking in him." These Corinthians were thus the "seal of his apostleship" (v. 2).

2. *Paul's right to the maintenance and support of the Lord's people declared* (vs. 4-6).

(1) *He had a right to eat and drink* (v. 4). He was doing the work of the Lord, therefore he was at least entitled to food to sustain him in his service.

(2) *He had a right to do as the other apostles.* He could not only require that they support *him*, should he so desire; but he was at perfect liberty, if it was the will of the Lord, to have a wife to travel with him even as the other apostles.

(3) *He had the right to freedom from secular service* (v. 6). While it was true that Paul, rather than be under the patronage of, or obligation to the Corinthians, had labored with his own hands; yet he only did this in order to shut the mouths of those who would have accused him of benefiting himself at their expense. (Acts 18:1-3). He did the same thing at Thessalonica (I Thess. 2:8-9). At other times, and under different circumstances, he gladly accepted gifts sent to him as from the Lord Himself. His letter to the Philippians was occasioned by such a gift which he gratefully and beautifully acknowledged (Phil. 4:10-19).

Let no one imagine that it is a backward step for a full-time preacher to take secular employment in order to honestly support himself, when such an act becomes necessary. Paul did not think it was beneath his dignity to take a job, when the circumstances warranted such a course of action.

3. *Paul's fourfold substantiation of his right to the material support of the Lord's people* (vs. 7-14).

(1) *By an appeal to nature,* or the principle that obtains in human affairs. Many common illustrations are used to drive home this fact.

(a) *A Soldier* is supported by the country whom he serves. He rightly looks to his government to supply his needs, seeing his whole life is devoted to furthering its interests.

(b) *A farmer* is physically supported by the farm he cultivates. He plows, sows, harrows, fertilizes and reaps. Is it too much to expect that he will eat of the fruit he has toiled so hard to produce?

(c) *A Shepherd* is supported by the flock he cares for. He is surely entitled to some of the wool of the sheep and milk from the herd that he tends.

(2) *By an appeal to the Scriptures* (vs. 8-13). He goes on to say: Say I these things (merely) as a man? Does not the law also affirm the same principle? He then makes his appeal to the word of God. Again he uses some simple illustrations to clarify his points.

(a) *The lowly ox* treads out the corn in hope of eating some for itself. Therefore the ox is not to be denied its desire, for no muzzle must be put upon its mouth (Deut. 25:4). He then asks: Was this law written merely for the sake of the oxen, or did God not have a greater principle in view, even the support of His servants? (v. 9-10).

(b) *The plowman* does his work with the hope that he will partake of the harvest which his labor has made possible.

(c) *The thresher* of the grain does so with the expectation of sharing in the benefits of his toil and partaking of the bread.

(3) *By an appeal to common decency* (v. 11). Ordinary common decency demands an adequate return for labor expended. Christ declared: "The laborer is worthy of his hire" (or reward) (Luke 10:7). To receive the benefit of labor expended on one's behalf, and then make

no effort to contribute to the laborer's support is the basest form of ingratitude. Likewise, to receive spiritual ministry without feeling responsible to reciprocate in the way of financial and physical support, comes under the same category and deserves the same condemnation.

(4) *By an appeal to the Levitical precedent* (v. 13). The Levites depended for their support on the tithes of the people of Israel. Though the Aaronic priesthood has been done away in Christ (See Hebrews 9 and 10), yet the principle remains. Those who devote their entire time to the preaching of the gospel should be supported by the free will offerings of the Lord's people. If all Christians realized this fact and fulfilled their obligations in this matter, there would be no lack of support for those wholly engaged in Christian service.

God wants the willing gifts of His redeemed people (Exod. 25:2). He particularly emphasized that He only desired gifts "of every man that giveth it willingly with his heart." It is remarkable that, in response to this appeal, the people gave so liberally that they had to be restrained from further giving! (Exod. 36:6). It is not without the deepest spiritual significance that two whole chapters of the New Testament are devoted to the subject of willing, liberal and sacrificial giving. See II Cor. 8 and 9.

4. *The inevitable conclusion* (v. 14).

Mark it well: "Even so hath the Lord ordained that they which preach the gospel should live of the gospel." The Scripture teaching is quite clear. He who has been called by the Lord and sent by the Lord, will be supported and supplied by the Lord, through whatever means He sees fit, preferably through the medium of the Lord's people. If the Lord has not called and sent a preacher, then the sooner that person is "starved out" the better!

The servant of the Lord, who goes forth obediently at His command, "taking nothing of the Gentiles" (III John 7), but looking alone to the Lord for his supplies, will have all his needs met. He may, and probably will, have trials, in which the reality of his faith, love and obedience will be tested. In this path of simple dependence on the Lord alone lies true blessedness for the full-time servant of the Lord. It may be "a hand-to-mouth existence"; but so long as it is the *hand* of the *Lord,* and the *mouth* of the Lord's *servant,* who would want to introduce a better mode of supplying his needs?

Supposing a modernist, who denies the essential and eternal Deity of Christ and the Divine inspiration and infallibility of the holy Scriptures, went out into whole-time ministry, looking alone to the Lord for support; how much support would he get from the One whose Deity he denied, and whose word he discredited? Such a modernistic "minister" would soon be out of a job and compelled to do something useful in life, and thus earn an *honest* living!

While those in full-time service are urged to "look to the Lord for their support;" those not so fully engaged are, in turn, urged to "look to themselves" that they do not fail in fulfilling their obligations. Thus by their systematic, proportionate, liberal and cheerful giving, God will use them to supply the needs of those engaged in full-time work for Him.

III.   This right to support is waived, by grace, on the part of Paul (Vs. 15-23).

1.   *The preacher must be independent of man* (v. 15).

Though Paul has proved his right to be supported by them; he would rather die than force the issue, or demand his "rights" from those who were unwilling, or too unspiritual, to give. Thus the idea of a person bargaining with a church for a stipulated salary per year, finds no support here, or in any other part of the Scriptures. It is foreign to the very principles of Scripture. The only instance of a "hired ministry" is found in Judges 17: 6 to 18: 31; and this occurred at a time in Israel when "every man did that which was right in his own eyes." Surely no one would wish to follow the example of this miserable Levite and sell his services to the highest bidder!

It is to be feared that many have done so, and have consequently degenerated into the "servants of men" (I Cor. 7: 23). These men, because they have been *"hired,"* may also be *"fired"* by those who "called" them. Because of this fact, the strong temptation for the salaried preacher is to suit his preaching to those who were influential in securing his position and now pay his salary. These men, in turn, act on the assumption that those who "pay the piper" can also "call the tune." How much better is the Scriptural method of doing things! It leaves the preacher free to be the Lord's messenger and to declare the Lord's message, none daring to make him afraid. Thus he gets his authority, directions and support from the Lord Who has sent him.

2. *The preacher is responsible alone to the Lord.*

Of each preacher of the Word it can be said that a "dispensation (stewardship) of the gospel" has been committed to him; and he is thus directly responsible to the Lord who gave it to him (I Cor. 9: 17). In this way each preacher is individually accountable to God:

(1) *For the field in which he labors.* It may be the home field, or the foreign field. It is all the Lord's work, and part of the one great harvest field.

(2) *For the nature of his work in that field.* It may be evangelistic work, or it may be a teaching ministry. It may be amongst boys and girls, or with adults.

(3) *For the methods he uses in that work.* He may use charts, lantern slides, blackboard, flannelgraph, object talks, etc. Let not him that useth them not judge him that useth them, and vice versa! The Divine exhortation is: "Who are thou that judgest another man's servant? To his *own* Master he standeth or falleth." See Rom. 14: 1-13.

3. *The preacher's determination should therefore be:*

(1) *To preach the gospel freely* (v. 18). He is to make "the gospel of Christ without charge." To solicit money in the form of collections, from a mixed audience of saved and unsaved, has no warrant in the word of God. While it is true that God sometimes uses the unsaved to supply the needs of His people when the occasion demands, it is the *exceptional* thing. The ravens, which were ceremonially unclean birds, were used of God to supply the need of His servant, Elijah (See I Kings 15: 6). The "barbarians" of Melita showed Paul and his companions "no little kindness" (Acts 28: 2). Many a pioneer foreign missionary has had his needs supplied through the unsolicited help of the heathen to whom he preached the gospel, as missionary biographies will testify.

However, this help from the unsaved should not be solicited. Paul did not pass the plate around after preaching the gospel and urge his audience to contribute generously to his support. When Simon, the sorcerer, offered Peter money for the power to confer the Holy Spirit on whomsoever he laid his hands, he was roundly rebuked by the apostle and informed that he "had no part nor lot in this matter" (Acts 8: 18-23). Furthermore, we are told that: "The sacrifice of the wicked is an abomination unto the Lord" (Prov. 15: 8).

Paul did not hire out his services as a preacher, neither did he send any veiled hints in his letters regarding his needs. One has seen letters from so called "Faith Missions," describing their needs, asking for prayer and enclosing a blank check for the prospective donor's subscription! The words of our Lord should dispel any lingering doubts regarding this matter: "Freely ye have received, freely give" (Matt. 10:8). Surely, if it is the Lord's work, then the Lord who does the employing will also take care to supply the needs of His servants. We read: "Yea, he shall be holden up, for God is able to make him stand" (Rom. 14:4).

The following clever parody on modern mercenary methods in ecclesiastical circles appeared some time ago in a magazine. It consists of an imaginary letter coming from Paul in response to the "Macedonian Call." (Acts 16:9). It reads thus:

"Dear Sirs and Brothers,

Doubtless you recall the invitation you extended to me to come over to Macedonia and help the people of that section. You will pardon me for saying that I am somewhat surprised that you should expect a man of my standing in the church seriously to consider a call on such meager information.

There are a number of things I would like to learn before giving you my decision, and I would appreciate your dropping me a line, addressed to me at Troas.

First of all, I should like to know if Macedonia is a circuit or a station. This is important, as I have been told that once a man begins on a circuit, it is well nigh impossible to secure employment in station work. If Macedonia embraces more than one preaching place, I may as well tell you frankly, that I cannot think of accepting the call.

There is another important item that was overlooked in your brief and somewhat sudden invitation. No mention was made of the salary I should receive. While it is true I am not preaching for money, there are certain things that need to be taken into account. I have been through a long and expensive course of training; in fact I may say, with pardonable pride, that I am a Sanhedrin man—the only one in the ministry today.

The day is passed when you can expect a man to rush into a new field without some idea of the support he is to receive.

I have worked myself up to a good position in the Asiatic field, and now to take a drop and lose my grade would be serious.

Nor can I afford to swap 'dollar for dollar,' as the saying is amongst us apostles. Kindly get the good Macedonian brethren together, and see what you can do in the way of support. You have told me nothing about Macedonia, beyond the implication that the place needs help. What are the social advantages? Is the church well organized?

I recently had a fine offer to return to Damascus at an increase in salary, and I am told that I made a very favorable impression on the church at Jerusalem. If it will help with the board at Macedonia, you might mention these facts. Some of the brethren in Judea have been heard to say that if I keep on, in a few years I may have anything in the gift of the church. For recommendations, write to the Rev. Simon Peter, D. D., Jerusalem. I may say that I am a first class mixer and especially strong in argumentative preaching.

If I accept the call, I must stipulate for two months vacation, and the privilege of taking an occasional lecture tour. My lecture entitled: "Over the wall in a basket," is worth two drachmas of any man's money.

Sincerely yours,

Paul."

Arthur T. Pierson wrote: "Imagine Philip sending a financial agent to secure proper financial remuneration for his evangelistic work in Samaria; or Barnabas, that son of consolation, charging so much a week for his ministry to new converts at Antioch; or Peter, hesitating at Joppa, until he knew whether the fee for his visit to Caesarea would at least cover expenses and entertainment; or Paul, taking a collection at Mar's hill, to cover rent for his hired house in Rome! While it is lawful that they who preach the gospel should live by the gospel, that law may easily become a cloak for avarice."

(2) *To seek, by all means, to win souls for Christ* (vs. 19-22).

Here is a wonderful insight into the heart's desire of the apostle Paul. He longed to see precious souls brought to know Christ as their Savior and Lord. Would that verse 22 were true of every preacher! It is one thing to be *evangelical* and another to be *evangelistic*. The former serves the truth on *ice;* the latter presents the truth on *fire!* The preacher who makes it his aim, "by all means to save some," will not lack for fruit in his ministry.

In concluding this subject of the preacher's support, it can be stated that there are hundreds of full-time servants of the Lord, both at home and abroad, who are looking, and not in vain, to the Lord for their support. They are discovering each day that God does indeed "supply all their need, according to His riches in glory by Christ Jesus" (Phil. 4:19). How much better is this than the worldly-wise, and often sordid expedient of bargaining for a stipulated salary to preach the gospel. How much dishonor has been brought to Christianity by the pitiful appeals, directed to the unsaved, to support what is professedly the Lord's work! If we are to be preachers of the Book, then let us take our directions from the same Book in regard to this matter of temporal support.

CHAPTER TEN

The Perils of the Preacher

The remarks that follow have been drawn very largely from Dr. J. H. Jowett's book: "The Preacher, His Life and Work." This contains his lectures, delivered many years ago at Yale. This book, together with all his volumes of sermons, would make a splendid addition to any preacher's library, for they are characterized by deep spiritual insight, as well as being models of English prose.

It is well known that perils are attendant on privilege. The greater the privileges, the greater the perils associated with them. Many seem to think that a preacher lives a charmed life and basks in an atmosphere where little or no temptation can enter to mar or dim; where all is calm and bright and where "the wicked cease from troubling, and the saints are all at rest." This however, is not the case. Though his life may appear to be as secluded as a walled garden, yet often a garden can become a battlefield and a place of defeat, as was evidenced in Eden long ago.

The preacher is always in peril of losing his spirituality, his power, his vision, his usefulness and his life for God. Many a preacher has discovered this by tragic experience and has now been set aside, as being of no further use to his Master. In II Cor. 11, Paul describes the many perils through which he has passed as a herald for Christ. He spoke of being in "perils of robbers, in perils by my own countrymen, in perils in the wilderness, in perils in the sea, in perils among false brethren" (v. 26). In I Cor. 9:27 he speaks of a greater peril that far surpassed these physical dangers. He says: "I keep under my body, and bring it into subjection, lest that by any means when

141

I have preached to others I myself should be a castaway."
(or set aside, as unfit for the service of Christ.). This is
the spiritual peril to which every preacher is exposed.
Wise is he who, having been forewarned, forearms himself against this dire possibility.

The advice of Miles Coverdale, which he gave to
preachers of his day, is very much up to date: "If thou be
a preacher and hath oversight of the flock, awake to feed
Christ's sheep with a good heart and spare no labor to
do them good . . . and be ever reading, exhorting and
teaching in God's words; that the people of God run not
to other doctrines; and lest thou myself, when thou
shouldst teach others, be found ignorant."

Everything depends on what the preacher *is*. God is
far more concerned about this than what he *does*. In II
Cor. 6: 4-10, Paul draws up a list of the things that marked
his ministry as being approved unto God. This list does
not mention a thing about the *sermons* he preached, or
the *miracles* he performed; but only describes the *Christian* graces he displayed! The value of what we *say* and
do, is in exact proportion to what we really *are* in our
characters.

Hymns have very properly been written on behalf of
sailors who are in "peril on the sea." Others have been
composed for soldiers who face the dangers of the battlefield. A hymn might appropriately be penned on behalf
of those who are in "peril in the pulpit." What are these
peculiar perils to which preachers are exposed?

I. The peril of undue familiarity with divine things.

Just as it is possible to live in the midst of majestic
scenery and lose the sense of wonder and awe; so it is
possible to live in the realm of the sublime doctrines of
holy Scripture, and lose the sense of proper reverence that
such an environment must ever demand. It is possible to

be well acquainted with the majestic truths of God's sovereignty and grace, and even preach about them, and yet fail to appreciate their immensity, glory and beauty.

This was the fatal lack on the part of Nadab and Abihu, the sons of Aaron. Though they were the chosen, called and consecrated priests of God, and had witnessed the erection of the tabernacle and the glory of the Lord filling it; yet they had lost their sense of reverential awe, and failed to recognize and respect the intrinsic holiness of God. We are told they "offered strange fire" before Jehovah and died for their temerity (Lev. 10:1-3). The same was true of Israel as a nation. These people, though they had been redeemed from Egypt to the accompaniment of mighty signs and wonders, and had constantly brought before them the visible token of the presence of Jehovah in their midst, in the pillar of cloud by day and the pillar of fire by night; yet they allowed undue familiarity with Divine things to breed contempt in their souls, and turned aside into gross sin and idolatry.

When a preacher, who constantly handles Divine things, loses the spirit of humble and reverential awe in the presence of the holy and glorious Being whom he serves; he is in great peril of being set aside as unworthy any longer to "serve the living and true God," (I Thess. 1:9). John, the beloved disciple, as he neared the end of his long and useful life for Christ, was given a revelation of the outshining majesty, glory and power of his Lord. This wondrous vision caused him to fall at the feet of Christ "as one dead." At this, the glorified Son of God laid His right hand upon him and said: "Fear not, I am the First and the Last; I am He that liveth and was dead; and behold, I am alive for evermore!" (Rev. 1:10-18). Thus, in the evening of his days, this great apostle was not allowed to forget the surpassing glory of the One he served.

Paul, at the beginning of his Christian life, had the transcendent glory of the Lord indelibly impressed upon his heart. He never lost this sense of the greatness of Christ. As he neared the time when he should seal his testimony with his blood, he spoke of his Master as: "The King, eternal, immortal, invisible, the only wise God, to Whom be honor and glory for ever and ever, Amen!" (I Tim. 2:17). Though he knew the Lord as few men, he never allowed his close intimacy with Him to degenerate into undue familiarity.

Each preacher must therefore constantly have before him the fact that the One whom he serves is "the Lord Christ" (Col. 3:4). He must ever keep in mind that between the servant and the One he serves, is the immeasurable distance that exists between infinite Deity and finite humanity. The "treasure" of the gospel has only been placed in the "earthen vessel," in order that "the excellency of the power may be of God and not of us" (II Cor. 4:6-7). The message of God to Israel, in connection with the tragedy of Nadab and Abihu, should come home with force to the heart of every preacher: "I will be sanctified in them that come nigh Me, and before all the people I will be glorified" (Lev. 10:3).

II. The peril of inconsistent living.

It is tragically possible to be a guide *post* and not a *guide!* to be an *exhorter* and not an *example;* to point out the way to others and yet not walk in the way oneself. This was the sin with which Christ charged the Pharisees. Of them He said: "All therefore whatsoever they bid you observe, that observe and do; but do ye not after their works, for they say and do not" (Matt. 23:3). This also was Paul's indictment against the Jews: "Thou therefore which teachest another, teachest thou not thyself? Thou that preachest a man should not steal, dost thou steal? Thou that makest thy boast in the law, through breaking the law dishonorest thou God?" (Rom. 2:21-23).

The great peril of inconsistent living lies in the fact that it produces blasphemers of God's name and of His doctrine. Regarding the inconsistencies of the Jews, Paul had to say: "The name of God is blasphemed among the Gentiles through you" (Rom. 2:24). An altogether too common expression concerning some preachers is: "He preaches *cream* but he lives skimmed milk!" Christian *talk* should be backed up and balanced by Christian *walk*. Two brothers, one a doctor of divinity and the other a doctor of medicine, shared the same house and phone. A call came one day for "the doctor." The servant inquired: "Which doctor do you want: the doctor who *preaches,* or the one who *practices?*" In the case of the Christian preacher, he should be both! A preacher is never more effective for God than when he exemplifies in his life what he expounds with his lips.

It is to be feared that some preachers assume that the mere holding and teaching of correct doctrine is the equivalent of correct living; or that gift and grace are the same; or that orthodoxy of belief need not be balanced by orthodoxy of behavior. While standing and state must ever be kept *distinct* in our minds, they must be *harmonized* in our lives, if we are to be used of God in the proclamation of the gospel. Paul's two letters to his "son in the faith" are full of good counsel to preachers. He wrote: "Let no man despise thy youth, but be thou an example of the believers, in word, in conversation, (manner of life) in charity, in spirit, in faith, in purity" (I Tim. 4:12). To Titus he wrote: "In all things showing thyself a pattern of good works" (Tit. 2:7). No preacher will ever be despised because of his youth if he displays, in his life, that true godliness of character which adorns the gospel.

III. The peril of neglecting one's own spiritual development.

It is possible to guide others to the King's garden, describe the loveliness that lies within. and yet remain outside the gate himself. A preacher may wax eloquent on the fabulous riches of the Lord's treasury, and yet be poverty stricken in his own spiritual life. How many have had to sadly confess: "They made me a keeper of vineyards, but mine own vineyard have I not kept" (S. S. 1:6). A servant of the Lord can become so busy cultivating the spiritual orchards and gardens of others that his own garden, through neglect, degenerates into a wilderness of weeds.

The sober words of Alexander Maclaren, "the prince of expositors," are pertinent in this connection: "We who are ministers know the dreadful temptations of the ministerial office; how almost impossible it is to meet them unless on the condition of the most rigid discipline of soul; how almost impossible it is to avoid regarding the Bible as a dictionary of texts; how impossible to avoid looking at the magnificent truths of Christianity as weapons with which to assail our hearers. For one minister who fails by reason of what the world calls immorality, a dozen settle down into the perfunctory monotony of professionalism, because they fail to live alone with God, and because solitude of soul is forgotten and ceases to be the atmosphere into which they habitually withdraw. The river that is to bring freshness to many a league of plain must have its rise in the solitary cleft of the lonely hills, and draw its water from the snows that sparkle on their tops. The minister to be a man of power must live alone with God."

Our Lord's words are pregnant with spiritual import to all who handle the word of life: "What shall it profit a man if he gain the whole world and lose his own soul?"

(or life) (Mark 8:36). To gain the world of oratorical fame, or expository ability, or doctrinal exactness, or of popular appeal, and lose one's own spiritual power, through neglect, is a tragedy indeed. Again we quote Paul's words to Timothy: "Take heed unto thyself and unto the doctrine." Note the inseparable order here: first *thyself* and then the *doctrine*.

A great teacher of the word once wrote: "O the joy of having nothing, and being nothing, and seeing nothing but a living Christ in glory, and being careful for nothing but His interests down here."

The preacher must read, meditate in and study his Bible, not primarily with a view to impressing it, in sermon form, on the minds of his hearers; but to have the truth firmly *impressed* on his own heart and *expressed* in his own life. As he thus takes heed unto himself, the doctrine will logically follow. Electricity must flow *in* before it can flow *out*. The preacher's intake must be greater than his outlet, or spiritual malnutrition will result. God's word to Abraham is appropriate in this connection: "I will bless thee . . . and thou shalt be a blessing" (Gen. 12:2). The servant of the Lord must live in the good of what he preaches. What has proved to be a blessing and profit to his own soul, will doubtless become a blessing and a profit to others as it is passed on in preaching.

IV.   The peril of callousness to the needs of others.

Just as a doctor can become hardened to the suffering of his patients, so the preacher can lose his capacity for compassion and become inured to the pitiable spiritual and physical needs of others. It is a peril indeed when a preacher fails to appreciate and sympathize with suffering humanity as it comes to him for the counsel and comfort that he alone can give from the Word. There are many who are sick in body, mind and soul. There are the tempted, the discouraged, the doubtful and the despairing. There are the bereaved, who mourn the loss of their loved ones, and who are in dire need of Christian sympathy and the comfort of God's word. How tragic it is when such come to us and are sent empty away. They asked for bread and were given a stone, because of the callousness of the preacher.

This lack of sympathy to the needs of others was evidenced by the disciples of Christ, and drew from Him a stern rebuke. When the woman of Tyre and Sidon cried to the Lord to help her daughter, who was possessed of a demon, the disciples callously said to the Lord: "Send her away, for she crieth after us!" Her appeals annoyed the disciples, who failed entirely to appreciate her distress of soul. To them she was simply a nuisance who disturbed their convenience, and therefore needed to be silenced; but the Lord dealt wondrously with her (Matt. 15:21-28). On another occasion these disciples asked their Master to send away the hungry multitude; but Christ, in His deep compassion, met their need with the miracle of the multiplied bread and fish (Matt. 14:13-21). Still again, because certain people did not welcome Christ into their village, James and John inquired: "Lord, wilt Thou that we command fire to come down from heaven and consume them, even as Elias did?" At this evidence of their revengeful spirit Christ rebuked them and said: "Ye know not what manner of spirit ye are of, for the Son of Man is not come to destroy men's lives, but to save them" (Luke 9:52-56).

It is a sad day when a preacher loses the keen edge of his sympathy and compassion, and is no longer able to "weep with them that weep, and rejoice with them that rejoice" (Rom. 12:5). We all need to spend much time in the school of Christ and learn of Him. The whole of our Lord's life was characterized by a deep and tender-hearted compassion for those who needed Him. He was never too busy, or too weary, to minister Divine comfort to suffering humanity. The servant of the Lord must therefore beware of being too busy, or too much wrapped up in himself and his own interests, to be able to enter into the sorrows, sufferings and needs of others. This is a very real peril and one to which every preacher is exposed.

V.   The peril of professionalism.

Here the peril consists in the possibility of a preacher saying and doing things, not because of any inward urge of the love of Christ, or the leading of the Holy Spirit; but from a mere sense of duty, because it is the "proper thing" for him to do or say. Preaching can easily become a perfunctory affair, and clothe the preacher with a professional air, so that he becomes cold and distant, and imagines he is in a class by himself.

There is always the danger that a preacher may become austere and intolerant of friendly criticism, and resent needed correction, and even good advice from those in the position to give it. Such an one imagines that because he has been wholly engaged in the work of the Lord over a period of years, he is now beyond the possibility of criticism from "ordinary Christians," who are not "out in the work!" This atmosphere of professionalism is conveyed to others in a subtle way that is difficult to define, but which nevertheless produces a most adverse effect. The preacher may exude an attitude of condescension, or assume a patronizing air, or even introduce an artificial intonation of voice. He creates the impression that he is conferring a great favor on the audience by gracing the meeting with his presence. The preacher may not be aware of what is happening, but the audience quickly senses this spirit of professionalism and rightly resents it. It is hardly necessary to point out that such a thoroughly unjustified superiority complex is a smoke in the nostrils of God, Who hates pride in any shape and form.

Clerisy is a direct result of this spirit of professionalism in the things of God. It started early in the history of the church, when those gifted by the Lord to teach and preach began to form themselves into cliques, and became a separate class from their brethren. They adopted a particular form of dress to distinguish them from the "common people," and assumed a title befitting their superior status from those who did not publicly teach or preach. They soon became a caste and resented any intrusion into their privileged domain. They also began to assume a proprietorship over the people of God and to exercise a "lordship over God's heritage," in direct contradiction to the Scriptures (I Pet. 5:3). From such ecclesiastical pretention and prideful professionalism, may the Lord deliver us! May it be ours to walk humbly before, live holily amongst and be mutually helpful to our brethren and sisters in assembly fellowship.

It may be in order, at this juncture, to address a frank and friendly word to preachers on the subtle danger and the abysmal folly of taking themselves too seriously. This is particularly true of those individuals who seem to have lost, or perhaps never had any sense of humor. These unfortunate people appear to labor under the misapprehension that sobriety of conduct means solemnity of manner.

With the view of maintaining "the dignity of their profession," as preachers, they adopt an unnatural attitude of stiff and starchy formality, assume a super sanctimonious and priggish air of conscious superiority, and apparently utterly fail to realize that, in their attempt to appear dignified, they have only succeeded in becoming ridiculous. What a mercy it would be to themselves, and a greater relief to their brethren, if they could only be brought to see themselves as others see them!

These preachers appear to have neither the desire nor the ability to view a situation in the light of all its attendant circumstances, nor to correctly estimate the right and proper proportion of things, or even to intelligently form and maintain a balanced sense of judgment. Every event which comes before their notice is viewed from the same standpoint, interpreted according to their rigid and prejudiced standards which, like the laws of the Medes and Persians, admit of not the slightest possibility of change, relaxation or readjustment.

It was one such individual who, when he saw a small boy playing baseball who had professed to be saved the night before, remarked gloomily to a friend: "Do you see that? It's just as I thought: I *knew* there was no reality to his profession!"

This sanctimonious attitude is usually coated with a thin veneer of assumed humility, and combines to produce a smug and self satisfied air, plus a condescending and patronizing attitude toward others. Their speech abounds with ultra pious phraseology, well sprinkled with a generous supply of worn out religious clichés. A bumptious and pontifical air of papal infallibility accompanies their pronouncements, which admit of no possibility of error or contradiction. Their attitude is: "I have spoken: let the earth keep silent!" They never seem to be able to come down from the platform or pulpit, and unfortunately have allowed their position, as preachers, to go to their heads.

Should anyone have the temerity to criticize their style of preaching, or take exception to their line of teaching, or question their ethics, or express disapproval of their behavior; they view all such criticism as being motivated by envy and jealousy because of their mental, moral and spiritual superiority. That such criticism could possibly arise from a genuine desire to correct their faults is, of course, unthinkable to them. Consequently, with a martyr-like air, they receive it as part of "the cross" they have been called upon to bear because of their "separation" and "faithfulness" to the Lord, and their determination to walk in what they term "the old paths"!

It goes without saying that such nauseating smugness and proud pretention ill becomes a sinner saved by grace. It is strongly reminiscent of the attitude adopted by the Pharisees of Christ's day, and which called forth His severest words of rebuke. One is reminded of the story of an extremely egotistical United States senator who contracted a severe cold which necessitated his absence from the senate for a few days. During this brief period of his absence, a political crisis arose in the nation. On the first morning after his recovery from his cold, as he took a stroll through the streets of Washington, a man approached him and inquired anxiously: "Senator, what is the latest news about the national crisis?" The great man paused in his stride and then replied ponderously: "Thank you, I am feeling much better today!"

No preacher should take himself too seriously, or consider himself beyond criticism and, least of all, behave like a martyr if he is criticized. Nor should he, for one moment, imagine that his gift of teaching or preaching has rendered him sacrosant, or elevated him to a position of superiority above and beyond his fellow saints. Each preacher should resolutely resist, and turn with loathing from the temptation to "think of himself more highly than he ought to think" (Rom. 12:3). We do well to keep in mind the words of a wise man who declared that: "regeneration is that process by which God makes a *natural* man *spiritual,* and a *spiritual* man *natural.*"

May each one determine that, by the grace of God, he will stedfastly refuse to take himself too seriously, or attempt to stand on his dignity, or even be guilty of spiritual snobbery, or behave in an unnatural manner; but will seek humbly, sincerely and consistently to be "a good minister of Jesus Christ, nourished up in the words of faith and good doctrine." (I. Tim. 4:6).

A reporter once asked Bernard Stanley, White House Special Counsel, if President Eisenhower laid down any hard and fast rule for the staff's behavior. "Yes, and they are very simple," he replied. "He laid them down to the staff right after he was inaugurated, and he tells them to each new staff member. They are: 'I want everybody smiling around here. Always take your job seriously, but never yourself! Don't forget to pray'."

It was Robert Burns, the great Scotch poet, who wrote:

> "O would some one the gift would give us,
>   To see ourselves as others sees us;
> It would from many a blunder free us,
>   And foolish notion!"

Another poet has put it thus:

> "Just stand aside, and watch yourself go by!
>   Think of yourself as "he" instead of "I."
> Pick flaws, find fault; forget the man is you,
>   And strive to make your estimate ring true.
> The faults of others then will dwarf and shrink,
>   Love's chains grow stronger by one mighty link,
> When you, with "he" as substitute for "I,"
>   Have stood aside, and watched yourself go by!"

VI. The peril of compromise.

Here the danger lies in the avoidance of frankly and honestly facing unpleasant situations, truths and duties. When such an occassion calls for faithful dealing and straight talking, the subject is dodged under the guise of "tact," "diplomacy" and "geniality." The truth is thus sacrificed on the altar of compromise, and this usually results in the situation degenerating from bad to worse. This spirit of compromise can be evidenced in many ways by the preacher; and he must be continually on the watch lest he fall into this snare. He must beware of compromise:

1. *In relation to his own life.*

Life is made up of the sum total of many little things. A preacher's ethics should therefore be of the highest order. He must resolutely refuse to compromise with sin in his own life. Once sin is trifled with, it is tolerated and then practiced. One must therefore rule himself with an iron hand and not temporize with evil in any shape or form. It is fatally easy to condemn in others what one allows in one's own life. Herein is seen the constant need for individual prayer, devotion, self examination, humility of heart, self judgment and a life of self sacrifice on behalf of others. This is not easy, but it is the price each must pay for usefulness. Then he must beware of compromise:

2. *In relation to others.*

Particularly should this be true in his relationships with the opposite sex. In this, *friendliness* and not *familiarity*, should be the key note. Many preachers have failed here, and have had to be laid aside from further public service for their Lord. Then again, the preacher's business dealings should be above board. Many a preacher has ruined his testimony by contracting debts he was unable and, in some cases, unwilling to pay. It was said of a certain preacher, greatly gifted in the ministry of the Word, that he had "no sense of financial responsibility." This ultimately became his ruination. It is a good principle to "owe no man anything," and to resolve that no debt shall be contracted unless there is every prospect of honorably discharging it. Finally, he must avoid compromise:

3. *In relation to his ministry of the Word.*

Each preacher will do well to keep constantly before him the fact that he is living in a world characterized by agnosticism, modernism, liberalism and unbelief. These things have also made great inroads into the professing Church, so that in many pulpits the fundamental truths of Christianity are either ignored, belittled, or flatly denied. The modern church, so-called, has largely lost its grip on God; its love for Christ; its implicit reliance on the Spirit of God; its knowledge of the word of God; its sense of the sinfulness of sin; its zeal for the salvation of souls; its realization of the awfulness of hell, and the hope of the personal and literal coming again of the Lord Jesus Christ. As a result of this state of affairs, there is a marked indifference to eternal realities in Christendom.

This calls for uncompromising faithfulness to the truth of God's word. There is always the peril of developing into a "twilight preacher." Twilight is a mixture of light and darkness, so that it is neither one nor the other. There is a color of cloth which tailors call "parson gray." It is neither white nor black, and is consequently suitable for either a marriage or a funeral! The temptation will always be present to avoid certain lines of ministry that need to be presented, lest offence be given to certain influential people in the audience. This "soft pedalling" of needed truth develops into suavity and urbanity and these, in turn, pave the road which leads to spiritual impotence.

There are occasions, of course, when it is the best part of wisdom to avoid certain controversial subjects, lest the ears of our audience be cut off, or the hearers unnecessarily offended. It is not this which is in view here, but rather a question of the *motive* that lies behind one's ministry. Was this particular truth held back because of the fear of man, or the fear of the loss of popularity, or the fear of the lack of financial support? If so, then it is compromise, and must be viewed as obnoxious to both God and man.

God's word to Jeremiah emphasizes this need for faithfulness on the part of the bearer of the Divine message: "Speak unto all . . . the words that I command thee to speak unto them; diminish not a word" (Jer. 26:2). Notice those last four words: *"Diminish not a word!"* It was to be the truth, and the *whole* truth that Jeremiah was to proclaim. He was instructed to keep back nothing. Happy is the preacher who can say to his audience, as did Paul: "I kept back nothing that was profitable unto you." (Acts 20:20) Such can also say with him: "I am pure from the blood of all men." Acts 20:26 cp. Ezek. 33:8).

VII.   The peril of popularity.

The lure of the limelight, and the courting of the praises of men has also been the ruin of many. There is always the danger of being more anxious to catch the approving eye of the audience than of God. We read of those in the days of our Lord who "loved the praise of men more than the praise of God" (John 12:43). It is much easier to become a man of *popularity* than a man of *principle*. Many a preacher has sacrificed his spiritual power on the altar of secular popularity, and lived to regret his absymal folly.

This desire for popularity provides a fertile breeding ground for the twin evils of envy and jealousy. Instead of praising God for other preachers of equal, or superior gift to his own, the green eyed monster is allowed to do its evil work in the soul and eat away the spirituality of the life. Years ago, stars of the movie world used to suffer from a form of blindness caused by undue exposure to the brilliant lights of the studio. The preacher must also take heed, and beware lest over exposure to the blazing lights of the approval of men, blind him to the supreme importance of the approval of God.

He needs ever to remember that often what is "highly esteemed among men, is an abomination in the sight of God" (Luke 16:15). Both self confidence and self esteem combine to dim one's spiritual vision to the value of unseen, but eternal realities. It causes the preacher to degenerate from a servant of God to a servant of man. Paul determined that, by the grace of God, this should never be true of him (Gal. 1:10).

These, then, are some of the peculiar perils to which every preacher is exposed. The prominent place is indeed the perilous place. The Devil will seek, by all the means in his power, to bring about the downfall of a servant of the Lord. How good it is to know that the One Who saves, calls, commissions and equips the preacher, is also able to "keep him from falling," and to present him "faultless before the presence of His glory with exceeding joy" (Jude 24). The task is not easy, the enemies are both wily and powerful and the perils are very real. To each preacher comes the heartening words of his Lord: "My grace is sufficient for thee!" (II Cor. 12:9).

We could not conclude this subject better than by quoting this poem by J. J. Penstone. It is entitled: *"The Servant's Path."*

Servant of Christ, stand fast amid the scorn
    Of men who little know or love thy Lord;
Turn not aside from toil; cease not to warn,
    Comfort and teach. Trust Him for thy reward:
A few more moments' suffering, and then
Cometh sweet rest from all thy heart's deep pain.

For grace pray much, for much thou needest grace;
    If men thy word deride—what can they more?
Christ's weary foot thy path on earth doth trace;
    If thorns wound thee, they pierced Him before;
Press on, look up, though clouds may gather round;
Thy place of service He makes hallowed ground.

Have friends forsaken thee, and cast thy name
  Out as a worthless thing? Take courage then:
Go, tell thy Master; for they did the same
  To Him, who once in patience toiled for them:
Yet He was perfect in all service here;
Thou oft hast failed: this maketh Him more dear.

Self-vindication shun: if in the right,
  What gainest thou by taking from God's hand
Thy cause? If wrong, what dost thou but invite
  Satan himself thy friend in need to stand?
Leave all with God. If right, He'll prove thee so;
If not, He'll pardon; therefore to Him go.

Be not men's servant: think what costly price
  Was paid that thou mayest His own bondsman be,
Whose service perfect freedom is. Let this
  Hold fast thy heart. His claim is great to thee:
None should thy soul enthrall, to whom 'tis given
To serve on earth, with liberty of Heaven.

All His are thine to serve; Christ's brethren here
  Are needing aid; in them thou servest Him.
The least of all is still His member dear;
  The weakest cost His life's blood to redeem.
Yield to no "party" what He rightly claims,
Who on His heart bears all His people's names.

Be wise, be watchful. Wily men surround
  Thy path. Be careful, for they seek with care
To trip thee up. See that no cause is found
  In thee thy Master to reproach. The snare
They set for thee will then themselves inclose,
And God His righteous judgment thus disclose.

Cleave to the poor, Christ's image in them is;
  Count it great honor, if they love thee well;
Naught can repay thee after losing this.
  Though with the wise and wealthy thou shouldst dwell,
Thy Master oftentimes would pass thy door,
To hold communion with His much-loved poor.

"The time is short": seek little here below;
  Earth's goods would cumber thee, and drag thee down;
Let daily food suffice; care not to know
  Thought for to-morrow; it may never come.
Thou canst not perish, for thy Lord is nigh,
And God's own care will all thy need supply.

CHAPTER ELEVEN

The Sermon and Its Structure

Having discussed, at some length, the qualifications of the preacher, his call, the matter of his support and somewhat of his perils; let us now proceed to the subject of the sermon itself and its structure. This will fall into three main divisions: its definition, structure and modes of delivery.

Many object to the word, "sermon," as being too "ecclesiastical." Such say: "I don't preach sermons, I only give a simple word in the gospel." Or: "I just try to open up the Scripture in my humble way." The difference between this and a sermon is the same difference as between six and half a dozen! To paraphase a famous saying: "A sermon, by any other name, is just as good—or bad!"

The word "Sermon" has its origin in a Latin word, which means a stab, or a thrust. This indicates the purpose of it—to pierce the hearer with "the sword of the Spirit which is the word of God." (Eph. 6:17).

I. The definition of a sermon.

Perhaps the simplest definition is: "A sermon is a form of discourse on Scripture truth, designed to save or edify the hearer." A. T. Pierson defined it as: "A speech spoken in behalf of, or in the name of God." Another has described it as: "That which is born of the union of truth wedded to knowledge, matured in meditation and sent forth, clothed in the beauty of diction." Dr. Jeff Ray has it as: "An oral address to a general audience, with a view to unfolding, elaborating and enforcing scriptural truth."

Perhaps the best definition has been given by Dr. Phelps, who states it thus: "A sermon is an oral address to the popular mind, upon scriptural truth contained in the Bible, elaborately treated and with a view to persuasion." Let us notice five points in this excellent definition.

1. *It is an oral, or spoken address.*

It is not something to be read by an audience, but *heard* by it. This, of course, necessitates that it be spoken sufficiently loud and enunciated so clearly that all can hear distinctly. In Nehemiah 8:8 we are told that those who addressed the people: "read in the book in the law of God *distinctly,* and *gave the sense,* and caused them to *understand* the reading." Would that every preacher followed this example!

2. *It is to the popular mind.*

Therefore it should be couched in language which can be understood by all present. Words "easy to be understood" should be used to convey the message (I Cor. 14:9). Christ spoke in language His audience, composed mostly of common people, could easily understand. Lincoln once remarked that: "God must have loved the common people, for He made so many of them!" An old lady, returning from a preaching service, was asked how she had enjoyed the sermon. She replied: "Not very much, for I took the wrong book with me. Instead of taking my Bible, I should have taken a dictionary!"

3. *It is upon Scriptural truth contained in the Bible.*

This eliminates, with one blow, those thousands of so-called sermons that are nothing more than a disquisition upon the most recent scientific discovery, or a discussion of the latest sensational novel, or a summary of the current political situation, or the setting forth of the virtues or follies of some famous personage. Read I Cor. 15:1-5. It is good to remember that the preacher has not been sent to *reconstruct* society, but to *regenerate* it, and this can only be accomplished through the preaching of the living word of God.

A preacher once said: "Though I have a scientific mind and a university degree in sociology and philosophy, and though I am an expert in social service and an authority on Browning, and though I use the language of the scientific laboratory, so as to deceive the very elect into believing I am a scholar, and have not a message of salvation and the love of Christ, I am a misfit in the pulpit and no preacher of the gospel!" See I Cor. 1:21-24.

Many a preacher has been turned aside from his God-given commission to "preach the gospel" and "teach the word," in order to catch the eyes and tickle the ears of intellectual worldlings. Jeremiah 23:28 is appropriate in this connection. Here God declares: "The prophet that hath a dream, let him tell a dream; and he that hath My word, let him speak My word faithfully. What is the chaff to the wheat? saith the Lord." The only remedy for this poor, sin-blasted, Satan-blinded, proud, self sufficient and pleasure-loving world is the gospel of God, preached by a man of God, in the power of the Spirit of God, as he is constrained by the love of God. Such a preacher will not lack for an audience, for there is nothing so attractive as "the old, old story of Jesus and His love." Christ's words are still true: "I, if I be lifted up . . . will draw all men unto Me" (John 12:32).

Christ is the mighty Magnet. As He is presented, in all the attraction of His Person, the abundant sufficiency of His saving power and His satisfying presence, souls will be drawn to Him. "He will draw the miser from his gold, the sensualist from his lusts, the worldling from his pleasures and the sinner from his follies." Like Paul, the preacher should be able to testify: "I have not shunned to declare unto you the whole counsel of God" (Acts 20:27).

The preacher is not called upon to entertain worldlings by lecturing to them on secular subjects, but to proclaim to sinners "the unsearchable riches of Christ" (Eph. 3:8; I Cor. 2:1-5). A certain evangelical minister of a church called "St. Peter's," was approached by some of his worldly parishoners with the request that the church building be opened for some frivolous entertainment. He replied: "Like the apostle, after whom this church is named, I have been commissioned by the Lord to feed His sheep and not to amuse the goats!" He had learned that the business of a preacher is not to *amuse* an audience, but to cause it to *muse*.

Preaching is the setting forth of Scriptural truth before the hearer and this demands, of course, that the preacher be well acquainted with the holy Scriptures. It has been well said that "preaching is, to God's word, what the feather is to the arrow: it is that which directs it to the mark." Let it not be said of us, as one man said of a certain preacher: "He has two faults: first, he has no delivery, and second, he has nothing to deliver!"

4. *It is elaborately treated.*

That is to say, the scripture truth is closely examined in relation to its context, the passage is carefully analyzed, the real meaning of its words explained, its truth illustrated and the lesson applied in a logical, intelligent and edifying manner. All this necessitates close and connected study, an orderly arrangement of the material and a clear presentation of the address. We shall discuss this orderly arrangement later.

For this elaborate treatment of the Scripture truth, three things are essential: rhetoric, grammar and logic.

(1) *Rhetoric* has to do with the use we make of the material, its choice, adaptation, arrangement and expression. In other words, rhetoric simply consists of putting the right words in the right places. It is the art of discourse and skill in the use of language. The word comes from "rhetor," orator.

(2) *Grammar* has to do with the choice and use we make of the words that form the medium by which the sermon is preached, and also to the correct use and pronunciation of these words.

(3) *Logic* concerns itself with the right use of thought and of the rational powers. It implies that the arguments we use are based on good and sound reasoning, which proceed, in orderly sequence, from the less to the greater, until the hearer has been convinced of the reasonableness and logic of the argument.

5. *It is with a view to persuasion.*

The supreme goal of the preacher is to gain the attention and win the hearer to an acceptance of, and obedience to the truth that has been presented. It should be the preacher's aim to see that the hearer is not merely "almost persuaded," but "altogether persuaded" to accept the truth (Acts 26:28-29). However eloquent, logical and orderly the sermon may be, it has missed its mark if it fails to move the audience for God.

Someone has pointed out that if we remove the initial letter of the word *"preach,"* we have the word *"reach."* If the initial letter of this word is removed, we have the word *"each."* Thus to *preach* is to so present the truth that it will *reach each* person in the audience. Preaching is not merely the testimony of one's own experience of the truth of God's word, nor does it consist only of exhortation; but it is the clear, orderly, definite exposition and application of the truth God has been pleased to reveal in the holy Scriptures.

II. The structure of the Sermon.

The sermon has been likened to a bridge which spans the gulf that separates ignorance from knowledge; indifference from interest; unbelief from faith, and inaction from decision. It is the preacher's business to bridge this gulf by means of his sermon and conduct the hearer safely across. The *approach* to the bridge, on the hearer's side, we may call the *introduction*. The body of the sermon, or the *discussion,* forms the *main structure* of the bridge, with each division as a supporting column. The *near side* of the bridge is the *conclusion,* or the application, by which the hearer is conducted to the ground on which the preacher stands. Surely such a service, with so exalted a purpose, demands the best we can give in the way of careful preparation of the material, and the powerful presentation of the truth to the audience.

Properly speaking, there are five parts to a sermon:
1. *The Text*: that is, the portion of Scripture to be considered.
2. *The Theme,* or the subject to be discussed.
3. *The Introduction.*
4. *The Discussion,* or the body of the address, consisting of the main divisions or points.
5. *The Conclusion.*

We shall now proceed to examine each of these parts of the sermon separately, and go into considerable detail in the description for the next fifty pages.

1. The text.

(1) *Definition of the text.*

The word "text" is derived from the Latin, "textus," which means something woven. For instance, see the word "texture." It denotes therefore the web of the discourse. We speak of the "text of Scripture." By this we mean all the words of holy writ. Thus any part of the Bible selected for exposition is called "the text."

This text may consist of a single verse, or even part of a verse, or a whole passage from the word of God, consisting of many verses. The text, then, is our authority, of the foundation on which the sermon is built. The purpose of preaching is to expound the word of God which, in turn, is to indoctrinate the hearers. The importance of the text will therefore be readily appreciated. We shall now consider three things regarding the text: its necessity, the principles governing its selection, and its rules of interpretation.

(2)   *The necessity for the text,* or why should we select a definite portion from the word of God?

(a)   *It gives authority to the message.*

It is the: "Thus saith the Lord!" that carries the weight in the sermon. The audience is made to realize that it is the truth of God's word to which it is listening, and not the mere vaporings of man.

(b)   *It confines, or should confine the preacher to his subject.* This certainly will be the case if it is properly treated. Alas, in many cases, the sign outside a certain wood-turner's shop would be appropriate to many a sermon: "All kinds of twisting and turning done here!" Happy is he who sticks to his text, for the text will then probably stick to his audience. There are altogether too many preachers who firstly, take a text; secondly, depart from the text; and thirdly, never return to the text!

(c)   *It gives unity to the sermon,* presenting a complete thought that can be retained by the audience. The sermon exists only for the text, and the preacher's business is to press it home to the heart of the hearer.

(d) *It prepares the hearers for the discussion* that is to follow.

It should start a train of thought in their minds as to what the speaker has to say about this particular text. The text, to the preacher, is what a "brief" is to a lawyer: it is the basis of his argument. He first succinctly states his brief to the judge and jury, and then proceeds to prove his statement and, if possible, win his case.

(e) *It promotes variety in preaching.*

There is no lack of texts, each of which has its own message addressed to the heart of man. There are, however, some preachers who seem to preach the same sermon, whatever their text may be! Of them it can be said:

> "Although ten thousand are their texts,
> Their sermons are but one!"

(3) *The selection of the text.*

There are certain broad principles governing the selection of texts. These are well worth considering.

(a) *Be careful about choosing texts*, the sentiment of which is not inspired. For instance, the *record* of what Satan said is inspired but his words were certainly not. Job 1:9; 2:4. Inspiration guarantees the truth of the *record,* but not necessarily the truth of the *sentiment* expressed. This is true of much that Job's friends said, concerning which God declared: "Ye have not spoken of Me the thing that is right" (Job 42:7). Again: the key to a correct understanding of Solomon's observations recorded in the book of Ecclesiastes, is that they are based on his viewpoint of things as they appear "under the sun." Eccl. 9:1-6. Note v. 1, "I considered in my heart." Here is the inspired account of the working of a man's deceitful heart. This book is the favorite hunting ground for false cults. Make sure the sentiment is inspired before using it as an authoritative message from God. Above all, beware of drawing the attention of an unsaved audience to any alleged flaws of the copyists. Never state: "This word should have been translated so and so," for this only awakens a doubt in the minds of the unsaved as to the authority and integrity of God's word.

(b) *Texts, on the whole, should express a complete thought.* The text must have a verb. It should not be a form like the infinite, or participle. For instance, the expression: "The glorious gospel of God," may be used as a theme, but hardly as a text, for it is only a phrase.

(c) *Avoid, as a rule, the use of odd texts.* It is recorded of Dean Swift that he once preached to an audience of tailors from the text: "A remnant shall be saved." Another preacher, at the funeral of a child who had been bitten by a mad dog, took for his text: "Beware of dogs." Both Spurgeon and Broadus quote instances where the oddity of the text used detracted from the message preached. It must be remembered that the text is not an *excuse* for the sermon, but the *cause* of it.

(d) *Be careful about choosing texts that promise a great effort that we cannot fulfil in the sermon.* Some texts are marked with a grandeur of expression and lead to an expectation that the sermon may disappoint. In other words, we should keep within the limits of our own capabilities as preachers.

(e) *We should not be afraid to choose familiar texts,* for the last word has not been said on any text of the Bible, for truly "the well is deep." If, however, a less familiar text will serve the purpose and carry the same truth, it would be better to choose it.

(f) *One should avoid using texts, the interpretation of which is not clear to the preacher.* What is not plain to the speaker, is not likely to be made clear to the hearer. If there is any doubt in one's own mind as to the interpretation of the text, it would be best to wait until further light is obtained on it before attempting to preach from it.

(g) *Only those texts that personally appeal should be taken.* Spurgeon was once asked to preach from a certain text. After some consideration of it he refused and gave at his reason: "It doesn't bite." In other words, we must only choose texts that choose us. We must beware of what has been described as "trafficking in unfelt truth." Job had to confess what many a preacher has had to acknowledge since: "I uttered that I understood not." (Job 42: 3; 38: 2).

(h) *The text should be selected with one's audience in mind.* The kind of audience and its particular needs should enter largely in the selection of the text. The *character* of the meeting should also be taken into account. It may be a gospel meeting, or a Bible reading, a wedding, or a funeral. It may be for children, or for adults. It may be an open air meeting, etc. All these things should be taken into consideration in the selection of the text for the sermon.

CHAPTER TWELVE

The Sermon and Its Structure

(Continued)

(4) *The interpretation of the text.*

This is, perhaps, the most important part of the sermon. By "interpretation" is meant: "The process of ascertaining the mind of the writer." What did the writer *mean* to convey? Once this has been discovered, the interpretation will be clear. One can therefore easily realize how vitally important it is to discover the true interpretation of the text. A sermon may be homiletically correct, but if its interpretation is wrong, it is not only a failure, but becomes a *menace to the hearer*. The preacher must beware of "handling the word of God deceitfully" (II Cor. 4:2).

In thinking of the interpretation of the text we must distinguish between *exegesis* and *exposition*. Exegesis refers to the *discovery* of the material, while exposition consists of the *display* of what has been discovered. "Exegesis comes from a Greek word that means to lead and guide. Exposition, from a Latin word, that means to place out. Exegesis draws out the hidden meaning; exposition places that meaning out in logical, appropriate and effective order. Exegesis is the task of the commentator; exposition is the task of the preacher." (Jeff. Ray.)

The illustration has been used of a diver who recovers from a sunken vessel a large quantity of jewels. As he emerges from the water, he throws these gems in a heap upon a table. This is exegesis. An expert jeweler now takes this jumbled heap of precious stones and skillfully arranges them in such a way that each jewel enhances the beauty and charm of the one next to it. This is exposition. To put it simply: exegesis is the *discovery* of the material *for* the sermon; exposition is the *display* of the material *in* the sermon.

There are certain guiding principles that must be observed in the correct interpretation of the text. These should be noted very carefully, for they are essential to the mastery of *Hermeneutics*, which is the science and art of interpretation, especially of the Scriptures. The word comes from the Greek "hermeneutes," an interpreter. We shall spend some considerable time on this subject, because of its great importance. How should the text be interpreted so as to discover its true meaning?

(a) *The text should be interpreted honestly.*

That is to say, we should credit the writer with meaning exactly what he says. How often a text has been twisted to suit the viewpoint of the *preacher* instead of the *writer!* Someone has said: "If the first sense makes good sense, seek no other sense!" An old preacher used to say: "If it's *new*, it's not *true*. If it's *true*, then it's not *new!*" There is a good measure of truth in this. Some people have a mania for the esoteric, or the mysterious. Others love the spectacular and the unusual. Many suffer from what might be termed "Athenitis." Like the people of Athens, they spend their time in nothing else, but "either to tell or hear of some new thing" (Acts 17:21). This is a mischievous malady indeed.

Charles Simeon, a great teacher of many years ago, said regarding the apparently contradictory truths of God's sovereignty and man's free will: "I deplore what is called 'the golden mean' in matters of Biblical interpretation, and maintain that the truth is not in the *middle*, and not in *one extreme*, but in *both extremes*. Thus I am a high Calvinist sometimes, and a low Arminian at other times; so that if extremes please you, I am your man. Only remember, it is not one extreme we are to go to, but both extremes. So, my beloved brother, if I find you at the *zenith* at one side, I shall hope to find you at the *nadir* at the other."

Concerning this same problem, J. B. Watson has said: "An antinomy is a contradiction between two laws. In theology, when two teachings face each other irreconcilably, it is said we have an antinomy. Scripture antinomies are not unreasonable, they are *super*-reasonable. The way of faith, in regard to them, is to take all Scripture evidence and testimony on both sides, at one hundred percent of its face value; and believing the truth to lie at both extremes, account *both* wholly true."

(b) *The text should be interpreted in the light of its context.* By this is meant what precedes and succeeds the text under consideration. It has been well said that: "Text, without context, is a pretext." Just as a gem is enhanced by its setting, so the text of Scripture will scintillate with spiritual significance when interpreted in relation to its context. Many questions could be asked in regard to the text, all of which are calculated to throw light on it. Let us suggest a few: *Who* made the statement, or asked the question? To *whom* was it made? What were the *circumstances* under which it was said, as to *time* and *place?* What was the *purpose* in the writer's or speaker's mind?

Take, for instance, the first word of Malachi 3:16: "Then." This is the hinge on which the truth of this particular verse turns. It demands that the whole book be examined for its setting. When this is done, it will be seen that Malachi lived in days of apostasy, declension, doubt, darkness and depression. What did this

godly remnant in Israel do? Did they sit down, with
folded arms and passively let things go to the dogs? No,
indeed! "*Then* they that feared the Lord spake often
one to another."

Note also the setting of Luke's account of the Lord's
prayer. Luke 11:1: "As *He* was praying." What light this
gives on the words that follow! Take that oft quoted
text by those who believe in the "falling away" doctrine:
"He that endureth to the end shall be saved." This would
never be used to bolster up that unscriptural doctrine if
it was interpreted in the light of its context. Take also
that favorite verse for the legalistic preacher: "Touch not,
taste not, handle not" (Col. 2:21). The context clearly
indicates that Paul was merely quoting the legalistic
phraseology of those whose teaching he was condemning;
for he went on to say: "Which are all to perish with the
using."

Wycliffe, "the father of the British reformation," deserves the closest attention on this matter of interpretation. He wrote: "It shall greatly help to understand
Scripture if thou mark, not only what is spoken or written,
but of whom, to whom, with what words, at what time,
where, to what intent, and with what circumstances, considering what goes before and what follows."

(c) *The text should be interpreted in the light of
its language.* We shall think of three things in this connection.

(i) *Its grammatical construction.* Melancthon wrote:
"The scriptures cannot be understood *theologically* unless they are understood *grammatically.*" Immer has said:
"Grammar is, and must remain the foundation of all
exegesis." We must apply the simple rules of English
grammar to the text we are studying: we must note the
parts of speech, the nouns, verbs, adverbs, prepositions,

adjectives, etc. We must observe the *tenses,* past, present and future. We must study the *syntax,* or the construction of the sentence. We must pay heed to the *punctuation* of the text in question.

Each word exists for some definite reason. The "therefores," "wherefores," "thens," and "thats," etc. are all worthy of the closest attention. An old Christian used to say: "Whenever I see a 'therefore,' I always ask myself the question: "What is that 'therefore,' there for?"

(ii) *The exact meaning of the English words.* The English language is in a continual state of flux, or change, for it is a "living" language. The Hebrew, Greek and Latin are "dead" languages, and the meaning of each word is fixed. The meaning of some English words have completely changed, and in some cases have come to mean the exact opposite! Take the word, "profane" (Heb. 12: 16). Today it refers to bad language; but when the Authorized Version was published, it meant "common." A field that is open to the public is called a "common," because it is common property and all have a right to walk upon it. Esau's mind was not kept sacred for God, but was common to any thoughts that wished to enter and dwell there.

Then again the word, "let," which used to mean, "hinder," now means "permit" (Rom. 1:13; II Thess. 2:7). The word, "by and by," used to mean immediately; but now it means "at some other time" (Mark 6:25; Luke 21:9; 17:7). The word, "condescend," which now means: "a patronizing waiving of real or assumed authority;" used to mean: "to walk hand in hand with the lowly" (Rom. 12:16).

Some words have many meanings that only the context can determine. Take the word "since." It can mean "after," "if," "because" and "inasmuch."

A good English Dictionary is indispensable for a study of the etymology or derivation of words; for it is with words that the preacher has to work. They are his bricks and stones, with which he builds his sermon. Therefore the need for skill in using them. Words are the preacher's coins by which he does business for his Master.

(iii) *The meaning of the words in the original.* Should there be any doubt as to the exact meaning of a word in the English translation, a Strong's or Young's concordance will give its meaning in the Hebrew or Greek. Wigram's "English-Hebrew, and English-Greek Concordance" will also prove very useful. By the aid of these books shades of meaning, not found in English, can be discovered. However, we must beware of what has been aptly called, "amateur Greek." By this is meant the quoting of the original as though the preacher were an expert Greek scholar. It is far better to quote the authority and say: "Strong's concordance renders the word thus, etc." It is good to remember that, in no case, is the truth of any doctrine affected by referring to the original. The Authorized version is good, but it is well to consult the original for the shades of meaning, which throw light on the text, and thus aid in its correct interpretation.

It is also helpful to notice the various occurances of a certain word in the original, and then note the many different English words the translators used in rendering the same Hebrew or Greek term. Often a wealth of good sermon material may be unearthed in this way. For instance, the words: "rejoice," "glory" and "joy" in Rom. 5:2, 3 and 11 is the same word in the original, and really conveys the thought of "boasting." It is so translated in II Cor. 7:14; 9:2 etc. W. E. Vine's: "Dictionary of New Testament Words" is a treasure house of helpful information regarding the use of the words in the original text, and is warmly recommended.

(d) *The text should be interpreted in the light of Biblical history, manners, customs and geography.*

Many ridiculous statements would never have been made if the preacher had only taken the time and effort to consult a good Bible dictionary as to the meaning of the terms involved.

(i) *Local color, customs and history* explain many otherwise difficult situations. Let us look at a few: "Suffer me first to go and bury my father" (Luke 9:59). This was a common saying in Christ's day. It did not mean that this person's father was dead, or even dying; but he wanted to delay his response to Christ's call until after his father had died. Hence our Lord's words: "Let the dead bury their dead." We have already referred to the matter of the napkin, in which the unfaithful servant hid the talent.

The incident of the roof broken in, which is recorded in Mark 2:4 is a good example. On one occasion a Sunday School teacher described to his class how these four men, at great risk of their lives, crawled up the steep slopes of the pitched roof, and removed some of the heavy tiles in order to let the man down! One boy asked incredulously: "But how could they do it?" The teacher replied solemnly: "With man this is impossible, but with God all things are possible!" Of course, the roof was flat, reached by stairs and the thatching easily removed.

(ii) *Bible geography is a most helpful study,* and every preacher should have a good Bible atlas in his possession. (Hurlburt's is quite useful). Note the "ups" and "downs" of Scripture. "A certain man went *down* from Jerusalem" (Luke 10:30). This is both literally and spiritually true, for Jerusalem is 2,500 feet above sea level, while Jericho is around 1,000 feet below sea level. Note also that Christ "went *down* to Capernaum;" then "*up* to

Jerusalem" (John 2:12, 13). The distance between certain places is also of great significance, as also is the character and contour of the country through which a person is said to pass. Thompson's: "The Land and the Book" will supply much material in this direction.

(e) *The text should be interpreted in the light of the general teaching of the word of God.*

(i) *No doctrine can be based on an isolated text,* but must have the support of all the other scriptures that relate to the same subject.

This is the meaning of that verse: "No prophecy of the scripture is of any *private* interpretation" (II Pet. 1:20, 21). Almost any false teaching can find *apparent* support from a solitary scripture quotation, wrested from its context; but it can never stand the test of *all* the Scripture revelation on that particular subject.

For instance, Roman Catholicism uses Eccles. 9:1 to prove that no one can know that he is saved in this life. Seventh day Adventists use verse 5 to support its false theory of "soul sleep." The fatalist uses verse 2 to show "all things come alike to all." The libertine uses verse 2 to prove "As is the good, so is the sinner." The infidel bases his denial of future existence on verse 5, which states: "The dead have no reward." He could also use Psalm 14:1, which states: "There is no God." Others could take Rom. 3:8, which declares: "Let us do evil that good may come." Or, "Let us eat and drink, for tomorrow we die!" (I Cor. 15:32). There is no end to the mischievous use to which the Bible can be put by unscrupulous men, when a text is interpreted in the light of *itself,* and not in the light of Scripture as a whole.

It is impossible to exaggerate the importance of grasping the exact *Biblical* meaning of the great words of Scripture, and also having, at one's finger tips, a clear,

concise and complete definition of these words. It is one
of the fundamental laws of philology (the study of words)
that the correct definition of a term will always make
good sense when placed *instead* of that term.

With this fact in mind, the preacher should make it
his business to learn the meaning, and also get a good
definition of the following words:

Atonement, reconciliation, propitiation, sanctification,
justification, salvation, remission, righteousness, redemption, regeneration, acceptance, mercy, love, grace, faith,
hope, glory, eternal life, predestination, ordain, election,
calling, inspiration, prayer, worship, praise, the old man,
the new man, carnal, spiritual, flesh, spirit, body, soul,
repentance, offering, sacrifice, cross, death, blood, priest,
sin, judgment, heaven, hell, eternity, world, church,
Gentile, Jew, truth, unbelief, walk, standing, pilgrim,
stranger, Christian, etc.

(ii) *The spiritual must be compared with the spiritual.*
(I Cor. 2: 12-14). The Bible is not a collection of isolated
texts, but is an organic whole. The best commentary on
the Scriptures is the Scriptures! A person once remarked:
"Isn't it remarkable the amount of light that the Bible
throws on commentaries!" Campbell Morgan said: "More
and more, as I get older, and go on preaching, I find that
if I take a text, I need the whole Bible to explain it."

(iii) *An obscure statement should never be allowed to
contradict, or nullify, a clear, definite and unmistakably
plain statement of Scripture.* James McConkey puts it
thus: "There is a rule of legal interpretation in the United
States of America to the effect that where a clear statement is made in a document, no subsequent and obscure
statement shall be permitted to turn it aside. Thus, if a
clause in a will gives all a man's property to a certain
heir, no subsequent clause, which seems to give a part

of the property to another, shall stand. The plain shall not give place to the doubtful."

This is a most important rule to remember. The "falling away" doctrine, or the teaching that a truly regenerated person can fall away and be eternally lost is based on certain obscure statements, and these are allowed to contradict such plain statements as John 10:27-30; Rom. 8:29-39; John 5:24; I John 5:10-13, etc.

(f) *The text should be interpreted in the light of its typical significance, when such is warranted by other Scripture passages.*

(i) *The definition of a type.* Scofield's definition is good: "A Divinely purposed illustration of some scriptural truth." Words may convey a truth, and yet not express a literal fact. For instance, when Christ said: "I am the door," He expressed a fundamental truth, but not a fact, for Christ was not a door; but the use of the word "door" did express the essential truth. "Figurative language is a mode of expressing an idea by the use of words that suggests pictures, or images of the idea." (Ray).

A type may consist of various things. It may be a person, as Adam; (Rom. 5:14) an event, as the crossing of the Red Sea (I Cor. 10:1-11); a thing, as the veil of the temple (Heb. 10:20); an institution, as the tabernacle, priesthood, and the offerings (Heb. 9:11); or a ceremonial, as the Passover (I Cor. 5:7).

(ii) *The existence of these types is obvious to all believers.* The history of Israel is God's picture book for Christians. Read I Cor. 10:6-11; Rom. 15:4. The Tabernacle, the offerings and the priesthood are redolent with typical significance, as the whole epistle to the Hebrews clearly indicates. See Heb. 9:23; 10:1. In this epistle, God uses both comparison and contrast to convey spiritual truth and show the superiority of Christ to all the types of the Old Testament.

Solomon, Jonah, Aaron and Moses are among the many typical characters (Matt. 12:42; 12:40; Deut. 18:15; Heb. 3:5-6; 7:11). The book of Revelation is full of "signs," as the word "signified" clearly indicates (Rev. 1:1). In fact, the Old Testament is utterly incomprehensible apart from the New Testament and vice versa. The *"shadows"* of the Old Testament, demand the *substance* of the New Testament. (Heb. 10:1). There cannot be one without the other.

(iii) *The rule of typical interpretation.* It is difficult to lay down any hard and fast rule, but the following statement may serve as a general guide: "Whatever thing, incident, or person described in the Old Testament, is used in the New Testament in a typical, or spiritual sense: this can be used without question."

(iv) *The tremendous value of the types cannot be overestimated.* Dr. Griffith Thomas has finely said: "The Old Testament is largely a book of unfulfilled prophecies, unexplained ceremonies and unsatisfied longings." As one opens the pages of the New Testament, these prophecies are seen to be fulfilled in Christ; the ceremonies are explained by Christ; and the longings are satisfied through Christ.

Christ is the grand Key to all the types. They cannot be understood apart from Him. There must be a knowledge of the *reality* before a type, or picture, can be appreciated. Christ is seen in all the types. His character, offices and relations with His church are presented in these types. Consequently it is essential that they be studied for a thorough knowledge of Him. In the types, Christ, as it were, is taken to pieces, closely examined and all His many perfections laid bare for the soul's appre-

ciation and worship. Many seem content to limit their
typical teaching to the Passover type, but this is only one
of the very many of these divinely purposed illustrations.
With the writer of the epistle to the Hebrews, "let us go
on" to further study and greater use of this most fruitful
field of Scripture teaching.

A few of the more obvious types are: The formation of
Eve from Adam; the coats of skins; Abel's offering; the
ark; the sacrifice of Isaac; the search for the bride for
Isaac; Joseph; the Passover; the Red Sea; the firstling of
the ass; Marah; Elim; the manna; the smitten rock; the
Tabernacle; the priesthood; the offerings; the brazen ser-
pent; Jordan; the cleansing of the leper; Joshua; Ruth;
David; Solomon; etc.

(v) *The danger of extreme spiritualizing.* The church
has suffered much from the over spiritualization of the
incidents and types recorded in the word of God. Origen,
one of the early fathers, went to great lengths along this
line, and practically spiritualized *everything.* Many plain
and literal truths that refer to Israel's future of national
restoration and blessing have been spiritualized, and
wrongly made to apply to the Church's present position.

It must also be kept in mind that *no doctrine should be
based upon these types.* They may, and indeed do serve
the excellent purpose of *illustrating* doctrinal truth, but
they must be kept in their God-appointed place and used
for this purpose only. Seventh Day Adventism bases one
of its false doctrines on the entirely wrong assumption that
Christ came in 1884 for the purpose of "cleansing the
sanctuary." They refer to the ritual of the day of atonement for confirmation of this error! (Lev. 16).

(g) *The text must be interpreted in the light of its
dispensational aspect.*

(i) *The definition of "dispensation."* By a dispensation
is meant the *basis* of God's dealing with mankind, or a

portion of mankind, through various periods of history. Andrew Jukes has stated the matter very succinctly: "God has dealt with mankind at various periods since the fall of man, in different degrees of intimacy and, in a certain sense, also on different principles. Through all, He has had one purpose in view; to reveal what *He is,* and to show what *man* is; but this one end has been brought out in different ways, and under varied and repeated trials." Scofield's definition is also good: "A dispensation is a period of time, during which man is tested in respect of obedience to some specific revelation of the will of God."

(ii) *The value of dispensational teaching.* It is one of the essential keys to a sound grasp of the Scriptures. It is that which gives us the ability to "distinguish things that differ" (Phil. 1:10 marg.). In this sense, each believer should be a "D. D." This does not mean "doctor of divinity," but something far more important and infinitely better: a "distinguisher of differences." It is essential for every Christian to know where he is in relation to God's program for this present age, for only then will he be able to "rightly divide the word of truth" (II Tim. 2:15).

The question of the Sabbath day, and of divine healing, with its many extravagances, and the confused ideas regarding the Christian's relation to the law stem from a failure to rightly appreciate dispensational truth.

For instance: one has only to do a little Bible study to learn there is a vast difference between law and grace (John 1:17; Gal. 2:16); between the Jew and Gentile and the Church of God (I Cor. 10:32); between the Sabbath and the Lord's day: one at the end of a week and the other at the beginning (Exod. 20:8-11; Acts 20:7; Rev. 1:10; Ps. 118:22-24). (Note particularly the setting of: "This is *the day* which the Lord hath made"); between

God's gifts and His rewards (Eph. 2:8-9; I Cor. 3:10-15). He will discover that God's program today is not the conversion of the world, but the taking out of the world a people for His name (Acts 15:14; John 10:14-16). He will discover that there are at least *seven* distinct judgments: John 12:31; I Cor. 11:31; II Cor. 5:10; Matt. 25: 32; Ezek. 20:37; Jude 6; Rev. 20:11-15). C. I. Scofield's little book: "Rightly Dividing the Word of Truth," is good for a start in the study of dispensational truth.

(iii)   *The dangers of dispensational truth.* There exists today what is known as "Ultra dispensationalism." This school of interpretation swings to the other extreme, and arbitrarily puts the Scriptures into water tight compartments of their own making. It hands back to the Church a few of Paul's prison epistles as its sole means of guidance for this present day. The baptism of believers is voted out and, in some cases, the observance of the Lord's supper is eliminated, as not belonging to the present order of things. Such extremists simply go to prove that it is possible, as Paul puts it, to be "wise above that which is written" (I Cor. 4:6). William Hoste has written a good pamphlet exposing the errors of this school of interpretation. It is entitled: "Ultra-Dispensationalism Examined" and can be obtained from the publishers of this book. H. I. Ironside has also written an excellent pamphlet on this subject entitled: "Wrongly Dividing the Word of Truth."

A sanctified imagination can also play a useful part in the interpretation of the Scriptures. Historic characters can be made to live before an audience in this way. A sense of the dramatic is also necessary to make the Scripture narrative come to life in one's preaching. The fact that some abuse these gifts should not deter us from using them. "Wise men do not abandon a good thing because fools abuse it."

Broadus has an excellent article on: "Brief rules for interpreting the text," which will repay the student for reading. We can do no more than give his outline. "Interpret the text (1) Grammatically, (2) Logically, (3) Historically, (4) Figuratively, (5) Allegorically, (6) In accordance with the general teaching of Scripture."

We have purposely enlarged on this matter of the interpretation of the text, because of its extreme importance. It must ever be kept in mind that the sermon exists for the sole purpose of interpreting the word of God, and in such a way as shall enlighten and edify the hearer.

Since writing this book, a series of articles by Albert E. Horton, missionary in Portuguese West Africa, appeared in "The Witness," under the title of: "The Teaching, Interpretation and Application of Scripture." These were so excellent that, with his very kind permission, they have been inserted as an appendix to this book. This should now be turned to and carefully read. It will further emphasize the vital significance of, and the absolute necessity for the right interpretation of the text.

CHAPTER THIRTEEN

The Sermon and Its Structure

(Continued)

Having discussed the question of the text: its definition, necessity, selection and interpretation; let us now proceed to look at the second part of the sermon, namely:

2. The theme.

(1) *The Definition of it.*

By this is meant that part of the sermon which **defines** the main truth to be expounded from the text. The theme is, therefore, the *most striking truth* contained in the text, not necessarily the *whole subject-matter of the text.* It is a concise statement of the principal truth which the preacher sees in his text, and which he proposes to expound in his sermon. The theme is the discourse *condensed*: the *discourse* is the theme *unfolded.* Prof. Phelps says: "The theme is to the discourse what the heart is to the physical system, the relation is organic." The theme, therefore, should state exactly what the preacher intends to discuss, without any involved clauses or explanatory terms. Sometimes the theme is called the proposition, or statement.

(2) *The choice of the theme.*

This will depend entirely on the viewpoint of the preacher. It will be a case of "many men, many minds." Four preachers may select the same text and yet each have a different theme.

Take, for instance, the best known text of the Bible: John 3:16. Let us suppose that four preachers decide to take this as the text for a sermon. After careful consideration, each writes out what he believes to be the theme of this verse.

(a)   The first preacher states the theme thus: "The love of God is the ocean, from which the river of salvation takes its source." In this theme, the emphasis is on the love of God, and the outline he prepares will have this particular thought in view. His outline might be something like this:

  I. It is a Divine love. "God"
  II. It is a superabounding love. "so loved"
  III. It is an unmerited love. "the world"
  IV. It is a sacrificial love. "that He gave . . . His . . . Son"
  V. It is an inclusive love. "whosoever believeth"
  VI. It is a delivering love. "not perish"
  VII. It is a bestowing love. "have . . . life"

(b)   The second preacher states his theme thus: "The gift of everlasting life is conditioned by faith in Christ." Here the emphasis is on everlasting life. This fact will color his outline, which he states thus:

  I. The Giver of this life. "God"
  II. The source of this life. "love"
  III. The Channel of this life. "Son"
  IV. The cost of this life. "gave . . . Son"
  V. The scope of this life. "whosoever"
  VI. The condition of this life. "believeth"
  VII. The character of this life. "everlasting"

(c)   The third preacher is struck with the thought of "gift" as the predominant theme, and consequently states his theme with this in mind: "The revelation of God as a Giver is here demonstrated beyond all contradiction." He prepares his outline with this in view, as follows:

  I. It is an unasked gift. "God"

   II. It is an unmerited gift. "world"
  III. It is an unspeakable gift. "only begotten **Son**"
  IV. It is an inclusive gift. "whosoever"
   V. It is a conditioned gift. "believeth"
  VI. It is an insuring gift. "not perish"
 VII. It is an unsearchable gift. "everlasting **life**"

(d) The fourth preacher might see, in this **verse, the** four great dimensions of the love of God **and write his** theme accordingly: "The four dimensions of **the love of** God." His outline, following this theme, could be:

   I. The breadth of God's love. "God so loved the world"
  II. The length of God's love. "that He gave His . . . Son"
 III. The depth of God's love. "whosoever . . . believeth . . . not perish"
 IV. The height of God's love. "have everlasting life"

It will be observed that the viewpoint, in each case, is different. This, in turn, not only determines how **the** theme is stated, but also affects the preparation of **the** outline so as to best present the theme.

(3) *The advantages of stating the theme.*

It is essential that the speaker should know what he is going to speak about. He should therefore be prepared, if necessary, to state this theme to his audience, so that both speaker and hearer are aware of the subject to be discussed. It is therefore a good mental discipline for the preacher to write out what he believes to be the most important, or the most striking truth in the text; and then prepare his sermon with this in view. This, of course, will aid in securing the interest of his audience.

The theme should include all that he proposes to treat, or discuss, in the sermon. It is hardly necessary to say that this theme should be stated in the most interesting way possible. We shall discuss this later. There is a marked distinction between a *subject* and a *theme*. A subject is much *broader* than a theme. For instance, our general subject is "Homiletics," but our present theme is: "The sermon and its structure," and particularly that part of the sermon which is called "the theme."

(4) *Methods of stating the theme.*

There are two methods of stating the theme: the logical and the rhetorical.

(a) *By the logical method* is meant the expression of a *complete thought,* which would entail the use of a verb, either expressed or implied. For example: "The new birth is essential to entrance into the kingdom of God." Or: "Salvation is by grace, through faith in Christ." Or: "Eternal life is the gift of God." Or: "Is the coming of Christ imminent?" Or: "Can a person know that he is saved?" Or: "Can a true believer ever be lost?"

Thus, in the logical statement of the theme, the complete thought of the text is succinctly expressed. The advantage of this method is that it makes for clear thinking, close thinking, consecutive thinking and unity. It prevents the speaker from adopting what has been called the "butterfly method." This consists in flitting from one theme to another, in such a disconnected way, that the audience wonders just what lesson the preacher is trying to drive home.

(b) *By the rhetorical method* is meant the stating of the theme in the form of a phrase; that is, a group of words that do not express a complete thought. Let us illustrate this method by stating the *logical* themes, which we have already referred to in the *rhetorical* form: "The new birth," "Salvation's genesis," "God's gift," "Christ's coming," "Salvation's assurance," "Eternal security."

The advantage of this method is that it makes for both freedom and variety of treatment. It is well for the preacher to use both the logical and the rhetorical forms. However, if the latter is used, it would be advisable to express it also, for his own sake and private study, in the logical form. This will enable him to have it clearly in his own mind and aid in confining him more closely to his theme.

(c) *Some more examples.* Let the reader determine which of the following themes is stated in the logical or the rhetorical form. Mark each with either an "L" or an "R," according to his classification:

"The great Divider:" "Christ is the great Divider of men." "What does God mean when He declares: 'There is no difference?' " "No difference!" "Signs of life." "What are the evidences of the possession of eternal life?" "The wages of sin and the gift of God." "Wages or gift?" "The living sacrifice." "God desires the willing presentation of the believer's body."

It will be seen that each mode of stating the theme has its advantage. For the sake of variety, which has been described as "the spice of life," each should be used; but, as we have already pointed out, it is best for the preacher's own discipline of mind to state it, *for his own study and profit,* in the logical form.

We shall not introduce, at this time, the title of the sermon, for we shall devote a whole chapter to this interesting and important theme.

CHAPTER FOURTEEN

The Sermon and Its Structure

(Continued)

Now let us look at the third part of the sermon:

3. The introduction.

(1) *The definition of it.*

By this is meant that part of the sermon which leads up to the discussion and thus prepares the audience for the main part of the sermon, the discussion.

(2) *The purposes of it.*

It serves many excellent purposes.

(a) *To awaken the hearers' interest in the subject* that has been chosen. An introduction serves the same purpose to a sermon as a porch does to a house; or a prelude to a symphony; or the dawn to the actual rising of the sun above the horizon; or the approach of a bridge to the actual structure itself; or the bud to a rose. It is a *natural* approach.

(b) *To enable the speaker to surmount the obstacles that stand in the way of interest.* A teacher of public speaking used to tell his classes that there were four obstacles to overcome in winning an audience to the speaker's viewpoint. These obstacles he expressed in the common phraseology of the man in the street.

(i) *The first obstacle he styled:* "Ho-hum!" By this the indifference and apathy of the average audience is expressed. It looks at the speaker as he rises to address the meeting, yawns and sleepily murmurs: "Ho-hum! I wonder what this babbler will say?" To overcome this "initial inertia," it is essential that there shall be an introduction which will awaken the lethargetic, stir the apathetic and, at the same time, gain the sympathetic ear of all present. An introduction that does not arouse the attention of the hearers will leave the preacher without an audience, when he comes to the discussion of his theme.

(ii) *The second obstacle he expressed thus*: "Why bring that up?" The audience now challenges the right of the speaker to address it on the subject he has chosen. He must now proceed to take the audience into his confidence, and state clearly and succinctly why he has chosen his topic. He must show the audience how essential it is, to its best interests, that this subject be presented at this time.

(iii) *The third obstacle he designated*: "How do you make that out?" This is the obstacle of incredulity. It is the business of the speaker to overcome this by marshalling clear, forceful, well illustrated and well applied arguments, which he proceeds to state in logical sequence, until he reaches his climax and makes his application.

(iv) *The fourth obstacle he termed*: "So what?" By this the audience evidences the fact that it wants to know what is expected of it, and this the speaker should proceed to do in no uncertain manner. He should make his application as pointed and personal as possible, demanding a decision in favor of the truth he has presented. This should leave each hearer in no doubt as to his responsibility in the matter.

This common-sense advice, even though it comes from a man of the world, contains much that the gospel preacher and teacher would do well to take into consideration when addressing an audience. The words of our Savior are pertinent in this connection: He declared: "The children of this world are, in their generation, wiser than the children of light" (Luke 16:8). Many a Christian, if he served his worldly employer as he serves his heavenly Master, would long ago have been dismissed for laziness, incompetence and carelessness!

(c) *To prepare the audience for an understanding of the theme under consideration.* Let us suppose it is the new birth. The average unsaved audience has little or no understanding of this subject. Like the Eunuch, each hearer's unspoken question is: "How can I understand, except some man should guide me?" (Acts 8:31). The speaker must anticipate this ignorance and, with few but well chosen words, arouse his attention to the vital importance of this subject and enlighten him as to its meaning. Interest is simply *sustained attention.* Therefore it is essential that the hearer's attention be first *gained,* and then *sustained* to the end. The introduction should be an incline, by which an audience is brought from its low level, or inertia, to the higher plane of the speaker's thought. By means of this introduction, the preacher anticipates and clears away the obstacles which would otherwise hinder the audience from grasping the importance and meaning of the theme.

We will assume that the theme is new birth. Perhaps an introduction like this might serve the purpose: "What would your reaction be if someone, knowing full well that you were religiously inclined and moral in your life, looked you right between the eyes and said, with solemn and impressive earnestness: '*Ye* must be born again!' Such an incident actually took place nearly two thousand years ago. The person to whom the words were addressed was a ruler of the Jews named Nicodemus, and the Speaker was none other than the eternal and incarnate Son of God."

(d) *To secure the good will of the audience.* The hearers may be prejudiced against and even antagonistic to both the speaker and his theme. Therefore one can easily appreciate how necessary it is for the speaker, at the very beginning of his sermon, to dissolve their prejudices, disarm their doubts and take them into his confidence. Many a hearer who "came to scoff, remained to pray," because of a good introduction. First impressions are often lasting. How important, then, that he make that impression a favorable one for his message! A young preacher asked an older brother what was the best method of securing the attention of an audience. The somewhat brusque but wise reply was: "Give it something to attend to!"

(e) *Some examples from the great sermons of the Bible.* By a study of these, one may see for himself how the speaker sought to put himself "en rapport" with his audience. Note Peter's introduction in Acts 2:14-21. See how he sought to disabuse the false idea of the mockers, and then made his appeal directly to the Scriptures which they all acknowledged to be the word of God. Then came the explanation of the miraculous gift of languages by which every person heard, in his own tongue, "the wonderful works of God." Notice also the introductions to his other speeches in Acts 3:12; 4:8-9; 10:34-35. Look at Stephen's masterly approach in his address to the Sanhedrin, Acts 7:2. Note Paul's brief, but telling introductions: Acts 13:16-23; 17:22-23; 22:1-5; 24:10; 26:1-3.

(3) *The importance of it.*

The introduction has been well called "the crucial five minutes." In this period, the speaker will either gain or lose his audience. If the introduction fails to gain the sympathetic ear of the hearers, the sermon that follows will be lost on the audience. Napoleon attributed his successes against the Austrians to his expert use of the first five minutes of the battle.

"Well begun is half done," is good counsel. Therefore the great necessity for the most prayerful and careful preparation of the introduction. The preacher must master the art of getting away to a good start. This is just as essential in a sermon as in a foot race. It is possible, as we all know from painful experience, for a speaker to go round and round the mulberry bush and say nothing at extreme length. Just as salesmen are given a preliminary course of training in the art of approaching the prospective customer, with a view to gaining access into his home and pocketbook; so the preacher must study the best way to gain access into peoples' minds with a view to selling them the truth. There is certainly no doubt that the preacher has the finest product in all the world. Let him therefore so present it that the hearer's eye, ear and heart will respond to it with interest and faith. In order to catch a horse, one must first catch its eye. Only then can he slip a halter around its neck and lead it where he desires. The preacher must do likewise if he wishes to lead people into the way of life.

(4) *Some suggestions regarding it.*

In preparing the introduction five things should be observed.

(a) *It should lead directly to the discussion.* The audience should not be conducted on a tour from Dan to Beersheba. The introduction is but a gate that leads directly to the body of the address. The speaker should therefore lead the audience *through* it and not swing to and fro on the gate! Everything irrelevant to the theme should be rigorously eliminated. Remember: an introduction that leads nowhere always carries the audience with it! Every theme has a natural approach. This must be found and the audience led along it. D. L. Moody's introductions were brief and almost abrupt, but they were strictly to the point and no time was wasted on useless padding.

A teacher of Homiletics used to tell the story of a farmer who stopped his plowing to chase a rat. During the process, he wasted an hour of his time and tramped down a lot of young corn. In the meanwhile, his horses ran away and damaged the plow. Worst of all, he failed to catch the rat! The teacher would then point out his moral and say: "Don't interrupt your preaching to chase stray and inconsequential thoughts, but get on with your sermon!"

(b) *It should not promise more than the sermon can supply.* To prepare an audience, in one's introduction, for a demonstraton of the atomic bomb and then let off a pop gun in the sermon is, to say the least, somewhat of an anti-climax! The preacher should beware of following the example of the ballyhoo merchants of the midway of a county fair who, with raucous voices, announce to all and sundry that their particular exhibition is the "most stupendous and colossal show on earth!"

(c) *It should be simple and modest.* The preacher should not *capitalize* on his capital "I"s! The cross is the capital "I" crossed out! Note the five "I"s, of Gal. 2: 20. It will be observed that they are all crucified with Christ, and this is the proper place for that stiff little perpendicular pronoun. Christ must have the preeminence in the introduction, as well as throughout the sermon. The preacher should not be like the antiquated steam engine which used so much steam when it whistled that, while whistling, it couldn't draw its load; He should therefore take care not to use all his steam in the introduction, but leave some for the sermon. All tendency to be "high falutin" should be mercilessly scrapped and it will be good riddance to bad rubbish. Nothing is more likely to awaken resentment in an audience than for it to be impressed with the consciously superior air of the preacher in his introduction.

(d) *It should be varied.* The preacher should not only beware of *ritualism,* but also of *rutualism.* It has been often pointed out that the only difference between a rut and a grave is its depth! There are many different ways of introducing a sermon, and one should make himself master of them all. It is by constant practice that a speaker becomes proficient in this matter.

(e) *It should not be long.* Its length, of course, will be determined by the theme. Five minutes, or less, should be ample for a forty minute address. The sermon does not exist for the introduction, but visa versa. A long introduction is not only tiresome, but it defeats its very purpose, which is to *awaken* the attention and not *exhaust* the patience of the audience.

(5) *Some sources from which the introduction can be drawn.*

This will aid in securing that variety, so necessary in preaching.

(a) *From the text itself, as seen in the light of its context, or its historical setting.* Here are two examples:

(i) *"Joseph's four requests"* (Gen. 40:14). "Joseph is perhaps the most complete personal type of our Lord Jesus Christ in the whole of the Old Testament. One has only to read the story of his life to see in it countless similiarities to that of the life of our Lord. Just as the New Testament refers to Christ as the "greater than Solomon," the "greater than Jonah," and the "greater than Moses and Aaron;" so also He is the greater than Joseph. We shall see, in these four requests which Joseph made of the butler, a striking illustration of the four requests which Christ makes of His disciples in this present time."

(ii) *"The last words of the Bible"* (Rev. 22:20-21). "The Bible is a wonderful book. It has a magnificent opening: 'In the beginning God created the heaven and the earth.' It has a wonderful content: the history of God's dealings with humanity. It has marvelous ending, as we have already read. There are some people, chiefly of the feminine gender, who would not deign to read a book until they had first taken a cursory glance at its beginning, and then quickly switched to the closing pages. If it starts well and seems to end happily, they conclude that the book is worth reading. The Bible, by this test, should prove to be, and indeed is, the most interesting book in all the world."

(b) *From the book in which the text is found.*

That is, something could be said about the author and the circumstances under which it came to be written.

(i) *"Paul's last message"* (II Tim. 3:14-4:8). "The last words of men are given particular attention and are usually treasured by those who love and admire them. When a person faces death and eternity, all pretense is laid aside and reality and earnestness becomes the keynote of his words. These words of Paul, which we have just read, were penned about six weeks before his martyrdom when, like so many 'of whom the world was not worthy,' he sealed his testimony for Christ with his life's blood. In view of these circumstances, his last letter, written to Timothy, should prove to contain much for our spiritual profit."

(ii) *"The name of 'Jesus' in Hebrews"* (Heb. 2:9; 3:1; 4:14; 6:20; 7:22; 10:22; 12:2; 13:8). "The Jew, in turning to Christianity, left the law with its elaborate ritual, its material sacrifices, its altar and its temple. Now he worshipped by faith. But when persecution came, he began to wonder whether he had not made a serious mistake. Before, he had comfort and consolation in the law and the sacrifices. He could turn, when necessary, to the altar and the temple. Now, there was nothing tangible, nothing visible upon which he might lay hold for confidence. Doubting the advantages of conversion, many contemplated returning to the fold of Judaism. To such the writer sends this epistle to the Hebrews. The burden of its message, in brief, is this: 'You have given up all the material things associated with the Mosaic economy. True, but you can now turn to the Lord Jesus Christ. He is greater and better than all these things, for they were but shadows, pointing forward to Him' . . .

"The use of the name of Jesus, mentioned eight times in the epistle to the Hebrews sets eight beautiful lessons before the Jews who had espoused Christianity, each calculated to encourage them to hold fast their profession. And to us, 'upon whom the end of the age is come,' are these things also sent. Let us examine them that we, too, may find encouragement and solace in them." (J. Boyd, M. D., in "The Witness.")

(c) *By comparing the text with other texts that relate to the same theme, or which throw light upon it, either by comparison or contrast.*

(i) *"The Lord's Supper"* (I Cor. 11: 20, 23-26). "There are many suppers spoken of in Scripture, and each has its own spiritual significance. In Luke 14 we are told of 'a certain man who made a great supper, and invited many.' This might be termed: 'The *gospel supper.*' In Revelation 3: 20, Christ speaks of a supper He is prepared to enjoy with each individual who will hear His voice and open the door of his heart to Him. We could term this: 'The *supper of fellowship.*' In Revelation 19 the glad proclamation is made: 'Blessed are they that are called to the *marriage supper* of the Lamb!' What a grand supper that shall be, when all the redeemed of all the ages shall

198   THE PREACHER AND HIS PREACHING

sit down in the presence of the One whom they all adore!
But this supper, of which we have read, is distinguished
from these other suppers by the title: *'The Lord's supper.'*
Let us see why this supper is peculiarly the Lord's."

(ii)   *"The Heart's Desire"* (Psalm 37:4). "The most illuminating thing about any person is his desires. Let a
person write out on a sheet of paper what the supreme
desires of his heart are, and from that statement a correct
estimate may be formed as to what he really *is.* The mind
has ever been the measure of the man. No person can
rise any higher than his thoughts. As the Scripture puts
it: 'For as a man thinketh in his heart, so is he.' Someone
has said: 'You are not what you *think* you are, but what
you *think,* you *are!'* The heart, in Scripture is viewed as
the motivating part of man's being. How essential then,
that the desires of the heart be of such a nature that
God can grant them and, in so doing, bring both glory to
Himself and blessing to the believer!"

(d)   *By an arresting question that arouses the attention
and provokes thought.*

(i)   *"Life's Greatest Objective* (Col. 4:12). "What,
in your opinion, should be the supreme object of the life
of a Christian, to the attainment of which he should
bend every endeavor? Is it to occupy a good position in
the business world? To be happily married? To possess
the ability to preach the gospel or teach the word of God?
To be a martyr to one's scriptural convictions? No! all
these may be very good in their place, but the supreme
objective for each believer should be to desire, to know,
to do and to continually live in the enjoyment of the will
of God. Nothing can be greater than this. All lives are
equally great or small, according to the measure in which
they are either lived in, or out of the will of God. The
success of a person's life is not determined by the number

of years he has lived on earth, but by the amount of time he has spent in the will of God."

(ii) *"Something About Nothing"* (I Tim. 6:7; John 6:63; 3:37; Gal. 6:3; I Cor. 8:2; John 15:5). "What is that which men love more than life, fear more than death, which the rich man wants, and the poor man has; which a miser spends, and a spendthrift saves; which each person brings into the world, and which each person shall take out of the world? The answer to this riddle forms the subject of our theme, which is—nothing!"

(e) *By a reference to Biblical manners and customs, or the geography of the country.*

(i) *"The Good Samaritan"* (Luke 10:30-37). "Our story begins: 'A certain man went down from Jerusalem to Jericho.' To us, who live thousands of miles from these two places, these words have little significance. To those who heard these words from the lips of the Son of God, they were pregnant with spiritual meaning. Jerusalem is situated on a chain of hills 2,500 feet above sea level; while Jericho, close to the borders of the Dead Sea, is at least 1,000 feet below sea level. The word, 'down' can therefore be taken very literally.

"But more: Jerusalem was 'the city of the great King.' Its meaning is variously rendered as: 'the place of peace;' 'the place of vision;' and 'the place of blessing.' Jericho, on the contrary, was the city whose walls miraculously fell down before the people of Israel and upon whose rebuilding God placed a curse. Thus this certain man turned his back on the place of blessing to go to the place of a curse; he left the place of vision to go to the place of darkness; he travelled from the place of peace to the place of unrest. Thus he becomes a picture of all humanity by nature, who has turned, 'every one to his own way'."

(f) *An illustration, or story, that will serve to throw light on the text itself, or some incident in one's own experience in which this text has figured prominently.*

(i) *"The Unanswerable Question"* (Heb. 2: 3). "Some years ago, a Scotch friend of mine, while walking the streets of Johannesburg, South Africa, happened to glance in the gutter and saw a piece of paper on which was written in large letters: 'Five thousand pounds reward!' Moved with curiosity, to say nothing of a desire to possess the substantial reward, he stooped down and retrieved the paper. It turned out to be a four page gospel tract. On opening it he read: 'Five thousand pounds will be paid to the person or persons who can answer the following question: 'How shall we escape, if we neglect so great salvation? Needless to say, the reward remains unclaimed unto this day!"

(ii) *"Indispensable Things."* (Heb. 9: 22). "The story is told of a backwoodsman who, at the invitation of a wealthy New York friend, came to visit the great metropolis. It was the first time he had ever left his home in the hills and he was filled with wonder at what he saw. He spent the first day window shopping on Fifth Avenue. On his return to his friend's home, his host inquired: "Well, Bill, what do you think of our great city?" The backwoodsman hesitated a moment and then drawled: 'Well, George, I never saw so many things in all my life that I could easily do without!' He had learned, as most of us have, that civilization has added much to our lives with which we can quite easily dispense. Let us now look at certain things in the word of God that are described as being absolutely indispensable, and without which no one can possibly live a life that is well-pleasing to God."

The well known author, F. W. Boreham, has written many books concerning the influence of certain texts upon great men and women. His extremely well written essays are not only inspirational, but provide abundant material which can be profitably used for introductory purposes.

(g) *The present occasion may supply the material.*

It may be a wedding, or funeral; a New Year's Eve or a New Year's day, a Christmas celebration; Mother's day, Independence day, Labor day, Thanksgiving, Easter Sunday, the opening of a church building, etc. Each of these occasions will provide material for an appropriate introduction.

(i) *"Christ, the Problem Solver"* (John 14:1-3). This would be suitable for a funeral. "All are agreed that life is full of mysteries and unsolved problems. The wisest of men have spent their lives in a vain effort to pierce the veil that enshrouds these perplexing questions. Philosophers, from time immemorial, have grappled with them until they also have had to bow to the inevitable march of time and the hand of death.

"Perhaps the three greatest of these problems are: the problem of God's providential dealings with humanity; the problem of the presence of sin in the world; and the problem of the future and what comes after death.

"Nineteen hundred years ago there was miraculously born into this world One Who, in a few short words, solved these three tremendous problems of life. Let us examine His words and see how Christ, Who spake as no man ever spake, solved fully and satisfactorily each of these problems."

(ii) *"Hitherto And Henceforth"* (I Sam. 7:1-13; II Cor. 5:13-21). This is particularly adapted for the New Year season. "Cold and cynical indeed is that heart which remains unmoved at the passing of an old year and the birth of a new. Callous must be that soul who can sit by the dying embers of the fire of an old year, and remain untouched as memory holds back the door of the past days and weeks and months that have combined to form the year that has so quickly sped.

"Much has transpired since last we celebrated the passing of the old year and the dawn of a new one. There is much to regret in the way of failure; much cause to praise for the faithfulness of God, as seen in His preserving, providing and protecting care. Let us therefore look back over the past to see the 'hitherto' of the Lord's dealings with us for our *remembrance;* and then face the future, and see the 'henceforth' of our *responsibility* for the years that lie ahead."

(h) *Secular history, both past and present, will furnish much that can be used for this purpose.*

(i) *"Things Worth Knowing."* "Socrates, the great Grecian philosopher, who lived 440 B. C., once remarked: 'I have spent my entire life bringing people from a state of *unconscious* ignorance to a condition of *conscious* ignorance.' Surely no one will accuse him of having lived in vain; for a realization of one's ignorance is essential both to the desire and acquisition of knowledge. The first step into the hall of knowledge is the admission of one's own ignorance."

(ii) *"Peace"* (Rom. 5:1). It will be a long time before the incident is forgotten when Neville Chamberlain, with careworn face but triumphant gesture, stepped from a plane which had brought him from an interview with Hitler at Munich. Waving a paper, he shouted to the people who had come to meet him: 'Peace in our time!' Alas, it was a short-lived peace, for it was based upon the promise of an utterly untrustworthy person, to whom a solemn promise meant nothing. How different is the word of another Man, Who left His home in heaven to bring, to a sin-stained and war-torn earth, a peace that is eternal and, best of all, founded upon the perfect righteousness of a holy God! It is of this peace we would speak".

(i) *An apt quotation from the poets, or a hymn, will often serve the purpose of awakening attention to the message.*

(i) *"The Gospel In Seven Words"* (Eph. 2:8). "If there is one thing above anything else that distinguishes the gospel of God's grace from all humanly conceived schemes of religion, it is its extreme simplicity. William Cowper, the great Christian poet of 150 years ago wrote of this fact in the following lines:

> "O how unlike the complex works of man,
>   Heaven's easy, artless, unencumbered plan!
> No meretricious graces to beguile.
>   No clustering ornaments to clog the pile;
> From ostentation, as from weakness, free,
>   It stands like the cerulean arch we see,
> Majestic in its own simplicity.
>
> Inscribed above the portal, from afar
>   Conspicuous as the brightness of a star,
> Legible only by the light they give
>   Stand the soul quickening words: 'Believe, and live!'
> Too many shocked at what should charm them most,
>   Despise the plain direction and are lost.
> The plea of works, as arrogant as vain,
>   Heaven turns from with abhorrence and disdain;
> For Christ as soon would abdicate His own,
>   As stoop from heaven to sell the proud a throne!' "

(ii) *"The Greatest Discovery of Life"* (Prov. 2:1-5). "The greatest discovery of life is the knowledge of God. This discovery dwarfs into utter insignificance the so-called great discoveries of man. What can compare, for one moment, with a personal knowledge of that infinite and eternal Being, all wise, all powerful, all present and unchanging in all His Divine attributes! Binney has beautifully expressed this fact in the following hymn:

'Eternal light! Eternal light!
  How pure the soul must be
When, placed within Thy searching sight,
  It shrinks not, but with calm delight
Can live and look on Thee!

The spirits that surround the throne
  May bear the burning bliss;
But that is surely their's alone,
  Since they have never, never known
A fallen world like this.

O how can I, whose native sphere
  Is dark, whose mind is dim,
Before the Ineffable appear
  And on my naked spirit bear
The uncreated beam?

There is a way for man to rise
  To that sublime abode,
An Offering and a Sacrifice,
  A Holy Spirit's energies,
An Advocate with God.

These, these prepare us for the sight
  Of majesty above:
The sons of ignorance and night,
  May dwell in the eternal light
Through the eternal love;' "

These are not all the sources from which introductory material may be drawn, but these nine will at least aid in securing that necessary variety which is essential if the introduction is to serve the purpose for which it is intended.

CHAPTER FIFTEEN

The Sermon and Its Structure

(Continued)

4. The discussion.

Having defined and described the first three parts of the sermon: the text, the theme and the introduction; let us now consider the most important part of the sermon: the discussion, and the divisions that go up to make the body of the sermon.

(1) *The definition of it.*

By the discussion is meant that part of the sermon which presents the truth contained in the text and the theme. It is therefore the most important part of the sermon. It is that for which the text, theme, introduction and the conclusion exist. The preacher may be likened to a builder and his sermon to the building he wishes to erect in the hearer's mind. For this building he needs a definite plan. His business, in the sermon, is to work out his plan in the construction of the building. A foundation must first be laid and then, proceeding in orderly sequence, the preacher builds until the structure is complete.

(2) *The necessity for divisions in the discussion.*

Just as a building demands the three-fold division of foundation, superstructure and roof; so the discussion must have a definite order. Nature itself can teach us in this matter. (I Cor. 11:14). Time has three distinct divisions: past, present and future. Each day has its parts: dawn, morning, noon, afternoon, evening and night. Life also can be classified in many divisions: babyhood, childhood, youth, manhood, middle age and old age. Each year witnesses four distinct seasons: spring, summer, autumn and winter.

(3) The purpose of these divisions.

These divisions of the sermon serve the same purpose as the skeleton of the human body. The bones are the framework on which the body is built. One may have a skeleton without a body, but hardly a body without a skeleton, unless it be a jelly fish, and no sermon should resemble this! In his address the speaker must clothe the skeleton of his outline with the flesh and blood of his own thoughts and words. Note a threefold purpose of divisions.

(a) *They keep the speaker to his theme,* and thus prevent him from wandering into the fields of fancy; or generalizing, by the hour, from Genesis to Revelation.

(b) *They tend to retain the attention of the audience,* and make plain the logical process of the preacher's train of thought. The speaker's plan is perceived and his progressive argument appreciated, as he proceeds from point to point.

(c) *They help the memory.* God is a God of order, and not of confusion, and He has made men's minds orderly. (I Cor. 14:33, 40). The human mind instinctively demands order and dreads chaos. Order transforms a mob into an army. Order is "heaven's first law." As the speaker presents the truth in an orderly and connected fashion, it will make an orderly impression on the mind of the hearer, and enable him to recall the various points, or divisions, long afterwards.

Dr. James M. Gray used to liken a sermon to the packing of an order of groceries in a bag. When the bag is taken home, the goods are taken out in an orderly manner. We must therefore pack these divisions, in an orderly fashion, in the hearer's mind so that he can unpack the sermon when he is at leisure. It is possible to say a lot of good things in a sermon but, if there is no orderly sequence, the sermon will soon be forgotten.

(4) *Some rules governing the forming of these divisions.*

(a) *Each division should be clear and distinct from the other divisions.* Each division should carry a further thought which distinguishes it from any of the others. The second division should not be a rehash of the first, but distinct from it and progressive in its thought.

(b) *The sermon plan must possess three essential qualifications.* It must have *order, movement* and *progress.* Let us illustrate what is meant by these words. A merry go round has *movement* but no *progress.* Its only effect is to produce giddiness and this, most emphatically, is what a sermon should *not* produce on an audience! A company of soldiers, engaged in marking time, certainly exhibits *order* and *movement,* but there is no *progress.* Some sermons are of this type. The preacher used plenty of words and manifested a certain amount of movement but, to use the language of the man in the street, he "got nowhere fast!" A rabble mob has both *movement* and *progress,* but possesses no *order.* It moves as fancy dictates, surging here and there, but with no coherence, producing only confusion and, very often, damage to valuable property. An army on the march possesses all the three essentials of a good sermon, for it has *order, movement* and *progress.*

In warfare an attacking army, after careful deliberation, outlines its objectives. It has a first, second and third objective. When the first has been gained, it can proceed to the second and then to the third, until the battle plan has been consummated. The preacher, by means of his sermon, is out to capture the city of Mansoul for Christ. He must therefore plan his objectives, and let each division of his sermon be an objective. He must drive home division number one, before going on to number two and so on. The sermon is not to be a rabble of confused words, but an army, well disciplined and with a definite purpose in view.

(c) *They should be cumulative.* That is, they should gather volume, strength and value as they proceed, and also possess unity of thought. In other words, these divisions should not produce a series of little disconnected sermons; but combine to present an harmonious whole, each division being incomplete without the other.

Furthermore, no division should be allowed to stand out *too boldly,* thus attracting attention to itself at the cost, or the exclusion of the other divisions.

(d) *They should seek to fully comprehend the text and theme, and attempt to expound all the truth contained therein.* A simple illustration may serve to clarify what this means. The text, or theme, could be likened to an orange from which the juice is to be extracted. Each division represents a squeeze which the preacher should give that orange until all the juice, or truth, has been extracted. These divisions should therefore be successive squeezes, until no more truth can be obtained from the text. Naturally, the *fewer* these divisions are, the *more* truth must be extracted with each squeeze. The more these divisions are, the *less* truth will be obtained with each squeeze.

(e) *These divisions should be natural.* They should not be *forced,* or artificial. If there are only three natural divisions, they should not be forced to make five. If there are only five, they should not be stretched to make seven. The grammar of the text will aid largely in determining the correct number.

(f) *They should not be too many in number.* There is no hard and fast rule regarding the number of divisions in a sermon. One preacher will see more and another will see less in the same text. Some think that three is the ideal number, while others favor seven. The more there are of these divisions, the greater will be the need for them to follow in logical sequence, or else the audience will be unable to recall them. In determining these divisions, each preacher must be "fully persuaded in his own mind;" and he should also be prepared to give a reason for the existence of each division in his sermon.

(g) *They should be orderly.* Four things should be observed.

(i) The negative should precede the positive. We should first state what a thing is *not*, before we describe what it really *is*.

(ii) The abstract should be stated before the concrete.

(iii) Conviction must always go before the appeal.

(iv) The false must precede the true. First show the wrong idea and then state the true.

It will be observed that in the formation of these divisions common sense plays no small part. A "sound mind" will result in logical divisions. This calls for concentrated study and constant practice until, what has been aptly termed "the Homiletic Habit," has been acquired.

The reading of sermons by the best of preachers will prove to be very helpful in sermon construction. Such pulpit masters as Alexander Maclaren, C. H. Spurgeon, J. H. Jowett, James Hamilton, Matthew Henry, Griffith Thomas, etc., will combine to show what can be done in this direction. Spurgeon, in advising his students to read other men's sermons said: "It is good to feed in other people's pastures, providing you give your own milk!"

(5) *Three methods of stating these divisions.*

First, by a series of propositions, or terse statements, called the *Logical* form. Second, by a series of phrases, called the *Rhetorical* form. Third, by a series of questions, called the *Interrogative* form. Let us examine each of these methods and illustrate just what is meant by each term.

(a) *The Logical Form.* This consists of a series of propositions, or concise statements, which emerge as the text is examined. These propositions constitute the main divisions of the sermon and should be indicated, in the sermon, by the use of Roman numerals: I, II, III, IV, V, VI, VII, etc.

Let us take a text that will easily yield its main divisions. We shall choose Rom. 13:11-14 for our example. It reads thus: "And that knowing the time, that now it is high time to awake out of sleep: for now is our salvation nearer than when we believed. The night is far spent, the day is at hand: let us therefore cast off the works of darkness, and let us put on the armor of light. Let us walk honestly, as in the day; not in rioting and drunkenness, not in chambering and wantonness, not in strife and envying. But put ye on the Lord Jesus Christ, and make not provision for the flesh, to fulfil the lusts thereof."

As one reads and rereads these words, a certain theme is seen to dominate the whole passage. Let us state it thus: "In view of the return of Christ, God calls His people to a godly, self-denying, consistent and Christ-glorifying life before the world." In this statement of the theme, the 97 words of the text have been condensed to 22 words. The theme, as we have already stated, is the sermon condensed. This theme, stated rhetorically, could be: "The awakening summons." The title we shall state as: "The Divine Tocsin," (or "God's Call to Arms").

As one continues to read the passage, a certain order or pattern will appear. This pattern will indicate the main divisions. Let us see how this works out in this particular scripture. Seven distinct and imperative injunctions are mentioned. Let us name them:

    I.   "It is high time to awake out of sleep."
   II.   "The night is far spent, and the day is at hand."
  III.   "Let us therefore cast off the works of darkness."
  IV.   "Let us put on the armor of light."
    V.   "Let us walk honestly . . . not in rioting, etc."
  VI.   "Put ye on the Lord Jesus Christ."
 VII.   "Make not provision for the flesh."

These seven injunctions, or commands, will therefore form the main divisions of the sermon. Now let us state these same divisions in the *logical form,* by a series of propositions or statements of fact. We shall indicate them by the use of Roman numerals:

    I. *There is an arousing injunction, to awaken from spiritual indolence and lethargy.* "It is high time, etc."

   II. *There is a sobering anticipation of the imminency of the day of Christ.* "Night is far spent . . . day is at hand."

  III. *There must be a definite renunciation of evil doing.* "Let us cast off the works of darkness."

  IV. *There must be a personal appropriation of the armor of God's providing.* "Let us put on the armor of light."

   V. *There must be a practical manifestation of the Christian life before the world.* "Let us walk honestly, etc."

  VI. *There must be the transforming occupation of putting on Christ.* "Put ye on the Lord Jesus Christ."

VII. *There must be the resolute self-mortification of the flesh and its lusts.* "Make not provision, etc."

It will be seen that each of these divisions is distinct from the other, yet all combine to present the one theme. These divisions, moreover, possess the essential qualifications of *order, movement* and *progression* of thought, and also combine to present *unity* of expression.

(b) *The Rhetorical Form.* By this is meant a series of phrases. Let us now state these same divisions in the rhetorical form:

   I. *An arousing injunction.*
  II. *A solemn anticipation.*
 III. *A definite renunciation.*
 IV. *A personal appropriation.*
  V. *A practical manifestation.*
 VI. *A transforming occupation.*
VII. *A resolute self-mortification.*

It will be perceived that this mode of stating the divisions makes for brevity and certainly has the advantage of being more easily retained by the hearer. However, as was pointed out in regard to the statement of the theme, each preacher should at least *privately* state his divisions in the logical form, as he prepares his sermon. This makes for that necessary discipline of his mind, for it demands a close reading of the text, plus a clear conception and statement of its teaching.

(c) *The Interrogative Form.* By this is meant a series of questions which the text answers. Let us now put these same divisions into the interrogative form and turn them into a series of questions.

  I. *What is this awakening summons?*
 II. *What circumstances make it so urgent?*

III. *What does it involve in the way of renunciation?*
IV. *What does it urge in the way of appropriation?*
V. *What practical effect should it have on the life?*
VI. *How is this transformation to be effected?*
VII. *What must be our attitude to the flesh?*

This form makes for variety of treatment, but it is not the best method to state *these particular divisions.* Other texts will be better adapted for the use of this form, and particularly topical subjects, which we shall consider later. Each of these forms of stating the divisions has its value, and all may and should be used for the sake of variety. The best method, as far as the preacher himself is concerned, is the logical form.

(6) *Modes of discussion, or the different methods of presenting the sermon.*

There are two: the explanatory and the observational.

(a) *The Explanatory.*

As its name indicates, it means informing and instructing. This method seeks to make clear what is more or less obscure in the text. It seeks to explain things in their logical and chronological order. We will take Malachi 16-17 as our text and, in this case, enlist "alliteration's artful aid" in the statement of the divisions. The natural discussion along explanatory lines would be something as follows: We shall entitle the sermon: "Light at eventide," or it could be called: "The Gleam in the Gloom."

I. *A Choice Company.* "Then they that feared the Lord."

II. *A Fragrant Fellowship.* "spake often . . . with one another"

III. *An August Auditor.* "Lord hearkened and heard"

IV. *A Recorded Remembrance.* "book of remembrance"

V.   *A Precious Possession.* "they shall be Mine"

VI.   *A Striking Simile.* "jewels"

VII.   *A Divine Discrimination.* "I will spare."

Thus, by this mode, the words are taken in their order and explained to the audience.

(b)   *The Observational.*   This discusses the text and the theme by a series of observations, which bring out the prominent thoughts of the text.   We will use the same text and maintain the same divisions, but state them in a different way, suitable to this mode of discussion.

I.   *However dark the days may be, God has a remnant of His people who fear His name.*   "Then they that feared the Lord."

II.   *The godly will take advantage of every opportunity to meet for fellowship together.*   "they spake often," etc.

III.   *This gathering together of the godly remnant is of great interest to the One, in Whose name they have met.*   "And the Lord hearkened."

IV.   *The Lord treasures up this appreciative remembrance of His people.*   "and a book of remembrance."

V.   *God promises a peculiar intimacy to those who thus honor Him.*   "and they shall be Mine."

VI.   *God likens such a godly remnant to rare and precious jewels.*   "when I make up My jewels."

VII.   *To such He reveals Himself in family relationship.*   "and I will spare."

Thus, by a series of observations, the text has been divided and the main truths set forth.   There is value in each method, and both should be used for variety of presentation.

Martin Luther, when speaking of the preacher said: "When he preaches on any subject, a man must first distinguish it. Secondly, he must define, describe and show what it is. Thirdly, he must produce sentences from the Scripture to prove and strengthen it. Fourthly, he must explain it by examples. Fifthly, he must adorn it with similitudes. Lastly, he must admonish and arouse the indolent, correct the disobedient and reprove the authors of false doctrines."

(c)   *The elements of a satisfactory sermon.*

The late Dr. Griffith Thomas, himself a great teacher and homilist whose books should be read by every preacher, has put the matter very succinctly: "The following four elements will probably be found essential to every satisfactory sermon:

(i)   *There will be propositions.* We must state our case and show the people what we intend to do with our subject.

(ii)   *There will be explanations.* We must interpret, elucidate and justify our propositions.

(iii)   *There will be observations.* We shall comment on and apply our text in all suitable ways.

(iv)   *There will be illustrations.* There are very few sermons that will not be benefited by some illustrations to let in the light and impress the subject on mind and heart." These words, from a past master in the art of preaching, are worthy of the closest attention on the part of all preachers.

Sometimes it is advisable for a speaker to take the audience into his confidence and, at the very beginning of his address, to give his hearers an outline of the main divisions of his subject. They will then be prepared to follow him intelligently as he proceeds with his sermon, and appreciate the order, movement and progress of the sermon.

CHAPTER SIXTEEN

The Sermon and Its Structure

(Continued)

We have considered the matter of the text, the theme, the introduction and the divisions. Now let us discuss:

5. The Conclusion.

(1) *The definition of it.*

This is sometimes called "the *application*," but this is somewhat of a misnomer, for the application of the truth contained in the text should not be confined to the conclusion, but made continuously during the address, as the occasion demands. This is the drawback of many gospel tracts. The incident is interestingly told, but the application is confined to the conclusion. It appears as an appendix and the reader, more often than not, performs an appendectomy!

(2) *Some suggestions regarding it.*

(a) *It should be short.* A conclusion with no terminal facilities is entirely out of place. Many a good sermon has been ruined because of a long drawn out conclusion which has wearied the audience, and dissipated whatever good effect the sermon may have had. In view of this, the conclusion should be as carefully prepared as the introduction.

(b) *It should be varied.* Sterotyped endings should be avoided. There are other ways of ending an address than by saying: "And now, friends, in conclusion," etc.

(i) *The quoting of a verse of a hymn,* or an impressive poem that sums up what one has been seeking to impress upon the audience is good.

(ii) *An apt quotation from some pose writer* will often serve the purpose of clinching the message. If possible, give the source of the quotation.

(iii) *A searching question can be left with them,* as a challenge to their own responsibility in the matter.

(iv) *A solemn incident* will also serve to drive home the message.

(v) *A summation of the main points of the sermon* is often used to seal the truth upon the mind and heart.

(c) *It should be real.* The preacher should only speak as he really *feels.* All forced and artificial emotion should be avoided like a plague, for it is verily an abomination unto the Lord. Such artificiality may be all very well for the stage, which acts *fiction* as though it were *fact,* but it should have no place whatever in the Christian pulpit. A preacher's notes were once found, and in the margin were various annotations such as: "Here wipe the eyes;" "Here let the voice break," etc. If the heart of the speaker is really moved, it will be conveyed *naturally* in the voice and the manner and, in turn, communicated to the audience. All should sedulously avoid "the pulpit tone." This consists of a kind of religious whine that is entirely unnatural to the speaker, but which he fondly but mistakenly imagines harmonizes with the religious atmosphere of the pulpit.

Some preachers are more emotional than others, but these emotions should be kept under control and not allowed to run riot. The story is told of a very uninteresting speaker who wept profusely as he addressed a crowd of boys. One boy whispered to a companion: "What's he crying for?" The other replied: "If you were up there and had nothing to say, you'd cry too!" Above all, the speaker should remember to be natural, and in earnest.

(d) *It should be personal.* The conclusion is no time for mere generalities. The speaker must be specific. Nathan left David in no doubt as to the application of his parable of the ewe lamb. With outstretched hand and flashing eyes, he addressed himself to the king and fearlessly charged: "Thou art the man!" Like an arrow from the bow of God, it pierced David's soul and brought forth the humble and frank confession: "I have sinned!" Note also Peter's sermon: *"Ye* yourselves . . . *ye* have taken and by wicked hands have crucified and slain!" (Acts 2: 22-23). It has been well said: "He who preaches to broken hearts, preaches to all generations and to all degrees of intelligence." (Parker)

The "horrible example" in the art of evasion is attributed to a bishop, who is reported to have said to his stylish congregation: "Unless we repent, as it were, in a measure; and believe to a certain extent, we may possibly be damned, so to speak, to a certain degree." From all such beating around the bush and banal verbal equivocation, may the Lord deliver us! It takes courage to apply the message in a personal manner, but the Master's "well done!" will amply compensate for the loss of any earthly prestige which may result.

(e) *It should be pointed.* The conclusion enables the speaker to briefly recapitulate the arguments and apply them to the audience in a most pointed way. Therefore the preacher should be specific and faithfully and fearlessly, yet courteously, drive home the truth to the intelligence, emotions and will of the hearers. The speaker is out to get a verdict in favor of his Master and for the truth he has presented. He should therefore press for an immediate decision for Christ and leave the audience in no doubt as to its responsibility in the matter.

Perhaps a word may be in order, at this juncture, regarding the matter of what is called "the appeal." These are the days of the "professional evangelist," who specializes in the art of getting people to "express themselves" in some way, as either desiring prayer, or salvation, or who have definitely experienced salvation. These people can count their converts by the thousands, as they move from place to place. The only difficulty about the vast majority of these converts is that they cannot be found six months afterwards! They were emotionally moved and swept away by the atmosphere of religious fervor, and allowed their emotions to dominate their intelligence and will. Thus they "made a decision," with no true knowledge of what they were doing. Such so called "results" are worse than useless: they are a *spiritual menace,* for these souls have been given to understand that they are "saved," when all the while they have never been regenerated by the Spirit of God! Thus they are mere empty professors who lack true possession of Christ.

All preachers of the gospel should give an opportunity for anxious souls to remain behind after the meeting and be dealt with, if they so desire; but to *trap* souls into making a premature profession of Christ, by an expert use of psychology, is reprehensible to the last degree. Each preacher must ever keep before him that verse from the Book: "Salvation is of the Lord!" Unless the Spirit of God does His convicting and regenerating work in the human soul, all man's efforts are utterly in vain. It is far better to see a few souls genuinely saved by the grace of God, than a host of converts who have been mistakenly led to believe they are Christians, but who prove the unreality of their profession by going back into the world. Let us go in for *quality* and not quantity.

(f) *It should conclude.* This may sound obvious, but this fact does not appear to be clear to many preachers. A conclusion that fails to conclude merely serves to awaken resistance to the message. The speaker's *finishing* point should coincide with his *stopping point*. All should beware of going on after they have finished.

We will conclude this section on the sermon and its structure by a brief summary on:

(g) *The elements that go to make up a good address.*

(i) *It should be well studied.* The preacher should be saturated with his subject.

(ii) *It should be well prayed over.* Like Hezekiah's letter, it should be "spread before the Lord" (Isa. 37:14).

(iii) *It should be well introduced* and thus gain the ear of the audience.

(iv) *It should be well expressed,* in good, clear forceful language, so that the hearer may not only *hear,* but *understand* what he hears.

(v) *It should be well illustrated,* so as to both clarify and enforce the truth.

(vi) *It should be well applied* and leave the hearer in no doubt as to his responsibilities regarding the message.

(vii) *It should be well concluded.* Having delivered the message, he should stop.

Again we would emphasize that each preacher should ever keep before him the fact that diligent preparation, plus humble supplication, plus powerful presentation is as far as he can go. Only God can provide the spiritual regeneration essential to the hearer's entrance into the kingdom of God. Read John 1:11-13.

CHAPTER SEVENTEEN

Modes Of Delivery

Having considered the matter of the sermon and its structure, it may be well to inquire as to the best mode of delivering the sermon. We shall examine three methods and see the advantages and disadvantages of each. The three methods are: first, *reading;* second, *reciting;* third, *extemporaneous.*

I. Reading.

Probably all will agree that a good sermon read from manuscript is better than a poor sermon preached extemporaneously. Doubtless all will also agree that a good sermon preached, is better than a good sermon read, or recited.

1. The advantages.

(1) *It necessitates the writing out of the entire sermon.* This is a splendid preparation for two reasons. First it disciplines the mind and compels the preacher to express himself clearly and fully on his subject matter. Second, it develops his ability as a writer, which is no mean accomplishment. Such a preacher certainly cannot be accused of laziness, for it requires considerable physical and mental effort to write down the five thousand or more words that a thirty minute sermon requires.

(2) *There are occasions when the reading of a sermon is essential.*

(a) *It is particularly useful when giving a radio address.* Such an address is best read, providing it is *well read.* The reasons for this are: First, the necessary time limit, which must be meticulously observed, and often this is a matter of seconds. Second, the great need to make this precious time count to the best advantage. A discriminating audience, unseen by the speaker is ready, at a moment's notice, to switch him off if he fails to gain its interest. Third, the absence of a visible audience eliminates a great deal of the inspiration that a seen audience supplies. A microphone, in a broadcasting studio, has poor inspirational properties! It doesn't lean forward, look interested or otherwise respond to the message given.

In preparing the manuscript to be read for a radio address, several things should be observed. It should be typed, double spaced, with a wide margin for annotations and the words in the script *underlined* that should be emphasized in the address. Needless to say, this should be read and re-read several times before it is given and the exact time of its reading carefully noted.

(b) *Writing is especially needful when giving some particular definition,* or of clarifying some mooted question which calls for an exact statement; or of making some fine distinction on which a great deal depends. Careful writing will tend to eliminate any ambiguity of speech, which might easily create misunderstanding in the minds of the hearers. To be able, when challenged, to show to the challenger the exact words which were uttered, will do much to settle a controversy.

(c) *It would be a good thing for every preacher to write out his sermon,* for it would enable him to sympathize with the audience that will have to listen to it. While this sermon should not be read, the very writing of it will fix it in his mind as nothing else. An old Scotsman once observed: "There is one advantage at least of a written sermon. The audience will know that the preacher will end when his paper ends!"

(3) *Many famous preachers have adopted this method.*
Jonathan Edwards' famous sermon: "Sinners in the
hands of an angry God!" was *read* to his audience. This
shortsighted preacher stood in the pulpit holding a candle
in one hand and his manuscript in the other. As he
read, sinners were so convicted of their lost and undone
condition, that they actually clung to the pillars of the
church building to keep themselves from slipping into
hell! This was not due to the fact that the sermon was
read, but to the intense *spirituality of the speaker* and
this is of paramount importance. It is the Holy Spirit
alone Who can produce conviction of sin and lead the
soul to an apprehension of Christ as Substitute, Savior
and Sovereign.

J. H. Jowett, perhaps the most polished of evangelical
preachers, used to read his sermons, but did it with such
skill that it was never conspicuous. Dr. Graham Scroggie
read his addresses at Keswick in 1935 and 1950, and they
were both excellent and inspiring.

2. The disadvantages.

(1) *Artificiality.*

It tends to make preaching a mechanical process. True,
it is accomplished smoothly and efficiently, but it lacks
that element of spontaneity, so essential to any sermon.

(2) *Limitation.*

The reading of a sermon makes no provision for the
fresh light that often comes at the moment of speaking.
No allowance is made for the mental quickening that an
audience will often aid in producing. Then again, the
Holy Spirit, Who guides into all truth, may impress the
speaker to emphasize a certain line of truth to meet the
needs of someone in the audience. A read sermon lacks
this possibility of alteration to suit the needs of the
moment. The story is told of a preacher who wrote out

his sermon very carefully, but forgot to take his manuscript with him to the meeting.   Much perturbed because of his loss, he apologized to his audience and said: "Inasmuch as I have forgotten my manuscript, I shall have to rely on the Lord for the delivery of my sermon this morning; but this evening, I can assure you, I shall come better prepared!"

(3) *Failure to look at the audience.*

Then again, the reading of a sermon keeps the preacher's eyes on his manuscript and not on his hearers, and this is a fatal defect in any address.   Many preachers try, but with little success, to hide the fact that they are reading; but the audience is not so easily deceived and soon becomes aware of the fact.   If a sermon is read, there should be no attempt at deception in the matter. Above all, if the sermon is read, it should be *well read* and, more important still, it should be *worth reading!* On being asked his opinion of a sermon to which he had listened, a person replied: "I didn't like it for three reasons: first, because it was *read;* second, because it was *poorly read;* third, because it wasn't *worth reading!*" There is nothing like speaking to an audience, eye to eye and heart to heart.

II.   Recitation.

By this is meant the memorization of one's written manuscript and the reciting of it, word for word, before an audience.   This method is adopted by quite a few preachers.

1.   The advantages of it.

(1) *It aids greatly in developing the memory.*

This certainly is a splendid thing.   All preachers could do with considerable improvement along this line.   However, the strain of such a task on the mind and nervous system must be tremendous.

(2) *Recitation is a most useful thing when making an exact statement regarding some misunderstood doctrine, or truth, before a discriminating audience.*

It is necessary also for defining the great words of Scripture and for the clear setting forth of the great fundamental doctrines of the Christian faith.

(3) *It is needed for the correct quotation of verses from the Bible.*

It is impossible to overestimate the value of being able to quote *correctly* the words of holy Scripture. This should and, indeed, *must* be done during the course of an address. It is hardly necessary to say that such scriptures cannot be recited from memory until they have been memorized. Hints on how best to memorize these verses of Scripture are given in chapter two. The speaker should inform the audience when he is quoting from the Scriptures, otherwise many will not be aware of that fact. It is the Bible that gives authority to the message.

(4) *Recitation is essential for the repeating of the lines of a hymn, or a whole poem.*

The benefit of being able, at will, to recite appropriate verses of hymns, or poems can easily be appreciated. Thus recitation can serve a very useful purpose in preaching.

2. The disadvantages of it.

As in the read sermon, the same two fatal defects are evident.

(1) *Artificiality.*

This impression of artificiality communicates itself, in some subtle way, to the audience. True, as in the case of the read sermon, the audience is treated to a polished address, in perfect English, with well rounded periods, and even oratorical flights: but somehow there is an appreciable lack that only spontaneity of thought and expression can give.

One cannot imagine a lawyer pleading for the life of his client, or an ambassador presenting the claims of his country on this principle. Stale emotion, six days old, and "served as directed," seem to be the very quintessence of artificiality.

(2) *Limitation.*

It leaves no room for the inspiration of the moment, or the Spirit's leading for that particular audience. The preacher thus becomes the slave of his sermon, and this naturally imposes a tremendous strain on him lest he forgets what he has memorized. Thus memory rules the sermon like a depot. The imagination and the emotions are not permitted to have free play, and memory alone is allowed to have its own way. By this mode of delivery, the preacher becomes bound by the chains of his memory. He dares not disgress from his memorized sermon, lest he be unable to recall it again.

III. Extemporaneous.

The primary meaning of the word is to speak without preparation, but it also includes the expression of thoughts that have been the subject of much careful preparation. In fact, all things being equal, the more careful the preparation, the better the speech will be. It is good to write out the sermon, but not to read it; to memorize the sermon, as an exercise for the memory, but not to recite it. Even though one wrote out his sermon and then reproduced it, *without an effort to repeat the language* of his manuscript, it could still be termed an extemporaneous sermon.

1. *The advantages of it.*

(1) The speaker can accustom himself to think more rapidly and with less dependence on external helps. He can turn to advantage any fresh ideas that occur to him as he preaches, as led by the Holy Spirit of God. This will sometimes lift him into an exaltation of mind that almost amounts to rapture, until he wonders where the words are coming from. Such an experience is better experienced than described.

(2) *The preacher can look at his audience.*

He can then watch the effect of the sermon on the faces of his hearers. Thus the audience itself will aid him in his preaching. He can see the dawn of conviction upon this one, or that one. Sometimes he may actually be able to see conversion taking place, as a person grasps the soul-emancipating truth of the finished work of Christ. The preacher's humble, but careful and prayerful preparation of the sermon is now rewarded, as he sees the interest shown and the blessing resulting from his message.

2. *The disadvantages of it.*

(1) *The temptation to neglect prayerful and careful preparation.*

This snare is ever present and should be resolutely and consistently resisted. The preacher should continually remind himself that God does not encourage spiritual indolence. The Holy Spirit does not supply the lazy preacher with thoughts and words that were within his own power to provide through diligent study, but which he failed to do because of the effort involved. The man who relies only on the inspiration of the moment, is apt to be left with nothing to say when that moment arrives.

(2) *It tends to prevent the excellent habit of writing.*

Each speaker must cultivate this art if he would widen his horizons, learn to express himself intelligently and clearly, and discipline himself to think carefully and logically. For a preacher to read a stenographic report of his sermon is often a humbling experience! Though this is liable to be hard on the flesh, it will be good for the spirit, for it will help him to appreciate what the audience has to put up with each time it listens to him! Incidentally, it will be a great aid in correcting his grammar.

Sometimes the question is asked: "Is it right to preach the same sermon over again?" The late Peter Hynd of Troon, Scotland, when asked this question, replied: "Yes, providing it has been born again!" One famous preacher declared he did not consider a sermon was really his until he had preached it twenty times. Another says: "Do not repreach old sermons without warming them over in the oven of prayer and study."

CHAPTER EIGHTEEN

The Types of Sermons

Let us now consider some of the various types of sermons, with examples of each kind and note their advantages and disadvantages.

By way of introduction, let us notice two examples of these various types of sermons.

1. The Example of Christ.

Christ came into the world, not primarily to preach the gospel, but to *make it possible* for a gospel to be preached. As the greatest Preacher and Teacher the world has ever known, He, "Who spake as never man spake;" used many types of sermons with which to impress His life-giving words upon the hearts of His hearers. He taught by means of *parables*. He told *stories*, unsurpassed for brevity of speech and depth of meaning. He used *similies* and often used the word, "like," in His addresses. He also adopted the *question and answer* method. Sometimes he emphasized and illustrated His meaning by means of a *miracle*. At other times He used a *plain statement* which admitted of only one meaning. Lastly, He used *His own example* to enforce His teaching and said: "As I have done, so also do ye."*

2. The example of Paul.

We have already noted that the apostle Paul used many methods of presenting the truth of God's word to an audience. Sometimes he gave his personal testimony, as we shall see later. In Acts 17:3, we find him "opening

* For a fuller development of this, see author's pamphlets, "The Teacher as a Student," and "Lessons from the Great Teacher."

and alleging." That is to say, he would open up the Scriptures and expose and expound what was contained therein. He would allege, adduce, claim and advance certain truths, which he would then proceed to prove.

In Acts 18:4 he described as "reasoning and persuading." This indicates that he sought to logically present and enforce his arguments from Scripture and thus prove the reasonableness of God's revelation. From this appeal to the reason, he would proceed to persuade the hearer to act upon that which he had been convinced was right; and thus not only be "almost," but "altogether persuaded" to believe the gospel and receive the Savior (Acts 26:28, 29).

In Acts 28:31, it is stated that Paul was busy "preaching and teaching." By "preaching" is meant the *proclaiming* of the facts of the gospel. By "teaching" is meant the *explaining* of the word of God to those who had received the message.

In Col. 1:28, Paul himself describes the many means he used in seeking to win the hearer to the truth. Speaking of Christ, he said: "Whom we preach, *warning* every man, and *teaching* every man in all wisdom; that we may *present* every man perfect (or mature) in Christ Jesus." Wise indeed is that preacher who adopts Paul's method, and so warns and teaches his hearers, that they shall be brought to Christian maturity.

While there are many methods of preaching and types of sermons, the end in view is exactly the same; the regeneration of the lost and the edification of the believer. We shall consider six types of sermons, or methods of preaching, in the following order. 1. The personal testimony. 2. The expository sermon. 3. The textual sermon. 4. The topical sermon. 5. The historical-incident sermon. 6. The biographical sermon.

I. **The Personal Testimony.**

1. *The definition of it.*

By this is meant the telling of one's own personal experience of God's saving grace. It involves a description of the circumstances surrounding it, the experiences in appropriating it and the effects resulting from it. The world's adage: "An ounce of experience is worth a ton of theory," well summarizes its importance as a factor in preaching the gospel.

2. *The value of it.*

(1) *It is the best and most natural way to begin to preach.*

The Savior once said to one whom He had delivered from Satan's power: "Go home to thy friends, and tell them what great things the Lord hath done for thee" (Mark 5:19). Notice the *sphere* of his ministry: his own home, the most difficult of all spheres of Christian service. His *audience*: his family circle and his friends. His *subject*: "how great things the Lord had done for him." As the believer tells what God has done for his own soul, he will soon be able to tell what God did for Paul and Peter, etc. Before long, he will find himself telling what God can do for every guilty sinner who owns his need and trusts in Christ.

(2) *It is interesting to an audience.*

People like to hear of a personal experience, if it is told in an interesting manner. One has only to read the advertisements of some patent medicines to see how large a place is given to the personal testimony of those who have benefited from the remedy. There is something particularly interesting to others in the relating of a personal experience. There are certain characteristics which are common to the whole human family. As human beings we share, to a certain extent, the same fears, doubts, hopes and aspirations of others. The Scripture puts it thus: "As in water, face answereth to face (or reflects the image exposed to it), so does the heart of man to man" (Prov. 27:19).

Here is a person who claims to have had an experience with God that has broken the power of sin in his life, and which has given him a peace, joy and satisfaction he never knew before. How did all this come about? Where did it take place? When did it happen? An audience is ready and quite willing to hear the description of this greatest event of his life.

(3)   *It has been greatly used of God.*

Many a soul has been won to Christ as the speaker has described his own experience of God's salvation: of his conviction of sin, his attempts to resist the Spirit's strivings, his vain efforts to obtain peace through his good resolves, good works, prayers and religious exercises, and his final deliverance through faith in the finished work of Christ, acceptance of Him as his own personal Savior, and confession of Him as the Lord of his life.

Many a cloak of self righteousness has been stripped from a self-satisfied and religious sinner by this method of preaching. Numbers of people, in the grip of some habit, have been encouraged to trust Christ, because of the testimony of another who used to be bound by the some chain. Many, who were blinded by the false teaching of some particular cult, have been delivered from that delusion because of the testimony of another who was saved from the same snare. Thus the testimony of a person saved from Roman Catholicism would be likely to have great weight with one who was still enmeshed in that false religious system.

3.   *The importance of it.*

(1)   *The place it is given in Scripture.*   Personal testimony is given quite a prominent place in Scripture.

David said: "Come and hear, all ye that fear God, and I will declare what He hath done for my soul" (Psa. 66:16). The Scripture further enjoins the believer to "give thanks unto the Lord; . . . let the redeemed of the Lord *say so*, whom He hath redeemed from the hand of the enemy" (Psa. 107:1, 2). The Psalms is a book very largely devoted to the record of David's *personal* experiences with the Lord. Surely none will question the importance and value of this part of the holy Scriptures.

(2) *Paul gave it great prominence in his preaching.* The Apostle Paul realized the great importance of giving his testimony. There are altogether six accounts of it in the New Testament.

(a) The historical account, in Acts 9.

(b) The Hebrew narrative, in Acts 22.

(c) The Gentile narrative, in Acts 26.

(d) Its relation to the sovereignty of God, in Gal. 1.

(e) To discountenance all thought of human merit, in Phil. 3.

(f) As a pattern, or model, in I Tim. 1:12-17.

(3) *The fact that it cannot be denied.* It is often a good thing for a preacher, when addressing an audience for the first time, to describe briefly the facts relating to his own conversion. This will serve to secure both the attention and sympathy of the hearers. While an audience may call into question some interpretation of truth which he makes from the Scriptures, they cannot very well refuse to accept the testimony of his personal experience, when this is simply, humbly, interestingly and sincerely told.

4. *Hints on the telling of it.*

(1) *As the speaker rises* he should explain briefly why he does so. He should mention that the Lord has

done something for him which he is convinced God is able and willing to do for others. He could begin something like this: "I am glad to be able to stand before you and *testify* to my own personal experience of God's salvation." This should be spoken in a tone that all can hear and while facing the majority of the audience. All apologies should be avoided, for the purpose of the testimony is to speak of Another, his Savior, Redeemer and Lord.

(2) *Avoid all exaggeration and overstatement.* A witness should tell the truth, the whole truth and nothing but the truth. The speaker should therefore stick closely to the actual facts of the case. In the attempt to be spectacular some simple, and very ordinary testimonies, have gradually developed into wild flights of imagination. If the speaker has been saved from the depths of sin and shame, let him tell it humbly, but in such a way as not to offend the good taste of the hearers.

Some people have been saved from the midst of the muck and mire of outward vice and unspeakable sin. Others, young in years, have been saved from such a life of outward shame. Let each tell his story simply, briefly and truthfully. Sometimes when very young men are giving their testimony, the audience is led to suppose they had run the gamut of sin, plumbed the very depths of every conceivable form of vice, and been saved from the lowest dregs of society, whereas the exact opposite was true in their case.

If one has been saved from the gross forms of sin, it is neither necessary nor nice to go into all the gory details of it and drag the audience through the mire. A *hint* should be enough. There are things in life that are "not so much as named" (I Cor. 5:1). One should not gloat over the past sins, or put on exhibition that which was his shame.

(3) *The dangers of two extremes in a personal testimony.* Two extremes must be avoided in the giving of a testimony. The first is to advertise one's self to such a degree that Christ is practically eclipsed. The second is to think that because one's experience at conversion was not extraordinary, therefore it has no value. The fact of the matter is that both are needed, and can be equally used of God to bring blessing to others. The experiences of Lydia and the jailer of Philippi were totally dissimilar. The first was a quiet unostentatious affair, while the other was a most spectacular event, accompanied by an earthquake and an attempted suicide! Imagine listening to these two persons giving their testimonies. Though each had an entirely different experience, yet each emerged from it a "new creation in Christ Jesus." See Acts 16.

(4) *Try to recall the details of the case.* It is these little details that count in a testimony. For the speaker to rise and say: "I'm glad to tell you that Christ has saved my soul," does not convey any definite impression; but to tell, if possible, how, why, when and where the Lord saved his soul, will awaken the interest of the audience. He should begin at the beginning, and tell how he was awakened from his carelessness about eternal realities to a sense of his need as a sinner.

Was it a verse from the Bible; some striking incident; a kindly word from a friend; the reading of a tract; or the hearing of a gospel message from some faithful preacher? Let him describe his fears, hopes, doubts, the attempts to shake off the conviction of sin, the vain efforts to justify himself before God, the excuses he offered and the futile attempts to *"feel* saved," etc. He should describe how the light dawned upon his soul and the great truth of the finished work of Christ was seen and grasped by faith, and how the Lord Jesus was received as his own

Savior and confessed as Lord of his life. The speaker should then tell how he knows he is saved and what effect this has had on his life. All these varied details combine to make the story interesting and living, so that God can use it to help someone in the audience who is passing through a similar experience.

(5) *Keep Christ preeminent.* The purpose of a testimony is to magnify Christ and not to draw unnecessary attention to one's self. It exists for the purpose of focusing the attention of the hearer on the wonderful Savior, His marvelous grace, His infinite power and His satisfying presence, and not on the speaker's experience. "We preach not ourselves, but Christ Jesus, the Lord" (II Cor. 4:5). The speaker should be careful not to set himself up as a classic example of what a true and faithful Christian should be, or draw attention to his own faithfulness as a believer; but seek to center the attention of the hearers on the Lord Jesus Christ.

(6) *The truth should be applied to the hearers.* After the testimony has been given, the speaker should then press home to the audience the fact that what Christ has done for him, He is able and willing to do for all who will trust Him as Savior and own Him as Lord. The application will necessarily be short, but it must be very much to the point; for his testimony should have presented the need of the sinner and the reality of Christ's redemptive work. The advice of a colored preacher to those about to give their testimony is good. He said: "First, tell them what you were. Second, tell them what you now are. Third, tell them how you got that way! Fourth, then sit down!"

5. *The dangers of it.*

This may sound strange, yet the telling of one's personal experience also has its dangers.

(1) *To allow it to supercede God's word in the preaching of the gospel.* While a personal testimony is good, it should never be allowed to become a substitute for the scriptural setting forth of God's way of salvation. A testimony is but a personal witness to the truth of God's word in one's own experience; but the principal thing is the word of God, and nothing must be allowed to displace its authority in the minds of the hearers. It is a poor thing to substitute the personal pronoun "I," for a "thus saith the Lord." A testimony is only of value as it magnifies the grace of God, the Person and work of the Lord Jesus, makes clear the way of salvation and emphasizes the truth of the word of God.

Many a soul has been made to grope on in spiritual darkness while trying to get an experience similar to the person whose testimony he has heard. He looks in vain for some "vision," or waits to "hear a voice" saying: "thy sins are all forgiven." He tries to get some wonderful "feelings," such as the speaker described himself as having. All the while he is occupied with these things, his attention is diverted from the Savior, through whom alone salvation can come. Thus he is made to flounder in the bog of despondency, through trying to get another person's experience instead of one of his own! It must ever be remembered that it is not an *experience* that saves, but the *Savior Himself.*

(2) *To make it a mould for everyone else.* God is a God of infinite variety. No two persons are saved under exactly similar circumstances. There are no spiritually "identical twins." For a speaker to insist on every one having an experience of God's salvation similar to his own is not only foolish in the extreme, but positively *dangerous.* It directs the attention of the audience to his *experience,* instead of *Christ's Person* and work. It has been pointed out that there are many ways to Christ,

but only one way to God, and that is through Christ.
(John 14: 6).

It is both interesting and instructive to notice the different experiences of conversion recorded in the first chapter of John. First was the preached word: "Behold the Lamb of God!" (vs. 35-36). Next came personal work when Andrew brought Peter to the Lord. (vs. 40-42). Following this was the direct approach of the Savior Who said: "Follow Me." (v. 43). Lastly came personal experiences of Christ Himself on the part of those who responded to His invitation to: "come and see" (vs. 45-46). Some come to Christ because of their fear of hell. Others trust the Savior because of His goodness and grace in giving His life for them (Rom. 2: 4). Still others because of a desire for peace and satisfaction.

Whatever the means may be that God uses, the result is always the same; for the soul is led to trust Christ as Savior and own Him as Lord. It has been well said that some people are *kissed* into salvation, while others have to be *kicked* into it! We must ever remember that, in the regeneration of a soul: "the wind bloweth where it listeth, and thou hearest the sound thereof, but canst not tell whence it cometh or whither it goeth: so is every one that is born of the Spirit." (John 3: 8). God is absolutely sovereign in all His acts, and He knows just the right experience to give to each person. The experience of a little child in coming to the Savior is vastly different from that of an adult. Those who insist that unless a person knows the how? why? when? and where? of his conversion, he is not saved; are faced with the impossible task of explaining away the godly and consistent lives of many Christians who cannot recall the when and where of their conversion! We must constantly keep in mind the fact that salvation is not in an *experience,* but in a

Person, for it is written: "He that hath the *Son* hath the *life!*" (I John 5:12).

(3) *To never get beyond the initial experience of one's conversion.* A speaker would do well to avoid an undue repetition of his testimony before the same audience. Moreover it is important that his testimony be kept up to date. While it is good for a speaker to be able to tell what the Lord did for his soul years ago, when he was first saved; it is also necessary that he be able to tell what the Lord means to him at the *present time,* as he enjoys conscious communion with Him through his study of God's word, prayer and service for Him. It is good to be able to testify to His *present* faithfulness, His comfort in sorrow, His restoring grace, His friendship in all the vicissitudes of life and of the satisfaction Christ gives each day to His own.

Let us not be like the man who was so afraid he would forget his testimony that he wrote it out in full and kept it in a drawer in his bedroom, where it lay unused for some considerable time. One day, when asked to give his testimony, he went to take it out and discovered, to his chagrin, that the mice had nibbled it away. As he viewed the work of destruction the mice had wrought, he exclaimed dolefully: *"O wife, whatever shall I do, the mice have eaten my testimony!"*

God's mercies are "new every morning," and each day should witness some fresh realization of His love and some new aspect of the glories of our blessed Lord and Savior. The writer of the epistle to the Hebrews gives the heartening word: "Let us go on!" This should come home to the heart of every believer. We should not move in a monotonous cycle or dwell in the experiences of the remote past, or be constantly and wistfully reminiscing about "the good old days," when there were "giants in the earth." What about the *present days?* Is not Christ "the same, yesterday, today and forever?" It is written in the good Book: "The path of the just is as a shining light which shineth, *more and more,* unto the perfect day" (Prov. 4:18).

Each preacher should therefore so seek to study the Scriptures and live for Christ, that he shall *grow, go* and *glow* for Christ, and thus be enabled to pass on the bread of life to others. God's promise to Abraham was: "I will bless thee, and thou shalt be a blessing" (Gen. 12:2).

> "If the Savior's won your heart,
> And for heaven you've made a start,
> Keep your eye upon the chart—
>   *And go on!*
>
> Buy the truth and sell it not,
> Hold for God the bit you've got;
> Be content whate'er your lot—
>   *And go on!*
>
> Feed on Christ the living Bread,
> Drink of Him, the Fountain Head;
> Think of why His blood was shed—
>   *And go on!*"

—W. Luff.

CHAPTER NINETEEN

The Types of Sermons

(Continued)

II. The Expository Sermon.

Of all the types of sermons this, though perhaps the most difficult, is the very best. "There may have been a great expositor who was not a great preacher, but there has never been a great preacher who was not a great expositor." (Ray)

1. *The definition of it.*

By exposition is meant the opening up, (exposing) or the unfolding and explaining of a passage of Scripture. The word comes from two Latin words: "ex" meaning "out," and "pono," to place. Thus it means to place out, to display, to exhibit. An "exposition" is a public exhibit of arts and manufacturing. An exposition of a Scripture portion is therefore the placing out, or the displaying of the truth contained in the passage selected. This passage usually consists of a paragraph, or a number of verses which combine to present a main thought, or theme. These paragraphs are indicated clearly in the Revised Version. An expository sermon takes the central thought of this portion of Scripture and then seeks to expose, explain and supply it, in the light of its context, in this *particular passage*. It must not be confused with a series of running comments on the verses of a chapter of the Bible. This is properly called "commenting." Spurgeon was a past master of this art.

Let us glance at two other definitions of the expository sermon. "In preaching, exposition is the detailed interpretation, logical amplification and practical application of a passage of Scripture." (Ray). "An expository sermon is one based on a passage of Scripture, which it seeks to illuminate; from which it seeks to draw a concise and comprehensive theme and sermon points, and which applies to the lives of the people. The theme must cover all, and all the points must come out of the message." (Byington)

An expository sermon has been well likened to a *wheel*. The *main theme* of the passage is the *hub*, and the *contributing thoughts* in the passage, which throw further light upon the theme, or which spring from this theme, are the *spokes* of the wheel which radiate from the hub, thus presenting a complete unit. The method by which an expository sermon is prepared is to first discover what is the central, or main theme of the paragraph. This should be stated in one's own words. Then the contributing material in the paragraph, which relates to the theme, should be gathered and arranged in its logical order.

By this method of preaching, all the truth contained in this particular paragraph of Scripture is dealt with, opened up and applied to the hearer. Thus the audience is left in no doubt as to what the theme is, or what God's word has to say about this particular subject in the passage under consideration.

2. *The advantages of it.*

(1) *It puts the supreme emphasis on the word of God itself.* It "magnifies the Word," and gives it the place of supreme authority, even as God Himself also does (Ps. 138:2). Furthermore it demands direct contact with the Scriptures. While this style of preaching does lend itself to as great an opportunity for the display of oratorical ability as some other types of sermons, it serves the far better purpose of edifying the people of God as the Scriptures are applied to their everyday lives.

(2) *It makes for a broad knowledge of the Scriptures as a whole.* This applies to both preacher and hearer. The relationship of each part of Scripture to the whole of God's revelation is emphasized, and the hearers are thus built up on their most holy faith.

(3) *It provides an opportunity for speaking on many passages of Scripture which would otherwise be neglected.* There are quite a number of passages in the Bible that receive very little, or no attention. By means of this method of preaching these little known truths will be given their rightful place, and it will be demonstrated that "all Scripture" is essential to fully furnish the man of God (II Tim. 3: 16-17).

(4) *It will also make for variety in the ministry of the Word.* It will deliver the preacher from the common fault of harping on one string, or of over-emphasizing one line of teaching to the exclusion of other truths which are equally needed.

(5) *It enables the preacher to deal with current evils.* Evil practices can be reproved in this way, which would otherwise seem to be too personal, or even impertinent to the audience. The Bible will be seen to be very much up-to-date, for man's heart has not changed through the passing of time. Solomon knew what he was talking about when he declared that there was "no new thing under the sun" (Ecc. 1: 9-10).

(6) *It will deliver the preacher from the tendency to a fanciful use, or abuse of isolated texts.* These will now be seen in their proper setting and their real meaning discovered, appreciated and expounded to the hearers.

(7) *It will furnish the preacher with enough material for a lifetime of preaching.* There will be no need to scrape the barrel for sermon subjects. The expository preacher need never fear he will exhaust the resources

of God's word. He will discover there is "bread enough to eat and to spare" for all who come to it for sustenance, and also a superabundance of Scriptural material for preaching to others.

3. *The dangers of it.*

The chief danger of an expository sermon is that it may easily degenerate into a collection of little and disconnected sermonettes, which have no relation to the central theme. In this type of sermon, *unity* is the great aim and should be in keynote. In other words, each sermon should be a *complete wheel* in itself. It should not consist of a collection of separate spokes, with no hub to bind them together and give completeness to the whole sermon. The sermon must not become involved, or have "wheels within wheels," but must form one complete wheel.

4. *Some hints regarding the preparation of the Expository Sermon.*

(1) *The mode of procedure.*

(a) Select the passage to be expounded.

(b) Discover its main theme, or subject.

(c) This theme should be written out in one's own words, using the logical method of statement.

(d) Discover the contributing thoughts in the passage that throw light on the theme, or spring from the theme.

(e) These should now be written down in one's own words.

(f) Arrange these contributing thoughts, in their logical sequence, as the main divisions of the expository sermon.

(g) Prepare the sermon with these main divisions in view.

(2) *Study books by the masters of this method of preaching.* F. B. Meyer's book entitled "Expository Preaching, is perhaps the best. Alex. Maclaren has been termed "the prince of expositors." His sermons may be secured second hand for a reasonable price, and these will prove to be rich in suggestion, as well as a blessing to one's own soul. It will show how the word of God can be made to speak for itself on any subject necessary to "life and godliness." (II Pet. 1:3).

(3) *Prepare some outlines of Scripture passages for practice.* Constant practice will develop one's ability to analyze and outline. The following passages will be found useful for this purpose. They are all taken from the New Testament, and lend themselves fairly easily to the discovery of the theme and the preparation of an outline for an expository sermon. There are very many more in the Old Testament, particularly the Psalms, that will serve the same purpose.

John 1:1-5; 1:6-14; 1:35-51; 10:1-18; 15:1-27; 17:1-26; Rom. 1:14-17; 3:19-28; 5:1-11; 10:1-11; 12:1-2; I Cor. 9: 16-23; 11:23-34; 13:1-13; 15:1-10; II Cor. 5:1-8; 18-21; Gal. 5:16-26; Eph. 1:1-14; 1:15-23; 2:1-10; 3:14-21; 4:17-32; 5:15-21;6:10-20; Phil. 2:5-11; 2:12-18; 3:4-14; Col. 1:9-17; I Thess. 1:1-10; 4:13-18; 5:14-24; II Thess. 1:11-12; I Tim. 1:12-17; 4:12-16; 6:1-12; II Tim. 1:6-14; 2:1-7; 3:14-17; 4:5-8; Titus 2:11-15; 3:3-7; Heb. 1:1-14; 4:12-14; Heb. 4: 14-16; 7:23-28; 9:11-17; 9:18-28; 12:1-4; 12:18-24; James 1:1-7; 1:12-16; 2:14-18; 5:16-20; I Pet. 1:11-12; 2:11-25; 4:10-11; II Pet. 1:1-11; I John 1:1-10; 3:1-3; 4:7-12; 5:9-13; Rev. 1:10-18; 5:1-14; 22:1-5.

The young preacher would be wise not to attempt the exposition of an entire book of Scripture, but to confine himself to paragraphs that lend themselves, without too much difficulty, to an outline. Later on, as knowledge and ability increases, he could attempt some of the simpler epistles and, from these, go to the more profound.

5. *Some examples of outlines for Expository sermons.*

Three suggestive outlines for an expository sermon follow. Needless to say, all these outlines are merely suggestive. They have purposely been made *much fuller than an experienced preacher would require.* In fact, these outlines could easily be made the subject of *a series of sermons.* The great problem of the beginner is to find sufficient material for the body of the sermon; hence this suggested material is more than will be required as one advances in the experience of preaching. They have also been made as simple as possible, lest a too elaborate treatment of the passage, text, or subject should discourage the beginner.

The persevering student will soon discover for himself the fundamental principles underlying homiletics which, as we have seen, is the science which treats of the preparation and delivery of sermons, or gospel messages. From this elementary beginning, the young preacher should go on to the more involved outlines that will be found necessary as he progresses in his knowledge of the word of God and his ability to expound it.*

(1) "THE DIVINE BENEDICTION."

Our first outline will be Hebrews 13:20-21 Let the reader now turn to this passage and read and re-read it for himself. We shall first seek to discover the central theme of the passage. This could be stated in these words: "God's supreme desire, in this benediction, is for the spiritual maturity of His people." Various titles will suggest themselves. We might call it: "The God-pleasing life," or "The Divine Benediction." We will take the latter as the title, noting as we do that the word benedic-

* See author's book, "Through the Scriptures."

tion comes from two Latin words: "Bene," meaning "well"; "Dico," meaning "saying." This is one of many such benedictions found in the Scriptures, and in our introduction this fact could be touched upon.

Now let us discover the main divisions of this passage which contribute to the theme. These divisions, as we have mentioned before, may be stated in three ways, but each must relate itself to the main theme. It can be in the form of (1) *A proposition,* or the logical form, (2) Or a *phrase,* or the rhetorical form, (3) Or a *question,* or the interrogative form. Each of these methods will aid in making for variety of presentation. The preacher would be well advised, as he prepares his address, to state each main division of his subject in the form of a logical proposition. This will aid him in getting a clear, logical and progressive grasp of his subject.

In this first outline we shall give examples of each of the three methods of stating the main divisions. The main divisions of the outline should be indicated by *Roman numerals* I, II, III, IV, etc. The sub-divisions should be marked by *Arabic numerals* 1, 2, 3, 4, etc. Divisions of these sub-divisions should be noted *by Arabic numerals* in brackets (1), (2), (3), (4); while further divisions of these should be indicated by *small letters in brackets* (a), (b), (c), (d). Still further divisions can be indicated by small Roman numerals in brackets: (i), (ii), (iii), (iv), (v), (vi), (vii).

Now let us examine the passage of Scripture carefully and see, first, what are its *main divisions.* When we have discovered these and stated them we can then determine whether these main divisions, in turn, should be subdivided. In this way, the theme can be closely examined in the light of Scripture and made to yield its full quota of truth in the exposition.

Under Roman numeral I, let us state the first division, first of all in the form of a logical *proposition*.

I. God is the Divine Author of this Benediction.

This is found in the words: "Now may the God of peace."

Now let us state it in the form of a rhetorical phrase:

The Source from Whom it originates.

Thirdly, let us put it in the interrogative form of a question:

From Whom does this Benediction come?

Thus the same thing has been said in *three* different ways. For the sake of variety, each method may be used, but the propositional form is the best, if only to compel the speaker to clarify his thoughts.

Under Roman numeral II, let us now state the second main division:

II. The power of God, behind this Benediction, guarantees its effective operation in the believer.

This arises from the words: "That brought again from the dead our Lord Jesus."

As a phrase it could be stated thus:

The power for its operation.

As a question:

By what power is this Benediction accomplished?

The third main division, stated in this threefold way, could read:

III. Christ, the great Shepherd of the sheep, is the Mediator of this Divine Benediction.

This is deduced from the words: "That great Shepherd of the sheep."

THE TYPES OF SERMONS

As a phrase:
The Person through Whom it is made possible.

As a question:
Who is the Mediator of this benediction?

The fourth main division is:

IV. The procuring cause of this Benediction is the blood of the everlasting covenant.

We learn this from the words: "Through the blood of the everlasting covenant."

As a phrase:
The cost of its provision.

As a question:
By what means was this Benediction procured?

The fifth main division is:

V. The purpose of this Benediction is the spiritual maturity of the believer.

This arises from the words: "Make you perfect (mature) . . . well pleasing in His sight."

As a phrase:
Its effect upon the recipient.

As a question:
What is God's purpose in this Benediction?

The sixth main division is:

VI. This Benediction comes to us through a Divine Person—our Lord Jesus Christ.

This is clearly shown by the words: "Through Jesus Christ."

As a phrase:
The Channel through Whom it is made available.

As a question:
Through Whom does this Benediction come?

The seventh main division is:

VII. This Benediction will bring eternal glory to Christ.

This is seen in the words: "To Whom be glory for ever and ever."

As a phrase:
The ultimate consummation of it.

As a question:
What shall be the outcome of this Benediction upon the One Who made it possible?

The last main division is:

VIII. This Benediction should have the hearty endorsement of every believer.

This is found in the word "Amen," or "So be it."

As a phrase:
The hearty acquiescence of it.

As a question:
What should be the response of the believer to this Benediction?

Thus each main division, whether stated logically, as a proposition: rhetorically, as a phrase; or interrogatively as a question, has a vital bearing on the central theme: "God's supreme desire, in this benediction, is for the spiritual maturity of His people." By this means we have been enabled to discover the main natural divisions, or parts of this passage of Scripture.

Now let us further examine these main divisions and see if they, in turn, can yield further material for the exposition of the passage.

Under the *first division* something could be said about God's other titles, by which He has been pleased to reveal Himself, such as "The God of Consolation" (Rom. 15:5); "Love" (II Cor. 13:11); "Patience" (Rom. 15:5);

"Hope" (Rom. 15:13); "Comfort" (II Cor. 1:3); "Glory" (Acts 7:2), etc.

The distinction could also be drawn between "Peace *with* God" (Rom. 5:1), "The Peace *of* God" (Phil. 4:6, 7), and "The God of *peace*" (Phil. 4:9).

These could be stated in this way. Under Arabic numeral one:

1. *The significance of God's titles.* By them, He reveals His character.

Under Arabic numeral two:

2. *The meaning of this title: "peace."*

Under the *second division* we could show that the supreme exhibition of God's power was manifested in the resurrection of Christ, and that this power is now placed at the disposal of every believer (Eph. 1:19, 20).

We might further show that this power of God is used in at least four ways on the behalf of the believer and express it so: God's:

1. *Power unto Salvation* (Rom. 1:16).

2. *Power unto Stabilization* (Rom. 16:25).

3. *Power unto Preservation* (I Pet. 1:5).

4. *Power unto Presentation* (Jude 24, 25).

Under the *third division,* the emphasis is on the title: "the great Shepherd of the sheep." We could now point out that Christ is the Shepherd in a three-fold sense:

1. *As the good Shepherd,* He laid down His life for the sheep (John 10:11).

2. *As the great Shepherd,* He is risen and ascended, and ever lives to guard and lead His flock (Heb. 7:25; John 10:16).

3. *As the chief Shepherd,* He will come again to reward His flock (I Peter 5:4).

Under the *fourth division,* reference could be made to the everlasting covenant.

1. *The Parties to it.* The triune Godhead: **Father,** Son and Holy Spirit; the eternal counsel (Eph. 1:11; Acts 2:23).

2. *The Period of it.* "Before the foundation of world" (Eph. 1:4; I Pet. 1:20; Rev. 13:8).

3. *The Cost of it.* The blood, i. e., death of Christ. See Luke 22:20, cp. Heb. 9:15-28. Through this blood

(1) *God has been satisfied* (Acts 17:31).

(2) *Justice has been gratified* (Rom. 4:25).

(3) *The law has been magnified* (Heb. 9:22).

(4) *The believing sinner is justified* (Rom. 3:25).

(5) *The believer is sanctified* (Heb. 10:10, 14).

(6) *All the saints shall be glorified* (Rev. 5:9).

Under the *fifth division* something could be said about Christian maturity.

1. *Christian maturity is desired by God:* "Make you mature in every good work to do His will." To do the will of God should be the supreme object of life.

This will of God should be—

(1) Desired (Ps. 143:10).

(2) Known and proved (Rom. 12:1, 2).

(3) Delighted in (Ps. 40:8).

(4) Obeyed (Heb. 13:21).

2. *Christian maturity is produced through God's indwelling power.* He works *within* the believer, "Working in you," cp. Phil. 2:12, 13. The believer is only the channel.

3. *Christian maturity is pleasing to God:* "Well pleasing in His sight." Surely this should be every Christian's

ambition (Col. 1:9; II Tim. 2:4). Illustration: Enoch (Heb. 11:5).

Under the *sixth division* we could note that, through this Person, every blessing flows out to the believer.

1. *Every blessing has been purchased by Christ* (Eph. 1:7, 8). His blood has made them all available.

2. *Every blessing for the believer is in Christ* (Eph. 1:3).

3. *Every blessing comes to us through Christ* (Heb. 13:21).

The prominent word in the *seventh division* is "glory," which means "displayed excellence." We could notice the glory of Christ—

(1) *At His birth* (Luke 2:9-14).

(2) *During His life* (John 17:1-4).

(3) *For eternity* (Rev. 5).

Under the *eighth main division,* little need to be said, except to point out that every true believer, with glad accord, joins to say: "so be it," when glory is ascribed to the Lord Jesus Christ.

This outline, as can be easily appreciated, is very *much fuller* than the average preacher would require. There is enough in it to provide material for *many addresses;* but this has been *purposely done* in order to provide *plenty of material* for the beginner. It will also serve to indicate the many ways by which contributing thoughts may be expanded and developed in the sermon.

By this expository method, with the aid of its divisions and subdivisions, the whole passage of Scripture may be opened up, or expounded, in orderly fashion. Thus the audience is left in no doubt as to what the theme is and what God's word has to say about the passage selected.

(2) "GOD'S RIGHTEOUS SALVATION."
Romans 10: 1-17.

Our second example of an expository sermon shall be Romans 10: 1-17, which should now be read several times by the reader. We shall state the theme: "God's salvation, based on perfect righteousness, is available to all through faith in Christ as Savior, and acknowledgment of Him as Lord." The title could be termed: "GOD'S RIGHTEOUS SALVATION." We shall indicate the main divisions and the subdivisions without any further explanations regarding their presence in the outline.

I. Paul's Passion towards it. Verse 1.

1. *His passion.* Not for Israel's culture, growth, national spirit, sincerity, or religion; but for their *salvation.* See Rom. 9: 1-3. For this he gave himself (I Cor. 9: 22).

2. *His plea.* Directed to God, earnest and continuous. He laid hold upon God for them. (Cp. Isa. 64: 7; 27: 5).

II. Israel's Ignorance of it. Verses 2 and 3.

Four fatal things characterized Israel, which are true of many today.

1. *Zeal without knowledge.* Verse 2.

2. *Ignorance of God's provision.* Verse 3 (Cp. I Cor. 2: 14).

3. *Eagerness to establish their own righteousness.* Verse 3.

4. *Refusal to submit to God's righteousness.* Verse 3.

III. Christ is the Provider of it. Verse 4.

1. *He came to fulfil the law* (Matt. 5: 17).

2. *He lived to magnify it* (Isa. 42: 21).

3. *He took the place of those who had come short of it* (Rom. 3: 23; Isa. 53: 5, 6).

4. *He endured the full penalty of God's righteous judgment* in our stead (Gal. 3:13).

5. *Thus the claims of the law having been satisfied,* a righteousness, apart from the law, has been provided. Verse 4. Cp. Rom. 3:20, 21. It is not an *attained* righteousness through the sinner's own efforts; but an *obtained* righteousness through the merits of Christ's Person and work.

IV. The Scriptures contain the revelation of it.
Verses 5-8.

1. *The righteousness, which is of the law,* is based on perfect obedience to its demands. (Verse 5. Cp. Gal. 3:10, 11). This perfect obedience none has given; therefore all are guilty and condemned.

2. *The righteousness, which is of faith.* Verse 6. This has been

(1) *Bought by Christ.* Verses 6, 7. His precious blood paid the price in full.

(2) *Brought near through the gospel.* Verse 8. Note the word is in the heart and mouth. All that is left for the sinner to do to be saved is to swallow it!

V. Faith is the condition of it. Verses 9, 10.

1. *There must be a heart admission of the truth of the gospel.*

2. *There must be a heart reception of Christ as Savior.*

3. *There must be a heart submission to the Lordship of Christ.*

VI. Confession is the evidence of it. Verses 11, 12.

1. *This confession is Scriptural.* Verse 11.

2. *It is essential.* There is no salvation apart from the confession of the Lordship of Christ in the life. Matt. 10:32, 33.

3. *It is evidential.* It is the proof of an experienced realization of God's righteous salvation. Cp. II Cor. 4:13. True faith always evidences itself. See Heb. 11:13. "Out of the abundance of the heart." Matt. 12:34.

VII. Salvation is the result of it. Verse 13. "Saved."

1. *God's rich provision.* Verse 12, "rich." Cp. James 1:17; Eph. 1:3; Phil. 4:19.

2. *God's great invitation,* "whosoever," Jew or Gentile.

3. *God's wondrous salvation,* "shall be saved."

(1) *Saved* from what? Hell. Job 33:24.

(2) *Saved* to what? Holiness of life. Rom. 6:18.

(3) *Saved* for what? The glory of Christ and service for Him. II Thess. 1:12; Luke 1:74, 75.

VIII. Preaching is the means of it. Verses 14-17.

1. *There must be a preacher.* Verse 14.

2. *The preacher must be sent.* Verse 15.

3. *The preacher must preach the gospel.* Verse 15.

4. *Those to whom he is sent must hear.* Verse 14.

5. *Those who hear must believe.* Verse 14.

6. *Those who believe must call.* Verse 14.

7. *Those who call are saved.* Verse 13.

8. *Those who are saved confess Christ as Lord of their lives.* Verses 9-10.

9. *The conclusion.* Verse 17. "Faith cometh by hearing and hearing by the word of God."

(3) "THE GOSPEL ACCORDING TO PAUL."
I Cor. 15:1-8.

The third example of an outline for an expository sermon, we shall entitle: "The gospel according to Paul." This scripture portion should now be read and re-read.

The theme can be stated thus: "The gospel, given by Divine revelation to Paul, is based on the death, burial, resurrection and glorification of Christ; and is conditioned by faith on the part of the sinner and results in his salvation."

We shall adopt the alliterative style in stating these divisions. That is, the main word will begin with the same letter. This is a good aid to memory, but the preacher should be careful not to overwork this method, for it tends to result in strained and artificial divisions. Inasmuch as "variety is the spice of life," this will also apply to the presenting of the gospel message. In "The Gospel According to Paul," several things suggest themselves in the Scripture portion.

I.   It was a Divine Presentation.

It was revealed to Paul by the glorified Lord, who gave it to him. "I have received," verse 3. It was not something Paul had thought up for himself. Note the other revelations given by the Lord to Paul. Eph. 3:3; I Cor. 11:23; I Thess. 4:15; cp. Gal. 1:11, 12.

II.   It concerns a Divine Person.

"How that Christ," verse 3. Christ is the essence of the gospel. Christianity is Christ and apart from Him there is no Christianity, and no gospel of the grace of God. Paul:

1. *Knew Christ.* He met Him on the Damascus highway (Acts 9).
2. *Lived for Christ* (Gal. 2:20; Phil. 1:21).
3. *Served Christ,* "bond slave" (Rom. 1:1).
4. *Preached Christ* (I Cor. 2:2).

III.   It unfolds a Divine Passion.

"Christ *died.*" This is the great central fact of the gospel.

1. *The Creator of the universe, died* (Col. 1:16-17).

2. *The One "in Whom was life," died* (John 1:4).

3. *The One Who had no sin, knew no sin and did no sin, died* (II Cor. 5:21).

IV.   It reveals a Divine Purpose.

"For our sins." Christ died for, or because of something. Why did He die? He did not die as an Example, or a Reformer, or a Teacher; but as a Divine Substitute for the sinner. The words: "Christ died for our sins" does not represent an offer, appeal, or invitation; but is a *positive statement of an accomplished fact.* This surely implies at least four things:

1. *That we are all sinners.* Christ had no sins of His own, therefore death had no claim on Him. He was therefore bearing the sins of others. Cp. Rom. 3:10-19, 23.

2. *That we were in danger of dying in our sins* and thus being lost eternally; for it took Christ's death to put away our sins (Heb. 9:26; Rom. 6:23).

3. *That Christ assumed the liability of our sins* and, by His death, satisfied all the claims of God against the sinner (Rom. 4:24, 25; 5:1; Isa. 53:5, 6).

4. *That Christ's death is the alone foundation* for the believer's acceptance before God (Rom. 3:24, 26; I Pet. 2:24, 25).

V.   It was according to a Divine Pattern.

"According to the *Scriptures.*" Here is an excellent opportunity to show how Christ was prophesied, pictured and presented in the Old Testament. He was the paschal lamb of Exod. 12. The "serpent lifted up" of Numbers 21. The smitten rock of Exod. 17. The five offerings of Leviticus 1-7, etc. (Illust. Acts 8:35). Cp. Luke 24:25-27, 44; Rom. 3:21.

VI.   It was based upon Divine Proof.

"And that He was *buried.*" There was no doubt as to the death of Christ. The Roman soldiers made sure of

their work of execution and we may be certain it was the
dead body of Christ that was taken down from the cross
and buried in the sealed and guarded tomb.

VII. It was attested by a Divine Proclamation.

"And that He rose again." The resurrection of Christ
is God's proclamation to the world of His entire approval
and eternal acceptance of the finished work of His Son.
See Acts 17:31. The resurrection is God's "amen" to
Christ's: "It is finished" (Rom. 4:25). Note how the early
Christians emphasized this great fact in their preaching.
Acts 2:32; 3:15; 4:2, 10, 33; 5:30; 10:40; 17:18, 31, 32; etc.

1. *The witnesses to the resurrection.* Note the list
given of the actual eyewitnesses to the resurrection in
verses 5-8, of I Cor. 15.

(1) *Peter,*

(2) *Five hundred brethren,*

(3) *James,*

(4) *All the apostles,*

(5) *Paul himself.* Thus the resurrection becomes one
of the best authenticated facts of history.

2. *The resurrection of Christ demonstrates* at least
four things:.

(1) *His essential and eternal Deity* (Rom. 1:4):
Christ prophesied both His death and resurrection (John
10:17, 18; Matt. 16:21).

(2) *The truth of the Old Testament Scriptures,* upon
which Christ placed His Divine seal of approval (Matt.
5:17, 18).

(3) *The certainty of the believer's resurrection,* of
which Christ is both the pattern and pledge (I Cor. 15:12-
25).

(4) *The fact that Christ is to be the ultimate Judge of
all humanity* (Acts 17:30-31).

VIII. It was made known by a Divinely Ordained Preacher.

" I (Paul) preached unto you." This gospel had been

1. *Blest to his own regeneration* (Acts 9:16; Rom. 1:16).

2. *Committed to him as a sacred trust* (Acts 26:16-19; I Tim. 1:11).

3. *Proclaimed by him lovingly and faithfully* (Acts 20:18-24).

4. *Preserved by and defended against error by him* (Gal. 1:6-10; Phil. 1:7; Gal. 2:5).

IX. It resulted in a Divinely assured Possession.

"By which also ye are saved," verse 2.

1. *The certainty of this salvation.* "Ye are saved."

2. *The consequence of this salvation.*

(1) Saved from the *doom* of sin, the lake of fire forever (Rev. 20:12-15).

(2) Saved from the *dominion* of sin in the daily life (Rom. 6:14).

(3) Saved from the *domain* of sin at Christ's second coming (Rev. 21:27).

3. *The continuance in this salvation.* "If ye keep in memory" (or hold fast), verse 2. Continuance is the proof of the reality of one's discipleship and profession (John 8:31). Cp. I John 2:19; Phil. 1:6; Acts 26:22.

These examples should be sufficient to indicate the extreme value of this form of preaching, which thus exposes what the word of God actually says, and makes it possible for all the truth of God to be applied to the audience. Each preacher is earnestly urged to adopt this method, for it is fundamental to sound and profitable preaching.

CHAPTER TWENTY

The Types of Sermons

(Continued)

III. The Textual Sermon.

1. *The definition of it.*

This method of preaching, as its name implies, consists of selecting verses, a verse, or even the part of a verse as a text. After the theme of the verse has been discovered and stated in one's own words, it should be analyzed, divided and expounded in the light of its context. It is similar to the expository method, except that instead of selecting a paragraph containing many verses, the preacher has only one verse, or even part of a verse from which to speak, and must confine himself to impressing this upon his hearers.

2. *The advantages of it.*

(1) *The actual words of Scripture are brought before the people.* This gives Divine authority to the message.

(2) *A short text is more easily retained by an audience.*

While a whole paragraph of the Bible is difficult to retain in the memory, a short text is easily memorized and carried away by the audience.

(3) *It makes for variety in preaching.*

This, in itself, is a desirable thing.

(4) *It is good sometimes to take a number of different verses which contain the same word or thought.*

These may be combined to present the one truth it is desired to emphasize. This is particularly helpful to a beginner who may not be able to preach from a single text, but who would be able to speak briefly from a number of texts, and still feel that he was preaching the word of God. There are many such combinations of texts. D. L. Moody began this way. C. H. Spurgeon was essentially a textual preacher, and all would do well to read his sermons and study his method of treating his texts.

3. *The disadvantages of it.*

The unity of the Bible is not so apparent with this method, as it is with the expository sermon. Texts which are selected here and there throughout the Scriptures, are not likely to impress an audience with the unity of the Bible as a *whole*. The Bible is made to appear to be a book of isolated texts, instead of an organic whole and a complete revelation. Not only so, but the tendency of a textual preacher is to wear out his audience.

4. *Some hints regarding the preparation of an outline for a textual sermon.*

(1) As with the expository sermon, the young preacher would be well advised to take a number of texts that easily lend themselves to divisions, and prepare an outline on these texts for practice purposes. Faithful study, close application and constant practice will bring encouraging results.

(2) *These outlines should be filed away for future reference.* Like the ant, which "prepares its meat in the summer," the young preacher can lay in a good store of very useful material which will stand him in good stead when his mind is not so active. An old preacher, of outstanding ability, was once asked how he managed to prepare such a great variety of sermons. He replied: "I am preaching today from outlines that I prepared before I was twenty years of age." He had used his youth to good advantage: "Go thou and do likewise!"

(3) *Notes should be taken of other preachers treatment of texts.*

It is always advisable to take a notebook and pencil when listening to some other preacher. One can profit by his virtues and be warned by his vices! Be sure and put the name of the preacher on the notes taken of his address.

5. *Some examples of outlines for textual sermons.*

(1) "THE GOSPEL IN SEVEN WORDS." Eph. 2:8.

We will take part of this verse and entitle it as above. The text is: "By grace are ye saved through faith." The theme can be stated thus: "God's salvation, which originates in His infinite grace, is made good in the experience of the sinner on the simple condition of faith." As we examine these seven words, they naturally divide themselves into five main divisions as follows:

    I. "By grace,

    II. are

    III. ye

    IV. saved

    V. through faith."

Now let us look at them closer:

I. "By grace."

This surely indicates the *Source* of salvation.

II. "Are."

This denotes the present *Certainty* of salvation.

III. "Ye."

This defines the *Objects* of salvation.

IV. "Saved."

This opens up the subject of the *Content* of salvation, or what is implied by the term, "saved."

V. "Through faith."

This surely points out the *Medium* by which this salvation is received.

Now let us take the five points one by one and enlarge. For example:

I.   The Source of Salvation: "By grace."

The first question is, "What is grace?" So we place under the Roman numeral "I," the Arabic numeral "1," and thus we have

1. *Its Definition.*

The second question under this first main division is: "Where did it originate, or come from?" So now we put

2. *Its Origin.* God. See I Pet. 5:10.

The third question naturally is: "Through Whom did it come?" or

3. *Its Manifestation.* Christ. See John 1:17; II Cor. 8:9, etc.

II.   The Certainty of this Salvation: "are."

The word, "are," suggests other present tenses of salvation as I Cor. 1:18; 6:11; Acts 13:38; I John 4:17, etc. The subdivisions could therefore be somewhat as follows:

1. *It is a present salvation: "are* saved," not "are *going to be* saved."

2. *It is an assured salvation.* "are." No doubt is suggested. It is not "hope to be," or "might perhaps be," but *"are* saved."

3. *It is a contrasted salvation.* Note the words: *"are* lost," II Cor. 4:3; John 3:19. There are but two classes. Those who "are saved," and those who "are lost."

III.   The Objects of this Salvation: "Ye."

Who are the "ye" spoken of? See Eph. 2:1-3. They were at one time:

1. *Dead in sins,* verse 1.
2. *Depraved through sin,* verse 2a.
3. *Deluded by Satan,* verse 2c.
4. *Disobedient to God,* verse 2c.
5. *Defiled by sin,* verse 3a.
6. *Darkened in mind,* verse 3b.
7. *Doomed because of sin,* verse 3c.

IV. The Content of this Salvation: "Saved."

This word indicates a threefold deliverance of the believer:

1. *From sin's Penalty,* cp. John 5:24.
2. *From sin's Power,* cp. Rom. 6:14.
3. *From sin's Presence at His coming,* cp. Rev. 21:27.

V. The Medium of this Salvation: "through faith."

This naturally demands three subdivisions:
1. *Faith's definition,* or What is faith?
2. *Faith's Object,* Christ.
3. *Faith's result,* the salvation of the believer.

Thus, in a textual sermon, the words of the text must be analyzed, separated into their proper divisions, expounded and applied to the audience. This method applies to all textual sermons.

Now let us take another textual sermon which we shall call:

(2) "CHRIST'S WONDROUS INVITATION."
Matt. 11:28.

The theme could be stated as follows: "Christ invites each laboring and burdened sinner to come to Him and receive, from Him, rest from his labor and ease from his burden." As we examine the words of the text, at least eight things suggest themselves:

I. The Person Who Invites: Christ ... "Me."
Show His Divine authority.

II. The Invitation He Extends: "Come."

A beautiful word. Cp. with other "comes" of the Savior, and of the Scriptures.

III. The Stipulation that He Makes: "Unto Me;"

Not "near," but into living vital touch with Him. Note: not to a religion, to a church, to a rite, form, or ceremony; but to a living Person.

IV. The Description that He Gives: "laboring and heavy laden."

Truly a graphic picture of all by nature—laboring to merit God's favor on the basis of their own efforts, and heavy laden with the load of their sins.

V. The Authorization that He assures: "and I."

Cp. Some of the other "I am's" of Christ.

VI. The Determination He expresses: "will."

All the power of Omnipotence is behind His promise.

VII. The Presentation He Offers: "give."

Not sell, or pay as wages, or temporarily loan; but a free, frank and eternal *gift*.

VIII. The Possession He Guarantees: "rest."

Note the various rests, such as rest of heart, conscience, mind, etc.

For our third textual sermon we shall take the well known words of our Savior as found in John 10:9 and entitle it:

(3) "SEVEN FACTS REGARDING SALVATION."

The theme we shall state as follows: "Christ presents Himself as the alone entrance into salvation and promises, to all who enter, salvation, liberty and satisfaction." The text could be divided as follows, with credit to C. I. Scofield:

I. The Illustration of Salvation: "I am the Door."

A door serves a threefold purpose: 1., Admittance; 2, Protection; 3, Exclusion.

II. The Personification of Salvation: "By Me."

Cp. Acts 4:12; John 14:6; John 6:47; Acts 13:38; Acts 8:35; I Cor. 2:2. "Christianity is Christ."

III. The Invitation of Salvation: "If any man."

Cp. "Whosoever," John 3:16; John 7:37; Rev. 22:17.

IV. The Qualification, or Condition of Salvation: "Enter in."

Not by prayers, penance, good resolves, ordinances, church membership, sincerity, etc.; but a definite entering in. (Illust. Entering into a ship, or stepping through an open door.)

V. The Possession of Salvation: "he shall be saved."

This salvation is assured by His infallible word.

VI. The Emancipation of Salvation: "and shall go in and out:"

i. e., into the presence of God to worship, out into the world to serve Him. See John 8:32, 36; Gal. 5:1; Heb. 10:19 (margin).

VII. The Satisfaction of Salvation: "and find pasture."

Cp. Psa. 23:1, 2.

We have before mentioned that sometimes it is a good plan to take a *number of texts*, which contain the same word, or thought. For example, take Luke 13:23; Mark 10:26; Acts 16:30. Here are three questions about salvation. We could entitle our sermon: "The three questions." The outline would be as follows: I. *An inquisitive question.* II. *An incredulous question.* III. *An imperative question.* Spurgeon preached a famous sermon on seven verses, each of which had in it the words: "I have sinned." There are many other groups of texts awaiting the diligent searcher.* For suggestions on how to interpret the text, look under that heading in a previous chapter.

* See author's book: "The Uplifted Christ."

CHAPTER TWENTY-ONE

The Types of Sermons

(Continued)

The fourth method of preaching is by means of:

IV. The Topical Sermon.

1. *The definition of it.*

This type of sermon consists of choosing a certain subject, or topic and then searching through all the Scriptures to discover what light can be thrown on the subject under consideration. The great doctrines of the Bible would come under this classification.

The topic, or theme, may be likened to a river, and all the Scriptures that throw light upon the topic to the tributary streams that flow into that river. Each division of the topic must have a vital connection with it. Thus every topical sermon, properly prepared and delivered, should possess the threefold quality of unity, coherence and emphasis.

2. *The advantage of it.*

(1) *It enables both preacher and hearer to grasp a subject of the Bible as a whole.*

The Bible is not a book of systematic Theology, where all the teaching on a certain doctrine is grouped together; but these fundamental doctrines are woven into the warp and woof of the Divine revelation from the beginning to the end.

(2) *It affords ample opportunity for a thorough discussion of the subject.*

This, if necessary, can be dealt with by a *series* of sermons. This should serve to create a sustained interest on the part of the hearers.

(3) *It impresses an audience with the unity of holy Scripture.*

They will be brought to see that the Bible is one harmonious *whole*. As one scripture passage is compared with another scripture quotation, the Divine unity of God's revelation will be emphasized.

(4) *The great doctrines of the Bible can best be studied by this method.*

The vital fundamental truths of Scripture can be examined, expounded and applied in this way. Within this Book is found the doctrine of God, Christ, the Holy Spirit, the inspiration of the Bible, the Church, Redemption, Salvation, Faith, Regeneration, Sanctification, Prayer, Worship, Heaven, Hell, etc.

(5) *It makes for variety of presentation.*

This method of preaching therefore deserves a place in the ministry of God's word.

3. *The disadvantages of it.*

(1) *The range of topics is necessarily limited.*

It must be remembered that the Bible is not a mere compilation of topics for preachers.

(2) *This method of preaching will soon exhaust the preacher.*

Sooner or later, if he persists in limiting himself to this method of preaching, he will find himself running out of topics for his sermons.

4. *The method of preparing an outline for a topical sermon.*

A different plan of preparation is required for this type of discourse. The theme has already been determined by the selection of the topic, and now the whole Bible must contribute material for its elucidation.

(1) *A series of questions should be asked in relation to the topic.*

These are seven in number and should be asked in the following order of sequence.

(a) *What?*

This will define the subject and answer the question: "What am I going to talk about?" This will also serve to introduce the topic.

(b) *Why?*

This will take care of the necessity for, or the reason why this particular subject has been selected and is to be expounded.

(c) *How?*

This will answer all the queries as to the essential circumstances under which this subject was made available; the conditions upon which it can be received and its promises fulfilled in the experience of the hearer.

(d) *Who?*

This will include both the origin of the topic and the people to whom it is made available. Who provided it? Who may receive it? Thus the *personal element* is indicated by this question.

(e) *Where?*

This will suitably describe, either the source from which the topic comes, or the place where the subject may be received or experienced.

(f) *When?*

This will take care of the time element. When may this thing be received?

(g) *What then?*

This will adequately provide for the application of the topic to the hearer.

It will help to remember these questions if the following rhyme, somewhat adapted, is memorized:

> "I have seven faithful serving men,
>   Who taught me all I ken;
>   Their names are What, Why, How and Who,
>   And Where, When, and What-Then."

(2) *Any topic under the sun may be logically arranged and presented in an orderly fashion, by answering these seven questions.*

Take, for instance, a watch. Using these questions, here is an outline for a talk on this subject.

(a) *What is the subject?* A watch.

(b) *Why talk about it?* It is a most necessary thing. It tells time and enables us to keep appointments, etc.

(c) *How did this watch come to be?* Describe its manufacture. Its various parts, the skill required, the cost of its construction.

(d) *Who supplies this watch?* Or, *Who may have a watch?* Describe the manufacture and the people who may possess one.

(e) *Where can such an article be obtained?* Describe the location of the shop where the watch can be purchased.

(f) *When can it be secured?* Point out the splendid opportunity that is theirs of getting one immediately at this favorable price.

(g) *What then?* Urge upon each to get one right away.

It matters not what the subject may be. A workable outline of an address on it may be prepared by answering these seven questions.

(3) *An outline that embodies these questions.*

These will serve *the same purpose* as these questions and provide variety in presentation.

(a) *The Introduction.* This takes care of the "What?"

(b) *The Necessity for.* This will answer all questions under the "Why?"

(c) *The Nature of.* This corresponds to the "How?"

(d) *The Person who.* Here is the "Who?"

(e) *The Place Where.* This answers the question "Where?"

(f) *The Time when.* This takes care of the "When?"

(g) *The Conclusion.* This provides for the "What then?"

(4) *By following this method,* an orderly, logical, and full treatment of any topic is assured.

5. *Now let us consider some examples of Topical Outlines.*

(1) Subject, *"THE NEW BIRTH."** Scripture to read: John 3: 1-19. The Scripture to be read should be selected as the one that best presents the subject. It is impossible, of course, to read all the scriptures to the audience that relate to this or any other subject.

I. Introduction, or What?

Our subject is one of vital importance to all, for apart from it no one can either see or enter the kingdom of God.

1. *It is one of the great "musts" of the Bible.* Boiled down to the irreducible minimum, there are only three musts for humanity.

(1) We *must* die.

(2) We *must* meet God.

(3) If we are ever to see or enter the kingdom of God, we *must* be born again, or from above.

2. *What the new birth is not:* It is not

(1) a *social* change.

* See author's book: "Ye must be born again."

(2)   a *physical* change.

(3)   a *local* change.

(4)   a *religious* change.

(5)   a *moral* change.

(6)   an *intellectual* change.

3.   What the new birth is.

It is a *spiritual* change, or the communication of a spiritual life.

4.   *Notice the person who came* and to whom this truth was stated.   He was not immoral, or irreligious but, on the contrary, was most religious, moral and sincere *but* he had not been born from above.

II.   The Necessity for the new birth, or Why must a man be born again?

1.   *The flesh is flesh,* verse 6.   The flesh is that principle of enmity against God which every person receives by natural birth.   Like can only produce like.   It may be educated, religiously inclined, etc., but it still remains "flesh."   While in the flesh no one can please God.   See Romans 8:5-8.

2.   *Man, by nature, is dead in his sins;* cp. Eph. 2:1; 4:18; etc.   He therefore needs a new *life.*   The new birth is the impartation of this new life to the believing sinner.

3.   *The kingdom of God is a spiritual experience* (Rom. 14:17), therefore the sinner must be spiritually prepared for it by the Spirit of God.   The new birth is "from above." (Margin)

III.   The nature of the new birth, or How can a man be born again?

1.   *By the word of God, believed and obeyed.* "Water," verse 5; cp. I Pet. 1:23; James 1:17.   God's word reveals both the sinner's need and the remedy God provides for it.

2. *By the Spirit of God,* verse 5. He it is who applies the word, convicts of sin and regenerates the soul who believes. (John 16:13, 14; Eph. 1:13; John 7:38).

3. *By faith in the substitutionary sacrifice of Christ,* i. e.. "The Son of Man lifted up." Verse 14.

4. *By believing on Christ.* Verse 15. i. e. Appropriating Him, as one's own personal Savior.

IV. The subjects of the new birth, or Who must be born again?

1. *The religious,* moral, and sincere, like Nicodemus, the ruler of the Jews.

2. *The educated,* like Paul.

3. *The immoral profligate,* like the thief on the cross.

4. *All people,* irrespective of race, color or creed.

V. The place of this new birth, or Where can a man be born again?

1. *It must take place on earth, for after death* it is too late.

2. *Wherever* a guilty sinner believes the gospel and trusts the Savior, *there* the new birth takes place. Eph. 1:13.

VI. The time when the new birth may be experienced? or Where can a man be born again?

1. God has only one time; *Now.* Cp. II Cor. 6:1, 2; Prov. 27:1; James 4:13-15.

2. *The danger of procrastination.* Heb. 2:3.

VII. The results of the new birth, or What then?
It produces:

1. A new *creation* (II Cor. 5:17).

2. A new *designation* (Isa. 62:2). "Christians," etc.

3. A new *occupation* (Eph. 4:24; I Pet. 2:2).

4. A new *inspiration* (Psa. 40:2, 3; Rev. 5:9; new songs).

5. A new *ambition* (II Cor. 5:9) to please Him.

6. A new *adoration, worshipping God,* (Heb. 10:19-22; John 4:23, 24).

7. A new *habitation* (Rev. 21:1; John 14:1-3; II Pet. 3:13).

Now make the application to the audience and inquire: "Have *you* been born from above?"

(2) For the second topical sermon we will take the subject of *"REDEMPTION."*

Scripture to read: Rom. 3:19-31.

Introduction: The Bible is not a book of history, science, philosophy, or morals, etc., though all it says on these subjects is absolutely authoritative; but it is a book devoted to the revelation of one Person: Christ, and the exposition of one theme: Redemption.

I.   Its meaning:

1. *To buy back.*
2. *To ransom or deliver.* Illus. Exod. 13:13.

II.   Its necessity.

1. *Man is sold under sin* (Rom. 7:14; Isa. 52:3).
2. *He is the slave of sin* (Rom. 6:16; John 8:34).
3. *He is condemned through sin* (John 3:18; Rom. 3:19; Job 36:16).
4. *He is helpless to deliver himself from sin* (Rom. 7:18, 19; 5:6; Eph. 2:1).

III.   Its Accomplisher: Christ.

The Redeemer must possess at least four qualifications according to Scripture.

1. *He must have the will to redeem.* This He proved by His coming (Luke 4:18; Mark 10:45; Luke 19:10, etc.).

2. *He must have the right to redeem* (Lev. 25:48; cp. Ruth 2:20; Heb. 2:14). He became Man to obtain this right.

3. *He must have the power to redeem.* All power is His. (Heb. 7:26; Luke 5:24; Rom. 1:4; Matt. 28:18, etc.).

4. *He must have the price to redeem* (Heb. 9:22; Lev. 17:11; Gal. 2:20; Heb. 9:12).

IV.   Its condition.

1. *Faith in the fact of His redemptive work* (Rom. 3:24, 25).

2. *Acceptance of the Redeemer's Person* as one's own personal Savior (John 1:12).

3. *Acknowledgment of the Redeemer's Ownership and Lordship* (Rom. 10:9, 10).

V.   Its results.

1. *Freedom from sin's slavery* (Gal. 3:13; 5:1; John 8:36; Rom. 6:18-22).

2. *Forgiveness of sins* (Eph. 1:7; II John 1:9; Col. 1:14; Acts 13:38).

3. *Justification before God* (Rom. 3:24; 5:1).

4. *Peace with God* (Col. 1:20; Rom. 5:1).

5. *Assurance from God* (Luke 1:77; I John 5:13).

6. *Godliness of walk with God* (Titus 2:14).

7. *Heaven with God for eternity* (Rev. 5:9).

CHAPTER TWENTY-TWO

The Types of Sermons

(Continued)

The fifth method of preaching the gospel and teaching the word of God is:

V.   The Historical Incident Sermon.

1.   *The definition of it.*

In this type of sermon, a Bible incident is taken as the subject, and the spiritual lessons it contains applied as the story is unfolded.   It is thus allied to the expository method, in that the whole passage containing the incident is taken, and its spiritual meaning expounded and applied. The difference, of course, is that *the story* is the theme, and the parallel spiritual truths are discovered and applied, right through to the end of the sermon.

2.   *The advantages of it.*

(1)   *All the world loves a story.*

The stories of the Bible are incomparable.   They reveal almost every phase of character and present practically every situation that can arise in human experience. Roy L. Laurin, in his excellent book: "Meet yourself in the Bible," states that there are around thirty-six basic dramatic situations found in literature and drama.   All the plots of novels and plays are based on either one or more of these fundamental situations such as fear, frustration, inferiority, anxiety, hatred, envy, etc.   All these various situations are found in the Bible, so that one has only to read the Scriptures to "meet himself" in the Bible.

(2)   *A wide range of sermon material is here provided.*

277

This includes all the Old Testament stories, the New Testament incidents and the parables of Christ. George Goodman has written three books, each containing seventy outlines of Bible stories. These should be in every preacher's library, for they are full of rich suggestive material for this type of preaching. His book: "What to teach and how to reach the young" is the classic on the subject, and all preachers should "read, mark and inwardly digest" it.

(3) *The incidents of the Bible, particularly the Old Testament, have been specially recorded for this purpose.*

We are left in no doubt as to this fact, for we read: "For whatsoever things were written aforetime, were written for our learning, that we through patience and comfort of the scriptures might have hope." Regarding the turbulent history of Israel, it is written: "Now all these things happened unto them for ensamples: (or types) and they were written for our admonition, upon whom the ends of the world (age) are come" (Rom. 15:4; I Cor. 10:11). Augustine's well known comment is to the point: "In the Old, the New is *latent;* in the New, the Old is *patent.*" Thus teaching the word of God from these incidents recorded in both Old and New Testaments has the full endorsement of Scripture.

3. *The disadvantages or dangers of it.*

The chief danger is the over spiritualization of the incident, and pushing the application of it to an extreme that is not warranted by the teaching of the rest of the Bible. Particularly is this true of the parables, which only serve the purpose of *illustrating* a doctrine, and clarifying but *one aspect* of a *truth.* For instance, there is no atonement in the parable of the prodigal son. Some preachers have felt it necessary to include this in the story, and have consequently used the killing of the fatted calf to illustrate this doctrine! The parable of the wise and foolish virgins has been used to teach the false theory of a partial rapture of Christians. The preacher should beware of forcing any story beyond its proper limits, and making it teach what is not substantiated by the *general* teaching of all the Scriptures.

A parable has been likened to a sphere and a doctrine to a plane. When a sphere is placed upon a plane, it touches the plane at *one point only*. In order to make that sphere touch the plane at more than one point at a time, the sphere must be broken. A parable therefore touches a doctrine at one point only. It serves the excellent purpose, designed by the Lord, of illustrating just one phase of doctrinal truth. Almost any false theory can be taught by using a parable for its *basis* of doctrine instead of using it as an *illustration* of Scripture teaching.

For instance, the parable of the prodigal son illustrates the love of God for sinners, and His willingness to pardon, cleanse and relieve them. The wise and foolish virgins points out the necessity for preparation in view of the second coming of Christ. The sower and the seed drives home the responsibility of the hearer of the word to both hear, receive and reproduce the good seed sown upon his heart. The Bible has been made to suffer at the hands of its "friends" as well as its enemies, as evidenced by the multitude of sects and cults, all of which claim support from its pages. Truly: "the abuse of the best is the worst."

4. *The preparation of the outline.*

(1) Consult parallel accounts.

In preparing an outline for this type of sermon, it is necessary to consult other references to the incident which are recorded in other books. For instance, an incident described in I and II Kings may be referred to again in I and II Chronicles. The same is true of the four gospels. The miracle of the feeding of the five thousand is common to each gospel. It will therefore be necessary to consult each account to get the overall picture of this event.

(2) *The divisions are determined by the movement of the story.*

Each main movement will become a main division. Proceed, in chronological order from the beginning to the end, and discover and apply the spiritual lessons from the *historical record*. The whole picture must be kept firmly in mind and one's sanctified imagination used to the best advantage to make the story and its application *live* in the minds of the hearers.

Let us now consider some examples of outlines on historical-incident sermons.

(1) "THE TEN LEPERS." Luke 17:11-19.

I. Their Condition, verses 11, 12.

Typical of the unsaved.

1. *Unclean.* Cp. Lev. 13:45; Isa. 64:6; Psa. 14:2, 3; Job 15:14-16; Isa. 6:5.

2. *Afar off.* Cp. Eph. 2:13; Isa. 59:2; Luke 18:13; Rev. 18:10; Luke 16:23.

3. *Without hope.* There was no cure by human means and they were helpless to save themselves; cp. John 3:18, Jer. 17:9; Rom. 5:6.

II. Their cry, verse 13.

1. *In the right spirit*: earnest, "lifted up;" cp. Jer. 29:13; Isa. 55:6; Rom. 10:13.

2. *In the right attitude*: humble, "mercy." They didn't demand their "rights," for they had none; but pled for mercy; cp. Micah 7:18, 19; Psa. 103:8, 10, 11; Matt. 9:13.

3. *To the right Person.* "Jesus." See Matt. 1:21; Acts 4:12; John 14:6, etc.

4. *At the right time.* While Christ was present. Cp. Prov. 27:1; Isa. 55:6; II Cor. 6:2. The opportunity of a lifetime must be grasped in the lifetime of the opportunity.

III.   Their Cure, verse 14.

1. *The word given;* "go," cp. Rom. 10:6-9; cp. "Come," Matt. 11:28; "Look," Isa. 45:22; "Hear," John 5:24, and "Receive," John 1:12.

2. *The word obeyed*—the obedience of faith; Rom. 16:26; 6:17; Heb. 4:2.

3. *The cleansing experienced.* Note it was "as they went" they were cleansed. They had no *experience* of the change at the time, yet they acted as cleansed ones. It was not by their "feelings" or by "sight," but *faith* in the bare word of Christ. cp. John 6:47, I John 5:13.

IV.   The Thankful One, verses 15-19.

His gratitude was expressed by—

1. *His turning back from the types* and shadows of law to the Antitype Himself; cp. Matt. 8:4; Gal. 4:9; Heb. 10:1-14.

2. *His hearty giving of thanks,* verse 6; by this he glorified God. CP. Psa. 50:23, 14, 15; Eph. 5:20; Phil. 4:6; Col. 1:12; I Thess. 5:18.

3. *His humility,* "at His feet;" cp. Luke 7:38; 8:35; 10:39.

4. *His worship,* "on his face;" cp. John 4:23, 24; Heb. 10:19-22.

The next historical incident we shall consider is:

(2)   "THE TOUCH OF FAITH." Mark 5:25-34.

I.   Her Condition, verses 25, 26.

1. *Defiled.* Verse 25; cp. Isa. 6:5; Prov. 30:12.

2. *Outcast.* Verse 25; cp. Lev. 15:19, 20; Isa. 59:2; Habak. 1:13; Amos 5:12.

3. *Suffering.* Verse 26; cp. Prov. 5:22; Gen. 3:17; Gal. 6:7; Num. 32:23.

4. *Penniless.* Verse 26; Illus. Luke 7:41, 42; Matt. 5:26, 27; Luke 15:14-20; Rom. 5:6.

5. *Hopeless.* Verse 26; cp. Eph. 2:12; Rom. 8:5-8.

II.   Her Faith, verses 27, 28.

1. *Faith's basis.* Verse 27. She had doubtless *heard* of the healing of the demoniac, which had just occurred previously; Mark 5:15; cp. Rom. 10:17.

2. *Faith's Simplicity.* She *believed* in His ability to save, verse 28; cp. Heb. 11:6; Mark 9:23; Luke 8:50.

3. *Faith's boldness.* She came *in spite of the crowd,* verse 24; cp. Prov. 29:25; Ezek. 2:6; Jer. 1:8; 29:13.

4. *Faith's attitude.* She came *as she was,* verse 24; cp. Matt. 11:28; Isa. 46:12, 13.

5. *Faith's Objective.* She came to *Him,* the only One that could meet her deep need, verse 27; cp. Acts 5:31; John 3:16; John 1:12.

III.   Her Blessing, verses 29-34.

1. *She was cured.* Verse 29.

2. *She confessed.* Verse 33. Based on knowledge. Rom. 10:5-10; Mark 8:36; I John 4:16.

3. *She was comforted and assured.* Verse 34; cp. Luke 8:48; Rom. 5:1; 4:5; Gal. 2:16, etc.

As in the case of the other types of sermons, it is good to select a number of these stories and prepare an outline on them for practice purposes.

CHAPTER TWENTY-THREE

The Types of Sermons

(Continued)

The last type of sermon we shall consider is:

VI. The Biographical Sermon.

1. *The definition of it.*

This consists of the study of a person's life and the lessons to be learned from it; how we may be warned by his failures and encouraged by his successes. It is really the study of a person's character which, in turn, determines his career.

2. *The advantages of it.*

(1) *Biographies make both interesting and valuable reading.* They are profitable for a three-fold purpose.

(a) *Information.*

Human nature is perhaps the most fascinating of all studies.

(b) *Inspiration.*

The study of the life story of a man of God is, in itself, a spiritual stimulus. It awakens and develops a desire for greater godliness of life.

(c) *Imitation.*

It should lead to a desire to follow the example of this godly person. Paul could say: "Be ye followers (imitators) of me, even as I am of Christ" (I Cor. 11:1).

(2) *Much sermon material is available from this source.*

The eleventh chapter of Hebrews has been aptly termed: "The Westminster Abbey of the heroes of faith." Many of the biographies therein described contain enough material for a series of addresses.

(3) *Biographical preaching makes for that variety which is so necessary to effective preaching.*

It provides an opportunity to present needed truth in a different form, and the hearers may be brought to see themselves, as mirrored in the life of another.

3. *The mode of procedure in preparing the outline.*

After the character has been selected:

(1) *Read all the Bible has to say* regarding him or her, again and again, until every detail of the life has become familiar.

(2) *Select what appear to be the outstanding events of this person's life.*

(3) *Draw up a list of his chief characteristics.*

What were his weaknesses and what were his good points?

Jeff D. Ray suggests three questions to ask of a character. whether good or bad.

(a) What sort of person was this?

(b) What made him this sort of person?

(c) What resulted from his being this sort of person?

(4) *Discover the cause, preventative and cure of his weaknesses.*

These weaknesses must not be glossed over, or minimized, for much can be learned from these things.

(5) *Learn the secret of his virtues.*

(6) *The lessons learned must be applied,* first to one's own life, and then passed on to the audience.

(7) *Prepare an outline of his life in its chronological order.*

Make each outstanding event, or characteristic, a main division.

(8) *Read the best of biographical sermons.*

Alex. Whyte's "Bible Characters" is good. F. B. Meyer's books on this form of preaching are perhaps the best, and are of real inspirational and devotional value. Edersheim's, "Life and Times of Jesus, the Messiah," is the classic on this subject. Kraumacher, on Elijah and

Elisha are excellent examples of what can be done in this line.

4. *Example of a biographical sermon outline.*

We will consider the life of

Enoch.

The Scriptures are Gen. 5:18, 21-24; Heb. 11:5, and Jude 14.

Introduction.

Though Enoch is one of the best known characters of Scripture, yet his biography is limited to four verses in the Old Testament and three in the New Testament. Compare this with the ponderous tomes that describe the lives of the worldly great.

I.   His birth. Gen. 5:18.

He was the seventh from Adam and was born 622 years after the Fall. He was therefore contemporaneous with Adam for over 300 years. Thus he heard all about sin's entrance, its judgment and God's provision of salvation from its penalty.

II.   His Conversion. Gen. 5:22.

1. *The circumstances.* At birth of Methusaleh, when he was 65 years of age. He had faith, but "faith cometh by hearing." Therefore God must have spoken to him and he believed and walked with Him. Doubtless God spoke to him in the birth of his son. Perhaps, as Enoch took the baby in his arms he wondered: "Is this child to grow up and follow the wicked example of the men that surround me?" He thus began to think of God and reach out after Him. He repented of his sins and turned from them to walk with God and live for Him. God uses many methods to bring eternal realities before the soul, and thus lead the sinner to Him. See Job 33:14-24.

2. *The result.* He walked with God. This is always the effect of a true conversion, whatever the circumstances surrounding it may be.

(1)   His previous walk was similar to that described in Ephesians 2:2, etc.

(2)   His present walk. Cp. Eph. 2:10; 4:1-3; 5:1, 2, 15.

III.   His walk or manner of life.

1.   *The implications of this walk.* Walking with God was no easier then than now, and it implies at least three things. See Matt. 7:13, 14.

(1)   *Reconciliation.* One must be united to God. How? By virtue of a sacrifice provided, offered and accepted. Cp. Romans 5:11 (marg.).

(2)   *Harmony,* Amos 3:3. *Oneness of purpose,* I John 1:7; Deut. 23:14.

(3)   *Continuance.* For 300 years; cp. John 8:31.

2.   *The description of his walk.* Cp. Titus 2:14.

(1)   *He walked with God* before his family in the home. Gen. 5:22.

(2)   *He walked with God* before the world. See Jude 14.

(3)   *He walked with God* in his own soul. Heb. 11:5. He had "the testimony," which consisted of a peace, joy, satisfaction and fellowship that is better experienced than described. Paul had it too (Phil. 3:8).

IV.   His Testimony.

He pleased God; Heb. 11:5, 6.

1.   *By his faith.* Heb. 11:6.

2.   *By his life.* Cp. Col. 1:10; I Tim. 6:11. A clean, honorable and truthful life.

3.   *By his witness to the world.* Jude 14. He confessed his faith and boldly stood for God against the world. Matt. 10:32.

V.   His Prophecy.

Jude 14, 15.

1.   *His denunciation* against false teachers.

2.   *His proclamation* "The Lord cometh." Here is the first prophecy of Christ's second coming.

3. *His condemnation*. Verse 15. The absolute certainty of future judgment to be visited on (1) the ungodly deeds, (2) the ungodly words, (3) of ungodly sinners.

VI. His Translation.

Gen. 5:24; Heb. 11:5.

1. *The Translation*. Taken up into God's presence without dying.

2. *The Type*. The translation of the Church (I Thess. 4:13-18).

These six types of sermons will serve to suggest the variety of presenting both the gospel and teaching message. It would be well to use each method as led by the Spirit, for each has some particular virtue to commend it; but the foundation of all preaching is the *expository* method, particularly if one is ministering to the same congregation regularly.

Each preacher would do well to covet ardently and develop assiduously the ability to become an able expository preacher. In this way, the *whole word of God* can be opened up, and he can give all the word of God to all the people of God. Someone has said: "The topical preacher soon wears *himself* out. The 'text tag' preacher soon wears his *hearers* out. The expository preacher has a field so wide and rich that one lifetime is not long enough to till and reap it."

The Bible offers a marvelous scope in the variety of sermon material, with its great doctrines, dispensations, types, prophecies, psalms, proverbs, incidents, conversations, ethics, warnings and commendations, etc. Inasmuch as all Scripture is necessary to the complete furnishing of the man of God (II Tim. 3:16, 17); each preacher of the word of God should seek to draw from this enexhaustible mine of Divine truth that which will lead souls to Christ, and also build up his hearers in their most holy faith.

CHAPTER TWENTY-FOUR

The Title of the Sermon

It is not enough to discover the theme of a passage of Scripture, draw up an outline of its main divisions and prepare a sermon on it. It is also necessary to find a suitable *title* for this sermon.

I. The advantage of it.

Its chief advantage is for advertising purposes. Some do not believe much in advertising, but D. L. Moody aptly said: "Some preachers think it undignified to advertise their services. I think it is a great deal more undignified to preach to empty pews!"

God wants people to hear the gospel. The evangel is not a secret thing to be whispered in strict privacy, but a glorious proclamation to be heard by the whole world. God declares: "I have not spoken in secret, in a dark place of the earth: I said not unto the seed of Jacob: 'Seek ye Me in vain;' I, the Lord, speak righteousness. I declare things that are right." In another place He says: "Cry aloud and spare not, lift up your voice like a trumpet, and show My people their transgression and the house of Jacob their sins" (Isa. 45: 19-22; 58:1).

If advertising will bring out the unsaved to hear the gospel, then by all means advertise. Needless to say, this should be made as attractive as possible. The Lord's work demands the best we can give. A good title for a sermon has real advertising value; therefore it is of no small importance to choose a title that will arouse attention and bring hearers under the sound of the regenerating word of God.

II. Some principles that should guide in its selection.

(1)   In the first place, one should avoid the fantastical, and the ultra sensational.   A preacher once advertised that he would speak on: "The Man in the Moon."   Just what he had to say about this non-existent gentleman is difficult to imagine.

(2)   Secondly, the title should not promise more than can be delivered in the address.   To merely use some startling title to attract an audience, and then fail to fulfil the promise made in the title is to make the audience feel it has been tricked and its intelligence outraged.

(3)   Thirdly, the title should be designed so as to catch the eye, arouse the curiosity and awaken the desire of the man in the street to hear a message on that particular subject.   In the choosing of the title, our Savior's words should be heeded: "Be ye wise as serpents and harmless as doves" (Matt. 10:16).

To this end, each preacher should be a careful observer of how other preachers advertise their subjects.   He can gain much valuable information in this way and also be warned what not to do along this line.

III. Methods of stating the title.

There are many ways of stating the title.

1.   *It could be put in the form* of an arresting question, such as: "After Death—What?"   "Where are the dead?" "Where is heaven?"   "Who is the greatest Man alive?" (Christ).   "Can a man be sure he is eternally saved?" "What is the world's greatest sin?"   "Where do we go from here?"

2.   *Then again, it can be stated in the form of a common phrase.*   A talk on the word "own" in Scripture, as found in Deut. 24:16; Mark 8:36; Acts 1:25; Phil. 2:12; could be entitled "Your Own Business."   A sermon on

the world "Behold," could be termed "Sights Worth Seeing." Such titles as "Things Worth Knowing," "Things Worth Having," "Things Worth Taking," "Bad Bargains," "Dead Certainties," "Excuse Me!" (Luke 14: 16-24), "Stop, Look! Listen!" (Habak. 2: 1), all have an interesting value.

3. *The title may also be expressed* in terms of interesting topics such as: "God's Dynamite" (Rom. 1: 16); "The Unanswerable Question" (Heb. 2: 3); "Heavenly Welding" ("What God hath joined together"); "A Great General's Three Mistakes" (Naaman); "The Greatest Text in the Bible" (John 3: 16); "The Great Divide" (John 7: 43; 9: 16; 10: 19); "David's D. D.'s" (I Sam. 22: 1, 2). "The Man Who Didn't Die" (Gen. 5: 24); "The Failure of a Successful Man" (Luke 12: 20); "When Chickens Come Home to Roost" (Esther 7: 10); "A Failure Who Made Good" (Acts 15: 3; II Tim. 4: 11); "High Finance" (Mark 8: 36); "From the Pit to Paradise" (Ps. 40: 1-3); "Something About Nothing"; "How the Thief Got In" (Luke 23); "Cheering Cheers;" "The Freedom of Slavery" (I Cor. 7: 22); "Seeing the Invisible" (II Cor. 4: 18); "God's 'Who's Who' " (Phil. 4: 3); "God's Panoply" (Eph. 6: 10-17); "The Storm King" (Luke 12: 29); "The Soul's Migration" (John 5: 24); "The Last Call" (Rev. 22: 17); "Unbelieving Believers" (Luke 24: 25); "The man who played the fool" (I Sam. 26: 21); "The Unfinished Sentence" (Luke 4: 16-20); "Bankrupt Billionaires" (Rev. 2: 9).

4. *Lastly, the title could be suited* to some special occasion. *For Christmas Day*: "When God Came to Earth;" "The Celestial Anthem" (Luke 2: 9-14); "The Star-led Pilgrimage" (Matt. 2: 1-12). *For the New year* such titles as: "New Things for Old;" "Three Good Resolutions" (Habak. 2: 1; Luke 15: 17-19; Isa. 12: 2). *For Independence Day*: "The Liberty Bell" (Lev. 25: 10; Isa. 61:

1; Rom. 8:21; Gal. 5:1); "Independent Dependents" (set free from sin to serve God, Rom. 6:22). *For Thanksgiving day*: "The Ten-stringed Instrument" (Ps. 92:1-4); "The Directory of Praise" (Ps. 150); "The Profit of Praise" (Ps. 50:23).

IV. Some Titles gleaned from famous preachers.

From Alex Maclaren: "The delays of love" (John 11: 5-6); "The universal Magnet" (John 12:32); "The prodigality of love" (John 12:1-11); "Simeon's swan song" (Luke 2:29-30); "The limits of liberty" (Rom. 14:12-23); "The Three Tribunals" (I Cor. 4:3-4); "The sin of silence" (I Cor. 9:16-17); "The death of death" (I Cor. 15:20-21, 50-58); "Light at eventide" (II Tim. 4:1-5; 16-17); "The Secret of immortal youth" (Isa. 40:30-31); "Obedient disobedience" (Acts 4:19-31).

From G. H. Morrison: "Elective Affinity" (Acts 4:23); "The Opening Note" (II Chron. 29:27); "So near, and yet so far" (Mark 12:34).

From J. H. Jowett: "The Rear Guard" (Ps. 23:6); "Daybreak in the Soul" (Isa. 9:1-7); "A Fatal Divorce" (II Kings 17:23-34); "The Possibilities of the Unlikely" (Matt. 9:9-13); "Life's Real Values" (Prov. 8:10-19); "The Larger Outlook" (Gen. 15:5-18).

From Oswald Chambers: "The Constraint of the Call" (I Cor. 9:16); "The Relinquished Life" (Gal. 2:20); "Yes . . . But . . . !" (Luke 9:61); "The Sacrament of Sacrifice" (John 7:38); "The Transfigured Life" (II Cor. 5:17).

The late Dr. A. C. Dixon once preached twenty-one sermons from the text: "God forbid that I should glory, save in the cross of our Lord Jesus Christ" (Gal. 6:14). The following are the titles he gave these sermons, under the general heading of: *"The Glories of the Cross."*

"In its Deeper Meaning"—Phil. 2: 5-8.
"In its Dynamic"—I Cor. 1:18.
"In its Magnetism"—John 12: 32.
"In its Necessity"—John 3:14.
"In its Vicariousness"—I Cor. 5: 7, 8.
"In the Liberty It Gives"—John 8: 36; Rev. 1: 5, 6.
"In the Character It Builds"—Heb. 13: 20, 21;
    Phil. 3: 8-11.
"In the Enemies It Makes"—Phil. 3: 18, 19.
"In the Remission of Sins It Insures"—Luke 24: 45-47;
    Heb. 9: 12.
"In the Peace It Produces"—Col. 1: 19, 20.
"In the Atonement It Effects"—Rom. 3: 21-26.
"In the Redemption It Brings"—Rev. 5: 9, 10; Eph. 1: 7;
    I Pet. 1: 18, 19.
"In the Victories It Gains"—Rev. 12: 11.
"In the Soul-food It Furnishes"—John 6: 53-56.
"In the Standing before God It Gives"—II Cor. 5: 20, 21.
"In the Covenant It Confirms"—I Cor. 11: 25.
"In the Testings It Applies"—Gal. 5: 11.
"In the Love It Commands"—Rom. 5: 8.
"In the Heaven It Makes"—Rev. 5: 6, 7; Rev. 5: 9-17.
"In the Hell It Destroys"—I John 3: 8.

These suggestions should serve to show the possibilities and value of sermon titles, and all young preachers would do well to make the title the subject of much prayer and consideration. A perusal of the sermon subjects, as advertised in current newspapers, will be suggestive of what can, or what ought not to be done, in the way of sermon titles.

CHAPTER TWENTY-FIVE

The Preparation of the Sermon

We have considered, thus far, as our main topics: the qualifications of the preacher, his call and commission; the necessity for preaching; the sermon and its structure; the various types of sermons, and the title of the sermon. We now come to the important matter of the preparation of the sermon.

I. The necessity for it.

1. *It is essential.*

It will surely be admitted that if preaching is to be what God intends it should; then there must be time set apart for serious and honest preparation. Preachers are both *born* and *made,* both *gifted* and *developed.* This developing process represents a lifetime of conscientious study and application to "the ministry he has received in the Lord." (Col. 4:17). It is hardly necessary to say that this involves a great amount of labor. Study is work and the preacher must ever remember he is a "workman" for God. This "labor of love" will pay great dividends one day and, in the meanwhile, will bring multiplied blessing to both preacher and hearer.

An old preacher's advice is worth noting. He said: "Get to *know* your subject by study. Then *stow* your subject in your mind by meditation and prayer. See that you *show* your subject, by translating it into the terms of daily living. Finally, *go* with your subject and *sow* it in the hearts of the hearers by faithfully delivering the message God has committed to you.

2. *It is Scriptural.*

In this careful preparation, the preacher is but following in the steps of heralds who have gone before and "whose faith follow."

Solomon's words concerning this need for preparation should be carefully pondered. Let us look at Eccles. 12:9-12. We could well entitle an exposition on this passage: *"A Preacher on Preaching."* Three main things stand out:

I. The Character of the Preacher, verse 9. He was

1. *Wise.* "wise." We are to be

(1) Wise to salvation. II Tim. 3:15.
(2) Wise in the Scriptures. Matt. 13:52.
(3) Wise in dealing with souls. Prov. 11:30.

2. *Instructive.* "taught . . . knowledge." Cp. II Tim. 2:2; Hos. 4:6.

3. *Persevering.* "still taught." Here is patient, plodding endurance, everlastingly at the job, with one's eye on the goal. I Cor. 15:58.

II. The Conscientious Preparation, verses 9, 10.

Notice he was

1. *Attentive.* "gave good heed." He who would teach must attend. In the R. V. it is "pondered" or meditated. (I Tim. 4:15).

2. *Studious.* "sought out." Painstaking preparation is the price. (II Tim. 2:15).

3. *Systematic.* "set in order." Orderly preparation makes for orderly presentation and orderly retention by the hearer. (I Cor. 14:40).

4. *Judicious.* "find out acceptable words." This requires discrimination, and the separating of the precious from the vile." (Jer. 15:19).

5. *Scriptural.* "what was written." He had a "thus saith the Lord" for what he taught: "Preach the Word." (Jer. 23:28).

6. *Sincere.* "upright." There was no evasion, or hypocrisy, or text without context. (II Cor. 4:2).

7. *Truthful.* "words of truth." It is God's truth that alone can reach and win the heart for the truth. (III John 3, 4).

III.   The Convincing Presentation, verses 11, 12.

1. *It was pointed,* "as goads." His sermon did not consist so much of "heads," as *points* that pierced the armor of indifference, ignorance and self-complacency. (Heb. 4:12).

2. *It was impressive.* "nails *fastened.*" Every sermon should be like a nail, driven in by the hammer of God's word by the power of the Spirit and thus permanently impressed on the heart. (Jer. 23:29).

3. *It was authoritative.* "given from one *Shepherd.*" The preacher is only the mouthpiece, the voice. The authority is God's. (John 1:22-23).

4. *It was effective.* "admonished." Cp. Isa. 55:11. It was constructive and did the work.

5. *It was the result of hard work.* "much study." This study is hard on the flesh, which naturally loves ease and pleasure, but it results in much blessing. (Prov. 22:29).

Solomon's advice, though three milleniums old, is very much up to date and still holds good. Would that every one who desires to preach the Word to the profit of his hearers would seek to emulate him in this respect!

3. *It is sensible.*

God has given His people a "sound mind" and this must be used for His glory. (II Tim. 1:7). Common sense and decency demands that due preparation be made for any matter requiring an address to the public. A lawyer carefully prepares his brief. A builder keenly studies the plans and specifications of the building he is to erect. A doctor conscientiously reads up on his case. An inventor meticulously prepares his invention before demonstrating it to an audience. Someone has wittily observed: "The desire to preach helpfully, without making the necessary preparation for it, is not true ambition, but merely an inflammation of the wishbone!" It is good to remember, however, that the preacher should be more concerned with getting his sermon *down* and *in* than getting it *up* and *out!*

Having discussed the necessity for preparing for the sermon, let us now consider:

II. The selection of the subject.

Let us suppose an invitation has been received to preach and accepted. The great question now is: "What shall be the text or the subject of the sermon?" How can this vitally important matter be determined? Many factors will have to be taken into consideration before this can be settled. The following suggestions may prove helpful to this end.

1. *There must be definite and earnest prayer for Divine wisdom and guidance.*

Inasmuch as it is God's work, it is essential that the preacher get in touch with Him about it. This spiritual preparation should possess a four-fold quality.

(1) *It should be done humbly.*

The preacher must lay to heart his Master's words: "Without Me, ye can do nothing" (John 15:5). He must also remember that Christ said: "As the branch cannot bear fruit of itself, except it abide in the vine, no more can ye, except ye abide in Me" (John 15:4). There is no room for pride in the service of the Lord. It is written:

"The meek will He guide in judgment, the meek will He teach His way" (Ps. 25:9). The "High and holy One, that inhabiteth eternity" has declared: "To this man will I look, even to him that is poor, and of a contrite spirit, and trembleth at My word" (Isa. 66:1-2). Like Moses, the preacher must say: "If Thy presence go not with me, carry us not up hence" (Exod. 33:15). He needs constantly to keep in mind that the sermon, like the one who preaches it, needs to be "born from above." Therefore to get the sermon *up,* he must seek to bring it *down* from heaven by prayer.

(2) *It should be done believingly.*

God has promised to give wisdom to the one who asks "in faith, nothing wavering" (Jas. 1:5-6). We are told that: "He that cometh to God must believe that He is, and that He is a Rewarder of them that diligently seek Him" (Heb. 11:6). Thus the preacher must lay hold on Him "Whose love is as great as His power," for the guidance and power that He alone can supply and which He delights to give in answer to the prayer of faith.

(3) *It should be done conscientiously.*

The preacher must not neglect any avenue that will furnish him with the necessary equipment. Wisdom comes from study which, in turn, is born of a sincere desire to be one's best for God. In this way the believer, as it were, must endeavor to answer his own prayers.

(4) *It should be done perseveringly.*

As the preacher patiently waits upon God, there will be a response to his prayers. The indwelling Holy Spirit, Whose work and delight it is to guide into all truth, will do His part, if ungrieved, and impress the mind and heart with some particular text or subject. This guidance of the Spirit, in answer to humble and believing prayer, is better experienced than described. It is not pleasant to the flesh to wait upon God, but it is absolutely essential to the spiritual preparation of the preacher. Apart from this spiritual preparation all other preparation is worse than useless, for "the flesh profiteth nothing" (John 6: 63).

2. *The subject, or the text may have been previously impressed upon the mind.*

Perhaps it was through the daily devotional reading of the Word. It may have been some incident, topic, or text, or even a word in a text that gripped the soul, and impressed itself forcibly upon one's consciousness. After this text, or thought, has been enjoyed personally, the suggestion has come: "This would make a good subject for an address." Now, as one waits on God, this impression is deepened in the mind, and the conviction grows that this is the subject upon which the Lord would have him speak.

3. *Perhaps the subject has already been chosen.*

It may be a Sunday School lesson that follows a prescribed course through the Bible. It may be a Bible class with a prearranged topic, or a young people's meeting with the Scripture portion, or subject already assigned.

4. *The subject, or text, may have been suggested by* hearing some other speaker preach from it.

This address impressed itself upon the mind, or perhaps opened up a new train of thought, or even suggested an entirely new subject. This now rises before one's mind while waiting on the Lord.

5. *Perhaps the reading of a book of sermons,* or outlines of sermons, suggested a theme which appealed as being a suitable subject for a sermon. This outline or theme now comes with force to the soul.

6. *A current event may have suggested a certain line of teaching,* or illustrated a text. It may be that the season of the year will aid in the selection. Perhaps it is

Christmas, New Year's day, etc. It may be some tragic incident or calamity which suggests a subject. It may be that the occasion, such as the opening of a new chapel or a Sunday School treat, etc., may suggest the text or theme.

7. *The needs of the audience will also prove to be a factor in the decision.*

Is it to boys and girls? To prisoners in a jail? To patients in a hospital? Is it a funeral, or marriage, or an anniversary? To a company of old folks in a home? An open air meeting? Is it to the saved or to the unsaved?

This exercise of heart before the Lord is of tremendous spiritual value. It is still true that "they that wait upon the Lord shall renew (exchange) their strength" (Isa. 40: 31). This period of prayer will result in keener spiritual insight, a greater spiritual capacity to know, and an increased ability to do the will of God. Prayerlessness results in carelessness, listlessness, powerlessness and uselessness. May the Lord deliver us from this quintette of deadly and devastating evils!

CHAPTER TWENTY-SIX

The Preparation of the Sermon
(Continued)

III. The preparation of the outline.

Having selected the text, or topic, the next thing is the preparation of the outline. We shall now consider some suggestions as how best to accomplish this. It is difficult to lay down any hard and fast rules, but these suggestions may prove helpful, for they have been tried and proved in the crucible of experience.

Alex Maclaren, when asked for his method of preparing sermons, replied: "I have really nothing to say about my way of making sermons that could profit your readers. I know of no method except to think about a text until you have something to say about it; and then go and say it, with as little thought for self as possible." In this matter, the truth of the old adage will become evident: "One man's method is another man's confusion."

John Gregg's advice is good: "Throw *yourself* into your *subject* by *prayer*. Then throw the *subject* into *yourself* by *study*. Finally, throw *yourself* and your *subject* into your *audience* by *preaching*." Still another has said: "The preacher must *think* himself empty; *read* himself full; *write* himself clear; *pray* himself keen, and *preach* himself out.

1. *Begin early.*

(1) *Beware of procrastination.*

This is not only "the thief of time," but of sermons also! To put off until tomorrow what should be done today only spells disaster. Someone has said that "the greatest labor saving device in the world today is—tomorrow!" This witticism, however, is not true; for the work we shirk today will be much harder to do tomorrow.

To leave this essential preparation until the last moment, trusting that the audience itself may bring about an inspiration, is to lean on a broken reed. When the fateful moment arrives, the sight of the audience, instead of producing an *inspiration* may only lead to a *perspiration* of the cold variety! The promise: "Open thy mouth wide and I will fill it," has no reference whatever to preachers who neglect the necessary preparation of the sermon because of the hard work connected with it.

(2) *Overcome the inertia.*

The Divine law of preparation is study. One man once said to a friend: "I never know what I am going to speak about five minutes before I get up." His friend replied: "And that is the reason why no one remembers what you have said five minutes after you have sat down." The finest *after* dinner speeches are thought out *before* dinner! A lady once said to Turner, the great artist, as she looked at one of his pictures: "I wish I could dream a scene like that on canvas." The artist growled: "Dream, nothing! That picture took 10,000 strokes of my brush and it's thundering hard work!" The gospel preacher who desires to be his best for God, will also discover how true were Turner's words, when applied to the preparation of a gospel or teaching message.

The great thing is to get *started.* It is much easier to *contemplate* getting started than to actually *begin* to work. In this respect, it is similar to getting out of bed in the morning. One can waste a great deal of time *thinking* about getting up instead of *doing* it! This initial inertia is the most difficult thing to overcome.

(3) *Begin right.*

To settle down comfortably in a well cushioned arm chair is fatal. A wide desk, a hard chair, a good light properly placed in the right position, a pencil, plenty of paper and one's study books handy to the reach, is the correct set up. It is quite a convenience to have a couple of home made inclined book rests on the table, to hold a Concordance and a Dictionary or any other heavy books that require frequent reference.

(4) *There may be exceptions to this.*

Sometimes there are occasions when one is suddenly called upon to give a message and there is no opportunity provided for adequate preparation. Under such circumstances the Lord will enable the speaker to give the needed message, often with a great deal of liberty and power. We must beware, however, of assuming from this that painstaking preparation is not necessary.

2. *Read the passage, or passages of Scripture, frequently.*

Needless to say, the context must be included in the reading. In this way, the preacher will become perfectly familiar with what God's word *actually says*. It is good to read these scriptures *audibly*. This will not only aid in concentrating on the actual words, but will also enable one to note where the emphasis should be placed in the public reading of the Scriptures. The purpose of preaching is to impart the word of God to the hearer, and this cannot be done unless the preacher reads it carefully for himself, and also pays good attention to the actual wording of the passage.

3. *Look up the parallel passages in other parts of the Bible.*

In some cases, the same incident is recorded elsewhere, and often significant details are added. This is true particularly in Old Testament history, where the book of Kings should always be compared with the book of Chronicles. The same is true of the four Gospels. The Epistles should be read in the light of the Acts, which often gives the historical setting of the writing of the letter.

The marginal references should also be looked up, for by this means, one can "compare spiritual things with spiritual." (I Cor. 2:13). The best commentary on the Bible is the Bible!

4. *Read the Scripture portion in other versions.*

This will often help to clarify a statement which seems somewhat obscure. It will also serve the purpose of supplying additional material for the sermon. Some good versions and translations are: "The American Revised Version," "The New Translation" by J. N. D.; "The Revised Standard Version of the Bible," "The New Testament in Modern Speech," by Weymouth (Without the notes) "The Epistles of Paul and Hebrews," by Way; "The New Testament," by Williams.

5. *Use a Concordance.*

To find words, Cruden's is the quickest. To discover the *meaning* of the words in the original, and this is most important, use either Strong's or Young's. Perhaps Strong's is the best to find a certain text, and Young's to learn how words are used in the Bible.

Wigram's "English—Hebrew—Chaldee" and his "English—Greek" is very good for noting where the same Hebrew or Greek word is translated by a different English word in the Authorized Version. W. E. Vine's: "Expository Dictionary of Bible Words," will prove to be an invaluable asset to the student and every preacher is advised to get this book.

A "Bible Text Encyclopedia" is invaluable. This book groups texts together that relate to the same *general subject*. Thus: if the subject is "praise," all the texts that contained the same *thought* would be grouped under this heading. This list would include the verses that had in them such words as "thanks," "thanksgiving," "sing," "worship" and "adore," etc. Inglis': "Encyclopedia of Texts" is good.

6. *Concentrate on the topic, or text, with paper and pencil ready to hand.*

(1) *Discover the theme.*

That is, if it is to be a textual or expository sermon. State this theme in the logical form. This, of course, implies that the student has thoroughly familiarized himself with the Scripture portion under consideration.

(2) *Arrange the main divisions.*

These, of course should definitely relate to the theme in the passage of Scripture.

(3) *Concentrate on the passage to the exclusion of all else.*

This concentration of thought is not an easy thing, but it is absolutely essential to proper preparation. With practice and perseverance, it will be found possible to discipline the mind and refuse to allow it to wander aimlessly around. Try to avoid all interruptions during this meditation, for these will wreck the train of thought, and allow the mental fires to die down. A certain writer in dedicating his book wrote: "To my wife, apart from whose absence this book could never have been written."

Stephen Leacock was once asked by a young and ambitious author for his magic formula for successful writing. He replied: "All you have to do is to procure pen, paper and ink, and then sit down and write as it occurs to you." Then he added: "The *writing* is not hard, but the *occurring*: that, my friend is the difficulty!"

(4) *Meditate on the passage.*

The preacher must brood over his sermon as a hen broods over her nest. As he thus waits on God, while concentrating on the passage or subject, the thoughts will begin to come, probably slowly at first; but one thought will suggest another, until he will have David's experience: "While I was *musing,* the fire burned: *then* spake I with my tongue" (Psa. 39:3). Someone has aptly remarked: "Meditation is that process of thought which enables the soul to rise out of the grave of the body." Needless to say, musing requires time, and this people are usually loath to invest. It has been said: "There are

thousands who long for immortality who do not know
what to do with themselves on a rainy Sunday afternoon!"

Dr. McWatty Russell used to tell his students that, as
a boy, he was often made to take an old woolen stocking
and unravel it so that the wool could be used again. At
first he would only get short pieces on the foot, where it
had been repeatedly darned; but once he got over these
places, the yarn came in one long string. It is just so with
an address. As we sit down with our books, the thoughts
will gradually increase, until the "one long string" of the
message will be unraveled and we shall be enabled to
"rejoice as one that findeth great spoil" (Psa. 119:162).

(5) *Write down these thoughts as they come.*

The logical sequence of these thoughts is not important
at this stage. These can be sorted out and arranged later.
One should try to recall all he has ever read, heard, observed, or gathered on this particular subject, or Scripture under consideration. As this is done perseveringly,
a train of thought will open up. Other Scriptures will
come to mind, illustrations will suggest themselves and
soon there will be more material than can be used. *Do
not be afraid to write.* Paper is cheap, and the effort of
writing will impress it upon the memory as nothing else,
and will also be a great aid in developing conciseness of
style and clarity of expression.

7. *Now tabulate these thoughts and arrange them in
their logical order.*

After the thoughts have been written down and, of
course, several pages will now have been filled; sort out
this material and place it in its logical order. This implies that an outline has been prepared, by which the
subject, or text has been divided into its main divisions,
all of which relate to the text and theme. These thoughts
should now be arranged under the various divisions.
Always prepare *more material* than you can use in the
time allotted, for it is far easier to *condense* than to *ex-*

pand during the preaching of the sermon.

If it is a Topical sermon, arrange it according to the questions found under the headings: "What?" "Why?" "How?" "Who?" "Where?" "When?" and "What then?" If Expository, arrange the divisions as they relate to the central thought. If Textual, relate everything to the text in its proper order. If Historical incident, arrange it in the order of the Scripture narrative. If Biographical, begin from the beginning and take the main features of the life in logical sequence.

This will necessitate carefully going over and rewriting all that has been written. It will also involve the addition of further ideas, until several pages have been filled with these thoughts, which are now arranged in orderly sequence.

8. *An introduction should now be carefully prepared.*

This should be written out in full, having in mind the kind of audience that will be addressed. Dr. Jas. Black has finely said: "Behind all our preparation in the study, there should be the shadow of a listening people.' Remember how important it is that the introduction shall anticipate and clear away as many obstacles as possible which would hinder the hearer from attending to the subject. Keep in mind also the fact that these introductory remarks will either gain or lose the attention of the audience.

9. *A conclusion should be planned.*

By this, the truth which has been set before the audience, is to be applied in a very personal way. Remember, eternal issues are at stake and each person in the audience should be made to feel that the message is for him or her alone. While it is true that there should be a constant application of the truth during the sermon, the conclusion should be the final summing up of the argument, and the appeal made for an immediate decision for Christ, or for the truth that has been presented.

CHAPTER TWENTY-SEVEN

The Preparation of the Sermon

(Continued)

10. *Suitable illustrations should now be prepared.*

In view of its importance, let us devote a little space to this matter of illustrations.

(1) *Their purpose.*

They exist for the purpose of clarifying the truths to be presented. Illustrations are like windows that let in the light, but these should not be too numerous, for one's sermon should not resemble a glass house! Quality here, as in everything else, is to be preferred to quantity. A gospel address should not consist of a long string of anecdotes, interspersed with a few odd texts to keep it from falling apart; but it should be a logical setting forth of the truth of Scripture, for this alone can give *authority* to the message. The sermon does not exist for the sake of the illustrations, but vice versa. These illustrations, though necessary, are secondary in importance.

Henry Ward Beecher has pointed out that illustrations serve a seven fold purpose.

(a) *They assist argument.*

When an argument is somewhat heavy, involved, or tedious to follow, it is good to be able to say: "For instance," or: "For example," or: "Let me illustrate what I mean," or: "Now let us suppose." One has only to watch the effect of such a statement on an audience to realize how valuable an illustration can be.

(b) *They help the hearer to remember.*

In fact an audience will often remember the illustration long after the sermon is forgotten!

(c) *They stimulate the imagination.*

The audience can visualize the picture presented by the illustration, particularly if it is well told, and all illustrations should possess this quality.

(d) *They rest the audience.*

An audience can only take in so much. Close reasoning can hold the hearers for a limited period. Consequently, they need a breathing space now and again, and an illustration serves this purpose admirably.

(e) *They provide for various classes of hearers.*

An audience is composed of individuals, each with a distinct personality. What may appeal to one, will make little or no impression on another. An illustration, however, will usually appeal to all alike.

(f) *They bridge difficult places.*

A profound doctrine of Scripture, difficult of exposition and explanation, can often be made clear by the use of a suitable illustration.

(g) *They enforce the truth.*

Take Nathan's parable of the ewe lamb. What could have been better fitted to drive home to David's heart the heinousness of his sin and reveal, in all its sordidness and hatefulness, his despicable crime?

Robert Hall once remarked to a preacher: "Your sermons do not have enough *"likes'* in them!" It is interesting to observe the numbers of times that our Lord used the word, "like." He said: "The kingdom of heaven is like," etc. The preacher who puts lots of "likes" into his sermons will, most likely, be liked by all alike!

(2) *Their selection.*

The ideal illustrations should be clear, telling and brief.

(a) *Avoid, as far as possible, the old stock illustrations.*

Somebody has suggested that a society be formed called the "S. D. W. S. P. I."; which, being interpreted, means: "The Society for Doing Without Some Pulpit Illustrations." Many of the illustrations used ought to be superannuated, for they have served their day and generation well and deserve a long rest from their strenuous labors!

(b) *Care should be taken not to repeat them too often before the same audience.*

A long suffering victim of too-oft-told tales put his complaint into verse, and wrote:

> "If he can remember so many tales,
>   With all the details that mould 'em;
> Why can't he remember with equal skill,
>   The many times he's told 'em!"

(c) *They should be carefully selected to specifically illustrate the exact phase of the truth to be conveyed.*

It would appear that some illustrations apparently exist only for their own sake, and serve no useful purpose in enlightening an audience regarding some particular Scripture truth. It is hardly necessary to point out that the purpose of an illustration is to *illustrate!* Other so called "illustrations" are so involved that they only succeed in "darkening counsel by words." Still others are so long drawn out, and accompanied by such an interminable succession of utterly inconsequential details, that the audience is bored beyond description.

Doubtless, we have all had inflicted upon us those illustrations which are commenced, but never completed. In the midst of the story, something occurs to the speaker and off he goes at a tangent, leaving his "illustration" hanging in the air with no visible means of support! This leaves the audience wondering how the matter ended, or if it was ever intended to have an ending, or what it was supposed to illustrate; or, what is more to the point, whether it should have ever had a *beginning!*

(3)   *Their source.*

The question may be asked: Where can these suitable illustrations be found? Let us suggest a seven fold source of such material.

(a)   *The Scriptures.*

Practically every truth of doctrine can be illustrated by a Bible incident, parable, or proverb.

(b)   *History.*

Both ancient and modern history is replete with countless incidents of actual happenings which can be turned to good advantage to illustrate Scriptural truth.

(c)   *Nature.*

The scripture: "Doth not nature itself teach you?" gives the preacher the warrant to search in the realm of nature for illustrations (I Cor. 11:14). Job's words are also in order at this point: "But ask now the beasts, and they shall teach thee; or speak to the earth, and it shall teach thee; and the fishes of the sea shall declare unto thee" (Job 12-7-8).

Thus Nature stands, ready and eager to pour into the preacher's lap her wealth of clear, telling illustrations. The great Teacher Himself drew many of His lessons from this source and which effectively clinched the lessons He taught. Madame Gatty's book: "Parables From Nature," will serve the purpose of indicating what can be done in this direction.

(d)   *Biblical magazines, the newspaper and secular magazines.*

These combine to form a treasure trove of illustrative material. Here is recorded a host of telling incidents and pithy sayings which are full of spiritual significance.

When clipping these items from a newspaper, it is good to retain the *name* of the paper and also the *date*. This will give added interest and supply authority and credibility to the story. "The Sunday School Times" has featured, for many years, a column called "The Illustration Round Table," and many excellent stories can be obtained from this source. "The Reader's Digest" also contains some good material for pulpit illustrations.

(e) *Good poetry.*

This will often furnish a well expressed thought, by which to make clear some obscure truth. Alex. Marshall, author of the well known tract: "God's Way of Salvation," was an adept at interspersing his address with most appropriate quotations from various hymns, which drove home the points he wished to make. The preacher should therefore become well acquainted with hymnology.

(f) *Gospel tracts.*

These contain an abundance of telling incidents and also serve the purpose of instructing the reader in the art of *how to apply* the illustration. It is one thing to tell a story and another to apply its spiritual significance to the audience.

(g) *"Suppose" illustrations.*

The preacher will be well advised to make his own illustrations. This can be done by *supposing* the existence of any situation he desires and then proceed, from his supposition, to his application. H. P. Barker was a past master in the use of illustrations, and his books should be read by all preachers who desire to excel in this most necessary art. Note how carefully these suppose illustrations are prepared, presented and applied. Every essential detail is taken care of and all unnecessary embellishments ruthlessly eliminated. They are admirably designed to effectively illustrate the exact *phase* of truth he desired to impart. Some of his apt illustrations can be found in a recently published book: "Windows in Words," published by Pickering & Inglis of London. Still another is his book: "The Vicar of Christ," which is replete with telling "suppose" illustrations.

The speaker must both use and develop his sanctified imagination. He must *learn to invent situations* that will illustrate the lesson he has in mind. Once he has pronounced the magic formula: "Let us suppose," the sky becomes the limit! The audience realizes that this is not an actual incident and will therefore grant him almost any liberty in this direction! That grand and much used tract: "Safety, Certainty and Enjoyment," owes much of its usefulness to its simple, but very telling "suppose" illustrations. We have gone into considerable detail regarding the value of illustrations. Now let us return to the next point regarding the preparation of the sermon.

11. *Now consult other writers.*

This is where the commentaries and other reference books will serve the preacher, not as a crutch on which to lean, but as a *supplement to his own efforts.* Fresh light will now be given and often, to his delight, he will find some of his own findings confirmed by authors who wrote long before he was born!

12. *Now condense the many pages of the sermon to one or two pages.*

This should be of a very good *quality* bond paper. Cheap paper will soon become brittle and fall to pieces. This should be 8½" x 10½" and punched for a loose leaf binder. A wide margin of at least 2½" should be left on the left side of the page to receive any additional notes it is necessary to insert afterwards. For those who do not use a typewriter, print the main heads and write neatly and small. Before filing this way, condense this large sheet to a small sheet of good bond paper which will fit

into the Bible which is to be used when preaching. This
paper should be around 7" x 4". Leave a margin on this.
Print the main headings and underline them with *two
lines* of red ink, and the subdivisions with one line of red
ink. This will facilitate quick reference, should that be
necessary during the course of the address. Having gone
over this sermon four times, the probability is it will not
be easily forgotten.

13. *This address should be rehearsed as often as
possible.*

The preacher should address himself, in audible tones,
(but not so as to disturb others!) to his bedroom furni-
ture, or better still, to the trees in the open air as he takes
a walk. This will not only accustom him to the sound
of his own voice, but will greatly aid in the clear and
forceful presentation of his subject when he faces an
audience.

Actors, who desire successfully to present fiction as
fact, spend very many hours in rehearsals. They count
the time well spent if the play turns out to be a success
and secures the approval and patronage of the public.
Surely the gospel preacher, who has the eternal truth of
God as his theme, should be no less eager that his message
shall go home to the hearts of his hearers and thus secure
the approval of God and the blessing of the audience.
Someone once asked a great actor why it was that thousands flocked to hear him acting out fiction, while only a
handful turned out to hear a preacher proclaiming God's
truth. The actor replied: "I act *fiction* as though it were
fact; many preachers preach the *fact* of the gospel as
though it were *fiction!*"

14. *He should now humbly and believingly commit
himself by prayer to God.*

Once the material has been studiously gathered and
conscientiously prepared, the preacher must now look to

the Lord to set it alight as he speaks. Wesley's advice to
young preachers was: "Catch fire for God, and the people
will come out to see you burn!" A good rule for a preacher
is to *pray* as though everything depended on *God,* and
then *preach* as though everything depended on *himself!*
This will make for that proper balance of prayerful
preparation and powerful proclamation which shall accomplish the purpose that God intends it should; the salvation of the lost and the edification of the believer.

CHAPTER TWENTY-EIGHT

The Gathering of the Material

This is a lifetime task. The preacher that is worth his salt never reaches the point where he no longer needs to gather material, or to add to his store of knowledge in the things of God. It will always be true to him what the Lord said to Joshua regarding the promised land: "There remaineth yet very much land to be possessed" (Joshua 13:1). Paul's words are also very much to the point in this connection: "If any man think that he knoweth anything, he knoweth nothing yet as he ought to know" (I Cor. 8:2).

Just as an efficient teacher needs to keep ahead of the class he is teaching, so the preacher needs to keep ahead of his congregation. This will necessitate that he be continually on the alert for anything that will contribute to his usefulness in preaching and teaching the word of God.

The price for an effective preaching ministry is the same as that of peace, namely: "eternal vigilance." The Scripture puts it thus: "Seest thou a man diligent in his business? He shall stand before kings, he shall not stand before mean men" (Prov. 22:29). In his diligent search for knowledge, the preacher must emulate the enthusiastic entomologist, or ornithologist who, when he walks abroad, is constantly on the lookout for new specimens to add to his collection, or to increase his fund of information concerning his particular branch of scientific investigation. In this connection, the best "helping hand" a person can have is the one at the end of his own arm!

D. L. Moody was an indefatigable searcher for Bible knowledge, and he counted no price too great to obtain

315

it. A Mr. J. Fegan described him at a conference of believers in England. After the addresses had been given, he approached the speakers and others, and with note book in hand, asked questions and carefully noted the replies in his book. He had an insatiable thirst for a better knowledge of the Bible he loved so well and used so powerfully. This is one of the explanations of his great usefulness as a preacher.

Youth is undoubtedly the best time to gather knowledge. The grain that is gleaned and beaten out in one's early days remains his possession for the rest of his life. Human beings grow proportionally faster in babyhood than at any other time in their history. It will take some time before one's *experience* catches up with his *knowledge*. Therefore the urgent need for collecting the material now, which will stand him in good stead for the years that lie ahead.

The preacher's "barrel" should be constantly replenished as a result of this continual inflow of knowledge. He should not wait until the barrel is empty of sermon material, for this will only result in worry and perhaps panic. A few hints on how to gather this material may be in order at this time.

In the first place, he should possess:

I. A carefully selected library.

Again we shall devote considerable space to this important subject.

1. *The necessity for it.*

Christ, the risen Head, has given gifts to the Church, which is His body, such as "Evangelists, pastors and teachers, for the work of the ministry and the edifying of the body of Christ" (Eph. 4:11-12). If such be true of *oral* ministry, it is doubly true of *written* ministry, for the latter is prepared and published with far more care than the former. We have before pointed out that the person who belittles written ministry should, to be consistant, also absent himself from all oral ministry. This, in turn, would be a denial of the truth of the Scripture we have already quoted, which affirms its necessity for the edification of the believer.

For one to speak disparagingly of books, written by gifted and godly servants of Christ, is to take issue with the Lord Himself Who not only gave these writers the gift of teaching, but also the desire and ability to sacrifice their time and energy to the onerous task of committing their thoughts to writing.

Seldom does one ever hear prayer offered on behalf of those who devote themselves to teaching through the medium of the printed page, yet their ministry is most necessary for the edification of the saints. J. N. Darby was prevented from disposing of his fine library, as being unnecessary, by a consideration of Paul's words to Timothy: "Bring the books, but especially the parchments" (II Tim. 4:13). He rightly argued: "If Paul needed these books, then how much more do I?"

Thus, whether the teaching be spoken or written, it comes from the same Source and exists for the same purpose. Each child of God is therefore well advised to take full advantage of this bountiful supply which God has provided for his spiritual edification.

2. *The value of it.*

A well selected library is a treasure, rich and rare, and of far more value than all the gold and silver of the earth! Through this library, gifted men and women of God will come into the preacher's study and, as it were, talk with him personally as often and for as long as he wishes! Voices, long silent in death, will again become vocal as they carefully and patiently expound the deep things of God, which they learned through much prayer and intensive study of the word of God. In this way they passed on to a generation, which was unborn when they wrote, the results of their many years of earnest Bible study, scholarly learning and spiritual discernment.

It can truthfully be said of every preacher today that his "lines are fallen unto him in pleasant places," and that he has a "goodly heritage" in the vast store of sound Biblical literature at his disposal. (Ps. 16: 6). Try to envision each book in the library as the writer himself, ready and willing, at a moment's notice, to step down from the shelf and commune with the reader. Imagine being able to say: "What do you think of this particular Scripture, Mr. Darby?" and have him answer as the book is opened! The same applies to any of the great teachers whose books happen to be in one's library.

3. *The dangers of it.*

(1) *To allow these books to displace the Bible as the supreme authority.*

Some of these men of God, though deeply learned in the Scriptures and most sincere in their convictions, were sometimes mistaken in their conclusions. The word of God must never be allowed to be superceded, as the preacher's supreme authority, by any writer however gifted and well taught. All these writings must be brought to the touchstone of holy Writ. The Scripture puts it thus: "To the law and to the testimony: if they speak not according to this word, it is because there is no light in them" (Isa. 8: 20).

The value of written ministry is in direct proportion to the amount of light it gives on the teachings of the holy Scriptures. The reading of men's books must never be allowed to become a *substitute* for the reading and study of *the* Book. God's word must be absolutely preeminent in one's reading and thinking, and the final court of appeal on all questions, irrespective of what men may think and say.

(2) *Many books are positively harmful.*

These teach positive error and thus become a spiritual menace. Much of the current religious literature is tainted with modernism, which denies the Divine, plenary and verbal inspiration of the Bible. In other books, great stress is laid on the denominational viewpoint of the writer and this is allowed to color many of his conclusions. Still others teach definite error, for they deny the fundamental doctrines of our most holy faith. These may well be labelled "poison," with the instruction written thereon: "From such turn away" (II Tim. 3:5).

One must therefore learn to discriminate between "the precious and the vile" (Jer. 15:19). The best preventative against error is *concentration on and a knowledge of the truth.* In order to be well grounded and established in sound doctrine one must "hold fast the form of sound words" (II Tim. 1:13). This will not only fortify the soul against error, but also impart a sense of *spiritual discernment,* which will make for quick recognition of any departure from the truth. Not only so, but it will enable one, "by sound doctrine, both to exhort and convince the gainsayers" (Tit. 1:9). The preacher must learn to test error by *the truth* and not truth by *error.* To fill one's mind with error, with a view to an appreciation of the truth, is not only most unprofitable but positively dangerous. Paul's advice is pertinent to this end: "Whatsoever things are true . . . honest . . . just . . . pure . . . lovely, and of good report: *think* on these things" (Phil. 4:8).

(3) *To sacrifice quantity for quality.*

There is a peculiar fascination about acquiring books, and the temptation is to secure them simply for the pleasure of seeing them on the shelves. These rows of books may present "a fair show in the flesh," and also serve the purpose of impressing our friends with the extent of our possessions; but they really only demonstrate our paucity in the matter of selection. As one has put it:

"A world of advice in this verse you will find,
    An impression, I trust, it will make on your mind;
I can speak for its worth, having proved it myself,
    That a book in the hand is worth ten on the shelf!"

Many a library remains unpossessed by its owner. It is one thing to own books and another to possess them. It is far better to become well acquainted with one book, than slightly acquainted with several. Robert Cecil once said: "I have a shelf in my *library* for tried *authors;* one in my *mind* for tried *principles;* and one in my *heart* for tried *friends."*

This library should be built up slowly, as one's means and tastes allow. Many good books can be purchased second-hand at half price and cheaper. These second-hand books are more likely to be better bound than new ones at double the price. A few will have to be purchased new, but such an investment of one's money will be more than amply rewarded by the benefit and blessing they will bring both to the preacher and those who will profit by his ministry.

CHAPTER TWENTY-NINE

The Gathering of the Material

(Continued)

4. The Content of this library.

What books should this "carefully selected library" contain? There will be a wide divergence of opinion regarding this matter. A book which will appeal to one person may have little value in the eyes of another.

The following list of books is given with this fact in mind. It is not intended to be exhaustive by any manner of means. It must also be kept in mind that all the contents of these recommended books is not endorsed. It will be necessary for the reader to discriminate. On the whole, all the books listed are good and should prove useful in "the work of the ministry."

Some preachers have libraries containing twenty thousand books. Spurgeon had a fine library, as also did Darby, Kelly, Griffith Thomas, etc. There are probably over four hundred thousand books written on theological subjects, and the end is nowhere in sight, for hundreds are added each year. The vast majority of these books are gathering dust on library shelves. Solomon said: "Of the making of books there is no end" (Ecc. 12:12). The subject of holy Scripture is inexhaustible, for the well of Divine truth is very deep. The problem of selecting a library from this vast supply of religious literature is not simple, and probably each person would compile a different list for his own particular library. The list that follows, arranged both topically and textually, is not large, but it is select. It is hoped later to issue a longer list in pamphlet form, and with the publishers' names and addresses.

(1) *Versions of the Bible.*

"The American Revised;" "The New Translation (J. N. Darby); "The New Testament in Modern Speech" (Weymouth, without the notes). "The Revised Standard Version." "The Epistles of Paul and the Epistle to the Hebrews" (Arthur S. Way). "The New Testament" (C. B. Williams).

(2) *Concordances.*

"Cruden's," for the English words. "Strong's" or "Young's" for the Hebrew and Greek; Inglis, "Bible Text Encyclopedia," for Bible topics. Wigram's: "Hebrew-Chaldee, and Greek Concordance."

(3) *Bible Dictionaries.*

"The International Standard Bible Encyclopedia." 5 Vols. (Edited by Orr); Davis "Bible Dictionary." I Vol. Third Edition. (Do not get the latest edition, as it is tinged with Modernism).

(4) *English Dictionaries.*

Funk and Wagnall's, Unabridged; Webster's "Collegiate," desk size. Roget's "Thesaurus" (for synonyms and antonyms).

(5) *Commentaries.*

"The Numerical Bible" 8 Vols. (F. W. Grant). "Commentary on the Holy Scriptures" (Jameson, Fawcett and Brown). "Students Commentary" (Williams). Also by Matthew Henry.

(6) *Doctrine, or Systematic Theology.*

"Systematic Theology" (By L. S. Chafer. 7 Vols.). "Lectures in Systematic Theology" (Henry C. Thiessen). 1 volume.

(7) *Harmonies.*

"Harmony of the Gospels" (A. T. Robertson). "Harmony of the Acts and Pauline Epistles" (Clark). "Harmony of Samuel, Kings and Chronicles" (Crockett).

(8) *Dictionaries of Bible words.*
"Expository Dictionary of Bible Words" (W. E. Vine). "Word Studies in the New Testament" (J. H. Vincent, 4 Vols.). The word studies of the New Testament, by Kenneth S. Wuest, will also prove valuable to the student who desires a knowledge of the meaning of the Greek.

(9) *Church History.*
"Short Papers on Church History" (A. Miller, 1 Vol.). "The Pilgrim Church" (Broadbent). "History of the Reformation" (D'Aubigne).

(10) *Secular History.*
"History of the Jews" (Josephus). "Rise and Decline of the Roman Empire" (Gibbon). "The Four Hundred Silent Years" (H. A. Ironside). "Handbook of Ancient History in Bible Light" (Ruth Miller).

(11) *Bible Geography.*
"Historical Atlas of the Bible" (Wright). "The Land and the Book" (Thompson).

(12) *History of the Bible, or Biblical Introduction.*
"Biblical Introduction" (H. S. Miller). "The Bible in the Church" (Westcott). "Bible Handbook" (Angus). "The Scripture of Truth" (S. Collett).

(13) *Evidences of Christianity.*
"The Bible, the Word of God" (Bettex). "The Cause and Cure of Infidelity" (Nelson). "The Secret of the Universe" (Nath. Wood). "A Lawyer and his Bible" (Linton). "System of Christian Evidence" (L. S. Keyser). "Many Infallible Proofs" (A. T. Pierson).

(14) *Prophecy.*
"Things to Come" (Pentecost), "Things which must shortly come to pass" (A. J. Pollock). "The Seven

Churches of Asia" (F. C. Jennings). "God's People and God's Purpose" (A. & W. Naismith).

(15) *Typical Teaching.*

"The Tabernacle, the Offerings and the Priesthood" (H. W. Soltau). "The Types" (Ada Habershon). "The Offerings" (A. Jukes), "Christ, in all the Scriptures" (Hodgkin).

(16) *The Second Coming.*

"The Redeemer's Return" (A. W. Pink). "The Second Coming of Christ" (I. M. Haldemann).

(17) *The Future State, or Eschatology.*

"Facts and Theories of the Future State" (F. W. Grant). "Human Destiny" (Robt. Anderson).

(18) *Angelology.*

"Satan" (F. C. Jennings). "Demon Possession and Allied Themes" (Nevius). "Angels" (A. C. Gabelein).

(19) *Dispensational Truth.*

"Ruling Lines of Progressive Revelation" (G. Scroggie). "Rightly Dividing the Word of Truth" (C. I. Scofield). "Ultra - Dispensationalism Examined" (W. Hoste). "Wrongly Dividing the Word of Truth" (H. A. Ironside).

(20) *Expository.* (General)

"Synopsis of the Books of the Bible" (J. N. Darby). "The Annotated Bible" (A. C. Gabelein. Many Vols.). All books by Harry A. Ironside. "Outline Studies of the Old Testament" (Moorehead). "The Dawn of Redemption," "The Triumph of the Crucified," "From Eternity to Eternity" 3 Vols. Erich Sauer. This triology by Sauer is highly recommended.

(21) *Expository.* (Particular).

The Pentateuch. "Notes on the Pentateuch" ("C. H. M."). Also "Notes," by (C. A. C.). "Gleaning in Genesis"

(A. W. Pink). "Studies in Genesis" (Geo. Henderson).
Also his "Studies in Exodus"; "Typical Teaching of
Exodus" (E. Dennett).

Joshua. "Joshua, and the Land of Promise" (F. B.
Meyer). "Joshua," by Carl Armerding.

Judges. "Lectures on Judges" (S. Ridout); "Judges
and Ruth" (F. C. Jennings). "How to Overcome" (J. T.
Mawson).

Ruth. "The Rich Kinsman" (S. H. Tyngs). "Ruth"
(H. Moorhouse). "Boaz and Ruth" (August Van Ryn).

The Books of Samuel. "Saul, the Man after the flesh"
(S. Ridout). "Samuel, the Prophet" (F. B. Meyer).
"First Samuel" (P. J. Pell).

The Books of Kings and Chronicles.

"The Kings of Judah and Israel" (C. Knapp).

Ezra and Nehemiah. "Ezra, Nehemiah, Zechariah, and
Malachi" (E. Dennett).

Esther. "The Book of Esther, and its Spiritual Meaning" (E. Cumming).

Job. "The Book of Job" (S. Ridout). "Eleven Lectures
on Job" (W. Kelly).

Psalms. "The Treasury of David" (C. H. Spurgeon,
7 Vols.). "The Titles of the Psalms" (Thirtle). "The Book
of Praises" (C. E. Stuart). "Analytical Studies in the
Psalms" (Arthur G. Clark).

Proverbs. "Laws of Heaven, for Life on Earth" (W.
Arnot). "Proverbs" (Chas. Bridges). Also H. A. Ironside.

Ecclesiastes. "Ecclesiastes" (Erdman). "Old Groans
and New Songs" (F. C. Jennings).

Song of Solomon. "Meditation on the Song of Songs"
(A. Miller). "Union and Communion" (Hudson Taylor).
"Song of Solomon" (H. A. Ironside).

Isaiah. "Studies in Isaiah" (F. C. Jennings). "Exposition of Isaiah" (W. Kelly). "Isaiah, One; and His Book, One" (Douglas).

Jeremiah. "Studies in the prophecy of Jeremiah" (G. C. Morgan).

Ezekiel. "Notes on Ezekiel" (W. Kelly).

Daniel. "The Coming Prince" (R. Anderson). Also by W. Kelly and E. Dennett.

The Minor Prophets. "Introductory to the study of the Minor Prophets" (W. Kelly). "Lessons from Jonah, the Prophet" (Willis). "Visions and Prophecies of Zechariah" (D. Baron).

The Four Gospels (General). "Guide to the Gospels" (G. Scroggie). A splendid volume. "The Four Gospels" (S. Ridout). "The Four Evangelists" (J. G. Bellett). "Four Portraits of our Lord Jesus Christ" (H. S. Soltau). "Expository Thoughts on the Gospels" (5 Vols., J. C. Ryle). "The Great Physician" (Campbell Morgan).

The Four Gospels (Particular).

Matthew. W. Kelly, Campbell Morgan, August Van Ryn.

Mark. W. Kelly, Campbell Morgan, Harold St. John.

Luke. "The Man of Sorrows" (J. N. Darby) (August Van Ryn).

John. "The Gospel of John" (A. W. Pink, 4 Vols.). (August Van Ryn). "Commentary on the Gospel of John" (Godet). "Tracings from the Gospel of John" (C. E. Stuart). Harold St. John.

Acts. "Introduction to Study of the Acts" (Stifler) (August Van Ryn). "Tracings in the Acts" (C. E. Stuart). "Exposition of the Acts of the Apostles" (W. Kelly). "Acts" (Rackham).

Romans. Books by W. E. Vine; W. R. Newell; Hodge; H. G. Moule; Griffith Thomas; Thos. Westwood.

First and Second Corinthians. "The Charter of the Church" (J. R. Caldwell). "The Corinthian Letters of Paul" (G. C. Morgan). "Notes on First and Second Corinthians" (W. Kelly). Also by W. E. Vine.

Galatians. "Galatians" (Hogg and Vine). Also by Martin Luther; Lenski.

Ephesians. "The Book of Ephesians" (H. S. Miller). "The Wealth; Walk; and Warfare of the Christian" (Ruth Paxton). "Ephesians" (August Van Ryn).

Philippians. "The Epistle to the Philippians" (F. B. Meyer). Also by W. Kelly.

Colossians. "Colossian Studies" (H. G. Moule). "Oneness with Christ" (W. R. Nicolson).

First and Second Thessalonians. "Thessalonians" (C. F. Hogg and W. E. Vine).

First and Second Timothy. "To My Son," and "A Leader Led" (Guy H. King). "The Epistles to Timothy" (W. E. Vine). Also by W. Kelly.

Hebrews. "Lectures on Hebrews" (S. Ridout). "Studies in the Hebrew Epistle" (G. Henderson). "Exposition of Hebrews" 3 volumes by A. W. Pink. "Expository Lectures on Hebrews" (Adolph Saphir). "Let us go on" (Griffith Thomas). Also by W. Kelly.

James. W. Kelly.

First and Second Peter. "Epistles of Peter" (W. Kelly). "The Apostle Peter" (Grif. Thomas). "Tried by Fire" (F. B. Meyer). "Simon Peter, His Life and Letters" (W. T. P. Woolston).

First, Second, and Third John. "The Epistles of John" (W. Kelly). "The First Epistle of John" (A. Van Ryn). Also by W. E. Vine.

Jude. "The Epistle of Jude" (W. Kelly). "Acts of the Apostates" M. Coder.

Revelation. "The Revelation" (W. Scott). "The Revelation of Christ" (F. W. Grant).

(21) *Church Truth.*

"God's Principles of Gathering" (Geo. Goodman). "The Church and its Order" (S. Ridout). "Bishops, Priests, and Deacons" (W. Hoste). "The Church" (W. E. Vine). Also by Arthur G. Clark. "Scriptural Principles of Gathering" (Alfred P. Gibbs).

(22) *The Life of Christ.*

"Life and Times of Jesus, the Messiah" (Edersheim). "Moral Glories of the Lord Jesus" (J. G. Bellett). "The Divinity of our Lord" (Lidden). "The Modern Student's Life of Christ" (Vollmer). "The Virgin Birth" (G. Machen). "The resurrection of Jesus" (Orr). "The Christ We Forget" Wilson.

(23) *Homiletics.*

"The Preparation and Delivery of Sermons" (Broadus). "Lectures to my Students" (Spurgeon, 2 vols.). "Expository Preaching, Plans and Methods (F. B. Meyer). "The Preacher, His Life and Work" (J. H. Jowett).

(24) *Heresies and False Cults.*

"Heresies Exposed" (W. C. Irvine). "Evolution at the Bar" (P. Mauro). "Seventh Day Adventism Renounced" (A. M. Canright). "Mrs. Eddy" (E. F. Dakin). "Holiness, the True and the False" (H. A. Ironside). "Divine Healing" (H. P. Barker). "Spiritualism, and the Fallen Angels" (J. M. Gray). "Comparative Religions" (J. Burrell). "The Two Babylons" (J. Hyslop). "The Mormon's and Their Bible" (M. T. Lamb). A well written expose of the absurdity of the Book of Mormon.

(25) *The Holy Spirit.*

"The Person and Work of the Holy Spirit" (S. Ridout). "The Vicar of Christ" (H. P. Barker).

(26)   *Difficulties in the Bible.*

"Talks to Men" (R. A. Torrey). "The Question Box" (C. I. Scofield). "Questions and Answers" (Loizeaux Bros.). "Bible Problems and Answers" (Hoste and Rodgers).

(27)   *The Gospel.*

"Grace and Truth" (W. P. Mackay). "The Gospel, and its Ministry" (Robt. Anderson). "The Way made Plain" (J. H. Brooks).

(28)   *Biographical.*

"Bible Characters" (Alex Whyte). F. B. Meyer, on Abraham, David, Elijah, Israel, Joseph, Moses, Samuel, Jeremiah, Joshua, Zechariah, John the Baptist, Paul and Peter; "Elijah, the Tishbite" (Kraumacher). Also on "Elisha," "Delivering Grace, Studies in the Life of Elisha" (J. T. Mawson). "Gideon" (P. Pell). "The Apostle John" (Grif. Thomas). "Moses" (A. C. Gabelein). "Life of Paul" (Stalker). "Paul, the Missionary" (W. Taylor). "The Life and Epistles of Paul" (Coneybeare and Howson).

(29)   *Personal Evangelism.*

"Soul Winning" (Soltau). "The Divine Art of Soul Winning" (A. O. Sanders). "Catching Men Alive" (Trumbull).

(30)   *Pedagogy and Child Evangelism.*

"Introduction to Child Study" (C. Benson). "What to Teach, and How to Reach the Young" (Geo. Goodman). "Seventy Lessons in Teaching and Preaching Christ" (Geo. Goodman). "The Sunday School in Action" (C. Benson). "Principles of Teaching for Christian Teachers" (C. B. Eavey). "Seventy Best Bible Stories" 3 vols. (G. Goodman). "Child Evangelism" (Alfred P. Gibbs). "Object and Blackboard Talks" (Hy. Pickering).

(31) *Poetry.*

"Hymns of Worship and Remembrance." Poems by William Cowper, F. R. Havergal, Annie J. Flint, Fay Inchfawn, "Hymns of Ter Stegan," "The Oxford Book of Verse."

(32) *Missionary.*

"The Progress of World-wide Missions" (Glover). "The Divine Plan of Missions" (W. E. Vine).

(33) *Biographies of famous men and women.*

"George Muller" (A. T. Pierson). "Hudson Taylor in Early Years" (Mrs. Taylor). "The Life and Explorations of F. S. Arnot" (E. Baker). "The Life of Murray McCheyne" (Bonar). "The Life of D. L. Moody" (W. Moody). "C. T. Studd" (N. Grubb). "Anthony Norris Groves" (J. H. Lang). "Chief Men among the Brethren" (Edited by Henry Pickering). "The Life of J. G. Paton" (Paton). "Madame Guyon" (Upham). "The Autobiography of C. H. Spurgeon" (4 Vols.). "David Livingstone" (Blackie). "The Splendor of God," the Life of Judson (Morrow). "Harold St. John," by Patricia St. John.

(34) *Classics.*

Bunyan's "Pilgrim's Progress," and "The Holy War." Plays of William Shakespeare. "The History of England" (Macaulay). "Rise and Decline of the Roman Empire." (Gibbon).

(35) *Devotional.*

"Power through Prayer" (Bounds). "The Three Fold Secret of the Holy Spirit" (McConkey). "Kept for the Master's use" (F. R. Havergal). "Letters of Samuel Rutherford" (Bonar). "Godly Self Control" (A. T. Pierson). "Life on the Highest Plane" (Ruth Paxton). "The Light of the Morning" (Miss Swain). "Morning by Morning, and Evening by Evening" (Spurgeon). "Grace and Power" (Grif. Thomas). "The Christian's Secret of a Happy Life" (H. P. Smith). "Worship" (Alfred P. Gibbs).

(36) *Sermons by famous preachers.*

James Hamilton; (6 vols.) C. H. Spurgeon; J. H. Jowett; D. L. Moody; "Other Little Ships" (T. T. Shields); F. W. Boreham; G. H. Morrison; A. T. Pierson; J. T. Mawson; W. T. P. Woolston, D. Martyn Lloyd-Jones. "Sermon on the Mount."

(37) *Archeology.*

"Archeology and the Bible" (G. A. Barton). "The Bible, and the British Museum" (A. Habershon).

(38) *Sermon Outlines.*

"Handfuls on Purpose (J. Smith, 13 Vols.). "A Thousand new Bible Readings," and "Pearls, Points, and Parables" (F. B. Marsh). "Through the Scriptures" (Alfred P. Gibbs).

(39) *Illustrations.*

"A Thousand Tales Worth Telling," and "A Thousand Acts and Facts" (Edited by Henry Pickering). "Three Thousand Illustrations for Christian Service" (W. B. Knight). "Curiosities of the Bible" (J. H. Vincent).

(40) *Bible study.*

"Knowing the Scriptures," and "The Bible and Spiritual Life" (A. T. Pierson). "How to study the Bible for the greatest profit" (R. A. Torrey).

(41) *Physical and Mental Health.*

"Nerves in Disorder," and "Christian Sanity" (Dr. A. T. Scofield).

(42) *Hymnology.*

"English Hymns, their Authors and History" (Duffield).

(43) *The Ordinances.*

"Baptism" (Johannes Warns) also by (H. A. Ironside). "The Lord's Supper" (Alfred P. Gibbs).

(44) *Current Magazines.*

There are many good magazines devoted to the exposition of the word of God. Many of these contain excellent articles, which will prove to be of great use to the preacher. It is almost impossible to preserve all these copies in their entirety, due to lack of space and difficulty of reference. With the aid of a pair of scissors and a little library paste, the most striking articles can be cut out and placed in a filing cabinet, of which more anon.

The following magazines have proved to be very useful for this purpose: "The Witness" (Published by Pickering and Inglis, London, England). "Light and Liberty" (Published by The Walterick Publishers, Box 2216, Kansas City, Kansas); "Help and Food" (Published by Loizeaux Bros., 19 W. 21st St., New York); "The Sunday School Times," 1211 Arch St., Philadelphia 5, Penna.; "The Gospel Herald" (Published by the Union Gospel Press, 200 Brookpark Rd., Cleveland, Ohio).

(45) *Pamphlets.*

Many excellent pamphlets have been published, which merit a place in one's library. Sometimes these pamphlets contain, in condensed form, more truth than a large book. These pamphlets should be filed away topically as suggested in the pages that follow.

CHAPTER THIRTY

The Gathering of the Material

(Continued)

II. This Library should be indexed.

Two systems of indexing will be necessary: a card index and a filing cabinet.

1. *A card index.*

This will facilitate quick reference to any subject, or text that is dealt with in any of the library books. There may be a passage in a book that gives light, clearly and succinctly, on a certain subject, or on some passage of Scripture. This may be too long to copy out, yet it may be needed in the future when studying this particular subject. Unless one is possessed of a phenomenal memory, the book and page number will probably be forgotten and many hours wasted trying to find the needed quotation. If, however, this book and its page number is noted in a card index system, it can be found in a few moments.

This necessitates that a book be read with a pencil in hand, to mark, in the margin, any illuminating thought, or well-put phrase, or striking illustration. These marked pages should also (be indicated at the back of the book and, when time permits, transcribed into the card index. It will be advisable to index these quotations in two ways: topically and textually.

(1) *Topically.*

Arrange the topics in alphabetical order, as Acceptance, Advocacy, Angels, Assurance, Assembly truth, Atonement, etc. Indicate on the topical card the title of the book, and the number of the page on which the quotation can be found which refers to this subject. Some preachers number their books and this saves the effort of writing out the title. Thus "26 (417)" would mean book number twenty-six and page 417.

This indexing entails considerable work but, in the end, it is a great time saver. It becomes the "open sesame" to that fabulously rich storehouse which is one's library. "The Wilson Index System Book" is quite good. It would be wise to go to a good library and examine its system of cross indexing, and then work out a system best suited to oneself.

(2) *Textual.*

Arrange the card index according to the books of the Bible and, should it become necessary, the chapters and even the verses. Often a quotation from one's library book, which would be difficult to classify topically, can easily be classified textually.

2. *A Filing Cabinet.*

This serves the purpose of filing all clippings from newspapers and magazines, as well as small pamphlets, which are often as valuable as books, but which are easily mislaid because they are so small.

A steel filing cabinet is ideal, with four drawers. Use one for topical, one for textual, one for sermons and one for pamphlets. As in the card index system, both topical and textual indexes should be arranged. The value of starting this filing system at the *beginning* of one's ministry cannot be over emphasized. It is important to begin right, for this is half the battle.

(1) *Topical.*

Of necessity, there will be a little overlapping of subjects in this topical index. It would therefore be good to indicate on the index title, where else to look for a subject which contains the same *thought.* For instance, under "Thankfulness," write "See also Praise, and Gratitude." Under "Hell," write: "See also Retribution, Punishment, Judgment."

The following alphatetical list for a topical index may prove helpful to the beginner. It is suitable for both card index and filing cabinet. Other subjects can be added as occasion demands.

"A" Acceptance, Advocacy, Agnosticism, Angels, Anger, Archeology, Assembly truth, Assurance, Astrology, Astronomy, Atonement, Atheism.

"B" Babylon, Backbiting, Backsliding, Baptism, Blessings, Blood, Boasting, Books, Burial.

"C" Calling, Carelessness, Carnality, Children (Characteristics of, Care of, Conversion of); Christ (Birth of, Deity of, Life of, Death of, Resurrection of, Post resurrection ministry of, Ascension of, Present ministry of, Second coming of, Future reign of); Christian Science, Christmas, Church, Compassion, Communion, Complaint, Comfort, Consecration, Conscience, Conviction, Conversion, Courage, Coveteousness, Covenants, Creation, Cross, Criticism.

"D" Death, Death bed, (Experiences of the saved, Experiences of the unsaved), Deliverance, Decision, Delay, Denominationalism, Discipleship, Discipline, Dispensations, Division, Divorce, Discouragement, Doubt (or unbelief), Drink (or Intemperance), Drunkenness.

"E" Earnestness, Elders, Election, Encouragement, Endurance, Envy, Eternity, Evolution.

"F" Fables, Faintness, Faith, Fasting, Father, Family, Flesh, Forgiveness (Of sins, Of one another), Fighting, Fruit.

"G" God, Good works, Gambling, Gentiles, Giving Gospel, Gossip, Glory, Grace, Gratitude, Greed, Growth, Guidance, Guilt.

"H" Habit, Happiness, Hatred, Healing, Heart, Heathen, Heaven, Hell, Holiness, Holy Spirit, Honesty, Hope, Home, Hospitality, Humility, Husbands, Humor, Hymnology.

"*I*" Idolatry, Imagination, Immorality, *Immortality,* Incarnation, Ingratitude, Indifference, Inspiration, Invitation.

"*J*" Jealousy, Jerusalem, Jews, Joy, Judgment, Justice Justification.

"*K*" Kindness, Kingdom of God, Kingdom of Heaven, Knowledge.

"*L*" Law, Liberty, License, Life, Light, Lord's Supper, Lost, Love, Lust, Lying.

"*M*" Malice, Man, Marriage, Martyrs, Meditation, Mercy, Messiah, Ministry, Miracles, Missionary, Modernism, Misunderstandings, Mormonism, Mother, Money, Murder.

"*N*" Nature, Neglect.

"*O*" Obedience, Offerings, Old age, Opportunity, Ordinances.

"*P*" Parables, Pardon, Patience, Paul, Peter, Peace, Pedagogy, Pentecostalism, Perfection (sinless), Persecution, Pity, Power, Politics, Praise, Prayer, Preaching, Predestination, Prejudice, Priesthood, Pride, Profession, Prophecy, Protection, Purity.

"*Q*" Quarrelling.

"*R*" Rebuke, Reconciliation, Redemption, Reception, Racialism, Regeneration, Rejection, Remembrance, Repentance, Responsibility, Restoration, Retribution, Revival, Revenge, Reverence, Rewards, Resurrection, Roman Catholicism, Ritualism, Righteousness, Russellism (Jehovah's Witnesses).

"*S*" Sabbath, Sacrifice, Salvation, Sanctification, Satan, Satisfaction, Second Coming, Sectarianism, Security, Self, Selfishness, Separation, Service, Seventh Day Adventism, Science, Shame, Sin, Sorrow, Singing, Sickness, Smoking, Spiritism, Soul winning, Stars, Standing, Stealing, Substitution, Sunday School, Swearing.

"*T*" Tabernacle, Temper, Temptation, Temple, Testing, Testimony, Teaching, Thankfulness, Thoughts (good and bad), Theosophy, Theater, Time, Tongue, Tracts, Trial, Translation, Tribulation, Transformation, Training, Types, Truth, Trust, Temperance.

"U" Unbelief, Unfaithfulness, Unity, Unity (false cult), Unitarianism, Universalism.

"V" Vengeance, Victory, Virgin Birth.

"W" Walk, War, Warnings, Wastefulness, Watching, Will, Wisdom, Wives, World, Worldliness, Worry, Worship.

"Y" Youth.

We have already pointed out that there will be a little overlapping in this topical file. Therefore be sure to indicate on the index title where else to look for a subject which contains the same thought.

(2) *Textual.*

Arrange this file in the order of the books of the Bible, 66 in all. As the clippings increase, it will become necessary to subdivide a book. Genesis could be divided into five sections or more, as: "Chapters 1-9; 10-19; 20-29; 30-39; 40-50." The great value of this system of filing will be particularly appreciated when preparing an expository or a textual sermon.

D. L. Moody used to keep a number of large and strong envelopes, each labelled with a topic. As he cut clippings from various magazines, he would file them in these envelopes. This plan, though somewhat primitive, is similar to the one we have described, and would prove useful until a filing cabinet could be secured.

III. Wide reading is essential.

Bacon's famous words are in order here: "Reading makes a *full* man, writing makes a *correct* man and speaking makes a *ready* man." Someone has also remarked: "The man who does not *read* will never be *read*, and the man that never *quotes* will never be *quoted!*"

1. *The Bible should be the preeminent book.*

Nothing should be allowed to displace this in one's reading. The supreme purpose of reading other books, is solely to increase one's knowledge of the Book of books. To neglect the Bible for other books is fatal. The preacher can only speak with authority when he is saturated with the Scriptures. The fundamental and final question is: "What saith the Scriptures?" not: "What saith the Commentaries?" It is nice to know what men say, but it is *essential* to know what God says. A library that displaces the word of God is a curse. It is far better to have no library, than to allow the books of men to turn away one's heart from the holy Scriptures.

Sir Wm. Jones, the eminent Orientalist said: "The Bible, independent of its Divine origin, contains more true sublimity, more exquisite beauty, more pure morality, more important history and finer strains, both of poetry and excellence, than could be collected, within the same compass, from all other books that were composed in any age or in any idiom."

2. *History, both ancient and modern.*

The preacher will find much useful information from this source, which can be turned into good account. History is but the record of God's dealings with the nations, of which He is still the "Governor." See Psalm 22:28; Daniel 4:34-37; Deut. 32:8.

3. *Poetry.*

This will serve the very useful purpose of increasing one's vocabulary, and also of providing new and choice forms of expression, to say nothing of developing the imagination.

4. *Biographies.*

These serve the admirable purpose of both instruction, inspiration and warning. Every preacher should read at least two good biographies each year

5. *The classics.*

The reading of secular literature will open up a wide field of various subjects, useful for cultural purposes, and the development of a better appreciation and use of the English language.

6. *Sermons.*

Sermons by great preachers is a *must*. These will not only prove to be a blessing to one's own soul, but will become an education in Homiletics, and develop both facility of expression, aptness of illustration and ability of exposition.

7. *Periodicals devoted to Scripture exposition.*

We have already touched on these. Here again quality is to be preferred to quantity. It is possible to subscribe to too many of these magazines. Three or four should be ample.

8. *Secular magazines.*

These deal with current world topics. While much of this form of literature is worse than useless, there are one or two publications that will prove worth while. "The Reader's Digest" often provides useful material for both informative and illustrative purposes.

9. *Good gospel tracts.*

These are very useful to file, for they can serve a most useful purpose in illustrating a gospel message.

10. *The newspaper.*

This, when used sparingly and judiciously, will supply still more material for the purposes of illustration. Be sure, when cutting out an item, to put the *name* of the paper and the *date* on the clipping. This will give authority to the quotation.

IV. A Thought Book.

This should be a fairly small and thin loose-leaf affair, which can easily be carried in the pocket and the leaves quickly replaced.

Suggestive thoughts can be jotted down as they occur in moments of special inspiration, for sermons are both born and made. Often a text will grip the soul, or some incident be witnessed which will suggest a theme. This book will therefore become a cage in which to imprison all the birds of paradise that fly into one's mental parlor.

This book is also useful to record any interesting conversations with others, while the details are still fresh in the memory. Choice thoughts, expressed by others, can also be recorded therein. These, in turn, may start trains of thought in the mind.

Dr. Torrey used to sleep with his thought book on a table near his bed. Sometimes, when he awakened in the night, some thought would come to him regarding the Scriptures and he would immediately jot it down and go to sleep again. When he awakened in the morning, there was his thought, all ready to be worked on still further.

V. Notes of other preachers' addresses.

An address worth hearing is worth remembering. The best way to bring this about is to take notes of the sermon. These should be filed away, with the preacher's name and the date. One should beware of plagiarism. This has been defined as: "The adaption of another's material, without any attempt at mental assimilation." Credit should always be given for a long quotation. This is why it is wise to put the preacher's name on the notes taken of his address. Do not be afraid to quote. The words: "I remember hearing So and So say," will arouse the attention of an audience, particularly if the preacher quoted is well known and respected. Charles Lamb, explaining how he wrote one of his entrancing essays said: "I milked twenty cows to get the milk, but the butter I churned is all my own." Originality consists very largely in the setting forth of old truths in a new way, *one's own particular way*. Someone has facetiously remarked: "Copying from one writer is *plagiarism*—copying from many writers is *research!*"

VI. The "Homiletic Habit" should be developed.

This is accomplished in a two fold way.

1. *By observation.*

Each preacher should carefully observe how other preachers behave in the pulpit and the reaction of the audience to what they see and hear. Observe the language they use, the styles they adopt and the illustrations they employ. In this way much can be learned as to what to emulate and what to avoid in one's own preaching.

2. *By practice.*

Constant practice in preaching, as in everything else, makes for improvement. Gift grows with exercise. When time permits, take some texts and prepare an outline on them and then file these away for future reference. One should beware of resting on his oars, or of becoming complacent with his store of knowledge. The preacher must go on and *keep on going on*. It has been said that there are three stages each preacher must avoid. First, of getting *tired* of the work. (Note, not tired *in* the work). Second, of *retiring* from the work. Third, of becoming *tiresome* in the work.

Caleb is a good example of one who started well, went on well and ended up well. He is recorded as saying at the age of eighty-five: "As yet I am as strong this day as I was in the day that Moses sent me: as my strength was then, even so is my strength now, for war, both to go out and to come in" (Josh. 14:6-14). Let each reader determine that, by the grace of God, he will follow in the footsteps of this man who thus "fully followed the Lord."

CHAPTER THIRTY-ONE

The Delivery of the Sermon

Having discussed the qualifications of the preacher; his call; the necessity for preaching; the structure of the sermon; the various types of sermons; the preparation of the sermon; and the gathering of the sermon material; let us now consider the no small matter of the delivery of the sermon.

Introduction.

The sermon, which has been prayerfully and carefully prepared, must now 'be preached, or it will profit no one. "How shall they hear without a preacher? . . . Faith cometh by hearing and hearing by the word of God" (Rom. 10:14-17). Much depends, not only on the *matter* which the audience hears, but the *manner* in which the matter is given. Many a good message has been spoiled because of the manner of its delivery. Just as "the vessel was marred in the hands of the potter;" so the message may be marred in the hands of the messenger. (Jer. 18:4).

1. *Some types of delivery.*

Bishop Wakefield has wittily described seven types of sermon delivery which have been inflicted, from time to time, on long-suffering audiences. Other types might be added, but these will suffice by way of "horrible examples."

(1) *The Sesquippedalian.*

This type is distinguished chiefly by the multitude of its jaw-breaking words which enabled the preacher to say nothing at extreme length. The big words were merely a camouflage to conceal his very little thoughts.

(2) *The Wishy-Washy.*

In this type, the few little thoughts are so diluted with empty phraseology and vague generalizations, that no one

342

can guess what the speaker is trying to convey. It was of
such a speaker that this story is told. As a man emerged
from a political rally, he was approached by a person who
inquired: "Who's speaking now?" He replied "Congress-
man Smiffkins." "What's he talking about?" was the next
question, and the man answered: "Well, he didn't say!"

(3) *The Pyrotechnic.*

This style consists of a veritable fireworks display. It
has plenty of blazing mataphors, scintillating epigrams,
thrilling illustrations and dramatic gestures, concluding
with a slight odor of gunpowder. It leaves the audience
slightly dazzled, but with very little idea of what it was
all about. The hearers were impressed with the *messenger,* but not with the message. All agree it was "a wonderful address," but no one seems able to recall what the
sermon was about.

(4) *The Anecdotic.*

In this, a lot of stories, mostly of the "chestnut" variety,
are strung together and told at interminable length. None
of them are very pertinent to the theme and the audience
is bored beyond description. Some are unkind enough
to suggest that perhaps there may be some connection
between *dotage* and *anecdotage!*

(5) *The Flowery.*

In this, there are lots of pretty expressions, well
rounded phrases, plenty of poetic quotations and with a
strong appeal to the esthetic. However, the sermon is
characterized more by rhyme than reason, by sentiment
than sense and by poetic quotation than practical exhortation.

(6) *The Mellifluous.*

Such an address is a smooth flowing affair, dripping
with honeyed phraseology and expressed in well modulated tones. It goes on and on, with calm unbroken flow,
but apparently with no conviction on the part of the

speaker, and certainly with no grip whatever upon the consciences of those who hear.

(7) *The Paregoric.*

Against this kind of preaching, the powers of wakefulness fail. It is like an anesthetic, which benumbs the senses, drugs the powers of concentration and leaves its victims unconscious. As the bishop· observes: "It is like a roll of ribbon, so much alike, that a yard can be cut off anywhere!" A guide, while conducting a visitor through a very ancient church building, in which many bodies had been buried, remarked: "A great many people sleep within these walls." The visitor enquired: "Why don't they get a more interesting speaker?"

From such types of delivery, we may well pray to be delivered, for they defeat the very purpose that preaching is intended to accomplish, namely: the *effective* presentation, to the soul of the hearer, of the living word of God.

2. *The need for the preacher's self discipline.*

Paul's letter to a young preacher named Timothy should have a special appeal to all who have the God-given desire and ability to preach and teach. In this first letter, Paul uses the word "thyself" seven times. Each time the word is used, some fresh spiritual significance is given to "the preacher and his preaching." Let us briefly note these seven occurrences of the word, "thyself," and see what we can learn to profit.

(1) *"Behave thyself"* (I Tim. 3:15).

The preacher must be an example of his preaching. He who would exhort his hearers to behave themselves "as becometh saints," must also behave himself as becometh a preacher, both in and out of the pulpit (Eph. 5:3). He who would be a good *conductor,* must be characterized by good *conduct.* As the inspired writer puts it: "In all things showing *thyself a pattern* of good works, in doctrine showing uncorruptness, gravity, sincerity, sound speech that cannot be condemned, that he who is of the contrary part may be ashamed, having no evil thing to say of you" (Tit. 2:7-8).

(2) *"Exercise thyself."* (I Tim. 4:7).

The word for exercise is "gumnazo," from which "gymnasium" and "gymnastics" is derived. The preacher, to be effective, must therefore enter upon and consistently maintain, a course of spiritual calisthenics.

(a) *He must have an exercised conscience* (Acts 24:16).

While the conscience is no true guide in itself, but must be enlightened and guided by the word of God; yet to go against an *enlightened* conscience is to court spiritual disaster. There is therefore a constant need for the conscience to be adjusted to the will of God, as found in His word. An exercised conscience will cost much to keep, but no expense is too great to maintain this priceless boon. It has been said: "He who loses his good conscience, loses the only thing that is worth keeping."

(b) *He must have an exercised mind* (Heb. 5:14).

The preacher has been given brains in order to use them. His lifetime task will be to educate himself along various lines, if he is to be his best for God.

(c) *He must have an exercised spiritual life* (I Tim. 4:7).

Anything that promotes godliness should be assiduously cultivated. It is possible to become spiritually stagnant through failure to add the Christian virtues enumerated in II Peter 1:5-7. Spiritual muscle, through disuse, degenerates into flabby self-complacency. This, in turn, is the precursor of spiritual impotency.

(d) *He must have an exercised physical body* (I Tim. 4:15).

"Bodily exercise profiteth for a little time." Judicious physical exercise is therefore necessary for the arduous task of preaching, and the preacher is well advised to keep himself physically fit for the work.

(3)   *"Give thyself!"* (I Tim. 4: 15).

Wholehearted and sacrificial service is surely the least the preacher can give to a cause as great as his. What costs nothing, gives nothing and does nothing is worth *nothing!* "How often we give God the dregs of our time, the sacrifices of our exhaustion and the mere scrapings of our superfluities!"

The preacher must *give himself* to and *deny himself* for the Lord. He should willingly give of his *time, talents, strength* and *money* to further the interests of the One Who sacrificed all for him (Rom. 12:1-2; Matt. 16:24; Eph. 5:16). The: "Well done, thou good and faithful servant" of his Lord, will more than compensate for all the toil of the way. (Matt. 25:21).

(4)   *"Watch thyself!"* (I Tim. 4:16).

"Take heed unto thyself and to the doctrine." The preacher will soon discover he is his own worst enemy and that he has a traitor within his breast. Unless restrained by diligent and merciless self-judgment, there is no limit to the possibility of both moral and spiritual disaster. George Muller used to pray: "Lord, keep me from becoming a wicked old man!" Our Lord's word to His disciples was: "Watch and pray, lest ye enter into temptation" (Matt. 26:41).

The preacher must therefore constantly watch his *thoughts,* for from these spring words, actions and attitudes. He must also watch his *words* lest, like Moses, he speak inadvisedly with his lips (Ps. 106:33). He must watch his *company,* for it is still true that "evil communications corrupt good manners" (I Cor. 15:33). He must watch his *actions,* avoiding the "very appearance of evil" (I Thess. 5:22). Furthermore, he must watch his *opportunities* for witnessing for Christ and of winning souls for Him (Gal. 6:10).

(5) *"Save thyself!"* (I Tim. 4:16).

This may sound strange but, of course, it has no reference whatever to the soul's eternal salvation. The thing in view here is salvation from present failure in one's ministry and of future loss at the judgment seat of Christ (I Cor. 3:10-15). Thus salvation, in this sense, is dependent on a faithful continuance in the doctrine and a conscientious discharge of one's responsibilities to his hearers.

(6) *"Keep thyself!"* (I Tim. 5:22).

While it is perfectly true that the believer is being "kept by the power of God;" it is equally true that he must keep himself from all that which would hinder his usefulness in the Lord's service. Each preacher should therefore:

(a) *Keep under his body* (I Cor. 9:27).

That is, the physical must always be under the control of the spiritual. The body must ever be the servant of the spirit. Both Samson and Solomon allowed their bodies to control them and disaster followed. "Self-control" is not the least of the nine-fold qualities of "the fruit of the Spirit" (Gal. 5:22-23).

(b) *Keep himself from idols* (I John 5:21).

These are the last solemn words of John's first epistle. An idol is anything that displaces God in the life, or which relegates Him to a secondary place. One does not have to bow down to a material idol to become an idolater. It is possible for a person to worship himself and become so wrapped up in himself that he lives for himself alone. Though it is true he makes but a very small parcel, yet such self occupation is idolatry. One can allow his position, pleasures, possessions or even his family to eclipse God.

(c) *Keep himself pure* (I Tim. 5:22).

Purity in thought, word and deed is essential to service for the Lord, *who* "loves righteousness and hates iniquity." Therefore care must be taken as to what is read, heard and seen and where one goes.

(d)   *Keep himself in the love of God* (Jude 21).

The lost sense of personal appreciation and enjoyment of the love of God produces a chilly formality, a cold politeness, an icy regularity and a frigid orthodoxy. The love of God has been "shed abroad" in the believer's heart, to be *spread abroad,* from his heart, in love-motivated and love-energized service for Him. God's love is like the sunshine and each Christian must continually bask in it until it permeates his whole being.

(e)   *Keep himself unspotted from the world* (James 1:27).

He must resolutely decline the world's seductive vanities, its sinful pleasures, its cunningly devised snares, its well concealed entanglements, its false standards of ethics, its prideful popularity and its corrupting friendships. The preacher is described as being a *"light"* in it, a *"stranger"* to it and a *"pilgrim"* passing through it. Thus, though he is *in* the world, he is, most emphatically, not *of* it (Phil. 2:15; I Pet. 2:11; John 17:14). He must therefore not 'be surprised if he is hated by it. (John 15:18-25).

(7)   *"Withdraw thyself!"* (I Tim. 6:3-5).

The preacher must withdraw himself from all that would hinder his usefulness in the Lord's work. He must refuse all unscriptural *doctrines* (I Tim. 6:5). He must avoid all unequal *partnerships* (II Cor. 6:14-18). He must forego all unlawful *amusements, habits* and *hobbies* (I Thess. 5:22). He must eschew all unprofitable *arguments* and *unspiritual companionships* (I Tim. 6:4). Thus, from anything and everything that would hinder him, comes the word from his Master: "From such *withdraw* thyself!"

This has been a somewhat lengthy introduction to the topic of the delivery of the sermon; but as it was pointed out in the beginning of the book, the preacher cannot be divorced from his preaching. He is linked with his message, even as the source of a river is with its flow.

CHAPTER THIRTY-TWO

The Delivery of the Sermon

(Continued)

As we consider the delivery of the sermon, we shall think particularly of Paul's word to Timothy: *"Watch thou* in all things." Let us note carefully seven things that each preacher should watch if he is to be his best for God.

I. He should watch his manners.

An old saying has it: "Manners maketh the man." The audience will undoubtedly be influenced, either favorably or unfavorably, not only by the *message* that is given, but by the *manner* of its delivery. What, then, should be the manner of the preacher as he delivers the message?

1. *He should be humble, but not servile.*

(1) *Pride ill becomes the preaching of the cross.*

The pompous, self important and over-confident air of a preacher carries its own condemnation. It dooms, from the very start, the effectiveness of his message. No audience likes to see a speaker strut, with a consciously superior air, to the platform. Nor does it care to hear him speak in a condescending manner. This justly awakens its resentment and earns its antipathy. The preacher should ever remember he is a servant of the One, Who "made himself of no reputation, . . . and . . . humbled Himself," and who declared: "I am among you as he that serveth." (Phil. 2: 7-8, Luke 22: 27).

Pride always "goeth before destruction, and an haughty spirit before a fall" (Prov. 16: 18). The story is told of an overconfident and self-sufficient young preacher, who mounted the pulpit with an overweening sense of his own importance and the assurance of his ability to impress the people with his knowledge and eloquence. His sermon, however, was a dismal failure, and he descended with the mortified realization that he had made both a fool of himself and a sorry hash of his well prepared sermon. An old brother, seeing this, remarked to him: "If you had gone *up* to the platform in the frame of mind that you came *down* from the platform; you would have come *down* from the platform in the way you went *up!*"

Still another story is told of a preacher named Samuel Smith. After he had delivered his sermon he asked a friend his opinion of the address. His friend replied: "Instead of preaching Christ and Him crucified, you preached Samuel Smith and him dignified!" Of a certain preacher it was said: "If we could buy him at the price we put on him, and sell him for a price he places upon himself, we would make a huge profit on the transaction!"

A young man, called to minister to a small country church, determined that his sermons should set a standard of excellence hitherto unknown in that community. With this in view, he prepared his first sermon with meticulous care. As he delivered it, he realized that Paul's sermon on Mar's Hill was sorry by comparison to this masterpiece he was delivering. The congratulatory comments of his audience, after the sermon, only served to reaffirm what he already knew: he was terrific! The last parishoner to greet him was an old lady who, as she took his hand in hers whispered softly: "Did anyone ever tell you how *wonderful* you are?" His answer: "No," lacked all vestige of conviction. "Well, then," continued the old lady: "Wherever did you get the idea?"

(2)   *Humility is enjoined upon the servant of Christ.*

The great scriptural principle holds good here; "He that exalteth himself shall be abased, but whosoever humbleth himself shall be exalted" (Luke 18:14). The way "up" in the things of God is always *"down"!* We must first humble ourselves under the hand of God and then the hand of God will 'be placed under us to lift us up (I Pet. 5:5).

Paul testified that he "served the Lord with all humility of mind" (Acts 20:19). The believer is exhorted to: "Put on therefore, as the elect of God, holy and beloved, bowels of mercies, kindness humbleness of mind, meekness, longsuffering," etc. (Col. 3:12). God's promise of guidance is conditioned to those who are "meek" (Psa. 25:9).

The preacher should be like an auctioneer who, when selling a painting, placed the picture in front of him while he pointed out its beauties to the audience. As he was thus hidden behind the picture, the people forgot the auctioneer and centered all their attention on the masterpiece he was describing, and each longed to possess it for himself. May it be ours to so describe and present Christ that the hearers shall long to know Him for themselves and forget all about us. The old adage: "children should be seen and not heard" should, in the case of the preacher, be altered to: "preachers should be heard and not seen."

The following poem will serve to illustrate the effect of this humility of spirit. It is called: "The Faithful Preacher."

> He held the lantern, stooping low,
> So low that none could miss the way;
> And yet so high to bring in sight,
> That picture fair, the world's great light:
> That gazing up, the lamp between,
> The hand that held it scarce was seen.
>
> He held the pitcher, stooping low,
> To lips of little ones below,
> He raised it to the weary saint,
> And bade him drink, when sick and faint.
> They drank, the pitcher thus between,
> The hand that raised it scarce was seen.

He blew the trumpet soft and clear,
To call the waiting soldier near;
And then with louder note and bold,
To raze the walls of Satan's hold.
The trumpet coming thus between,
The hand that raised it scarce was seen.

But when the Captain says, "Well done,
Thou good and faithful servant, come.
Lay down the pitcher and the lamp,
Lay down the trumpet, leave the camp,"
The weary hands will then be seen,
In His pierced hands, with naught between!
—Unknown.

(3) *The other extreme of apologizing for one's presence in the pulpit should also be avoided.*

While overconfidence is to be condemned, yet we must
not go to the other extreme and apologize to the audience
for our presence in the pulpit. Doubtless our friends
will be prepared to do this for us after we are through
preaching the sermon! Each preacher is an ambassador
and, as such, his message requires no apology. The divine
injunction is: "If any man speak, let him speak as the
oracles of God" (I Pet. 4:11). Very often these expressions of self-depreciation are merely a form of that pride
which apes humility, and serves only to detract attention
from the message and focus it on the messenger. It says,
as it were, to the audience: "Please notice how very
humble I am!" Both extremes of either self-advertise-
ment or self-depreciation should therefore be avoided.

The preacher has the holy Scriptures as his authority,
the Holy Spirit as his enabling redemption as his theme,
Christ as his supreme Subject, and the glory of God
as his aim. Such a message requires no apology. With becoming modesty, yet with holy boldness, the preacher
should deliver the message God has given him and then
be content to leave the results in the hands of his Master.

The poet has beautifully expressed it thus:

"When telling Thy salvation free,
Let all absorbing thoughts of Thee,
  My heart and mind engross:
And when all hearts are bowed and stirred
Beneath the power of Thy word,
  Hide me behind the cross."

2. *He should be earnest, yet self possessed.*

(1) *An audience will forgive almost anything in a preacher, except a lack of earnestness.*

The preacher may fail in the grammatical exactness of his speech; he may not possess eloquence; he may not present a good appearance in the pulpit; but all this will be forgiven if he is earnest in his manner and sincere in his presentation of the gospel.

A somewhat uncouth preacher saw many souls saved under his ministry, while his more cultured brethren saw little fruit in the gospel. On being asked to explain the reason, he replied: "You shoot at the *heads* of your audience and often miss; I fire at the *third button of the vest!*" Daniel Webster, the great lawyer and politician, while living in Washington, used to attend the ministry of a very ordinary preacher. When asked to explain why he went to hear this man, when there were so many better preachers in town he replied: "This minister preaches as if God were at his elbow!"

Dean Church once observed: "People are quick to discover whether the preacher speaks from his heart, or his library shelves." No speaker is more persuasive than when he speaks from the depths of his heart, as he is moved by an intense conviction of the verities he proclaims. This will be communicated by the tone of his voice, the expression on his countenance and the earnestness of his manner. This is particularly evident in Paul's letter to the Galatians. Note the tremendous earnestness with which he pleads with his readers, for he realizes their great peril and dire need to be delivered from the danger toward which they were drifting; hence his passionate outbursts as he thus delivers his soul.

Matthew Simpson said of the preacher: "His throne is the pulpit; he stands in Christ's stead; his message is the word of God; around him are immortal souls; the Savior, unseen, is beside him; the Holy Spirit broods over the congregation; angels gaze upon the scene and heaven and hell await the issue. What associations and what vast responsibility!"

(2)   *The ideal combination.*

Someone has pointed out that the two greatest aids in effective preaching consists of a balanced combination of self-possession and self-abandonment. Self-possession is the product of knowledge, belief and through preparation. Self-abandonment is the result of sincerity and earnestness. "Self-possession, without self-abandonment, will make a man a statue; self-abandonment, without self-possession, will make him a fanatic!"

Wycliffe, the "Father of the English Reformation," said: "Preaching should be apt, apparent, full or true feeling, fearless in rebuking sins, and so addressed to the heart as to enlighten the spirit and subdue the will."

A story from the ancients will serve to further impress this need for earnestness upon our hearts. Demosthenes was once approached by a person who complained to him that he had been beaten and abused. This man described the incident in such an uninteresting and dreamy fashion that the great orator, instead of expressing his sympathy with him exclaimed: "Beaten thee? Hath anyone beaten thee? I do not believe it!" The man, shocked out of his apathy, replied: "No? You do not believe me?" Then, growing more indignant and becoming increasingly vehement in his gestures and voice, he cried:

"See! He did this to me! Look at these bruises! Do you not call this a beating?" Demosthenes replied: "Yes, now I believe he hath beaten thee, for thou speakest as if thou felt the truth of what thou sayest!"

(3) *Earnestness is the product of real conviction.*

Each preacher would do well to ask himself the following questions: "Do I really believe the truth of the message God has given me to preach? Have I really grasped the reality of the sinner's helpless, hopeless and hell-deserving condition? Do I really believe that Christ, because of His redemptive work at Calvary, is able to save, instantly and eternally, every repentant sinner who rests in the efficacy of His substitutionary sacrifice, and trusts Him as his own personal Savior? Do I thoroughly accept the fact that God's way of salvation is the *only way* by which sinners may be saved? Do I sincerely believe that all who neglect, despise, or reject this salvation, will be eternally lost? Do I preach as a dying man to dying men and women?"

If a preacher really believes these things—and he should not be preaching if he does not—then let him speak *as though he did believe them.* The earnestness of his manner will communicate itself to the audience and convince the hearers of his sincerity. Paul quoted the words of the Psalmist: "I believed, therefore, have I spoken," and then added: "We also believe and therefore speak" (Ps. 116:10, II Cor. 4:13). Peter, when charged to refrain from preaching Christ, replied: *"We cannot but speak* the things we have seen and heard!" (Acts 4:20). It has been well said: "He who cannot but speak, will speak to people who cannot but hear!"

Cowper thus describes the ideal preacher. Would that each of us could fit this description:

"There stands the messenger of Truth; there stands
The legate of the skies! His theme divine
His office sacred, his credentials clear.
By him the violated Law speaks out
Its thunders; and by him, in strains as sweet
As angels use, the Gospel whispers peace.

　　·　　·　　·　　·　　·　　·　　·　　·

He that negotiates between God and man
As God's ambassador, the grand concerns
Of goodness and of mercy should beware
Of lightness in his speech. 'Tis pitiful
To court a grin, when you should woo a soul,
To break a jest, when pity would inspire
Pathetic exhortations; and t'address
The skittish fancy with facetious tales
When sent with God's commission to the heart."

An agnostic went to hear D. L. Moody preach. On his
return, one of his friends sneeringly asked: *"You* surely
don't believe what *he* preaches, do you?" The man replied: "No, *I* don't believe it, but *he* certainly does!" An
old preacher once remarked: "The power to convince and
persuade consists of being *convinced* and *persuaded!*"

J. B. Watson, late editor of *"The Witness,"* has finely
remarked: "Remember that the outward form and mould
of your message and the delivery of it, while important,
is secondary in comparison with its inward frame and
spirit. Transparent earnestness in rags, will accomplish
more than elocution decked in silks. A message with almost every technical fault of form and presentation, will
be blessed despite its blemishes, if it is the outgoing of
a heart that God has touched."

3. *He should be courteous, yet faithful in his presentation of the message.*

(1) *The preacher should be tactful, and not tackful.*
Tact means "touch" (as in "contact"). This means
that the audience must be touched in such a way as not
to unnecessarily offend it. The preacher who indiscrim-

inately distributes his "tacks," should not be unduly surprised if his audience "sees the point," and never comes out to hear him again! Someone has said: "Talent knows *what* to do; tact knows *how* to do it. Talent makes a man *respectable;* tact makes him *respected.*" To put it in still another way: Talent is *gift;* tact is *gumption.* Many an audience has been lost to the speaker because of his rudeness, which he mistakenly imagined was "frankness."

There is a vast difference between forthrightness and rudeness. To take advantage of an audience by exhibiting one's ill temper and bad manners before it, is surely inexcusable. Coarse illustrations, that offend the modesty of the audience, should be avoided. We may well learn a lesson from the successful salesman. He not only studies the merchandise he is to sell, but cultivates the right method of approach and the correct manner of presenting his goods to each person, so that the sale may be effected to the satisfaction of both his master and the customer.

Paul's sermon on Mar's Hill illustrates the value of tact. Instead of immediately censuring his audience for its idolatry, he began by saying: "I see you are very religious" (Acts 17:22 R. V.). Sometimes the *tone of the voice* used is offensive. An old song used to have a verse that ran: "It isn't exactly what he says, but the nasty way he says it!" Such expressions as: "You sinners," or: "My sinner friend," are surely not seemly.

(2) *The platform should not be used as a "Coward's Castle."*

Needless to say, the platform should never be used to hit someone in the audience that the speaker is afraid to speak to on the floor. Neither should the platform be used as an operating theatre for the cutting off of people's ears. That is to say, no preacher should go out of his way to stir up smouldering prejudices but, on the contrary, he should endeavor to dispel their false ideas by a winsome presentation of the truth.

(3) *Beware of naming and criticizing certain denominations before a mixed audience.*

To be continually knocking this sect or that, only serves to provoke the resentment of any hearer who may belong to that sect, or has sympathy with it. From that moment the ears of this person are closed to that particular speaker. Nothing is gained by such tactics and often much is lost. The gospel is a *positive* thing: therefore preach Christ and God's way of salvation, and the Spirit of God will use this to reveal the truth. It is the word of God that will cut and expose, for it is described as a "two edged sword." As this is used with wisdom and power, it will reveal the truth and expose the error. The combination of courtesy and faithfulness will be hard to resist. Paul expressed it thus: "Giving no offence in anything, that the ministry be not blamed" (II Cor. 6:3).

(4) *He should refrain from scolding an audience.*

It is both ridiculous and unreasonable for a preacher, who finds himself facing a smaller audience than he expected, to berate those who *are* there because of those that were *not* there! It is far better to commend the audience for its courage in coming out to hear him; and then give the hearers his very best in the way of preaching. This will have the effect of bringing more out the next time he is advertised to preach in that particular place.

4. *He should develop his powers of sanctified imagination and description, but avoid the habit of exaggeration.*

The ability to paint word pictures should be studiously cultivated. Reading will be a great aid in this direction. Take note how some speakers with a few, but well chosen words, can conjure up a scene that is almost visible before the minds of the audience. Herein lies the value of good poetry. Writing will also help to develop this gift.

Take, for instance, Galatians 1:18. Here Paul describes his visit to Jerusalem and says: "I went up to Jerusalem to see Peter and abode with him fifteen days." Here is an opportunity for the play of one's legitimate imagination. What happened during this period, when these two great men of God were together? What did they talk about? Where did they go? Doubtless the conversation often turned to the Lord Himself, whom probably Paul had never seen on earth. One can picture Peter taking Paul to some of the hallowed spots in that city and saying: "It was here that the Lord did so and so, or said this or that." One can envision them making their way to Calvary, and sense the effect of all this on Paul who thus heard, first hand, of the matchless life and ministry of his blessed Lord.

One must beware, of course, of *going too far* in this development of the imagination. The abuse of the best is the worst. It is in the description of *actual events* that the preacher must beware of both imagination and exaggeration. In an actual incident he must stick to the facts of the case and "tell the truth, the whole truth, and nothing but the truth." The judicious use of the phrase: "Let us suppose," will indicate to the audience that imagination is now at the helm and that the boundaries are limitless!

5. *He should be good humored, but not flippant.*

(1) *Humor has its part.*

Humor, if kept in its right place, can play a useful part in preaching and teaching. Spurgeon, the prince of preachers, used it to very good advantage. One has only to read his "Lectures to My Students," and his "John Ploughman" series, to appreciate what a valuable asset it is. He used it skillfully to show to the unsaved the senseless absurdity of their excuses, and the utter futility of all their attempts to merit God's favor by their own efforts. Archibald Brown, one of Spurgeon's famous pupils, after using a humorous illustration, remarked: "I don't mind you laughing, for when you do, your mouths are open and while they are open, I can pop the truth down!" He then proceeded to apply his illustration in a way the audience never forgot.

(2) *The Scriptures contain humor.*

Notice Elijah's grim humor as he taunted the prophets of Baal (I Kings 18:2). See Christ's reference to the Pharisees, who meticulously strained their drinking water, lest a tiny gnat should find its way therein, but who readily, and with apparent ease, swallowed a whole camel! (Matt. 23:24). Mark His reference to the children's songs in the market places and His application to the Pharisees (Matt. 11:16). Isaiah's description of the abysmal folly of idolatry is probably unequalled. Note his use of humor, in the form of irony, etc. (Isa. 44:9-17; see also II Cor. 11:16-21). We should certainly be thankful to the Lord for His gift to us of humor, and those who lack this sense are indeed to be pitied. It is still true that "a merry heart doeth good, like medicine" (Prov. 17:22).

(3) *The limits of humor.*

That form of humor, used in preaching, which merely draws attention to itself and which exists only for its own sake, should be avoided. That humor which belittles sin, or serves to tone down the eternal verities of the gospel, is entirely out of place. The preacher must remember that he does not occupy the pulpit for the purpose of entertaining an audience; but to preach and teach the word of God. The subtle temptation is always present to "play to the gallery," but this must be consistently resisted, for it is a dangerous snare.

Sarcasm, when rightly used, can become a potent weapon in the hands of a wise preacher; but when wrongly used, it can do him and his cause much harm. It is a weapon that requires much skill, for it cuts both ways. It should therefore be used very sparingly and with great discretion.

6. *He should be neat in appearance, but not foppish.*

In other words, the preacher should be neither *foppish,* nor *sloppish.* He should neither appear as though he had emerged from a bandbox, nor from a rummage remnant sale. Common decency demands that his body and his linen should be clean and his clothes neat. The Christian ideal of dress is that a person should be so attired, that he will not draw undue attention to himself, either through the extreme of uncleanness and untidiness on the one hand, or of fashionplate sartorialness on the other.

7. *He should be manly in his deportment, but not imitative of anyone else.*

(1) *He should avoid lounging over the pulpit.*

Some preachers have acquired the bad habit of leaning on the pulpit, as though they were on the verge of a physical collapse. Surely there is no need for a speaker to drape himself over the pulpit. The preacher should be able to stand up manfully on both his feet, if he has them, in such a way as will both commend the gospel and command the respect of the audience.

Ramrod-like stiffness is also to be tabooed. The "Let me-like-a-soldier fall" attitude is equally unsuitable. It should hardly be necessary to say that his hands should be kept out of his pockets and left free to enforce his remarks with appropriate gestures. For a speaker to address an audience with his hands in his pockets is not becoming to an ambassador of the King of kings who is presenting the message of his royal Master.

(2) *He should eliminate all odd mannerisms, and grotesque gestures.*

These only serve to detract from the message. Each preacher should read Spurgeon's, "Lectures To My Students." The wise and witty counsel contained therein will greatly aid in the avoidance of the peculiar mannerisms and gestures which provoke either amusement or resentment, and thus mar the effectiveness of the sermon. Some of these peculiar *motions* of the preacher, which produce an unfavorable *commotion* in the audience, could be described as follows:

(a) *"The pugilist."*

He stands with clenched fists and whirling arms, as though threatening his hearers with severe bodily harm. He leads first with his left fist and then with his right, until the audience wonders when the K. O. is to be administered!

(b) *"The village blacksmith."*

This preacher ceaselessly pounds the Bible, as did Longfellow's village blacksmith his anvil: "With measured beat and slow, like the sexton ringing the village bell, when the evening sun is low." Many a well-bound Bible has had the inside of it knocked out by these sledgehammer tactics!

(c) *"The tailor's dummy."*

There is no movement at all from this type. He stands motionless, with his hands at the side of his body. All that is needed to complete the illusion is a price tag on the lapel of his coat.

(d) *"The thumb twiddler."*

The hands are clasped and placed over the pulpit. Then the thumbs begin to turn, first in one direction and then in the other.

(e) *"The fly away."*

The only motion this preacher makes is the stretching out of both arms at unexpected intervals, and then moving them up and down like a bird in flight.

(f) *"The button twirler."*

This person can ruin a button overnight, as he nervously buttons and unbuttons his coat during the sermon. The "watch chain fumbler," is the first cousin of this gentleman, but fortunately the wrist watch has practically eliminated this type.

(g) *"The heel rock."*

He rises first to his toes and then rocks back on his heels, and continues this strange motion during his entire address.

There are many other peculiar motions that could be described, but these will suffice to demonstrate the fact that it is possible for preachers to become jesters by their gestures.

Inasmuch as a preacher usually stands behind a pulpit, his gestures are confined largely to his head and hands, principally the latter. The proper use of the hand will therefore aid considerably in conveying the thought the speaker desires to impress on the minds of his hearers. Montaigne says: "With the hand we demand, promise, call, dismiss, threaten, entreat, supplicate, deny, refuse, interrogate, advise, reckon, confess, repent, express fear, shame and doubt. With it we instruct, command, unite, encourage, swear, testify, accuse, condemn, acquit, insult, despise, defy, disdain, flatter, applaud, bless, abuse, ridicule, reconcile, recommend, exalt, regale, gladden, complain, afflict, discomfort, discourage, astonish, exclaim, indicate, silence, and what not, with a variety and multiplication that keep pace with the tongue." The use of the hands has been described as "the common language of mankind."

(3) *He should seek to be himself, and not an imitator of someone else.*

One of the many subtle temptations of a young preacher is to ape the mannerisms, voice and gestures of some other preacher, instead of being natural and allowing God to express the message through his own personality. While imitation may be "the sincerest form of flattery," it must be remembered that flattery has been likened to soft soap, and soft soap consists very largely of lye! This ministry creates an atmosphere of artificiality, which is surely a thing to be avoided. God is a Being of infinite variety and no one individual is the exact replica of another. The spider does not attempt to make its web out of borrowed spools of silk, 'but spins one out of his own body.

Preaching should reflect the speaker's own personality and not that of someone else. It will be recalled that Beecher defined preaching as: "Truth through personality." There has only been one Spurgeon and one Moody. While we may learn much from other preachers, yet each speaker must be himself as he stands before an audience. Spurgeon once expressed the fear that he would leave behind him a lot of "little Spurgeons!" May it be yours and mine to be our very best for God, and not attempt to imitate anyone else; for what may be perfectly proper in one person, becomes utterly ridiculous in another.

Someone once defined the qualifications of the ideal preacher as follows: "He should have the strength of an ox, the tenacity of a 'bulldog, the daring of a lion, the industry of a beaver, the versatility of a chameleon, the vision of an eagle, the disposition of an angel, the loyalty of an apostle; the heroism of a martyr, the faithfulness of a prophet, the tenderness of a shepherd, the fervency of an evangelist and the devotion of a mother." This may evoke the query: "Who is sufficient for these things?" (II Cor. 2:16). The satisfying reply comes from the same Book. "Our sufficiency is of God, Who hath also made us able ministers of the new testament" (II Cor. 3:5-6).

CHAPTER THIRTY-THREE

The Delivery of the Sermon

(Continued)

II. He should watch his language.

Inasmuch as the gospel, or teaching message, is conveyed from the preacher to the audience by means of *words,* it is imperative that these words should present the message clearly and forcefully. Paul, speaking of his God-given commission to "preach among the Gentiles the unsearchable riches of Christ," adds: "And to make all men see what is the fellowship of the mystery" (Eph. 3:8-9). This should be the aim of all preaching: "to make men *see.*" A good question for each preacher to put to himself after his sermon is: "What have I made the audience to *see? Illumination* is essential to *edification.*

The Bible is composed of Spirit-chosen words. We are definitely informed that it was not written: "in the words that man's wisdom teacheth, but which the Holy Ghost teacheth" (I Cor. 2:13). The Scriptures have a great deal to say about the value of right words. It likens *"fitly chosen"* words to "apples of gold, in pictures of silver"—a pleasing combination indeed! (Prov. 25:11). Job complained of the *"vain words"* of his so-called "comforters," and then exclaimed: "How forcible are *right words!"* (Job 6:25). The wise preacher is described as seeking out *"acceptable words"* by which to convey his message, even *"words of truth"* (Ecc. 12:10).

Paul urged those who ministered the word of God to do so by means of words that were *"easy to be understood"* (I Cor. 14:9-19). We also read of *"multitudinous words,"* in which there does "not lack folly" (Prov. 10:

19). The Bible also makes reference to *"troubling"* words, "profitless" words, that can quite easily be dispensed with; *"idle* words," *"smooth* words," *"fair,"* but *"deceiving* words," and also *"ignorant"* words. (See Acts 15:24; II Tim. 2:14; Matt. 12:36; Rom. 16:18; Ps. 55:21; Job 35:16).

Seeing that the actual words, used by "holy men of God as they were borne along by the Holy Spirit," were selected by God Himself; how necessary it is for the preacher to be in the mind of God with regard to the words he uses in presenting the message God has given him! How often a message has been made the object of ridicule, because of the poorly chosen, ungrammatical and badly pronounced words of the speaker. While it must ever be remembered that the gospel is described as "the foolishness of preaching" (or the thing preached), it certainly should not consist of *foolish preaching* on the part of the speaker! (I Cor. 1:21). A school boy once defined a prime minister as "a preacher at his best!" May we all seek to be "prime ministers" in this sense of the term!

Language is the incarnation of thought, or thoughts clothed with words. These thoughts can come from the lips of the speaker either well, or poorly dressed. It depends entirely on the preacher himself. The more study he gives to words and the greater discrimination he uses in their utterance will determine, humanly speaking, the effectiveness of his message to the audience. Words therefore represent the *coinage* of the preacher. He must learn to rightly appraise their tremendous value and skillfully use these coins to the best advantage for his Master. Fifteen minutes a day, spent in the study of words, will prove to be an invaluable investment of that precious commodity called time.

It has been estimated that the vocabulary of a five year old child consists of 3,000 words. At the age of ten he knows 5,000 words. At fourteen he is acquainted with 10,000. When he leaves high school this has increased to 15,000. A college graduate knows from 20,000 to 30,000. Should he go into law or medicine, he will need to know a few thousand more. Words, therefore, form an important part of a person's life.

The poet has recorded his impressions of the value of words in the following lines, culled from "*The New York Inquirer:*"

Trade words, made words, fit for money mart,
Rude words, feud words, rending men apart;
Bright words, right words, gracing printer's art,
    Words of every shade and meaning.

True words, new words, radiating light,
Calm words, psalm words, putting grief to flight;
Wise words, prize words, enlisted for the right,
    Words of every shade and meaning.

Queer words, mere words, wasting precious life,
Barbed words, garbed words, urging men to strife;
Mean words, keen words, like a whetted knife,
    Words of every shade and meaning.

Plain words, sane words, pleasing to the ear,
Sweet words, fleet words, dissipating fear;
Fair words, rare words, bringing good-will here,
    Words of every shade and meaning.

Pale words, frail words, slender as a vine,
Long words, strong words, words that glow and shine;
Just words, trust words, breathing love divine,
    Words of every shade and meaning.

Play words, gay words, used by passing throng
Best words, jest words, found in speech and song;
Straight words, great words, overwhelming wrong,
    Words of every shade and meaning.

—Anon.

Since language is of such vital importance to the preacher, perhaps a few hints may be in order regarding its proper use in the presentation of the gospel and teaching message.

1.	*The language used must be simple.*

The Divine dictum is: "Except ye utter by the tongue words *easy to be understood,* how shall it be known what is spoken? for ye shall speak into the air" (I Cor. 14:9). Especially is this true when addressing children. They have but a small vocabulary and do not understand many of the words and phrases which are common to an adult. In fact, all preachers would be well advised to speak as much as possible to children. This will greatly aid in developing their ability to express themselves clearly and simply. A boy once inquired of his father: "What makes leaves fall off the trees?" The father replied: "It is a phenomenon of nature that only occurs in decidious trees to protect them from cold temperatures. The leaf is sealed at the node, shutting off the food supply, so it withers and dies. Does this answer your question?" The boy replied: "I guess so, except what makes the leaves fall off the trees?"

(1)	*Avoid involved sentences.*

Victor Hugo, in his "Les Miserables," has one sentence which contains 823 words. In it there are 93 commas, 31 semi-colons, four dashes and one period! This monstrosity covers three pages! A well known preacher, now with the Lord, often used sentences that took a minute to give. Though perfectly framed and grammatically correct, they were so involved that the hearers had great difficulty in following him. A very helpful exercise, to correct this particular fault, is to speak to a foreign audience by means of interpretation. This demands the use of short declarative sentences, which must be used like building blocks to erect the sermon in the hearer's mind. Perhaps one of the longest sentences in the New Testament is **Ephesians** 1:15-23. This however, could easily be reduced to several sentences. I. M. Haldemann was a past master in the art of using short sentences. In fact, his sentences were almost abrupt.

(2) *The words must be simple.*

(a) *Unnecessarily long words defeat their purpose.*

The use of long words, when short ones would serve the purpose equally well, only succeed in drawing the attention of the audience to the *learning* of the speaker and not the *lesson* he is seeking to teach. You will perhaps recall Goldsmith's description of the village schoolmaster, famous for his ability to argue:

> "While words of learned length and thundering sound,
> Amazed the gazing rustics gathered round;
> And still they gazed, and still the wonder grew,
> That one small head could carry all he knew!"

It has been said that: "Big, high sounding words, are often but the graves in which men bury their little ideas." Many a sermon of this type, which the hearers imagined to be *deep* was, in reality, only *muddy!* Shallow, muddy water and deep, clear water are alike in one respect, the bottom cannot be seen: but there the likeness ends! Of a certain preacher it was reported: "He went down deeper, stayed down longer and came up drier than any other man!"

Our Lord so spake that "the common people heard Him gladly" (Mark 12:37). Though He could be so profound as to reduce the most learned of His critics to confused silence; yet His language was so simple that no one was left in doubt as to His meaning (Matt. 22:46). Profundity of thought should therefore be balanced by simplicity of expression. We must beware of becoming verbal gymnasts, and making a mere display of language.

Disraeli referred to one such as being: "intoxicated with the exuberance of his own verbosity."

The Authorized Version of the Bible is an example of this. Of its 810,697 words, there are only 6,000 different words, and the average length of these words is five letters. This same simplicity of utterance is also true of "The Pilgrim's Progress," which has been classed as the next best book to the Bible. Shakespeare required 20,000 words with which to gift his characters with speech. Mark the simple, yet sublime words, found in such Scriptures as John 3:16; 1:1-13; 10:9; 14:1-3, etc. Notice the large number of monosyllables therein.

(b) *Some horrible examples of verbosity.*

One should beware of overdressing his thoughts by the use of stilted and entirely unnecessary phraseology. Who would not prefer the simplicity of:

"Twinkle, twinkle, little star,
How I wonder what you are:
Up above the world so high,
Like a diamond in the sky."

to the highly scientific absurdity:

"Scintillate, scintillate, globule vivific,
Fain would I fathom thy nature specific,
Loftily poised in the ether capacious,
Strongly resembling a gem carbonaceous!"

Sometime ago there appeared in a magazine the following, which was entitled: "Advice to young preachers." It will speak for itself.

"In promulgating your esoteric cogitations, or articulating your superficial sentimentalities and amicable, philosophical or psychological observations, beware of platitudinous ponderosity. Let your conversational communications possess a clarified conciseness, a compact comprehensibleness, coalescent consistency, and a concatenated cogency. Eschew conglomerations of flatulent garrulity, jejune babblement and asinine affectations. Let your extemporaneous descantings and unpremeditated expatiations have intelligibility and veracious vivacity, without rhodomontade or thrasonical bombast. In other words, talk plainly, briefly and don't use big words!"

The following gem appeared some time ago on an instruction sheet that accompanied an income tax blank. It is a good example of how *not* to instruct! "The surtax of any amount of surtax net income not shown in the table is computed by adding to the surtax for the largest amount shown which is less than the income, the surtax upon the excess over the amount at the rate indicated in the table." Does this tax your ability to determine what this tax talk is all about?

An editor was once asked by a curious young lady: "Why do you always carry a big blue pencil on the back of your ear?" The editor, with a twinkle in his eye, replied laconically: "To make a long story short: to make a long story short!"

A copywriter, asked to describe Ivory soap for advertising purposes wrote: "The alkaline elements and vegetable fat in this product, are blended in such a way as to secure the highest quality of saponification alone, with a specific gravity that keeps it on top of the water, relieving the bather of the trouble and annoyance of fishing around for it in the bottom of the bath tub during his ablutions." When this reached the advertising manager, he crossed it out and substituted for it two words. They were: "It floats!" Which of the two descriptions was best?

A colored man was once asked by a friend if he had a job. He replied: "Ah's got better than a job: Ah's got a perfession, Ah's an orator!" When asked to explain what an orator was, he replied: "If Ah asks *you*: 'What is two and two?' and you says, 'fouh,' dat's conversation. But if you asks *me*: What is two and two?' Ah says: 'When, in de course ob human events, it becomes necessary to take de numeral of de second denomination, and add de figger two; den it can be said, widout any fear of successful contradiction, de result am invariably fouh!' " Then he added significantly: "Dat's oratory!"

A teacher of home economics in a state university was giving a cooking demonstration before a crowd of farm women. During the course of her address, she said: "Take an egg and carefully perforate it at the basal end. Duplicate the process in the apex. Now apply the lips to one of the apertures and, by forcibly exhaling the breath, discharge the shell of its contents." On hearing this, an old woman whispered to a friend: "It beats all how different these new fangled ways is! When I was a gal, we just poked a hole at each end and blowed!"

(c) *The value of simplicity.*

Lord Cockburn, a great English lawyer, who became an equally famous judge, when asked the reason for his success as a lawyer replied: "I always picked out the most stupid looking member of the jury and addressed all my pleadings to him. If I could convince him of the innocency of my client, I knew I had convinced and could easily carry all the rest." Surely the gospel preacher would do well to take a leaf from this great jurist's book, and so speak that the simplest and least educated of his audience can easily understand the message.

Of a colored preacher who used many big words during the course of his address, one hearer sagely observed: "Ah kinder think he uses dem big words 'cause he's afraid dat if people knew what he was talkin' about, they'd know he didn't know what he was talkin' about!' "

George Soltau once gave an address that captivated a large audience. A preacher approached him after the service and enquired: "What was it that made that address so impressive?" Mr. Soltau replied: "I only used words of one syllable!" A reading of C. H. M.'s "Notes on the Pentetauch" is an education in itself, for he wrote in a beautifully clear and expressive English, and yet in the simplest style. W. E. Gladstone said of him: "He writes the purest English in England." Macaulay's writings are famous for their diction. Someone has said: "It is impossible to impress an audience with one's own cleverness and with Christ crucified at the same time."

The "art" of preaching consists chiefly in concealing the "art" of it! As two people were leaving a preaching service, one remarked to the other: "I liked that *preacher*." The other replied: "I liked that *preaching*." May it be ours to earn the latter commendation! Marcus Dods once said to preachers: "Never *underestimate* the intelligence of people, but never *overestimate* the use they make of their intelligence!"

CHAPTER THIRTY-FOUR

The Delivery of the Sermon

(Continued)

II. He should watch his language. (Continued)

2. *The language used should be grammatically expressed.*

(1) *Language has a grammatical foundation.*

The least a preacher can do is to study the rules governing the use of correct English and then seek to carry them out to the best of his ability. While it is true that many preachers did not have the advantages of a higher education while young; yet this does not excuse them for being content to remain in that condition.

Grammatical errors only serve to draw the attention of an audience from the *message* to the *messenger;* so that any attempt to rectify this situation should be encouraged. One such preacher, when describing the fiery furnace said: "They hotted that furnace seven times hotter than ever it used to was!" and was surprised when his audience smiled out loud. Then again, there are those preachers who can quote Greek by the yard, but cannot talk English by the inch!

(2) *Many excellent books and also correspondence courses are available.*

Should one desire to improve his English, the remedy lies in his own hands. There are quite a number of excellent books written for this very purpose. It would be a most profitable investment of one's time, money and energy to secure such a book, or take a definite course of study in English by correspondence.

Still others have gone to the expense of taking special tuition under a capable teacher of English. Then again, there are free night schools where any deficiency in the use of language can be remedied. Truly: "Wisdom crieth without; she uttereth her voice in the streets: she crieth in the chief place of concourse, in the opening of the gates: in the city she uttereth her words saying: 'How long, ye simple ones, will ye love simplicity?'" (Prov. 1:20-22).

(3) *The value of wide reading and the habit of writing.*

We have already touched on the advantage of this in a previous chapter, and simply mention it again to give further emphasis to the great value of this means of improving one's education in this direction.

(4) *The value of a good mentor.*

It would be a very helpful thing if every preacher could arrange to have some capable person, who is well versed in English, sit in the audience and be instructed to take careful note of any lapse in his grammar, or mistakes in his pronunciation, and faithfully inform him of all these after the meeting. This person should sit well back in the audience, with paper and pencil in hand and carefully jot down all the errors as they occur. While this will not prove to be very complimentary to the preacher, or soothing to the flesh, (for there is every possibility of this *mentor* becoming a *tormentor!*) it would be an excellent discipline for his spirit, and certainly make for a more efficient use of language.

The Scripture declares: "Faithful are the wounds of a friend." Prov. 27:6. Surely it is far better for a person to have his feelings hurt, by having his faults exposed in a frank and friendly fashion, than to continue to inflict these hurts upon an audience. Solomon aptly said:

"A wise man will hear and will increase learning, . . . but fools despise wisdom and instruction" (Prov. 1:5-7).

Spurgeon, perhaps the greatest preacher the world has known, acknowledged his indebtedness to an anonymous critic who wrote him a letter each week, criticizing his sermon. Of him Spurgeon wrote: "An unknown censor, of great ability, used to send me a weekly list of my mispronunciations and other slips of speech. He never signed his name, and that was my only cause of complaint against him, for he left me with a debt I could not discharge. With genial temper and an evident desire to benefit me, he marked down, most relentlessly, everything which he supposed me to have said incorrectly. Concerning some of his criticisms, he was himself in error, but for the most part he was right. His remarks enabled me to perceive many mistakes and avoid them in the future. I looked for his weekly memoranda with much interest and, I trust, am all the better for them."

(5) *Some common lapses in English.*

(a) *The use of "You and I," and "You and me."*

Even the best of speakers sometimes slip up on this expression. This should be carefully watched and practiced, until it almost becomes second nature to use the right phrase. For instance, one sometimes hears a preacher say: "Christ died for you and I." This, of course, is wrong; it should be "you and me." The best way to discover which is the correct form is to use each pronoun separately and say: "Christ died for you and Christ died for me." If there is any doubt, the plural can always be used. It is always correct to say: "Christ died for *us;*" or *"We* are the subjects of God's grace."

(b) *The use of "their," with "everyone."*

It is quite a common thing to hear a preacher say: "Everyone has *their* own opinion," or "way of thinking," or "religion." It should be: "Everyone has *his* own opinion," etc. The Bible gives it correctly: "We have turned, everyone to his own way" (Isa. 53:6).

(c) *The use of "lay," "lie," "lain" and "laid."*

Again the Bible gives us the correct usage of these words. "I laid me down and slept." "He maketh me to lie down." "Let us lay aside every weight." President Coolidge, when asked if he ever had any difficulty with these terms replied: "When I was a boy and lived on a farm and heard a hen cackling; it was always a problem to me to know whether she had been really laying, or was merely lying!"

3. *The language used should be forceful.*

That is, the words should express exactly what the speaker has in mind. This is not quite so easy as it sounds, for it involves the use of *specific* words, by which to convey the right *shade* of meaning that is desired.

(1) *He should be a student of specific words.*

One has often been struck by a speaker's use of some choice phrase, that aptly and adequately set forth some phase of Divine truth. Perhaps few in the audience realized the tremendous amount of concentrated effort it required to coin that illuminating phrase, or to select that excellent definition, which clarified that obtuse doctrine or term.

Some famous secular writers have confessed that they have worked for hours over *one paragraph* in order to express their thought in as clear, succinct and forceful a way as possible. A friend of Thackeray once called on him in the early evening and found him working on a sentence. When he returned, four hours later, the author was still at work on that sentence, but it turned out to be one of the greatest sentences in the English language. Balzac, the French novelist, would frequently spend a week on a single page. Buffon, the French naturalist, was 50 years writing his great studies of nature, and he recopied it eighteen times before sending it to the printer. Bryant's "Thanatopsis" was rewritten a hundred times before it was offered to the world. Gerhard Dow, the famous Dutch painter, would spend five days painting a hand, and once took a whole day to paint a dewdrop on a cabbage leaf. Gray's famous "Elegy, written in a country churchyard," was polished for twenty years before it was released for publication. It is one of the few poems in the English language, a line of which cannot be altered to advantage.

There are words in the English language that will *exactly express* the shade of meaning that is necessary; but these words must be *dug out* in the study before they can be made to *come out* in the sermon. Mark Twain once said: "The difference between the *right* word and the *almost right* word, is the same difference that exists between lightning and a lightning bug!" David did not indiscriminately choose the five stones with which to face Goliath, but only those which *exactly* suited his purpose. The preacher must do likewise with the words of his sermon. Suitable words will not *pop out* of his mouth on the platform, that have not been *packed into* his mind in the study.

(2) *He should constantly seek to add new words to his vocabulary.*

If he can add but one new word every day, the results will be surprising. He should first find out the specific meaning of this new word, together with its correct pronunciation. Then he should write it out *ten* times and use it *ten* times in conversation. After this, the word is his for the rest of his lifetime.

The dictionary should never be far from a preacher's elbow. This study of words will become a fascinating as well as a most profitable occupation. An unabridged dictionary is invaluable, for by it one can discover the etymology, or derivation of words. Much sermon material can also be gathered in this way and fresh light thrown on Bible words. "The Reader's Digest" devotes two pages each issue to specific words and aptly entitles this section: "It pays to increase your word power."

The use of Roget's "Thesaurus" is practically essential to this study of words, for it gives a wide range of synonyms (or words that have nearly the same meaning) and antonyms (or words with the opposite meaning). Constant reference to it will save a speaker from that endless repetition of the same words, which becomes monotonous and mars so many addresses.

Wordsworth once said: "At the door of the lips, the invisible thought or emotion takes sensible form. Hence, it is the most skilled and trained tongue that can give thought its most perfect form of speech. How many an unuttered epic, or ethical system, or mighty oration lies behind an incompetent tongue, agonizing for competent expression!" Earnest, concentrated study and prayer will do much to open these lips to speak of he One, "Whom having not seen, we love." Like David, we too need to pray: "O Lord, open Thou my lips and my mouth shall shew forth Thy praise" (Psa. 51:15).

(3) *He should also make a study of the principal figures of speech.*

A figure of speech is a variation from the accepted usage of words and phrases, by which to simplify expression, or give unusual emphasis to an idea. There are many such figures of speech, with which every preacher should familiarize himself. Let us look at a number of the most important.

(a) *A Parable.*

This word comes from "para," =beside, and "ballo," =to throw. Therefore it means to throw beside, or along side, or compare. A parable teaches a certain truth by comparing it to a truth already known, or admitted. The object of a parable is to give greater point or imagery to the discourse.

(b) *Simile.*

This is the likening together of two things which, however different in other respects, have some strong points of resemblance to each other. It is an imaginative comparison. A symbol is one fact substituted for another. This is the simplest of all figures. When we say that one thing is *like* another, we use this figure. "As," and "like," are the words of similitude.

(c) *A Type.*

By this is meant a temporal, or physical fact which is used to illustrate a spiritual truth. It may be an object, place, event or person. It always bears an unmistakable likeness to the truth which it illustrates. For instance, an inventor makes a working model of the machine he has invented. This is more definite and accurate than any word description. This model is a type.

(d) *A Metaphor.*

This word comes from "meta" =over, and "phero" =to carry. It is a figure of speech founded on resemblance, by which a word is transferred from an object to which it properly belongs, to another, and in such a manner that a comparison is implied, though not formally expressed. For example: If a person says: "That man *is* a fox," this is a metaphor. If it is said: "That man is *like* a fox," this is a simile. In a simile the two subjects, "man" and "fox" are kept distinct in expression, as well as in thought. In a metaphor, they are kept distinct in the thought, but not in the expression. Christ said of Herod: "Go, tell that fox" (Luke 13:32). Here are a few more examples: "James and John, pillars of the Church;" "Destroy this temple;" "This is My body;" "I am the Door;" "I am the true Vine." In other words, a metaphor is a figure of speech in which one object is likened to another by asserting that it *is* the other.

(e) *An Allegory.*

This is an extended, or protracted metaphor. See Psa. 80: 8-15; Isaiah 5: 1-7. These are allegories. "The Pilgrim's Progress" and "The Holy War," are the most famous of allegories.

(f) *An Epigram.*

This is a pointed saying. It is an interesting thought, wittily enshrined in a few well chosen words. It is the art of putting a wealth of thought in a short sentence. For instance, here is one of the most famous. In commenting on the miracle of the water changed to wine, it was said: "The conscious water saw its God and blushed." This is attributed to Pope. Here is another: "We are saved by faith alone, but not by that *kind* of faith that is alone." Here is one from G. K. Chesterton: "Most evolutionists seem to know everything about the missing link, except the fact that it is missing!"

(g) *Antithesis.*

This is from "anti" =against; and "thesis," =a setting. In Rhetoric, it is a figure by which contraries are opposed by contraries. It is a contrast, or opposition of words, or sentiments. Thus we can sometimes better explain the meaning of grace by showing it in contrast to its opposite which, in this case, is law or human merit.

(h) *Hyperbole.*

This is derived from "hyper" =beyond; and "ballo," =to throw. It is a figure of speech which expresses much more, or much less than the truth. It is permitted, or understood exaggeration. The expression, used by Christ, must be so understood when He said: "They strain at a gnat and swallow a camel." Christ was here stating a truth but not an actual statement of fact. There are many such statements in the Bible.

(i) *Irony.*

This is a subtle form of sarcasm, in which apparent praise really conveys disapproval. See I Cor. 4:8-10; II Cor. 11:16-20.

(j) *An Analogy.*

In logic it is a form of inference in which it is reasoned that if two or more things agree with one another in one or more respects, they will probably agree in yet other respects.

(k) *Alliteration.*

This consists of words following each other with the same initial letter. For example: "Alliteration's artful aid."

(1) *Metonym.*

In this, a thing is described, not by its own name, but by that of some accomplishment, or incidental circumstance connected with it. For instance: "The *voice* said, 'cry';" or: "Go thy way in the *footsteps* of the flock."

(m) *Synecdoche.*

This means putting the part for the whole. For example: "All flesh is grass." This means, of course, human beings and the duration of their lives. In S. of S. 4:8 the words: "lions' dens," would refer to every place of danger. In I Cor. 14:9 the phrase, "Five words," is an *exact* number that is put for a *general* quantity.

(n) *Apostrophe.*

This consists of breaking off in a speech to address directly a person or persons, who may or may not be present; or to address oneself to an inanimate object. See Isaiah 14:12-20.

(o) *A Vision.*

A thing or event that is to come is described as happening before the eyes of the speaker. See Isaiah 24.

(p) *Personification.*

In this, inanimate things are credited with life. For instance: "The voice of thy brother's blood crieth" (Gen. 4:10).

(q) *Paradox.*

By this is meant a seeming contradiction. Quite a number of these are listed in II Cor. 6:8-10.

(4) *He should avoid hackneyed expressions.*

These, because of their oft repetition, have lost much of their value to the hearer. Clichés should also be used as sparingly as possible. A cliché is a stereotyped saying. There are also a great number of ultra pious expressions which, though current and well understood in certain ecclesiastical circles, are utterly meaningless to those outside that particular circle.

Here are a few of these hackneyed and over used expressions. "Each and every one." This is common parlance with the ballyhoo merchants of the midway of a county fair. "The broad and crowded path;" "I'm here to tell you;" "Beloved friends;" or worse, "Beloved." This is all very well from an aged brother, but utterly unsuited to a young preacher. "Listen to me!" "As I said before, and as I now again repeat." "I may state without fear of successful contradiction." This is quite a favorite with political orators. "My sinner friend," "Dear friends," etc.

Recently a secular writer gave a list of some of these trite and overworked phrases, and advised his readers to memorize them with a view to eliminating them from their vocabularies. The list was as follows:

Agree to disagree	To make a long story short
Clear as a crystal	Each and every one
Grim Reaper	Far from accurate
All in all	Few and far between
Green as grass	From bad to worse
Order out of chaos	If the truth were known

After all is said and done	Scared to death
Be that as it may	In the last analysis
Psychological moment	The heart of the matter
Take my word for it	It stands to reason that
Accidents do happen	Much as I hate to say it
At long last	Once and for all
By and large	Really and truly
Last but not least	So to speak
Adding insult to injury	Up to the hilt
As a matter of fact	Wear and tear
Bored to death	You know what I mean
Bright and early	A vicious circle
A bone of contention	When all is said and done
By word of mouth	It goes without saying

(5) *He should be careful in his use of Divine titles.*

A study of the many Scriptural titles for the Father, Son and Holy Spirit will prove helpful, and provide a *variety of expression* when referring to each. One sometimes hears addresses in which the full title of Christ, "The Lord Jesus Christ" is repeated at *every* reference to Him: sometimes in a dozen recurring sentences. How much better to refer to Him variously as: "The Lord," "The Son of God," "The Savior," "The Lamb of God," "God's dear Son," "Our Lord and Master," "Christ," "Christ Jesus," "The Son of Man," "The Lord of glory," "The Man of Calvary," etc.

When speaking of the Father, He could be referred to as "God," "Jehovah," "The Lord of Hosts," "The Father," "The eternal Father," "The holy Father," "The Almighty," "The most High," "The God of love," etc.

The Holy Spirit has many titles such as: "The eternal Spirit," "The Spirit of God," "The Comforter," "The Spirit," etc.

The Bible can be variously spoken of as "The Scriptures," "The word of God," "The Divine revelation," "God's word," "The word of truth," "The Divine oracles," "The Word," "The Book," etc.

4. *The language used should be correctly pronounced.*
Nothing is so calculated to distract an audience as well known words which are incorrectly pronounced. A speaker once held up, before a large audience, a big sheet of white paper which had a tiny black speck in the center of it. In answer to his question: "What do you see?" they all responded: "A black speck." As the speaker expected, they had concentrated on the small spot and missed the large expanse of pure white paper! So it is with a sermon. The hearers will be quick to mark the tiny black spot of a mispronounced word, and lose sight of the large white paper of an otherwise excellent address. The preacher should make it his business to eliminate the possibility of the audience having "spots" before his eyes!

A young man once solemnly assured his audience "that all Scripture had been given for their *abomination,* (admonition) and *insurrection* (instruction) in righteousness!" Satan is ever ready to snatch away the good seed of the word of God, and mispronunciations provide him with a splendid opportunity of doing his deadly work.

(1) *A good dictionary is essential.*
This should always be kept handy and within reach. Any word, concerning which there is any doubt, should be looked up and its real meaning and correct pronunciation learned.

(2) *A pronouncing Bible is useful.*
This will give the correct pronunciation of Bible names and places and thus save the preacher from a great deal of unnecessary embarrassment.

(3) *Be a discriminating reader.*
One should read with a pencil in hand and make a note of all words, the meaning of which are not clear, and look them up afterwards. In this way, one becomes both a student and connoisseur of words. Ripley, in his "Believe it or not" column, made the statement that not

one in a hundred thousand could correctly pronounce all the following words: "Data, gratis, culinary, cocaine, gondola, version, impious, chic, Caribbean and viking." There are books available containing lists of words which are most commonly mispronounced.

(4) *"The well dressed message."*

The following excellent article from the pen of the late Dr. Norman Bartlett, teacher in the Moody Bible Institute of Chicago, appeared in "The Moody Monthly," in 1946. With his very kind permission, the whole article is reproduced. It is a splendid example of the careful choice of words, by which he conveys clearly, concisely and convincingly, the message he wishes to impress on the heart. It is entitled: "The Well Dressed Message." It occupies the rest of this chapter, except the last paragraph.

"The importance of a good command of language on the part of those charged with giving forth the word of Life can scarcely be exaggerated. The gospel is of too noble a lineage to be sent forth in rags and tatters.

A well-dressed message is as much to be desired as a well-dressed speaker. Careless diction is as inexcusable as dirty linen. Since, as Scripture repeatedly and plainly declares, the eternal destiny of souls hinges upon their acceptance or rejection of the gospel message, the Christian worker can ill afford to curtail his influence and prejudice minds against this saving truth by the use of slovenly speech.

Other things being equal, a message given without notes has great advantages over one read from manuscript, or committed to memory. Naturalness is a prime requisite of eloquence, and most of all in *religious* discourse. Anything savoring of artificiality is ruinous. The speaker's style should be like an invisible glass window, that calls attention, not to itself, but to the truth enshrined in it.

How may we, in our speaking, master the art of artlessness in the use of good English? One or two suggestions may be of value.

The safeguard against affection in diction is to be found, not by giving free rein to natural carelessness, but through making carefulness natural. Effectiveness of speech must be made natural, if naturalness of speech is to become effective. Sloppy English may be natural, but it is a pretty wobbly vehicle of thought.

Just what is meant by command of language? Certainly something far more than the ability to rattle off long strings of polysyllables. Verbosity is not eloquence. There is such a thing as words being in command of the speaker rather than the speaker in command of words.

It is careful discrimination in the use of words rather than a reckless multiplication of them that marks the master of language. To employ words skillfully to express the subtlest shades and distinctions in thought, the speaker needs a well-stocked vocabulary.

The landscape artist does not use a house painter's brush. Beethoven's *Ninth Symphony* requires more than a penny whistle for its faithful rendition. The truth intrusted to us challenges us to spare no pains in the pursuit of proficiency in the use of our mother tongue.

This is not something that springs up overnight. It is the fruit of discipline. It calls for unremitting application. We must gain command of words off the platform to have command of words on the platform. Words wait on him who waits on words. He who waits on words in the study will not have to wait for words on the rostrum.

Writing much and revising ruthlessly, observing the handling of words and sentences by the best orators, noting and putting poison labels on violations of good usage, working at crossword puzzles, playing anagrams, thumbing books of synonyms and antonyms, versifying as a hobby—these are a few of many ways in which we can increase our vocabulary and improve our spoken style.

He who desires to speak acceptably will do well, furthermore, to immerse himself in the masterpieces of varied types of literature.

Some may find it helpful to keep a notebook ever at hand for jotting down new words as they come across them. But be sure, as soon as possible, to look up the definitions of these words in a standard dictionary.

Here is a further procedure that may prove to be of greater practical value than any of those mentioned so far—be exceedingly careful in the kind of English you employ in your ordinary conversation and in the contacts of daily life.

Carefulness in the use of English at all times is the most promising avenue of all these mentioned, for the attainment of mastery over audiences by the power and magic of words.

We frequently hear it said in praise of a renowned speaker that his addresses sparkle with epigrams. But just what do we mean by epigrams? Briefly, an epigram is a sentence with a wealth of thought packed into a few words. It is a capsule of truth, a verbal cartridge.

Having made effectiveness of speech natural through habitual practice, we must now see to it that from the pulpit, platform or teacher's desk, naturalness of speech has ample scope and freedom to operate effectively.

Feed the springs of thought and let the streams of speech dig their own channel. Through prolonged and prayerful brooding, heat your message until, figuratively speaking, it comes to a boil in a natural and irrepressible expression of impassioned thoughts.

If one puts into an address sufficient depth of thought and fullness of feeling, he may count on it to burst forth into beautiful expression, like the sparkling spray of a fountain.

In Spain, so we are told, are to be seen massive bridges thrown across tiny rivulets. The reason for such apparent incongruity in size is that in the early spring these streams, fed by the melting snows of distant mountains, are changed into swollen torrents whose raging impact these great bridges are scarcely able to withstand. Mighty rivers of eloquence that sweep audiences off their feet by the power of language are fed by the melting of vast verbal accumulations piling up over a period of months and years.

But a vocabulary to be melted into resistless rivers of eloquence in the thrilling hours of oratory, needs patiently and persistently to be stored up through long days of stern and faithful discipline." Thus ends Dr. Bartlett's sage advice to preachers.

A great preacher once said: "To be *listened to* is the first thing, therefore be *interesting*. To be understood is the second thing, therefore be *clear*. To be *useful* is the third thing, therefore be *practical*. To be *obeyed* is the fourth thing, therefore *speak as the oracles of God*."

CHAPTER THIRTY-FIVE

The Delivery of the Sermon

(Continued)

III. He should watch his voice.

The human voice is the God-given medium by which a God-given message is conveyed through a God-given messenger to accomplish a God-given purpose. As one considers the human voice he is led, with David, to exclaim: "I will praise Thee, for I am fearfully and wonderfully made!" (Psa. 139:14). What a marvelously intricate thing the human voice is! The multitudinous thoughts of the mind, as they pass through the delicate apparatus of the vocal chords, tongue and lips, are miraculously transmuted into words by which these thoughts are conveyed to others. More wonderful still, these words can be used of God to the regeneration of souls!

1. The possibilities of the voice.

It is impossible to estimate the tremendous possibilities of the human voice, either for good or evil. For good, when it is yielded to the Lord and used in speech or song; for evil, when it is allowed to become an instrument to accomplish the Devil's purpose. Peter realized something of its value for good when he said: "God made choice among us that the Gentiles, by my mouth, should hear the word of the gospel and believe" (Acts 15:7). How wonderful to be a mouthpiece for Deity!

God's commission to Isaiah was: "Cry aloud and spare not, lift up thy voice like a trumpet!" (Isa. 58:1). John the Baptist, when asked: "What sayest thou of thyself?" replied: "I am the voice of one crying in the wilderness"

(John 1:23). God wants His people to be voices for Him, backed up by a godly and consistent life. Paul likens the human voice to a trumpet and asks: "If the trumpet give an uncertain sound, who shall prepare himself for the battle?" (I Cor. 14:8). He realized, as all must do, that the trumpet which gives the commands during a battle must be unmistakably clear and distinct, so that each soldier can both hear and understand the message conveyed through it.

Some time ago there appeared a misprint in a magazine. In quoting I Cor. 13:1, it was made to read: "If I speak with the tongues of men and of angels, and have not *clarity*, I am become as a sounding brass," etc. Here is truth in an error! It has been well said: "There are three kinds of preachers: Those you *cannot* listen to, those you *can* listen to, and those you *cannot help* listening to." In reality, the third is the only one deserving the name of a preacher. Spurgeon once said to his students: "Remember, when you lift up your voice like a trumpet," that you also recall the injunction: "Do thyself no harm!"

2. *The four powers of the voice.*

The voice possesses four powers: compass, volume, penetration and melody.

(1) *The compass of the voice.*

By this is meant the *range of pitch* over which the voice extends. This varies with individuals. There are sopranos, altos, contraltos, tenors, baritones and basses. Nature decides the compass of the voice.

(2) *The volume of the voice.*

This refers to the *quantity* of the tone produced. Some have stronger voices than others; but weak voices, by proper exercise, can be considerably strengthened.

(3) *The penetration of the voice.*

This describes the *distance* the voice can be clearly heard. The voices of children, though not as loud as adults, are far more penetrating and can be heard much farther away.

(4) *The melody of the voice.*

This refers to the flexibility and the *sweetness* of the tone.

3. *The three pitches, or registers of the voice.*

The human voice has three pitches or registers: the low, high and middle. It is the latter pitch that is used in conversation and preaching is simply sustained conversation. The preacher should address his audience as though he was communicating something of great importance to an individual, but in a tone calculated to reach all in the building. This will make for naturalness of tone and gesture. The address should commence in the middle voice but, as it proceeds, should be altered to suit the emotion expressed. As one has put it: "The emotions and passions, such as joy, triumph, defiance and entreaty, are usually expressed in a high key; while solemnity, sorrow, awe and fear will require a lower tone of voice."

This can be observed in a conversation in which the speaker describes an experience through which he has passed. Note how he changes from one register to another, as he proceeds with his story. It is a perfectly natural proceeding, with nothing stilted or artificial about it.

4. *The purpose of the voice.*

Its purpose is to enable the speaker to *express to* the audience what he desires to *impress on* it. Thus, the preacher's own feelings should find expression in his tone and be communicated to the audience. The following good advice was given to a class in Homiletics: "Begin low, go slow, rise higher, take fire, wax warm and sit down in a storm!" Would that this were true of all who seek to preach the gospel, but alas this is often not so!

5. *Some poor examples of the use of the voice.*

As one thinks back, and calls to mind the many preachers he has heard at various times, at least eight types have impressed themselves somewhat unpleasantly on the memory.

(1) *The Mumbler.*

(a) *His description.* This person tries to speak with his lips closed, or gives the impression that he is holding a small potato in his mouth. As a result, the audience is left to guess just what the mass, or mess, of inarticulate words really mean. One such mum'bler, after he had addressed his audience, remarked to a friend: "Well, I made the gospel as plain as A B C." "Yes," replied his friend: "but you forgot the people might just as well have been D. E. F., for they scarcely heard a word you said!"

Let us hope that the following couplet will prove to be a deterrant to all such:

"If, from the pulpit, come inarticulate mumblings,
  Then, from the pews, rises legitimate grumblings."

It was said of our Savior that "He *opened His mouth* and taught them" (Matt. 5:2). One reason why "the people were very attentive to hear Him," was that He spoke so that all could hear (Luke 19:48). When the occasion demanded, He cried with a loud voice." (John 7:28, 37; 12:44).

(b) *His disservice.* Since it is true that "faith cometh by hearing" (Rom. 10:17), then it is imperative that the preacher be *heard* distinctly. If the preacher, by his inarticulate mumbling prevents this, then he is doing his audience the greatest disservice imaginable. In fact, he is positively *hindering* the word of God from accomplishing what God desires it should.

Such a speaker would be well advised to remain silent until he has remedied this slovenly ha'bit, and thus make room for some one who can speak intelligibly. Every mumbler should seriously consider the words of Paul: "There are . . . many kinds of voices in the world, and none of them is without signification. Therefore, if I know not the meaning of the voice, I shall be unto him that speaketh, a barbarian" (I Cor. 14:10-11).

(c) *His need of faithful criticism.* This is where our critical mentor in the audience (who ought to be sitting well back) will come in useful. It is surely far better to be rebuked by those who love us and profit by their rebuke, than to dwell in a fool's paradise, vainly imagining that our ministry is profitable when it is neither heard nor understood. If these words are used to turn a useless mumbler into a useful speaker, the effort will have been well worth while. Let each preacher honestly challenge himself in this regard, and critically examine himself, as to whether or not he is a mumbler.

(d) *His cure.* Mumbling *can* and *must* be cured. It might be a good plan to stand before a mirror and watch one's mouth as a verse of scripture is recited. By this means it can be seen whether or not the mouth is opened during the process. We are told that Demosthenes, the great Grecian orator, had a slight impediment in his speech. To cure it he visited the seaside every day and, in the teeth of the raging surf, he practiced clear enunciation, until he had cured himself of his impediment. He afterwards became a speaker whose name is to be conjured with, where clarity of thought and facility of expression is concerned. Persistent practice will yield astonishing results in this direction, and the compensation of addressing an audience who can really hear and understand, will be worth all the toil and labor involved.

(2) *The Yeller.*

(a) *His description.* This preacher is the exact opposite of the mumbler. While the latter cannot be heard

five feet away, the former can be heard within a radius
of two blocks! He begins his sermon with a roar, goes
on with a roar and ends up with a roar, until the nerves
of the audience are frayed and their ears literally ache
with the din, due to this entirely unnecessary "yeller
streak." Apparently this type of preacher has never
learned the difference between lightning and thunder,
and mistakes the latter for the former. If there were
any rightful cause for this ceaseless yelling, it would not
be so bad; but to inflict it on a small audience or in a
small meeting place is, to say the least, nonsensical in the
extreme. It was of one such preacher that a small boy
complained: "He talks so long that I want to go to sleep;
but he shouts so loud, that I can't!"

(b) *The cause of this yelling.* Strangely enough, this
yelling is sometimes a camouflage to cover up the speaker's own self-consciousness and nervousness, and he feels
he must shout or remain silent, but surely a happy
medium is possible.

Sometimes this shouting is the result of a speaker losing
the thread of his discourse, and he imagines that his
shouting will hide his embarrassed discomfiture from the
audience. This story is told of Dr. Henry Ward Beecher.
One day this distinguished preacher, while on vacation,
entered a little country church. The young preacher, who
was conducting the service, became so overawed at seeing
the great doctor before him that he lost the thread of his
discourse and began to shout, and finally ended his sermon in great confusion of thought and speech. After the
sermon Dr. Beecher invited the young preacher to ac-
company him to his lodgings. On the way the young man
inquired: "Dr. Beecher, did you ever lose the thread of
your discourse?" The great man replied: "Yes, I sometimes do." "What do you do under those circumstances?"

was his next query and Beecher replied gravely: "I always shout as loud as I can!"

There are times, of course, during an address, when a louder tone needs to be used to emphasize some particular point, or to drive home some truth of great importance, but for one's whole address to be couched in a shout is inexcusable.

(c) *The cure of the yeller.* Whatever the cause of this continual yelling may be, it ought to be eliminated, and the volume of the voice adapted to the size of the building. One building will require a louder, and another will necessitate a softer tone. Experience, plus our good friend the mentor, will aid in this direction. He should be seated right at the back of the building and, unseen by the rest of the audience, give his previously arranged signals. He could put his fingers in his ears if the tone is too loud, or cup his ears with his hands if the tone is not loud enough.

(3) *The Sing-song.*

(a) *His description.* This form of preaching consists of a kind of chant, the voice rising and falling with calm rhythmic flow, until it becomes a lullaby to many in the audience. Try as they will, they cannot keep their eyes open. At last, as the speaker's voice continues to drone on, as a gesture of self-defense one after another succumb to the lullaby, and are thus mercifully put out of their misery. Such preaching only succeeds in giving the audience a "nodding acquaintance" with the speaker. A famous preacher once said to one of the ushers: "If you ever see anyone asleep in the audience, please come to the pulpit and wake me up!" Of a preacher of this type a man once wrote:

"I never see my preacher's eyes,
  He hides their light divine;
For when he prays, he shuts his eyes,
  And when he preaches, mine!"

(b) *The cause.* This sing-song chant is anything but the *natural* voice of the preacher, for when he is off the platform he can converse intelligently enough, in a nice conversational tone; but the moment he ascends the pulpit, he feels it incumbent to adopt this peculiar sing-song intonation of voice, which has a fatally soporific effect upon the audience. This palpable artificiality of tone in the pulpit also serves to create resentment in the hearers, and thus hinders the favorable reception of the message.

A theological professor is recorded to have told his students that the test of a good sermon was that it accomplished a threefold effect: it *moved, soothed* and *satisfied* the audience. The following week one of the members of his class, being called upon to give a report of the sermon he had preached on Sunday said: "It must have been a good sermon, for I had only been preaching a short time when half the congregation rose and walked out, proving it was *moving.* As I continued, the remaining fell asleep, demonstrating that it was *soothing.* At the conclusion of the sermon, I overheard one man remark: 'I've had enough of *that* kind of preaching!' by which I concluded that the sermon had been *satisfying!*"

While on the subject of sleeping under a sermon, the story of the playwright and his critics may be in order. This playwright called a number of literary critics together, so that they might give him their opinion of a new play he had written. While reading his play to them, he noticed that one of them had fallen asleep. He stopped, awakened the sleeper and asked indignantly: "How can you give me *your* opinion of my play if you are asleep?" The critic replied promptly: "Sleep is an opinion!" Preachers, take notice.

(c) *The cure.* Once aware of his fatal tendency to chant, the sing-song preacher should take immediate steps to remedy the situation. He must resolutely deter-

mine that he will use only his *natural* voice in the pulpit.
It cannot be overemphasized that one's own naturalness
of expression is what is required in presenting the gospel
message.   The preaching should begin and continue in
the key of "B natural"; that is, the preacher should speak
in his own conversational voice, but in a tone calculated
to reach all in the building.   Once again the friendly
critic should be detailed to inform him of any departure
from this procedure.

(4)   *The Monotone.*

(a)   *His description.* This, if anything, is even worse
than the sing-song, for there is not even a rise and fall to
his voice.   There is practically no indication, either in
his face, voice, or gestures, of any emotion whatever. The
man in the street would refer to such a speaker as: "dead
pan." He recites his message in a flat, colorless, expressionless fashion, as though it is something that must be
concluded as quickly and painlessly as possible. The tone
of the voice is made to suggest: "the drowsy tinklings
that lull the distant folds," rather than the impassioned
speech of one who has an imperative message to deliver
to a lost and ruined race. It matters not what the theme
may be: the denunciation of sin, the warning of coming
judgment, the tender appeal of the Savior, or the description of the sufferings of Christ; each is described in the
same cold, expressionless tone, with no variation in the
speed of the delivery, or pauses to break the monotonous
insipidity of his sermon. It serves to convince the hearer
of the truth of the saying: "The face takes upon itself the
shape of the mind."

(b)   *The cause.* While it is true that some people are
more emotional than others, yet, if the theme really
grips the heart of the speaker, there should be at least
some emotion evidenced. Even the most monotone

preacher, if he saw his neighbor's house on fire would cry: "Fire! Fire!" in a different tone to what he uses in the pulpit when warning sinners to flee from the wrath to come. Surely one is as real as the other. The gospel message demands earnestness on the part of the speaker, and this earnestness is bound to find expression in his voice, which is the God-given medium for making his thoughts articulate.

If the speaker really believes the message he is seeking to impress on the audience, it will affect him. As his various emotions are stirred, they will be reflected in the expression on his face, the intonation of his voice, and also in the speed of the delivery. In this way, his feelings will be communicated to the audience. The tone of the voice used in warning, is surely different from that used when appealing to the sinner to trust the Savior. The monotone preacher leaves his audience with the impression that he has not entered into the real meaning of the message for himself.

An old preacher once wrote: "Be in earnest; let the fire burn in your soul; let the fire of love for souls be kindled and fanned in the presence of God! Then speak to men as one who knows and feels the power of the things he preaches. If you are not in earnest, you had better go to bed than speak for Christ!"

(c) *The cure.* General Booth, of the Salvation Army, declared it would be a good thing if every preacher could be sent to hell for a week, for he would return from there with a passion to save men from going to that dreadful place. The monotone preacher would do well to saturate himself prayerfully with the *reality* of his subject, and then speak as though everything depended upon himself as to the effectiveness of his message. Real conviction must lead to a corresponding expression in the voice and general demeanor. Perhaps the reciting aloud of poetry and the reading of descriptive narrative might be a material help in securing this needed variety and expression of tone.

(5)   *The Voice-dropper.*

(a)   *His description.* This kind of preacher drops his voice at the end of each sentence until it is barely a whisper, so that often the most important part of the statement is lost to the audience. Why a period at the end of a sentence should have this effect upon a preacher is difficult to say, but it does nevertheless. He begins well and the first part of the sentence is audible to all; but alas, as the fatal period is approached, the voice is lowered until the remainder of it is indistinguishable, save perhaps to those who might be sitting within three feet of him and, unfortunately, no one is that close! There are times, of course, when one's voice should be lowered for the purpose of emphasis, but it should never be so low that it cannot be heard distinctly by all. A "stage whisper" is designed to be easily heard by a large audience.

(b)   *The cause.* It may be that the intention of the whisperer is to produce an impression, but it merely creates a *depression.* It arouses a feeling of annoyance, on the part of his audience, at this aggravating habit of speech. The cause may be due to faulty breathing. This can easily be remedied by a few lessons in breath control by a capable voice teacher.

(c)   *The cure.* Each preacher, with this slovenly and annoying habit, ought to break himself of it by printing in large letters: *"I must keep my voice up at the end of my sentences,"* and place it on the pulpit, so that it is before him continually during the sermon. By this constant reminder, he will soon cure himself of this fault and, in so doing, will earn the gratitude of his hearers. One has tersely said: "Too many preachers are *giving* pains with their voices, instead of *taking* pains with them!"

(6) *The Repeater.*

(a) *His description.* This preacher persists in repeating his sentences, over and over again, as though his hearers were either deaf or mentally incompetent. By this means, a ten-minute address is stretched out into thirty minutes, and the audience is made to feel that its time has been wasted, its intelligence outraged and its patience sorely tried.

The favorite expression of this speaker is: "As I said before and as now again I repeat." Surely, if a thing has been plainly said once, would it not be better to say something else next time and thus get on with the business of declaring the message? Why move in a monotonous circle of endless and tiresome repetitions? A preacher's time is surely too valuable to be frittered away in such a totally unnecessary manner. It was of such a speaker that one wrote: "It took Sir William Ramsey 16 years to discover *helium,* the Curie's 30 years to find *radium;* but this man, in less than five minutes, can produce *tedium!*"

It is quite true that one of the rules governing emphasis is the use of repetition, but this does not refer to *everything* in the sermon. To be continually emphasizing the obvious, or illustrating what has already been illustrated, or clarifying what has previously been made clear, is to become ridiculous. We should all be on our guard against falling into this habit of preaching.

Again the poet comes to our aid. These lines are entitled, "Redundant."

> "The man I hate explains a fact
> In simple words, and then
> Beginning with: "In other words,"
> Goes through the thing again.

> I hate this man because I know
> He thinks that I am dense—
> In other words, he seems to think
> I haven't any sense!"

(b) *The cause.* Such preaching clearly indicates a lack of conscientious preparation on the part of the preacher, and he should be reminded of the exhortation: "Use not *vain repetitions* as the heathen do" (Matt. 6:7). The object of preaching is not to fill up thirty minutes of time, but to be God's messenger, with God's message, so that unsaved souls may be reached and won for Christ and believers built up in their most holy faith.

(c) *The cure.* After a point has been made clear to the hearers, the preacher should move to the next point and so proceed, in orderly progression to his conclusion. We should aim at brevity, so that every word will count. To do this, we must challenge the right of every thought ere we give it expression, and thus seek to blow out the chaff, so that the audience may be spared the trouble of doing so for itself. A large load of loose hay can be compressed into a very small bale. Let us make our sermons *bales* and *not hay stacks.*

Again, the usefulness of our mentor will become apparent. He should be instructed to make a careful note of all unnecessary repetitions and redundancies in the sermon. In this way the preacher will be put on his guard against this pernicious habit and, we fervently hope, permanently cured.

(7)   *The Throat-clearer.*

(a)   *His description.* This style of preaching consists of a slight, but entirely unnecessary clearing of the throat at the end of each sentence and sometimes in the middle of a sentence. His remarks, if stenographically reported, would read something like this: "My dear (ah) friends, (er er) it is (ahem!) with great (er er) pleasure that I (ah) stand before (ahem! ahem!) you (er, ah)"; and so on, far into the night, ad infinitum, ad nauseum.

(b) *The cause.* Very often this affliction is due to the extreme nervousness of the speaker. It may also be caused by a natural hesitancy of speech. Again, it may stem from a lack of proper preparation. Whatever the cause may be, it should be remedied, for "such things certainly ought not so to be."

(c) *The cure.* This crippling habit can be cured by resolute and painstaking care, plus rigid self discipline. Perhaps a step in the cure of such a preacher would be for him to read a word for word report of his address with all the "ahems," "er-er's," and "ah's" underlined in red ink. When thus faced with the record of his crime, it is to be hoped that he would realize the enormity of his guilt and the need for repentance and true conversion, and henceforth resolutely resist the temptation to insert an "er," "ah," or "ahem!" between his sentences, or even his paragraphs!

Another aid would be for him to practice reading aloud, with the mentor present to curb any tendency to throat clearing. Perhaps quoting verses from the Bible would help. The most heroic measures would be perfectly in order, for an audience wilts visibly as the throatclearer coughs his weary way through the sermon.

(8) *The Meanderer.*

(a) *His description.* This preacher's sermon consists of a series of disconnected remarks, which apparently occur to him as he speaks. It leaves the audience wondering what he is driving at, or if he really has anything definite in mind, or even possesses a mind capable of containing anything definite. He wanders from Dan to

Beersheba and has a little to say about everything in general, and nothing to say about anything in particular. This type of preaching reminds one of the description of the chaotic earth; for it is "without form and void and darkness was upon the face of the deep." (Gen. 1:2).

Like a tramp, who wanders from place to place, the meanderer seems to have no certain dwelling place. If the text he took contained a contagious disease, the sermon he preaches from it would be in no danger of contracting it! He reminds one of a butterfly hunter, as he chases the stray thoughts that flit before his anything but enraptured vision. He often begins an illustration but fails to conclude it, because another thought catches his fancy and off he goes in pursuit. Thus he meanders aimlessly on and then wonders why the audience does not seem interested in what he is saying, or refuses to come out the next time he is announced to speak. One teacher, speaking of this type of preaching said: "A text is like a gate opening into the Lord's garden. Many preachers however, instead of opening the gate and leading the people in to pluck the flowers and the fruit, content themselves with climbing on the gate and swinging to and fro."

After listening to one of these meandering preachers, one member of the audience was heard to remark: "That preacher's sermon reminded me of Columbus' voyage of discovery." On being asked to explain himself, he replied: "Well, when Columbus started out on his voyage, he didn't know where he was *going.* When he got there, he didn't know where he *was.* When, at length, he got back again, he couldn't tell where he had *been!*"

Perhaps this type of speaker bases his method of preaching on a wrong interpretation of that verse which describes the early disciples as "going *everywhere,* preaching the word!" Thus the meanderer ambles on his circuitous way and, like the camel in the desert, wanders on and on and never knows how dry he is!

(b) *The cause.* Undoubtedly this meandering is the result of a lack of adequate preparation. Having made no definite plan for his discourse, he has no definite theme for his address; consequently, when he rises to speak, he has nothing definite to say. Some preachers rise to speak in order to *say something,* while others do so because they have *something to say.* May we belong to the latter class!

(c) *The cure.* Such meandering can only be cured by a holy determination to *make* and *take* time for the prayerful and careful preparation that is so essential for preaching. The Scripture enjoins us to "let all things be done decently and in order." This includes preaching, as well as everything else that is done for the Lord. The orderly preparation of the sermon makes for the orderly presentation of the address, and this contributes to an orderly reception and retention of it by those who listen.

There are other types of preaching one may recall, but these examples will serve to show how it is sadly possible for the message to be marred by the messenger. Let us again quote Paul's weighty words to Timothy: "Take heed unto *thyself,* and unto the *doctrine*" (I Tim. 4:16). We have seen that the *man* and the *message* are closely linked. Often people's impressions of the *message* are determined by their opinion of the *messenger.*

If, with Paul, each preacher has the ambition that, by his voice, he "might teach others also;" then he must see to it, as far as it lies in his power, there is nothing to hinder his voice from being its best for God (I Cor. 14:19). Speaking of the gospel that has been committed to our trust, Paul reminds us that: "We have this treasure in *earthen vessels*" (II Cor. 4:7). By this our bodies, with all their faculties, are referred to. May these vessels be so yielded to the Lord and so fitted by diligent study and self-discipline, that God may be glorified in both the message and the messenger!

6. *Some hints on voice cultivation.*

(1) *Each individual is a distinct personality.*

No two preachers are absolutely identical in appearance, personality or voice. God delights in infinite variety. As the Word puts it: "There are diversities of gifts, but the same Spirit; and there are diversities of administrations, but the same Lord; and there are diversities of operations, but it is the same Lord which worketh all in all" (I Cor. 12:4-6).

A true sermon is part and parcel of the preacher himself, and should therefore be an expression of his own personality. Let us recall again Beecher's fine definition of preaching: "Truth through personality." Only as his personality is placed completely at God's disposal, shall the preacher fulfill God's purpose in his ministry. It must be true of him, what Paul affirmed of the Thessalonian believers: "For from you sounded out the word of the Lord" (I Thess. 1:8).

(2) *The value of voice cultivation.*

The Africans have a proverb: "God gives beauty, but we must help Him." While it is perfectly true that only God can impart the gift of preaching and teaching; yet this does not release the recipient of the gift from the solemn necessity to develop and improve it by his own persistent and self sacrificing efforts. The talents were given to the servants that their value might be increased for the Master (Matt. 25:14-30). Responsibility simply consists of our *response* to His *ability.*

(a) *Each should be prepared to remove any obstacle in the path.* An illustration of this is found in the raising of Lazarus. Christ conmmanded those that stood by to "take away the stone" that covered the mouth of the tomb. Our Lord could quite easily have had this stone miraculously removed, for He was omnipotent, but He did not do so. There are certain things which the Lord expects us to do for ourselves, for Deity performs no unnecessary miracles. Each preacher should therefore be much concerned as to what is hindering him from being his best for God. Once he realizes what this hindrance is, he should give himself no rest until he has taken this "stone" away.

If it is his voice, then he should attend to this disability at once, and seek to improve it by all the means in his power. Each believer is urged to "give diligence to show himself approved unto God" (II Tim. 2:15. R. V.).

This self-improvement means *work* and the sooner the Christian faces this fact seriously and gets busy, the better it will be.

(b) *A few vocal lessons would be helpful.* These should prove to be a great aid to those who have difficulty in enunciation, or have weak voices, or whose voices easily tire and become hoarse. Such would do well to go to a really competent voice specialist, submit to a thorough examination, and then follow faithfully whatever he prescribes in the way of exercises to remedy the disability. Whatever the cost may be, it is a good investment of time, money and effort.

Just as we go to a doctor, because of some weakness in the body and follow his advice; so let those who have trouble with their voices go to a specialist, with a view to having this organ, so essential to the preaching of the word of God, improved. Many who have followed this advice are now praising the Lord for the benefit they have derived from it.

Many preachers have never learned to use their voices properly. They have never learned the necessity for the use of the *diaphram* in speaking. They speak *from* their throats instead of *through* their throats. Consequently their voices soon tire, and they suffer from a complaint which is called "Clergyman's sore throat." To learn how to produce the tones from the diaphram would cause this trouble to disappear. By means of these vocal lessons, speakers will also learn the value of proper breathing, voice placement, tone production, the pitch, penetration, quality and speed of the voice, as well as the necessity for giving the consonants their proper value. The art of correct enunciation, as displayed by a good radio announcer, is certainly not to be lightly esteemed. One of the chief difficulties in enunciation is the proper use of the *consonants,* particularly "g," which is very often left out. The vowels give *richness* and the consonants give *brightness* to the tones.

Until fairly recently, no one could hear the sound of his own voice. With the invention of the tape recorder, anyone can now hear exactly how his voice sounds to other people. Each can now discover whether or not his enunciation is good.

Mere elocution, of course, is no remedy for poor speaking, for this tends to produce artificiality. The schoolboy who got "electrocution" mixed with "elocution," and defined the latter as "the means by which many innocent people were put to death," was not so far astray! A sermon should be something more than "a positive work of art," or "a great intellectual effort." It had far better never been born than to degenerate into this. H. I. Philipps caustically defined oratory as: "The art of making deep noises in the chest sound like important messages from the brain."

(c) *Some exercises to this end.* One of the best exercises to remedy any deficiency in the voice is to practice reading out loud, and give proper emphasis to each important word. He should also read sermons and classical literature and give particular attention to the sounding of the consonants. He should try to *feel* what he reads and, as this is done consistently, there will be a marked improvement, not only in the enunciation but in the *feeling* or tone of the voice.

Again, it is good to take certain words with which one has difficulty and practice repeating them, over and over again, until they are correctly articulated. The "g" endings should be given a good work over; such as going, reaping, sowing, doing, coming," etc. Then try the end sounds of "ip, it, ik," etc. Then practice the nasal sounds, with such a sentence as: "Morning winds among the lindens moan and murmur in the morn, mingling in my bosom's misery, making monotones forlorn." An old voice teacher used to get his pupils to pretend to yawn and, while their months were thus wide open, repeat: "It's far too early to get up!" Any good book on voice culture will give a list of helpful exercises by which these speech deficiences may be remedied. As these are practiced, (in private, of course!) it will be surprising and gratifying to see the improvements it will make in one's enunciation.

My friend John H. Manins, of Auckland, New Zealand, has kindly granted permission to reprint the following extracts from his most helpful article on: "The delivery of the sermon," which appeared in "The Bible Expositor," of New Zealand. The next seven paragraphs are taken from this article.

"By delivery is meant the manner of uttering a speech or address. In preaching, it is all that has to do with verbal expression. Matter has to do with *what* we say, delivery with *how* we say it. A good delivery is one of the greatest and most important elements in preaching. Demothenes said: "Delivery is the first thing, second thing and third thing in oratory" . . . Delivery is something we can develop, control and master . . . The art of elocution begins in the *mind,* not in the mouth. There are laws which govern the art of speech as well as those which govern the art of thought. Thought and expression must be fused together . . . The voice is the God-given organ of speech. There is nothing so musical, delightful and glorious as the correct utterance of human speech. It possesses a charm all of its own.

The human voice is produced by a complex system of organs, comparable to the mechanism of some grand organ. The Bellows controlling the wind system, the Lungs which regulate the amount of air used in speech; the Diaphragm, the organ of breath control; the Larynx, the upper part of the wind pipe containing the vocal chords is used in the production and modulation of sound; the epiglotis, the lid at the end of the Larynx; the Pharynx, the receiving space for the air to pass; the soft palate and nasal passages. It is the correct use and working of these voice organs which determine audible speech.

The sound originates with the vibration of the vocal chords caused by the passage of air from the lungs. It is the combination of the lips, tongue and teeth, etc., by which this sound is varied to make the different sounds of speech. The following examples will serve to illustrate this fact.

1. The lips, illustrated in the utterance of P. B., Posts, Rip, Bee, Board.

2. Tongue and Teeth, illustrated in the utterance of T. D., Tip, Eat, Did, Deed.

3. Lower Lips and upper Teeth, illustrated in the utterance of F. V., Fat, Feet, Eve.

4. Back of Throat, illustrated in the utterance of K., Gay, Gear, Gain.

5. Tongue and Teeth, illustrated in the utterance of S. Z., Sheep, Azure.

6. Nasal, illustrated in the utterance of N. M., Nine, Men, Ing, Ring.

7. Tongue and upper Teeth, illustrated in the utterance of Th., Theme, Thigh, Wreath.

8. Tongue and root of Mouth, illustrated by the utterance of All, Ill, Sell, Sail.

Practice of the use of these sounds can be made, as for example, A. pc., E. T., L. J., O. K., ON, V. L., etc.

We must speak so as to be heard. We can never hope to move the will or stir the emotions of people who cannot hear us. It is well nigh a crime to mumble and mutter and speak so indistinctly as not to be heard. How often in a public gathering the speaker has to be exhorted to "speak up." He really should have been told to speak *out*. It is not so much the lack of volume of sound that causes the difficulty, but the poor quality of the sound. A whisper can be heard if the quality of voice is behind it . . . To a large audience the rate of speaking must be slower than to a smaller audience . . . The sound produced within must be let *out*. Speaking with the lips partially closed is a bad fault.

Throat constriction is a real hindrance. It lessens the sound area and produces an unnatural tone making speaking tiring and hearing difficult . . . The tongue can be an offending member in more ways than one. To allow the sound to flow unobstructed, the tongue must be kept flat. The tendency is to arch the tongue and so produce a throaty, or guttural sound. Immobility of lips is another cause of inaudibility. This is evidenced in the common fault of speaking out of the side of the mouth. Notice the difference in effect of speaking with tightened lips, then with free.

Canon Fleming says: 'Take care of the consonants, and the vowels will take care of themselves.' A common fault is the mispronunciation of *and.* Most speakers leave out the "d" at the end. Care should be taken to articulate all the syllables in a word. Here is a list for practice: Opportunity, introduced, produced, innocent, difficult, particulars, telephone, purified, recognized, vehicular, issue."

To sum up this somewhat lengthy section on the voice: The preacher's voice should be clear and heard distinctly by all. It should reflect his innermost feelings and communicate them to the audience. The outcome will be an earnestness and sincerity of presentation that will impress those that hear that he wholeheartedly believes the truth of his own message. Paul puts it thus: "Seeing then that we have such hope, we use great plainness (or boldness) of speech" (II Cor. 3:12). As we "lift up our voice like a trumpet," let us remember that what we preach is not: "The word of man but, as it is in truth, the word of God that effectually worketh in them that believe" (I Thess. 2:13).

Recently, a booklet by Dr. Herbert Lockyer has been published, entitled: "Voice Culture for Speakers." It is published by Walterick Publishing Company, Box 2216, Kansas City, Kansas. All preachers would do well to secure a copy of this splendid pamphlet, for it contains further excellent advice regarding this important matter of improving one's voice.

CHAPTER THIRTY-SIX

The Delivery of the Sermon

(Continued)

IV. He should watch his audience.

In order to do this he must keep his eyes on them. Many find this a real trial and difficulty because of a natural timidity. To all such comes the heartening commission of the Lord to young Jeremiah: Speak unto them all that I command thee; *be not dismayed at their faces*, lest I confound thee before them" (Jer. 1:17).

1. *It commands the respect of the audience.* The human eye commands authority. An audience appreciates a preacher who, like the village blacksmith, "looks the whole world *in the face."* When the speaker's eyes are fixed upon some invisible spot on the ceiling, or some equally invisible place on the floor or, worse still, speaks with his eyes tightly closed; he loses, in a large measure, his personal touch with his audience. This looking at one's audience must be resolutely and persistently practiced, until it becomes a fixed habit. The speaker should not only speak from heart to heart, but from eye to eye and face to face. After all, the preacher is God's messenger to the people and this gives an authority to his message. Therefore, while having no confidence in the flesh, he should have every confidence in the message, and show this confidence by looking his audience straight in the eye as he proclaims the good news.

2. *It permits the speaker to see the reaction of his hearers.*

As the preacher looks at his audience, he will be abie to watch the effect of the message and see if they are following his line of thought. A puzzled expression will indicate he has not made himself clear, and this will be the signal for an illustration, or an example to clarify the matter. If there is a bored look, it will inform him that he is getting too prosy and something is required to revive the lagging interest. He may perceive that some are beginning to doze and this, or course, should have the effect of waking up the preacher. He may be able to perceive anxiety of soul depicted upon some countenances, and thus be guided as to whom he should approach for personal conversation after the meeting. Spurgeon used to speak of his delight as he actually saw people grasp the truth of the gospel and trust the Savior as he preached. He often saw the new life dawning on the faces of individuals in his audience.

3. *It also enables the preacher to perceive if the audience is comfortable or not.* Needless to say, the preacher should see to it that his audience can listen to him in comfort. If the room is too warm, windows should be opened, for the word must be mixed with *oxygen* as well as with *faith.* Beware of drafts, for these produce colds and create discomfort. Be on guard against lights, either at the *back,* or just *above* the pulpit. This glare is not only a discomfort to the hearers who wish to look at the speaker, but will also prove an additional incentive for many in the audience to close their eyes and thereby go to sleep. Put out all such lights before commencing to preach and thus earn the gratitude of all. Should there be a window at the back of the pulpit and the sermon is to be delivered in daylight, this window should be covered with a very dark shade.

The preacher should, at all times, be in command of the audience and be ready to act should any emergency arise. The speaker who does not look at his audience loses this command, hence the advice given at the head of this particular division: "He should watch his audience."

V. He should watch his time.

A French philsopher once said: "He who would live must watch his time, for time is the stuff out of which life is made." Time is therefore a most valuable commodity. Once it is lost, it can never be regained. Inasmuch as preaching involves the use of time, it is essential that the period alloted to this important task should be spent to the very best advantage.

1. *The preacher should inform himself as to the exact length of the service.*

(1) *He should plan the service within the limitations of the time alloted.*

The length of the opening song service should be determined by the time limit for the whole meeting, with enough time left for a closing hymn, if required. The principle business of the meeting is the reading and preaching of the word of God and not for the singing of hymns. For a one hour meeting, fifteen to twenty minutes should be ample for the opening hymns, prayer and announcements; with five minutes allowed for the closing hymn and prayer. For a longer service this could be altered. This will leave around thirty-five to forty minutes for the address. This should be ample, though no hard and fast rule can be adopted. Some sermons are altogether "too long" at fifteen minutes, while others are "too short" at sixty minutes. There are preachers—and preachers!

(2) *He should start the meeting on time.*

As a general principle, a preacher should begin the meeting on time, even though there is only a handful present. The audience will soon accommodate itself to this arrangement, except that band of incorrigibles who never seem to be able to come on time for anything and for whom it is only wasted time to wait. Surely it is only fair to those who have come on time, to begin on time. They came on the understanding that the service would begin at a specific time, therefore begin punctually.

(3) *He should conclude the meeting on time.* Tennyson's brook that murmured:

> *"Men may come, and men may go,*
> *But I go on forever."*

is no model for a preacher! He should make it his business to find out exactly how long he has to speak and, when the time for closing arrives, he should *stop*. Luther used to advise his students to: "Stand up *manfully,* speak out *clearly* and leave off *speedily."* On a certain pulpit a brass plate is fixed so that the preacher cannot help noticing it. On it is engraved the words: "Blessed is he that keepeth to his time. Verily, he shall be asked back again!" George Elliot once remarked: "Blessed is the man who, having nothing to say, refrains from giving wordy evidence of that fact!" A preacher once complained to a newspaper editor that in reporting a meeting at which he had spoken, he was referred to as the *"Neverend"* instead of the *"Reverend* Jones"!

If a meeting has been scheduled to begin and end at a certain time, it should be the preacher's duty to keep faith with the people who have come on that understanding. This will inspire confidence in the speaker as a man of his word. After a particularly long-winded address, a man was asked his opinion of it. All he replied was: "The preacher lost at least *five* excellent opportunities of closing his address." Someone once asked the

doorkeeper of a church building if the man, who was
scheduled to speak, had finished: "Oh, yes," replied the
man, "he finished ten minutes ago, but he hasn't stopped
yet!" Happy is the man who knows when he has finished
—and stops! We need to develop the fine art of making
the *finishing* point and the *stopping* point coincide!

The preacher who has a "train of thought," but no
"terminal facilities" for his train, only succeeds in out-
wearing his welcome. Is it any wonder that the exhausted
victim of a long-winded preacher once growled: "The man
who thinks by the *inch,* and talks by the *yard,* ought to
be dealt with by the *foot!*" To this, all fellow victims will
doubtless add a hearty "amen!" On being informed that
an instrument had been invented that would throw a
speaker's voice a mile; a man remarked: "Now all we
need is an instrument that will throw the speaker an
equal distance!" Years ago, a dull and long-winded member of Congress was speaking in the House. As he droned
on, at interminable length, he turned to Henry Clay and
said, very pompously: "*You,* sir, speak for the present generation, but *I* speak for posterity!" Clay replied: "Yes, and
it seems to me that you are resolved to keep on speaking
until your audience arrives!"

2. *When sharing a meeting with another speaker, he
should keep to his alloted time.*

If a meeting is to be shared by two speakers, it is surely
an inexcusable act of discourtesy for one to monopolize
three-quarters of the time allowed, leaving the other
speaker with but a small portion of the time that rightfully
belonged to him. To steal another person's time is to rob
him of that which can never be restored to him again; it
has gone forever. To paraphrase Shakespeare's famous
lines:

"Who steals my purse steals trash—
'Twas mine, 'tis his, and has been slave to thousands;
But he who filches from me *my good time*,
Robs me of that which nought enriches him,
And leaves me poor indeed!"

Not only is such an act cruel, but it represents the very quintessence of egotism. It proclaims, as it were: "*My* address is so important and *my* ability is so great, that I am sure you will not want to hear what anyone else has to say after *I* get through!" Though this time stealing is reprehensible in the extreme, it is to be feared that this act of platform robbery often takes place. This, most certainly, should not be so.

The story is told of three orators who were invited to share a political rally. As the meeting had to close at a certain time, each speaker was assigned forty-five minutes. The first speaker, however, occupied well over an hour. The second spoke for a full hour, and when the third speaker arose, he only had five minutes in which to deliver his oration. However, he rose, not only to his feet, but to the occasion, for he occupied the five minutes by telling a story. He began: "Some time ago a farmer friend of mine, who specializes in raising hogs, invited me to visit his farm for a few days. The first day I was there I accompanied him to the pens to see him feed the hogs. When I observed that he fed them *raw* potatoes, I remonstrated with him and said: 'Don't you know that if you cooked those potatoes, the hogs would digest them in half the time?' My farmer friend gave me a look of contempt and snorted: 'What do *hogs* care for time!' " As the speaker sat down, none of his audience was left in doubt as to the moral of the story! Let each preacher, too, lay it to heart and determine he will never become a platform hog!

An African tribe has devised a brilliant method of limiting the length of speeches during a debate, which has the virtue of being both simple and effective. As the person rises to address the congregation, he must stand, unsupported, *on one leg.* Only as long as he maintains this awkward position may be continue his speech. The moment he puts his other foot to the ground, his speech is over! It will surely be admitted that there is real merit in this system. It certainly would make for a "well balanced" address, and no one would be able to criticise the speaker by asserting he "hadn't a leg to stand on"!

3. *It is better to leave an audience longing rather than loathing.*

It is always an excellent principle to stop when the interest is still keen, rather than go on until the interest has been exhausted and gives place to boredom. C. H. Spurgeon once remarked; "It is a good thing to hit the nail on the head, but don't keep hitting if after it has been driven in, else the wood will split and the nail will fall out!"

4. *He should keep his promise to the audience.*

A particularly exasperating thing for a preacher to do is to promise a speedy conclusion and then go on at interminable length. The audience, hearing the words: "And lastly, my friends," plucks up courage and looks forward to a speedy release from its sufferings; but alas, it is doomed to disappointment, for having said, "lastly," the speaker proceeds to *last!* The truth of the old proverb: "Hope deferred maketh the heart sick," is thus exemplified, and many register the mental resolve: "I'll never come out to hear *that* speaker again!" It has been said that the longest word in the English language is that which follows the radio announcement: "And now, a word from our sponsor."

It is always a good principle to keep one's word with the audience. If the preacher announces: "I'll be through by nine o'clock," he should see to it, as a point of honor, that he fulfils his promise. Otherwise the audience may be pardoned for doubting his truthfulness and trustworthiness as a messenger of God. Should the speaker see that his time is running short, he can always condense his sermon so as to finish within the alloted time. The audience will not notice the condensation and will be favorably impressed with his reliability and punctuality.

CHAPTER THIRTY-SEVEN

The Delivery of The Sermon

(Continued)

VI. He should watch his theme.

While the *manner* of the preacher's delivery is important, it is secondary to the *matter* he delivers. The Scriptural injunction is: *"Preach the Word!"*

1. *The characteristics of this present age.*

This is an age when the latest is considered the most important and the best. The preacher will be tempted to invent and introduce something new and startling, instead of expounding what the word of God distinctly teaches. There are still plenty of people who, like certain of old, "spend their time in nothing else, but either to tell, or to hear some new thing" (Acts 17:21).

However ridiculous some of these new fangled theories may be, there are always plenty of people who will swallow whatever is told them without a moment's hesitation, for human beings are very credulous. Those who arrogantly refuse to accept the truth of God in the light, will greedily swallow the Devil's lie in the dark. In fact, when a person deliberately rejects the gospel, by that very act he opens his mind to hear and receive the most foolish of error.

The Bible itself speaks of this in II Tim. 4:3-4. We are told: "The time will come when men shall not endure sound doctrine, but after their own lusts shall they heap to themselves teachers, having itching ears: and they shall turn away their ears from the truth and shall be

turned unto fables." It is surely obvious that these days
have arrived. We are faced with literally hundreds of
"isms," and "ologies" which have sprung up, with mush-
room-like rapidity, on every hand.

The Devil is busy, together with his "host of wicked
spirits," in sowing the evil seed of false doctrines by which
to blind people to the truth of the gospel of the grace of
God. An apostate Christendom lends him every aid in
this direction, for it actually invites and shelters in its
pulpits men who openly deny the fundamental truths of
the faith which they solemnly promised to keep and for
which they are paid to preach!

2. *The necessity for Scriptural preaching and teaching.*

The paramount need of today is for God-gifted men who
will preach the word of God, without fear or favor, in the
power of the Holy Spirit. The chief aim of the preacher is
to present Christ as the sinner's Substitute, Savior, Sovereign, Securer and Satisfier. The words of that grand
old veteran should come as a challenge to each believer:
"Preach the Word; be instant in season, out of season;
reprove, rebuke, exhort with all long suffering and doctrine" (II Tim. 4: 2).

Note these directions: "Preach the Word:" not science,
philosophy, civic reform, better government, politics, or
the latest novel, etc. This will call for *persistency,* for it *is*
to be "in season and out of season." It demands *courage,*
for it involves reproving and rebuking. It implies *earnestness,* for there is to be longsuffering exhortation. It demands *watchfulness,* for he is urged to "watch . . . in all
things." It requires *patience,* for endurance is one of the
qualifications. It suggests *zeal,* for he is to "do the work
of an evangelist." Finally, it demands *faithfulness,* for he
is to "make full proof of his ministry."

Dr. Alex. Whyte, wrote to his fellow preachers as follows: "Is not the glory of God in the salvation of your hearers your main motive and chiefest end in setting out to be a minister? If we kept ourselves entirely true to that motive in our preaching, neither would the praise of men puff us up, nor would their blame embitter us and break us down. My sons in the service of our Lord Jesus Christ, begin from the very beginning of your ministry, and before it is begun, to have your hearts clean and pure within you on the matter of your motives in your preaching. Preach our Lord; preach Jesus Christ and Him crucified. And preach every single sermon of yours for the salvation of your hearers. Flee, like the very poison it is, every other thought, every other motive and breath of a motive in your preaching! Preach your absolutely very best every returning Lord's day. But no Lord's day make good preaching your motive or your end. Preach your absolute best, because the Lord of the day is your Lord and Master, and because He is the best Master, and the best text, and the best praise and the best reward for preaching."

An old gospeller once advised his younger brethren to preach: "A full gospel—Christ and nothing less. A plain gospel—Christ and nothing more. A pure gospel—Christ and nothing else." A famous preacher confessed: "I preached philosophy and men applauded. I preached Christ and men repented!"

If the Devil cannot get the preacher to swallow false doctrine, then he will seek to sidetrack him by switching him off into a discussion of non-essentials, or controversial issues that are of no importance to the audience. The preacher must therefore determine that, by the grace of God, he will devote his life to preaching Christ incarnate, crucified, risen, ascended, glorified, interceding and coming back again, even though such preaching is "to the

Jews, a stumbling block and to the Gentiles, foolishness"
(I Cor. 1:23).

3. *The qualities of an effective sermon.*

The effective sermon should be full of three things. It
should be full of the *Holy Spirit* and delivered in His
energy and power. It should be full of *the word of God,*
which gives it authority to the audience. It should be full
of *Christ, the Center* and Essence of the message. "We
preach not ourselves, but Christ Jesus the Lord; and ourselves your servants for Jesus' sake" (II Cor. 4:5). An
Irish preacher was once accused of wandering from his
subject. With ready wit he replied: "Yes, I may wander
away from my *subject* but, thank God, no one can accuse
me of wandering away from my *Object,* Christ!"

The late Dr. Archibald Brown advised young preachers
thus: "(1) The gospel is a fact, therefore tell it *simply.*
(2) It is a joyful fact, therefore tell it *cheerfully.* (3) It
is an entrusted fact, therefore tell it *faithfully.* (4) It is
a fact of infinite moment, therefore tell it *earnestly.* (5) It
is a fact of infinite love, therefore tell it *feelingly.* (6) It
is a fact difficult of comprehension to many, therefore tell
it with *illustration.* (7) It is a fact about a Person, therefore *preach Christ!*"

4. *The distinction between an evangelist and a teacher.*

These gifts are quite distinct. Broadly speaking, the distinction between the preacher and the teacher is that the
preacher *proclaims* the message while the teacher *explains*
the message. Many a good evangelist has been spoiled because he imagined that his years of experience in evangelism fitted him for a teaching ministry, whereas teaching
is a distinct gift from that of evangelism. It is true that
sometimes these gifts are combined in one person, as with
Paul for instance, but more often they are quite distinct.

5. *The seven cardinal truths of the gospel.*

What then, should be the theme of the preacher of the gospel? It should be his aim, in every gospel message, to set forth at least seven great cardinal truths of the gospel. It would be a good test if each preacher were to examine his gospel address to discover if these seven truths have been stated in some form or other.

(1) *The Need of the gospel, or Ruin by the Fall.*

This is anything but popular, but it is essential to proclaim it, if the need of the sinner is to be brought home to him. The truth of the total depravity of man is all too little heard from the pulpit today. By this is meant man's total incapacity to comprehend Divine truth, apart from a revelation from God Himself.

Man's need, as a ruined, lost, guilty, helpless, hopeless and hell-deserving sinner needs to be preached with no uncertain sound. See Roman 3:10-23. The mirror of the word of God must be held squarely before the sinner and he must be made to see that he is:

(a) *A sinner by nature and practice* (Rom. 5:12; Ps. 51:5; Eph. 2:1-3).

(b) *Alienated from God* (Eph. 4:18; Col. 1:21).

(c) *At enmity to God* (Rom. 5:10).

(d) *Incapable of pleasing God* (Rom. 8:5-8).

(e) *Astray, and lost in sin* (Isa. 53:6; II Cor. 4:3-4; Luke 19:19).

(f) *Guilty before God* (Rom. 3:19).

(g) *Helpless to save himself* (Rom. 5:6; Gal. 2:16; Eph. 2:8-9).

(h) *Deserving only of eternal death* (Eph. 2:3; Rom. 6:23; Rev. 20:11-15).

The natural man needs to be shown that he does not have to sin in order to *become* a sinner, but that he *sins* because he *is* a sinner by birth. Adam, as a result of his act of disobedience, acquired a sinful nature which he passed on to all his descendants. The difference between sin and sins, is the same as the differenec between the *source* of a river and its *flow*, or the *root* of a tree and its *fruit*: one stems from the other.

(2) *The Provision of the gospel, or Redemption through the precious blood of Christ.*

Once the sinner's need has been clearly set forth, then the preacher should make much of the redemptive work of the Son of God. Spurgeon said he always took a short cut to Calvary in every gospel sermon he preached. During the first great world war, when thousands of troops were entraining for the front, their friends and relatives shouted as the train left: "Give them (the enemy) hell!" At the same time a father bade farewell to his only son, who was returning to his lonely station in the foreign mission field. As the train started to move he called out: "My boy, give them Christ!" Let us make much of Christ and of the precious blood, and so set forth His redemptive work that souls shall be led to rest in His finished work, and trust Him as their own personal Savior and Lord. We must therefore preach:

(a) *The essential and eternal Deity of His Person* (John 1:1-3; Heb. 1:1-3; Col. 1:16-17).

(b) *The mystery and miracle of His incarnation* (I Tim. 3:16; Luke 1:35).

(c) *The grace and purpose of His advent* (II Cor. 8:9; Mark 10:45; Matt. 9:13; Luke 19:10).

(d) *The virtue and value of His substitutionary sacrifice* (I Cor. 15:1-3. Make much of the precious blood, and explain its significance (Levit. 17:11).

(e) *The full and final provision of His salvation* (Heb. 9: 24-28; 10: 12; John 19: 30). The work that saves has all been done. The gospel does not bring us a *work* to *do*, but a *word* to *believe* about a work that has already been *done*.

(f) *The significance of His victorious resurrection and glorification* (Acts 17: 31; Rom. 1: 4).

(g) *The efficacy of His present ministry in heaven* (Heb. 7: 25).

(h) *His second coming, as it affects both the believer and the unbeliever* (I Thess. 4: 13-18; Rev. 20: 10-15).

(3) *The Command of the gospel, or Repentance towards God.* Let us not fail in this.

(a) *Christ insisted on it* (Luke 13: 3).

(b) *God commands it* (Acts 17: 30).

(c) *Paul preached it* both publicly and privately (Acts 20: 21).

Repentance is a change of *mind*, produced in the sinner by the Holy Spirit, which results in a change of his *attitude* toward spiritual things, and issues in a change of *action* towards Christ as he responds to the gospel message.

(4) *The Condition of the gospel, or Reception of Christ as Savior and confession of Him as Lord of the life.*

This is the great end of the gospel. The preacher should so proclaim, prove, portray and persuade, that the repentant sinner shall be led to believe the good news, trust Christ as his own personal Savior and own Him henceforth as the Lord of his life. (Rom. 10: 9-10).

The sinner should be urged to:

(a) *Come to Him* (Matt. 11: 28; John 10: 9).

(b) *Believe on Him* (Acts 16: 31; John 3: 16).

(c) *Hear Him* (John 5:24).

(d) *Receive Him* (John 1:12; Rev. 22:17).

(e) *Obey Him* (Rom. 1:5; Matt. 7:24-27).

(f) *Look to Him* (Isa. 45:22).

(g) *Trust in Him* (Eph. 1:13), i. e. To commit himself to Him. (II Tim. 1:12).

Let us not fail to emphasize the Lordship of Christ and make clear what is involved by professing faith in Christ. To *believe* on Christ means that the believer henceforth *belongs* to Christ, spirit, soul, and body; and that he is to prove it by *behaving* as becomes a Christian (I Cor. 6:19-20).

(5) *The Result of the gospel, or Regeneration by the Holy Spirit.*

The need for spiritual life is declared by Christ in the words: "Ye must be born again (or from above)." This need is now met by the indwelling of the Holy Spirit and His impartation, to the believer, of a Divine nature. (Eph. 1:13).

(a) *His indwelling in the believer* (I Cor. 6:19-20).

(b) *His impartation of a Divine nature to the believer.* (Rom. 8:15; II Pet. 1:3-4).

Just as an earthly parent communicates his physical nature to his offspring by birth; so God imparts, in the new birth, a spiritual nature of His children.

(c) *His guidance of the believer* (Rom. 8:14; John 16:13).

The Holy Spirit guides through the word of God, which He has inspired and He never leads a believer to do anything contrary to it.

(d) *His fruit in the Christian* (Gal. 5:22-26).

As He is allowed to dwell ungrieved in the believer, the effect will be seen by others in this fruit, with its ninefold quality, Godward, manward, and selfward.

(e) *His empowerment for service* (Acts 1:8; Eph. 1:19-20; 3:16-21; Zech. 4:6).

Thus "The excellency of the power may be of God and not of us" (II Cor. 4:7). All needed power, for every needed task, is made available through the omnipotent Holy Spirit's indwelling presence.

(6) *The Solemnity of the gospel, or the Responsibility of the Hearer.*

This needs to be driven home, and the responsibility of each hearer of the Word made perfectly clear.

(a) *God desires the salvation of the sinner* (Ezek. 33:11; I Tim. 2:4-5; Rom. 2:4).

(b) *God has provided a salvation for the sinner* (John 3:16; Eph. 2:4-7).

God has gone to infinite lengths to make salvation possible to all.

(c) *God proclaims, through His servants, this salvation to the sinner* (Mark 16:15; Heb. 1:1).

(d) *God will hold each hearer of the Word responsible for his reaction to the gospel.* (John 12:47-48).

Far better never to have heard the gospel, than to hear and refuse the salvation provided. Mark the Savior's words: "Good for that man if he had never been born" (Mark 14:21).

(7) *The Penalty of rejecting the gospel, or the eternal Retribution upon the Christ rejecter.*

Care must be taken, when speaking of this, not to charge God with vindictiveness. There should be tears in the heart of the preacher when this solemn reality is proclaimed. It should be pointed out that:

(a)   *This retribution is factual.*

It is *real,* and not a mere figment of mythology to scare people. Our Lord Jesus Christ spoke much of it. See Matt. 11:19-24; 12:36-37; 12:41-42; Luke 16:19-31; Mark 9:43-48; Matt. 25:41; John 3:36; Mark 16:16).

(b)   *This retribution is eternal.*

The same word used in describing the eternal duration of the retribution on the lost is also used to portray the duration of the blessedness of the saved. "Everlasting" and "eternal," are grim words, when they relate to punishment and wrath.

(c)   *This retribution is deserved.*

To deliberately reject, despise, or neglect the Son of God, and the salvation He has provided at such definite cost, merits and results in eternal banishment from His presence. See Rev. 6:15-17. "These shall go away" (Matt. 25:46). An unbeliever once cried: "Hell were a refuge, could it but hide me from Thy frown."

6.   *Stewardship demands a faithful discharge of one's trusteeship of the gospel.*

Gospel preachers have not been left to themselves in the choice of their theme. This has been committed to them by the Lord. It is their solemn obligation to be faithful to the task, cost what it may. The Lord grant that, as His heralds, we may be loyal stewards of this secred trust and watch our theme, which is the theme of themes: Christ, the all sufficient Savior, able to save, secure, satisfy and sustain every sinner who believes on Him!

CHAPTER THIRTY-EIGHT

The Delivery of The Sermon

(Continued)

VII. He should watch for results.

The preacher must expect to see results from his prayerful and faithful presentation of the word of God.

1. *God has promised results.*

He has definitely declared: "My word shall not return unto Me void, but it *shall accomplish* that which I please and it *shall prosper* in the thing whereto I sent it" (Isa. 55: 11). He has also said: "He that goeth forth and weepeth, bearing precious seed, shall *doubtless* come again with rejoicing, bringing his sheaves with him" (Psa. 126: 6). The seed that we sow is described as *living* seed, which will germinate in the hearts of all who will receive it as the word of God. Not only has God *promised* results, but it must be remembered that only He can *give* these results. See I Thess. 2: 13.

2. *Only God can give results.*

The preacher must lay to heart the great fact that "Salvation is of the Lord" (Jonah 2: 9; Zech. 4: 6). No human being can manufacture genuine results for God. Unless the Holy Spirit wings home to the hearer the word of God, produces conviction of sin and reveals Christ to his soul, that person will remain in darkness, in spite of all our pleading. The preacher is shut up entirely to God in this matter of results. "Except the Lord build the house they labor in vain who build it." (Ps. 127: 1). The preacher's

431

sole task is to preach the gospel in the power of the Holy
Spirit sent down from heaven (I Pet. 1:12). It is God's
prerogative to give whatever results He pleases. Sometimes God uses what, to us, was a poor sermon; while often
a brilliant sermon goes unblessed.

An illustration of this is seen in the life of C. H. Spurgeon. He once preached what, in his judgment, was one
of his poorest sermons. He stammered and floundered,
and when he finally got through he felt that it had been
a complete failure. He was greatly humiliated and, when
he got home, fell on his knees and said: "Lord God, Thou
canst do something with nothing. Bless that poor sermon."
All through that week he repeated that prayer. He would
wake up in the night and pray about it. He determined
that the next Sunday he would redeem himself by preaching a great sermon. Sure enough, the next Sunday the
sermon went off beautifully. At the close, the people
crowded about him and covered him with praise. Spurgeon went home pleased with himself and, that night, he
slept like a baby. But he said to himself: "I'll watch the
results of those two sermons." What were they? From
the one that had seemed a failure he was able to trace
forty-one conversions. And from the magnificent sermon,
he was unable to discover that a single soul was saved.
Spurgeon's explanation was that the Spirit of God used
the one, and did not use the other. We can do nothing
without the Spirit who "helpeth our infirmities." (Rom.
8:26).

3. We must beware of creating results.

Professional evanglism, with its insatiable appetite for
"statistics" and "results," as distinct from fruit for God,
has been responsible for thousands of mere empty professors of Christ who have never been born again. These
professions have resulted from psychological mass appeals

by experts in this field. They have either "held up their hands for prayer," or "come forward," or "signed a card," or "taken the evangelist's hand;" but alas, have never been convicted by the Holy Spirit, or brought into living touch with the Son of God, whom to know is life eternal (John 17:3).

The modern tendency of professional evangelism is to extract a *maximum of reaping* from a *minimum of sowing,* The preaching of the word of God has been largely superceded by the singing of choruses, thrilling stories, personal charm, the "cheery and breezy" manner and the "team spirit." The audience is appealed to, on the basis of its "manhood," to come forward and take its "stand for Christ." Often the challenge is made: "Who will have the courage to come forward and thus show he has a backbone in him!" Sin is largely glossed over, the substitutionary work of Christ is relegated into a second place and what is called "the challenge of Christianity" becomes the dominant theme.

It is possible to secure the intellectual assent of almost any individual by putting to him a series of leading questions. When an affirmative answer is given to these questions, the person is assured he is now a Christian and urged to "keep faithful to the stand he has taken." By this "mass production" plan, converts are manufactured by the hundreds, to add to the already overstocked market of such dead professors.

4. *The preacher should expect results.*

He should therefore be continually on the alert and quick to perceive any signs of anxiety of soul on the part of any in the audience. A preacher once approached C. H. Spurgeon and inquired: "How do you account for the fact that though I preach the same gospel as you, I do not get anywhere near the same results?" Spurgeon replied: "But you surely don't expect results *every time* you preach, do you?" "O, no," answered the man. Then Spurgeon exclaimed: "Then that is one reason why you don't get any!" The farmer who sows his seed in the spring, does so with every expectation of reaping in the fall.

(1) *He should invite any who are concerned about their salvation to remain behind.*

It is a good plan to have an inquiry room to which any interested person may go and have further conversation regarding spiritual things. Some place a box at the door, in which those who desire a personal visit from the preacher may put their names and addresses. No gospel meeting, where unsaved people are known to be present, should conclude without an opportunity being given for an immediate decision for Christ, or at least further conversation regarding spiritual matters.

(2) *He should be prepared to do personal work with any who appear concerned.*

He must beware of two extremes: one, of rushing ahead of God and forcing the issue; the other, of lagging behind and allowing souls, who are really anxious, to go on groping despairingly in the darkness.

In view of this, it will be appreciated how much each preacher needs Divine wisdom as to just when to speak to a soul; to whom he should speak, and what he should say to a troubled sinner. It is a cause for great thankfulness that the preacher is not left to himself in this matter. The Holy Spirit of God dwells within him and it is His delight to lead and empower in this matter. In the measure in which the Spirit is allowed to dwell ungrieved within the believer, in that degree he will be susceptible to His Divine guidance. He will thus be able to testify with another: "I, being in the way, the Lord led me" (Gen. 24:27).

(3) *He should seek to do a thorough work with a soul.*

Here, as in everything else, "haste makes waste." In a kindly, courteous, yet faithful fashion, each step should be made clear to the inquirer until, of his own free will and choice, owning his lost and guilty state, he rests in the finished work of Christ, receives Him as his own personal Savior and acknowledges Him as the Lord of his life.*

This may take some time and may not be accomplished at this first interview. The word of God must be kept prominent, for it is this which gives authority. It should be kept open during the entire interview and all questions of the inquirer should be answered with a "thus saith the Lord." The inquirer should be allowed to read these scriptures for himself and, in this way, he will be anchored to the infallible Word for his knowledge. The believing soul should never be told that he is saved. Let him discover this for himself from the Bible. He will then be left in no doubt of his authority for believing himself to be a saved person. Happy indeed is that preacher who shall be able to say in a coming day: "Behold I, and the children whom the Lord hath given me" (Isa. 8:18)!

* See Author's booklet: "Child Evangelism—Its Delights, Dangers and Design." from this publisher.

1 6

CHAPTER THIRTY-NINE

The Public Reading of the Scriptures

There can surely be no doubt as to the importance of this essential part of a public service, which has been convened for the preaching and teaching of the word of God.

I.   It is Scriptural.

Way's translation of I Timothy 4:10 is very suggestive: "Until I come, give constant attention to the public reading of the Scriptures, to personal appeals and to exposition." Thus Timothy had a three-fold duty to perform as he faced his audience. He had to *read* intelligently, to *exhort* earnestly and to *expound* faithfully. The word used here for "read," is "anaginosko." This is used thirty-three times in the New Testament. In all the references, reading aloud would be permissable and in twelve of them, it is essential. See Luke 4:16; Acts 8:28-32; 13:27; 15:21; II Cor. 3:15; Col. 4:16; I Thess. 5;27; Rev. 1;3.

It is interesting to note that Hebrew scholars point out that Nehemiah 8:8 should be rendered: "Caused them to understand *in* the reading." In fact, those whose duty it was to read the Scriptures in public gatherings were called "anagnostes." Many, in those days, were illiterate and depended upon the public reading of the Word for their knowledge of it. Bibles were also very scarce, and it was a rare thing for a person to possess a complete copy for himself. Hence this public reading of the Bible filled a real need for the people.

II.   It is important.

The Scriptures are the Divinely inspired revelation of God to man. Though we do not read them publicly in the original language in which they were written, yet we have, in the Authorized Version, a wonderfully accurate translation of the original manuscripts. How important, therefore, that the Bible be read clearly, accurately, reverently and feelingly. It is to be feared that this is not always true of the public reading of the Scriptures.

Though Bibles are now both plentiful and cheap, it is little read by the unsaved. About all they know of it is what they hear when it is read at a preaching service; and this, in many cases, is quite seldom. It can therefore be appreciated how important it is that the living word of God be given due reverence, and read in such a manner that those who are present can be "caused to understand *in* the reading of it."

There was a time, in England, when Bibles were so scarce that a copy was chained to a desk in a church building, and people would gather simply to hear someone read audibly the word of God. It was in this manner that the seeds of the Reformation were sown, and which yielded such an abundant harvest to the glory of God.

III. This public reading is often performed carelessly and unprofitably.

Frequently, this preliminary reading of the Bible portion that is to form the basis for the sermon, is performed in a most uninteresting manner. It is treated as though it was a matter of minor importance, to be gotten out of the way as quickly as possible, in order to make room for the main attraction, the preacher's sermon. This certainly ought not to be. If the speaker is a man of the Book, then the Scriptures must be handled and read reverently and in such a manner as will enable all to hear the words of life.

IV.   Some causes for the unprofitable reading of the Scriptures.

1.   *The failure of the speaker to mention clearly the name of the book in the Bible, and its location in that book, at least twice.*

The result is that many in the audience are unaware of the book, the chapter in that book and the verse in that chapter, at which the reading is to commence. Such begin to ask their neighbors where the Scripture portion is. This naturally causes confusion and consequent inattention, and the Bible fails to command the place of preeminence, which is its right, as the word of God. It need hardly be said that the preacher, after clearly announcing the Scripture portion, should give the audience enough time to find it before commencing to read. He can easily determine this by looking at the hearers.

2.   *By the failure of the reader to enunciate clearly the words of the portion read.*

The words are either so mumbled, slurred, or run into each other that few can understand what is being read.

3.   *By the failure to give the correct emphasis, or feeling, to certain words or phrases in the portion read.*

Correct emphasis and feeling is the means by which the idea of the writer is made clear to those who hear. The inflection of the voice, the pause, the stress on this word or that phrase, will illuminate the Word and give its proper meaning. For example: It is possible to read I Kings 13:13, as: "So they saddled him, the ass." Luke 2:16 can be read in such a way as to suggest that both Mary and Joseph were in the manger. Then again, I Kings 18:27 can be read as though to suggest that Elijah himself believed that Baal was a god. Luke 23:32 was once made to read: "And there were also two other malefactors led with Him," etc. How much depends on the two commas before and after "malefactors." Romans 12:1 is often read as though the word was "wholly," instead of "holy." In I Peter 2:1, the stress is on the word "desire," and this is essential to clarify the passage. Take that best known of all verses, John 3:16. This can be made vapid and colorless by expressionless reading. Then again, take Numbers 32:23. "Be sure your sin will find you out." One can repeat this text in seven different ways, simply by stressing a different word each time it is repeated. First put the emphasis on "sure," then on the next word in the text and so on.

A recent writer has well observed: "True reading is interpretation, and true emphasis is exposition." Therefore the need, when reading the word of God publicly, to see that the right interpretation is given by the use of proper emphasis, inflection and pronunciation of the words.

4. *By the failure to pronounce the words correctly.*

Many a Scripture portion has been lost on an audience because of some ludicrous error of pronunciation. The beauty and dignity of the passage is forgotten because of this act of carelessness on the part of the reader. A brother once read Rom. 15:14 as: "Able also to *abolish* one another"; while still another read Phil. 3:10 as "Being made *comfortable* unto His death."

5. *By the failure to read deliberately.*

Quite often it is the speed at which the portion is read that makes it unprofitable. The passage is rattled off at express speed, so that the words of holy writ become a mere jumble of inarticulate words.

6. *By a failure to limit the length of the Scripture passage.*

This portion should not be too long. It should only contain that which is essential to the exposition of the passage.

Some preachers have been known to read two long chapters and the audience became wearied as a result.

V. Some suggestions for the remedying of this unprofitable reading of the Scriptures.

1. *The passage to be read publicly, should first be read, and reread, privately and audibly.*

This will insure that the reader will be well acquainted with the actual words of Scripture. How can one be expected to read the passage intelligently, until he has mastered the wording of it for himself? In this way, practice will make perfect.

2. *A careful note should be made of the words and phrases requiring special emphasis.*

If necessary, these words and phrases could be underlined in the Bible as a reminder. Often a little stress on this word and that, or a slower pace when reading a certain phrase, will serve to impress it on the hearer.

3. *All proper names should be studied for correct pronunciation.*

A pronouncing Bible is invaluable for this. Any other words, concerning which there is any doubt as to the correct pronunciation, should be looked up.

4. *Strict attention should be paid to the punctuation marks in the passage.*

Every comma, colon, semi-colon, period, question mark and exclamation mark, etc., is there for a purpose. The parenthesis, also should be carefully noted. All these marks are for the purpose of making the passage intelligible to both reader and hearer. This will mean that the preacher will have to watch his breathing, so as to read smoothly and with ease, and with a pause now and then as occasion demands.

The story is told of a lady who was much concerned about her husband who had joined the navy, and had just left by ship for active service. With a view to enlisting the prayerful interest of fellow Christians, she wrote a note to the preacher of the chapel she attended, with the request that it be read to the congregation. The note was as follows: "John Anderson, having gone to sea, his wife desires the prayers of the congregation for his safety." The note was handed to the preacher as he mounted the platform. After hastily glancing at the contents, to the amusement of the audience, and the embarrassment of the lady, he announced: "John Anderson, having gone to see his wife, requests the prayers of the congregation for his safety!"

5. *The passage to be read should be announced clearly and at least twice.*

Time should be given, for those who have Bibles, to find the place. The book of the Bible should first be announced, then the chapter and finally the verse in that chapter at which the reading is to commence. For example: "Let us turn to Romans, chapter ten and the first verse." Then, after a pause repeat: "Romans, chapter ten, verse one." It might also be well, after having read the portion to say: "May the Lord add His blessing to the reading of His holy word," or something similar.

6. *The passage should be read clearly, deliberately, reverently and feelingly.*

Thus the Scriptures will be allowed to speak for themselves. God often blesses this preliminary reading of the Word to the salvation of souls, while the sermon preached from it has left the audience untouched.

Years ago, an eloquent preacher in London used to set aside a night, now and then, and devote it entirely to the recitation, or the reading of the word of God itself. Such was his ability as a reader, that crowds flocked to hear him and sat spellbound under this delightful ministry.

It is now possible to purchase a set of phonograph records containing the whole of the New Testament. These may well serve as models as to how the Scriptures should be read. They are published by Audio Book Co., St. Joseph, Michigan.

7. *The Bible is a literary gem and is incomparable as pure literature.*

When it is well and reverently read, it never fails to command authority and arouse interest. May it be ours, as preachers, to give the Scriptures the place of honor, dignity and authority that is its rightful due as the inspired revelation of the living God! As this is done, "decently and in order," God will honor it and give our message authority through it.

VI. Some passages of Scripture for practice public reading.

The following passages should prove useful for practice purposes, and should be read *audibly*.

1. *Descriptive narrative.*

Creation, Gen. 1:1-31. *The Fall,* Gen. 3:1-24. *The Flood,* Gen. 7:11-24. *Babel,* Gen. 11:1-9. *Call of Abraham,* Gen. 12:1-8. *Destruction of Sodom,* Gen. 19:1-26. *Sacrifice of Isaac,* Gen. 22:1-19. *Esau and Jacob,* Gen. 27:1-40. *Jacob's Vision,* Gen. 28:1-22. *Joseph's revelation,* Gen. 44:18—45:15. *Finding of Moses,* Exod. 1:22—2:10. *Call of Moses,* Exod. 3:1-22. *The Passover,* Exod. 12:1-14, 29-36. *The Red Sea,* Exod. 14:5-31. *The Giving of the Law,* Exod. 19:1-25. *Breaking of the tables of the Law,* Exod. 32:1-28. *Balaam's commission,* Num. 22:1-35. *Joshua's commission,* Josh. 1:1-9. *Achan's sin,* Josh. 7:1, 16-26. *Gideon's victory,* Jud. 7:1-22. *Samson's death,* Jud. 16:4-31. *Ruth's confession,*

Ruth 1:1-22. *Samuel's call,* I Sam. 3:1-21. *Saul's disobedience,* I Sam. 15:9-31. *Anointing of David,* I Sam. 16:1-13. *David and Goliath,* I Sam. 17:20-52. *David and the Ark,* II Sam. 6:12-23. *Nathan's parable,* II Sam. 12:1-14. *The visit of the Queen of Sheba,* I Kings 10:1-10. *Elijah's provision,* I Kings 17:1-24. *Elijah on Carmel,* I Kings 18:17-40. *Elijah's complaint,* I Kings 19:1-18. *Elijah's translation,* II Kings 2:1-14. *Naaman,* II Kings 5:1-27. *Mordecai's triumph,* Esth. 6:1-14. *Haman's doom,* Esth. 7:1-10. *Job's testing,* Job 1:1-22; 2:1-13. *Job's triumph,* Job 42:1-12. *Ezekiel's vision,* Ezek. 37:1-14. *Daniel's purpose,* Dan. 1:8-21. *The fiery furnace,* Dan. 3:1-30. *The handwriting on the wall,* Dan. 5:1-31. *The den of lions,* Dan. 6:1-28. *Jonah and the whale,* Jonah 1:1-17. *The repentance of Nineveh,* Jonah 3-4. *The birth of Christ,* Luke 2:7-18. *Baptism of Christ,* Matt. 3:1-17. *Peter's confession,* Matt. 16:13-26. *Blind man healed,* John 9:1-41. *Woman at the well,* John 4:1-42. *The demoniac,* Mark 4: 35—5:20. *Nicodemus,* John 3:1-16. *The good Samaritan,* Luke 10:25-37. *The prodigal son,* Luke 15;11-32. *The rich fool,* Luke 12:13-21. *Dives and Lazarus,* Luke 16:10-31. *Zacchaeus,* Luke 19:1-10. *Raising of Lazarus,* John 11:1-45. *The Lord's supper,* Luke 22:1-23. *Gethsemane,* Luke 22:39-46. *Calvary,* John 19:1-30. *The resurrection,* John 20:1-18. *The commission of Peter,* John 21:1-25. *The Emmaus ministry,* Luke 24:13-35. *The ascension,* Acts 1:1-12. *Pentecost,* Acts 2:1-47. *Conversion of Saul,* Acts 9:1-22. *The Philippian Jailer,* Acts 16:16-40.

2. *Speeches.*

Elihu's, Job 33:1-33. *Christ's,* Matt. 5:1-16; 11:25-30; John 14:1-31; 10:1-18. *Isaiah's,* Isa. 55:1-13; 61:1-11. *Joshua's,* Josh. 23:3-16. *Hosea's,* Hos. 14:1-9. *Moses',* Deut. 32: 1-43; 30:11-20. *Peter's,* Acts 2:14-40. *Stephen's,* Acts 7:1-60. *Paul's,* Acts 17:16-34; 13:16-41; 26:1-32.

3. *The majesty of God.*

Isa. 40:1-31. Prov. 8:1-36. Job 28:1-28. Psalm 19:1-14. Psalm 8:1-9. Deut. 4:1-10.

4. *Rebuke.*

Jeremiah 13:15-24. Gal. 3:1-29. Matt. 23:13-39; 11:20-24.

5. *Judgment and warning.*

Matt. 25:31-46. Revelation 20:10-15. Ezek. 33:1-16.

6. *Prayers.*

John 17:1-26. Eph. 1:15-23. Ezra 9:5-15. I Kings 8:12-61. Dan. 9:1-19. Psalm 51:1-19.

7. *Songs and praise.*

Psalms 23; 15; 24; 32; 46; 84; 90; 91; 103; 116; 139; 150. *Moses',* Exod. 15:1-20; Deut. 32:1-43. *Hannah's,* I Sam. 2:1-10. *Deborah's,* Jud. 5:1-31. *Habakkuk's,* Hab. 3:17-19. *David's lament,* II Sam. 1:17-27.

8. *Argument and indictment.*

Romans 2:1-19; 3:1-31; 8:28-39. Isaiah 44:9-20.

9. *Prophecy and future glory.*

Isa. 11:1-16. Rev. 22:1-21; 1:4-20. II Cor. 5:1-21.

10. *Great passages.*

Love, I Cor. 13. *Faith,* Heb. 11:1-40. *Christian liberty,* I Cor. 8:1-13; Gal. 1:4-26. *Faith and works,* James 2:14-26. *The Second Coming,* I Thess. 4:13-18; I Cor. 15:49-58. *The Deity of Christ,* Heb. 1:1-12. Phil. 2:5-11. *Worship,* Deut. 26:1-11.

CHAPTER FORTY

Sermon Criticism

Though we do not go to hear a sermon in order to criticize it, yet unconsciously, as we hear it, we form our own opinion of its worth or otherwise, and *this is criticism.* The scriptural injunction is: "Let your prophets speak . . . and let the other judge" (I Cor. 14:29). Therefore it is perfectly right and proper to criticize a sermon, either to approve or otherwise.

Several things will impress us during the delivery of the sermon, either favorably or unfavorably. It has been pointed out that there is only one way by which a person can avoid criticism: and that is by his saying, doing and being nothing!

Let us imagine we are sitting in the audience, listening to an address. During the course of this address several things will impress us concerning both "the preacher and his preaching." Let us try to outline our reaction to both the man and his message. We shall think of seven things regarding the speaker and his message, and ask quite a number of questions.

I. The physical appearance of the preacher.

1. *His posture.* Careless? Slouching? Leaning on the pulpit? Hands in pockets?

2. *His clothing.* Neat? Gaudy? Untidy?

3. *His manner.* Pompous? Nervous? Indifferent? Humble?

4. *His gestures.* Appropriate? Grotesque? Funny?

5. *His eccentricities.* Any? Did they detract from his message?

6. *His attitude.* Was he earnest? Flippant? Cold and distant? Warm and friendly? Proud? Sincere? Artificial?

II.   The delivery of the sermon.

1. *The reading of the Scriptures.*
(1)   The portion, clearly and well announced?
(2)   Reverently read?
(3)   Pronunciation, good or bad?
(4)   Clearly heard by all?
(5)   Read with expression?
2. *The introduction.*
(1)   Gain your attention?
(2)   Appropriate to the subject?
(3)   Put you at your ease?
(4)   Pertinent to the theme?
3. *The language used.*
(1)   Suitable to the audience?
(2)   Any poor expressions? Ambiguous? Slang? Coarse? Sacrilegious?
(3)   Any grammatical errors?
(4)   Any mispronunciations?
4. *The order maintained.*
(1)   Were the divisions well arranged and stated?
(2)   Did they show signs of careful preparation?
(3)   Did these divisions follow in logical order, or were they haphazard?

III.   The teaching that was given.

1.   Were the terms clearly defined?
2.   Was the teaching scriptural?
3.   Was the text interpreted in the light of its context, or wrested from its context

IV. The illustrations that were used.

1. Were there any?
2. Were they to the point?
3. Were they too long, or involved?
4. Were they original, or stale?
5. Were there any "suppose" illustrations?
6. Were they well told?
7. Did they clarify the point he was seeking to make?

V. The application made.

1. Was it pointed, or vague?
2. Did it search, or challenge you?
3. Did it carry conviction?
4. Did it impress you as being from the Lord?

VI. The conclusion.

1. Did it sum up the points made?
2. Was it suitable?
3. Did it apply the theme?

VII. The sermon as a whole.

1. Was the theme well covered?
2. Was it too wordy, prosy, or dull? Or was it well put, pointed and interesting?
3. Was it a message from the Lord?
4. How would you grade it: good, bad, or indifferent?

CHAPTER FORTY-ONE

Public Prayer

Having touched on the subject of the public reading of the word of God, it is also necessary that we think of the public prayer which the preacher offers at the preaching service.

I. Its Definition.

This is a somewhat delicate subject, but one that should be faced. Public prayer is on an entirely different plane from private prayer. Private prayer is the expression of the believer's heart, as it goes out to God in worship, praise, prayer, supplication and intercession when he is *all alone*. Concerning this, we have nothing to say, except that it should be sincere.

Public prayer is the *audible* expression of the believer's heart, as he voices his desires to God in the presence of, and on behalf of others. As the Christian thus speaks to God he is, in reality, expressing the desires of all those believers who are assembled with him. Public prayer should therefore meet certain requirements. It should be reverent, clearly heard, intelligent, understood by all present and edifying to the assembly.

II. The scriptural requirements of public prayer.

We are not left in any doubt as to these, for this matter of public prayer is dealt with in the word of God. In I Corinthians 14, where the administration of the gifts of the risen Head of the Church is discussed; the question of public, or assembly ministry, praise and prayer is introduced.

Let us note carefully just what it says concerning this important subject. "If I pray (publicly) in a tongue, my spirit prayeth, but my understanding is unfruitful. What is it then? I will pray with the spirit, and I will pray with the understanding also: I will sing with the spirit, and I will sing with the understanding also. Else when thou shalt bless with the spirit, how shall he that occupieth the room of the unlearned say, 'amen,' at thy giving of thanks, seeing he understandeth not what thou sayest? For thou verily giveth thanks well, but the other is not edified." From this, it will be observed that public prayer, to be scriptural, must fulfill at least three requirements.

1. *The prayer must be intelligent.*

"I will pray with the understanding also." (v. 15). That is, the person who prays in public should understand what he is praying about. If *he* doesn't know what he is saying, then who can be expected to understand?

2. *It must be intelligible.*

The unlearned person, who is present, must be left in no doubt as to what has been said; for he must be able to say, "Amen," at the giving of thanks. This, needless to say, involves the use of clear enunciation on the part of the person who prays, and also demands the use of "words easy to be understood."

3. *It must be edifying to those that hear.*

It must build up the people of God. They must realize it was *their* prayer, and that the speaker was voicing audibly the desires of their own hearts. Such a prayer can lift an assembly spiritually, for it carries them into the presence of God and they are quick to realize this fact in a very real manner.

Thus every prayer, in addition to being reverent and clearly enunciated, should be subjected to this threefold test: Was it intelligent? Was it understood by all present? Was it edifying to the assembled saints?

III.   Some causes for unedifying prayers.

1. *The prayer was uttered in too low a voice to be heard.*

When a person is asked to lead an assembly in prayer, he should stand so that he faces the majority of the audience and speak so clearly that all may hear. Unless this is done, he merely wastes the time of those present. They hear a confused murmur which prevents them from praying themselves, and yet they cannot hear a word of what is being said.

2. *The prayer was too long.*

Sometimes the person who prays goes on and on, encompassing heaven and earth in his petition, until the audience is wearied beyond words and can no longer follow him. Their "amen," at the conclusion of such a prayer, is merely an expression of relief that it is over at long last. Usually those who pray long prayers in public seldom do so in private. Would that the order were reversed!

The longest prayer recorded in the Bible is that of Solomon at the dedication of the temple. This can be read, reverently, in about seven minutes. It is recorded that D. L. Moody once brought a long winded prayer to an abrupt conclusion by announcing: "While our brother is continuing and concluding his prayer, let us sing hymn number so and so."

We have all heard of the brother who was notoriously long in his prayers. After he had been praying for fifteen minutes, a stranger present inquired: "Is he nearly finished?" "No," was the reply: "He hasn't mentioned the Jews yet, and when he does, he's just half way through!"

Most prayer meetings would be very considerably improved if twice the number took part and each prayed shortly, and to the point, for some specific need.

3. *The prayer was too involved.*

The audience was unable to follow the prayer because of its extreme vagueness. The petitioner had nothing definite to pray for, so prayed about everything in general and nothing in particular. Prayer, to be edifying, should be definite. The petitioner should remember he is coming, as a child, to his Father in heaven and with something specific to ask for. We are told that Elijah was "a man of like passions as we are," and he prayed definitely and specifically about a certain thing, and God heard and answered his prayer. (James 5:17-18).

4. *The prayer was, in reality, a little sermon.*

There is always the temptation, when praying before an audience, to *preach* to it, instead of supplicating the throne of grace on its behalf. Many so-called prayers would just as appropriately serve the purpose of an address from the platform. A Christian once approached such a person at the conclusion of a prayer meeting and, to his surprise and embarrassment, thanked him very much for the nice sermon he had preached during his prayer!

Some prayers even go to the length of reminding God of what chapter and verse in the Bible a certain promise is found; and sometimes mention the number of a hymn and the name of the book, from which a verse has been quoted! Worse still, some have been known to administer a rebuke to someone present under the guise of a prayer. It is surely a shame and disgrace to use the throne of grace to criticize a brother or sister, whom one is afraid to speak to face to face.

It is recorded of Elijah that "in praying, he *prayed*" (James 5:17, marg.). Of some prayers it is feared it would have to be recorded: "In praying, he preached"; or, "In praying, he scolded his brethren"; or, "In praying, he exhorted." Let us determine that like Elijah we, too, in praying shall *pray!*

5. *The prayer contained too much repetition.*

Some prayers move in an endless circle, and the same thing is asked for repeatedly. True, each time the phraseology was slightly different, but it was merely putting the same thing in a different way. One wonders whether the injunction: "Use not vain repetitions as the heathen do," would apply in this case (Matt. 6:7). By this method of prayer, a five minute petition is unprofitably stretched to ten minutes, or longer.

6. *The prayer contained an over-use of the Divine names and titles.*

One hesitates to mention such a matter, but who has not heard prayers in which the same Divine title is used in practically every sentence. It would almost appear that these titles were used as a stop gap when the petitioner was at a loss for words, and thus gained time to think what he should say next. This certainly neither makes for reverence nor edification, but strongly savors of vain repetition.

One cannot imagine a child going to its father with a petition framed along these lines. If the child did, it would say something like this: "O father, I have come to you in order, O father, that you may allow me, O father, to go out, father." One could almost wish that a stenographic record could be made of such prayers, and the speaker presented with the record of what the saints have to put up with every time he prays. A study of the prayers of the Bible would do much to eliminate this type of prayer, and make for more reverent, intelligent and edifying prayers.

To sum up. Public prayer should be uttered clearly, so that all may hear. It would be far better to remain silent if one's voice is not capable of being heard. It should be brief and quite definite, so that no one is in any doubt as to what the petitioner has in mind. Finally, it should be reverent, earnest and sincere, so that the audience may realize that the person who prayed has led them into the presence of God. By such a prayer, the hearers will be prepared for any ministry of the Word which may follow.

The Conclusion

We could not end this book better than by quoting a poem, whose author is unknown. It sums up, in poetic form, those elements which together combine to make an ideal sermon. It is entitled: "What a sermon should be."

>"It should be *brief*: if lengthy, it will steep
>Our hearts in apathy, our eyes with sleep;
>The dull will yawn, the chapel lounger doze,
>Attention flag, the memory's portals close.
>
>It should be *warm*, a living altar coal,
>To melt the icy heart and charm the soul:
>A sapless, dull harangue, however read,
>Will never stir the soul or raise the dead.
>
>It should be *simple, practical* and *clear*,
>No fine spun theory, to please the ear;
>No curious lay, to tickle lettered pride,
>And leave the poor and plain unedified.
>
>It should be *tender* and *affectionate*,
>As His warm theme Who wept lost Salem's fate;
>The fiery law—by words of love allayed—
>Will sweetly warn and artfully persuade.

It should be *manly, just* and *rational,*
Wisely conceived, and well expressed withal;
Not stuffed with silly notions apt to stain
A sacred desk and show a muddy brain.

It should be *mixed with many an ardent prayer*
To reach the heart, and fix and fasten there.
When God and man are mutually addressed,
God grants a blessing: man is truly blest.

It should be *closely, well applied at last,*
To make the moral nail securely fast:
"Thou art the man!" and that alone wilt make
A Felix tremble and a David quake."

*　*　*　*

We have now reached the conclusion of the book. It is commended into the hands of "the Master of Assemblies," with the earnest prayer that He may be pleased to use it for His own glory, and also for the spiritual profit of both "the preacher and his preaching." The Lord enable us, as preachers of His word, to fulfill these conditions necessary to effective preaching, and then empower us to so present the gospel and teaching message that Christ shall be magnified, the unsaved regenerated, Christians edified and God glorified!

The Teaching, Interpretation and Application of Scripture

By A. E. HORTON, *Kavungu, Angola, Africa*

"Do your best to present yourself to God as one approved, a workman who has no need to be ashamed, rightly handling the word of truth."

—II Timothy 2:15, R. V.

It is our claim, as believers who seek to follow the pattern laid down in Scripture, that we have no creed but the word of God and that we are entirely subject to that Word. Generally speaking, this states our most earnest aim. But it is not always realized, for there are not wanting among us peculiar traditional interpretations of Scripture, tenaciously held as though they were the very teaching of the Word. Their acceptance is looked upon in some quarters as the very gauge of orthodoxy, though they may really be based on false principles of interpretation. True, these matters do not, as a rule, concern fundamental doctrine, for which we may thank God.

The tragedy is that these interpretations are often treated as if they were fundamental, so that failure to accept their implications cannot be atoned for, in the eyes of some of their proponents, by the most uncompromising adherence to the real fundamentals, and by the warmest love for the Person of our Lord Jesus Christ. A consideration of the legitimate principles of interpretation is thus of primary importance.

Let us contemplate our subject under three heads:

I. The teaching of Scripture, compared with our apprehension thereof.

II. The interpretation of Scripture and some of its governing principles.

III. The application of the typical, historical and figurative portions of Scripture.

I. The Teaching of Scripture.

The teaching of Scripture is that truth which the Scripture is intended to impart to the reader: the thought which was in the mind of Him Who gave it. It is, in other words, *what the Scripture actually means.* Our interpretation of Scripture, on the other hand, is our apprehension of its meaning: the impression made on our minds as we study it. It is *what the Scripture means to us.*

Now when we say that it is necessary to distinguish between these two things, we would not imply that there is necessarily a difference between them. The aim of all sincere study of the Scripture is to ascertain what the Book actually teaches. That is to say, the honest student's endeavor is ever to make his *interpretation* of Scripture synonymous with the *teaching* thereof. And it cannot be doubted that this aim is generally realized among Bible lovers where the fundamental doctrines of the Bible are concerned, in witness whereto we have but to recall the substantial accord of spiritually minded believers in Christ. They are matters so clearly stated in the Book that there cannot be any doubt concerning them where men are honest with themselves before God.

For example, every effort to deny the Deity of Christ must fail before the bar of the word of God. John 1:1 is inescapable here. And so with other vital elements of the truth. True faith cannot but produce uniformity of belief as regards basic doctrines.

If, then, all doctrines were so plainly stated, we would not find any difficulty in interpreting the Scriptures nor, if honest, any differences. We would determine what it is the Scripture has to say and accept it. But it is self-evident that not all the teaching of Scripture is so plainly presented. Some of its teaching is indirect or inferential; that is to say, it is to be inferred from truth clearly set forth that other truth underlies. Apprehension of the teaching thus to be deduced from the Scripture requires careful study, meditation, comparison of passage with passage in dependence upon the Spirit of God, Whose office it is to guide into truth. For the aim of the Word is primarily to present a Person to our hearts, thus resulting in life and godliness. It was not given as a mere statement of doctrine, or system of theology.

Now even in the case of doctrine to be gathered as a result of the indirect teaching of the Word there is a difference. Some are unmistakable. For example, the doctrine of the Trinity is not specifically expressed, but it cannot reasonably be doubted. It alone can account for some of the statements of Scripture, which presents the truth that God, Who is One, subsists in three Persons. There are other inferences, however, which are by no means so unmistakable and it is with these that differences of interpretation arise.

In my study of the Scriptures, a deduction which seems perfectly plain to me, may not be so to my brother. He may read the same passages and draw from them an inference quite different from mine. And he may be just as sincere, just as devoted and just as conscientious as I! I should be most careful about sitting in judgment on a fellow-Christian who is so very unfortunate as not to agree with me! It is not necessarily obstinacy or disobedience on his part. Indeed, the obstinacy may even be mine! But whosoever it is, it will be folly if I intolerantly insist that my deduction is *the* teaching of Scripture, and he holds his in the same way, neither allowing the other any latitude. Much of the mutual recrimination among believers has had no firmer basis than the unreasonable stand: "*I* am right, therefore *you* are wrong!"

Some profess themselves bewildered by such a lack of agreement on non-essential doctrines. They ask: "If we are all taught by the Spirit, why are there these differences?" The answer is not difficult.

First, *the teaching of the Spirit of God never rules out the operation of the human mind.* His office is to guide into the apprehension of truth, but He does so only as we exercise our own minds in dependence upon Him, in study and meditation. It is this necessary exercise of the human mind that differences arise. None of us can claim an entire subjection of all our powers to the Spirit's control, and so none of us has any business to lay claim to infallibility. As long as we are fallible, just so long will there be differences of apprehension among us. It would be cause for comment were it not so.

The Scriptures themselves recognize this difference of apprehension; as, for example, in the case of the "strong" and the "weak." The weak refuse to eat certain things; the strong feel free to eat all things. One regards certain days as of superior sanctity; another holds all days as alike holy. What is to be done about it? Why simply this— forbear with one another. Let not the one who eats condemn the one who does not; nor the one who does not eat condemn the one who does. Let every man be fully persuaded in his own mind. In other words, *the doctrine is not fundamental.* See Romans 14:1-12.

Second, *it should be remembered that we are finite beings, dealing with infinite things.* The teaching of the Spirit of God does not impart to us the comprehension of infinity. "Now we know in part"; we still wait for "that which is prefect" to come. We do not yet "know as we are known," but still "see as in a mirror, dimly." Our deductions are often imperfect because of our imperfect vision. Here note that some differences are caused by our apprehending but one side of a truth, which is beyond our comprehension, in its full-rounded infinity. Take, for instance, the vexed question of God's sovereignity and man's free will. How much argument there has been about these paradoxical truths, caused by "explanations" which try to explain away one or another of them! We are notorious in our tendency to be one-sided and unbalanced—always feeling that we must reconcile the infinite to our understanding and explain the incomprehensible. We will do well to remember the words of the late C. F. Hogg: "We can *apprehend* a great deal that we cannot *comprehend.*"

Third, *some things which are most confidently asserted are not the teaching of Scripture at all,* being nothing but speculations, extra-Scriptural rules, philosophies, reasonings about the Scripture and so on. If we were to test our doctrines consistently by what the Scripture actually *says,* to find whether they are really taught by the Word rather than by tradition, we might be surprised to find how many of our differences would vanish.

There is too much hasty and unquestioning acceptance of what someone else has to say. Few think for themselves. If someone states a doctrine with sufficient emphasis, it will often be accepted without any trial before the Word. Here is where denominational and sectarian doctrines arise. It is the explanation also of localisms of doctrine, certain teachings become current in certain places, so that it is not uncommonly possible to tell where a man hails from by noting the kind of doctrine he holds. Boldness of assertion is not necessarily a guarantee of conformity to the Scriptures. And it should be remembered that there is a very grave danger of being bound by the sayings or writings of others, and of making their words the final court of appeal.

There is thus only one logical attitude for us to take toward one another in the matter of our differences of understanding; that of tolerance and forbearance. Unfortunately, the plea for tolerance is not always happily received. Some seem to think that faithfulness to the truth demands a bitter and dogmatic bigotry, even on minor points of doctrine.

Here let us again call on sanctified common sense. Certainly we cannot plead for tolerance where fundamental error is concerned. We are not to be carried about by every wind of doctrine, but to stand fast in Christ. And we all recognize that there is a line beyond which tolerance would become trason. The trouble is that the line is too often drawn in the wrong place.

Here someone is likely to shout that oft-repeated shibboleth: "All truth is fundamental!" We would do better to be careful of parroting slogans: When you say: "All truth is fundamental," what do you mean by "truth"? Do you mean what the Scripture *actually teaches,* or do you mean *your apprehension* of its teaching? Very often when men say: "All truth is fundamental," what they really infer is that all the doctrine held by *them* is fundamental: that all *their* interpretations are *the* teaching of the Word, and that everything which differs therefrom is necessarily pernicious. This is nothing but the assumption of infallibility!

Then in what sense do you use the word "fundamental"? It may imply one of two things. First, a thing may be *individually* fundamental; that is, fundamental to me as an individual; or "fundamental to the Lordship of Christ."

APPENDIX

In this sense, all my understanding of Scripture is fundamental *to me*. *I* am bound to obey the Word in all things *as I apprehend it*. Others may understand differently, but their understanding cannot be the rule of practice for me. I must do as I have learned for myself, for that is what submission to Christ as Lord necessarily involves for me; but I have no right to make my understanding in such matters the rule of practice for others, nor the test of fellowship with them.

For instance, there are some of my brethren who feel that I am wrong in having fellowship with believers in Christ simply and solely on the ground of their being believers in Christ. But my position in this matter is quite fundamental to me, individually. For me to yield to the objectors would be to act purely from the fear of man. It would result in my being brought into bondage, in a guilty conscience, and in loss of fellowship with the Lord, for I would be disobeying what seems to me to be a vital doctrine of Scripture. But difference here does not prevent my having fellowship in Christ with some who do not agree with my position. My stand is not fundamental in that sense, *nor is theirs*.

Second, a thing may be *absolutely* fundamental. That is, it may be absolutely essential to any fellowship in Christ. These truths on which all who are born of God and love our Lord Jesus Christ will necessarily agree; whose denial involves a practical denial of the faith and raises doubt as to salvation: these are fundamental, not in a personal or individual sense, but in an absolute sense. Here, indeed, tolerance can have no place. But only confusion can result from confounding the *individually* fundamental with the *absolutely* fundamental, making all our inferences to be the inviolable rule for others.

If we are willing, then, to confess that we are not infallible, we ought to be more willing to listen to one another. The members of the body are not independent, but interdependent. None of us has all the truth, or even all aspects of one truth, and we must take from one another as well as give to one another. An intolerant or impatient attitude toward our brethren who differ from us will defeat God's purpose of ministry through all the members of the body (Ephesians 4:16), and will hinder our progress in the truth.

Let us, then, hold fast to the word of God and learn to consider one another, accepting one another as brethren dearly beloved; even though we may disagree with one another in our apprehensions of some points of the teaching of Scripture.

II.   The Interpretation of Scripture.

In dealing with the interpreting of Scripture, we would consider the strictly didactical qualities: that is, the doctrines which are definitely presented or clearly inferred. We shall leave the typical, figurative and historical portions for the next section, since the principles governing these are not strictly the same. For, in interpretation, we deal with the truth *presented* by Scripture; in application, we deal rather with the truth *illustrated* by Scripture.

Let us consider seven general principles which should govern our interpretation of the Scriptures:

1.   *Ascertain what the passage actually says.*

This is elementary, but surprisingly often neglected. It is vital to any intelligent interpretation that we should read our doctrines *out* of Scripture, and not read them *into* it. Here is a man, for instance, who reads I Peter 4:11: "let him speak as the oracles of God." He interprets it to mean that a man should speak as God's mouthpiece when he preaches, and that therefore it is wrong for one to prepare much beforehand, or to use notes when he speaks. This latter point particularly he presses, quite dogmatically, as the teaching of the text. Actually, the text says nothing concerning preparation or notes, and the matter of the use or non-use of notes must be one of individual exercise before the Lord.

Again, someone quotes: "Open thy mouth and I will fill it" (Psalm 81:10) in the same connection. But what does it really say? "Open thy mouth *wide*"—do not leave out or alter words in interpreting a text of Scripture. "Open thy mouth wide"—for what? to speak, or as a bird, for food? "And I will fill it"—with what? Extempore preaching, or with food? See what the passage really says, and do not make it say something different!

In seeking to ascertain what the Scripture really says, it must be remembered that our English Bible is a translation, and that no one version can give the exact sense of the original in every part. There are a number of good versions in English, and comparison of such versions is a very valuable means of ascertaining the actual sense of Scripture. The Revised Version has its faults, but is excellent as a "control text." The New Translation of J. N. D. is very good. Rotherdam is very suggestive, and can give much help. Weymouth is a paraphrase, and must not be trusted too far. Conybeare's *Epistles of Paul* often throws a flood of light on passages, but it also is a paraphrase, should not always be received as authoritative, and in at least one place footnotes are not devoid of error. Moffat and Goodspeed show modernistic bias, as can be seen by reference to the texts which state clearly the Deity of Christ in reliable versions. Commentaries may help, but none is infallible, and they should never be used to relieve one of the necessity of personal study, meditation, and dependence upon the Spirit's enlightening.

2.   *Do not interpret a passage of Scripture independently of its context, or apart from the general purpose and theme of the book in which it occurs, or of the teaching*

of Scripture as a whole. This is probably the most prolific source of misinterpretation. Many examples might be given.

Isaiah 1: 5-6 is often quoted as being a perfect picture of leprosy. Careful reading of the passage, in its entirety, will show that there is no reference whatever to leprosy. Jehovah has beaten His people with one sore judgment after another, until they are black and blue, covered with "wounds and bruises and putrifying sores." He has done nothing to mollify the stripes He has inflicted. And still stubbornly they rebel. In despair, He asks why He should continue to correct those who refuse correction.

Isaiah 63: 1 is another instance. How often it has been applied to our Lord's work of atonement! This is a misapprehension, for when read in its context, it will be seen that the reference is not to Calvary, but to the return of Christ in glory, when He shall tread down His enemies in His wrath, their blood being sprinkled upon His garment. This is confirmed by a reference to Rev. 19: 15.

II Corinthians 4: 10 is very often quoted as referring to the death of the believer judicially with Christ. The context shows that Paul is referring to his sufferings for Christ in the proclamation of the gospel. These were daily bringing him to an end of himself, thus making it possible for Christ to manifest Himself in him.

And then poor, persecuted II Corinthians 6: 17! It would never have been quoted in justification of the sinful practice of brother cutting himself off from brother, or assembly from assembly over non-fundamentals, except for this bad habit of making things mean what the context shows they were never intended to mean!

A passage should be interpreted also in the light of the general purpose of the book in which it occurs. The difficult passages of the book of Hebrews, for instance, become less difficult if it be borne in mind that the book was written to Hebrews who were on the borderline between Judiasm and Christ, who were addressed on the ground of their profession ,but who may not, in all cases, have had an actual experience of salvation.

A passage should be interpreted in the light of Scripture *as a whole.* I John 1:7: "the blood of Jesus Christ His Son cleanseth us from all sin," has been interpreted by some Christians as indicating eradication of sin in the believer. However, a study of the Scripture use of "blood" and "sin" and the believer's salvation as set forth in the Word, reveals that such an idea will not stand the test. "Blood" stands for death as satisfying judicially for the believer's "sin" (i. e., the condemnation and guilt produced by sin). The work of cleansing the heart in experience is that of the Holy Spirit. It is thus evident that the reference here is to the work of Christ on the cross, which avails to purge away all our guilt and condemnation before God.

3. *Take nothing for granted, whether it be the meaning of a word, the use of a phrase, or any such thing.* One should continually be asking, not only: "Is it Scriptural? but: "What does it mean?" Your appreciation of the words: "God is holy," will depend upon whether you understand what is meant by "holy" as applied to God. To many, "holiness" is a mere synonym for "sinlessness" or "purity," whereas its implications are far deeper and more vital. We constantly hear and repeat words without either having, or seeking a clear idea of what is really meant by them. Popular ideas are easily accepted, but are very often quite wrong. Hence, popular usages ought constantly to be brought before the bar of the word of God for trial.

Note here Matthew 16:24. The popular idea here is that our "cross" is some heavy burden, or trial which the Lord puts upon us. If we examine the subject carefully, we will see that the cross speaks rather of the world's rejection, hatred, and scorn, which is always the portion of the one who consistently follows the Lord, and that the Word nowhere speaks of "crosses" for the believer.

4. *Consider what the passage meant to those who wrote or spoke.* It is a very common error of interpretation to read into passages our present knowledge—to interpret them as having meant what we, with the complete revelation of God before us, would mean if we were to use similar words now. For example, Proverbs 18:16 is frequently quoted as indicating that a man's spiritual gift will make a place for him among the people of God. Well, if this be given as an *application,* it may pass; but it is not legitimate *interpretation.* The writer of Proverbs knew nothing of New Testament spiritual gifts, and there is no prophesy of the future there. He was speaking of the material gift which a man brings in his hand and which gains him the favor of others.

So, too, when John said: "He that hath the bride is the bridegroom" (John 3:29). This should not be interpreted as a conscious reference to the church, which was still unrevealed. John speaks rather of Christ as the One to Whom priority truly belongs, his own place being like that of the friend of the bridegroom, who prepares for the bridegroom and then withdraws. It is a figure used as an illustration, nothing more.

5. *Doctrines should not be founded on far-fetched inferences.* We have already seen that some things are necessarily to be inferred from the words of Scripture. But inference should be consistent, logical and not an offence to common-sense. One may have a certain measure of liberty of inference in non-essential doctrines, if it be remembered that such interpretations are only to be

inference and not necessarily authoritative. Inferences which stretch that liberty should be avoided.

6. *One should be cautious of interpretations which contradict the general understanding of spiritually-minded men, and those which contradict universal Christian experience.* The interpreter of Scripture must always remember that he is not the only one who is honestly intent on understanding the Scripture, nor the only one who is taught by the Spirit of God. It is not for nothing that believers generally have arrived at some settled conclusions concerning the truth of God. This is not to say that one may not be led to differ from the majority in some things; but merely that he should be very sure of his ground if he does so.

As for Christian experience, we grant that experience is no guide apart from the word of God. But, on the other hand, eternal life is more than a doctrine: it is a definite experience of fellowship with God. Any interpretation contrary to this experience cannot be true. It is one of the fatal objections to the doctrine of baptismal regeneration that it contradicts this universal experience of spiritual men. It is an evident fact that many have the enjoyment of everlasting life who have not been baptized, even as it is evident that many who have been baptized show no signs of life whatsoever. The right interpretation of certain passages of the New Testament must be one which harmonizes with the facts of Christian experience.

7. *Strange interpretation ("new light") should not be either hastily expressed or hastily accepted.* They should be left to mature. Careful study and prayerful meditation may show that a first idea was a wrong one, and that its promulgation would have been a teaching of error. Too many people rush hastily into speech or print, and then later are faced with the necessity, either of defending, re-examining, or abondoning their position; or, adopting an attitude of self-defense, become fixed in false doctrine.

So, too, new ideas presented by others ought not to be hastily accepted by the hearer. The Bereans are commended for not accepting the "new" gospel until they had tried it by the Word, "to find out if these things were so." We are commanded not to believe every spirit, but to "try the spirits whether they are of God" (I John 4:1). Haste in teaching or accepting strange ideas is a prolific source of error. *Haste* is one thing the *true* King's business does *not* require! (Another text frequently taken out of its context! I Samuel 21:8).

III. The Application of Scripture.

In treating of the application of Scripture, we might consider two things: the Holy Spirit's application of the Word to practical living, and our application of Scripture, as illustrating the truth of the didactical portions.

It should be noted first, that truth is not presented, and should never be studied or taught, from a purely theoretical standpoint, or as an end in itself. The purpose of the epistles, for example, is always practical: the truth is expected to produce fruit in the life, in devotion to the exalted Christ and in godly living. Hence, in dealing with such a portion as Colossians, our aim should be, not merely to understand its doctrine, but to give to the Lord His deserved place in our hearts and lives (Col. 2:6, 7).

Similarly, in dealing with such a portion as Phil. 2:5-8, the consideration of the doctrine must not be allowed to overshadow the purpose of the portion, which is found in the words, "Let this mind be in you." His self-humbling is set forth there, not merely for our contemplation, but for our imitation. Again, theorizing as to the doctrine of Ephesians 5:23-32 ought not to obscure the main purpose of the passage. For here also Christ is set forth as an example, this time to husbands, His love to the church being the pattern set before them to imitate in self-sacrificing love for their wives. The end in view is not mere doctrine, but behaviour.

Instances such as this might be multiplied. It is our purpose, however, to consider rather the parables, types and historical incidents of the Scripture, used as illustrations of spiritual truth. We may note at the outset that, especially in the case of the types and parables, it is not always easy to draw a distinction between application and interpretation. In type and parable, particularly, it is evident that the picture is of something definite, and so interpretation and application will blend to some extent, since the student is here also seeking to ascertain what was in the mind of the Teacher. But the principles which govern procedure will be similar, and so we thus group them together.

1. *It may be taken as a basic principle that the types and historical incidents do not teach doctrine.* This is a point not sufficiently realized. The function of these portions of Scripture is to illustrate truth presented elsewhere. The Bible is God's great sermon to man and, like the excellent sermon it is, it has its illustrations as well as its teaching.

Failure to make this distinction has led to not a little extravagance and confusion. Someone reads the story of the feeding of the five thousand, and evolves some wonderful theory as to the meaning of the fact that *twelve* basketsfull were picked up afterwards—a theory having no foundation whatever, except in an unusually vivid imagination—and then propounds this theory as unquestionable fact.

The question is asked in a Bible reading, "What does it *mean* when it says that the woman with the issue of blood was healed when she touched the hem of the Lord's garment?" Obviously the answer should be, "It means just what it says!" Surely it is taking most undue liberty when the leader responds: "It means power acting through circumstances" (whatever that means)!

A brother gives a series of addresses on the gates of the wall of Nehemiah. The name of each gate suggests to the speaker a rather intricate illustration of certain aspects of truth and experience. One man comments: "I had no idea the Scripture had so much to say about gates!" The obvious answer is that it hasn't! A woman says during the course of the meetings: "Isn't it wonderful that there is all that *teaching* in those Scriptures?" Again the answer ought to be evident—that teaching isn't there at all! What the speaker was doing was to use the names of the gates and the facts of history as allegorical pegs on which to hang teaching *gathered elsewhere.*

We may not all feel free to go to the same length of allegorization, but we may all use Scriptures in an allegorical manner. But we need to keep in mind the distinction between such application of Scripture, and what the passages actually teach in themselves. For an interpretation, we read passages to deduce their doctrinal content; in application, we read them as pictures of teaching found in other places.

Here again is a man who adduces the fact that the sons of Kohath, having the service of the sanctuary, were not allowed wagons to help them in the bearing of the holy things; whereas the sons of Gershon and the sons of Merari were given them (Numbers 7: 7-9). He seeks to "prove" by this that, since the assembly has "the service of the sanctuary," it is out of order to use a musical instrument in its services. But what has he done? He has merely *assumed* the wrongness of the use of a musical instrument, apart from any plain prohibition of Scripture, and then brought forward the passage referred to as an *illustration* of the doctrine whose truth he has taken for

granted. Utterly apart from the question of the rightness
or wrongness of the instrument, the application of the
passage is merely an application, and so has no authority
to decide the question. The principle of appeal is a wrong
one. On the same principle one might with equal justice
"prove" that it is wrong for the assembly to have a meet-
ing-hall, or to use chairs, or to have a heating plant, or
anything else with which the speaker did not happen to
agree.

There is evident, then, this first necessary principle of
the application of Scripture: it must be based upon and
be in accord with what the Word plainly teaches. This
is perfectly logical. If we are free to bring up applications
or arbitrary allegorizations of Scripture as proof of doctrines found elsewhere we have no secure ground what-
so ever.

2. *The second thing to note is that the Old Testament
does not present New Testament truth.* This truth is, according to the Scriptures themselves, a later revelation.
The truth of the gospel was, indeed, foreshadowed and
typified (Romans 3:21), and grace has been the principle
of salvation in all ages (Romans 4:1, 16). But only in the
New Testament is the gospel clearly revealed in all its
fulness, in the ground, means and result of salvation (Romans 16:25; II Timothy 1:19). As to the church, it is
nowhere in view in the Old Testament. It was not made
known in other ages (Ephesians 3:5). The binding together of Jew and Gentile as one body in Christ, all commonly partakers of one eternal life, is a purely New
Testament doctrine. Finally, the Old Testament has nothing to say concerning New Testament procedure. That
procedure is one consequent upon the presence of the
Holy Spirit, the existence of the church, and the understanding of the now fully-revealed gospel. The New

Testament is the dispensation of the Spirit; the Old is outstandingly that of the Law (see Galatians).

Now while this is true, we ought to avoid the extravagance of saying that "You can't preach the gospel from the Old Testament." That certainly is a complete misunderstanding of the facts. Granted that the gospel is not there fully revealed; but he is a poor student who cannot see the *foreshadowing* of it, nor find *pictures* of it there. God had that gospel in mind then, and all His working was to prepare men for its reception. It was no afterthought with Him.

However, it is a necessary conclusion that no Old Testament type or incident may teach gosepl truth where the New is silent. One sect, for instance, would have us believe that the two goats of Leviticus 16 represent, the one Christ, and the other Satan; and that Satan is to be the final sin-bearer, taking upon himself the sins of believers and bearing them off into oblivion. The basic fallacy of such an idea is seen in that the revelation of the gospel in the New Testament contains *not the slightest hint of it*. The Old Testament can only illustrate what the New clearly teaches where the gospel is concerned.

Then, as concerns Church truth, we ought to avoid extravagance which refuses to find, in the Old Testament, any *illustrations* of the relationship now existing between Christ and His people. True, the Old Testament contains no *teaching* concerning the church; but it has many beautiful pictures, and we are quite justified in using them as illustrations, always remembering that they are illustrative only, not doctrinal. Naturally, the same caution should maintain that the application of any such figures must be in strictest accord with the teaching of the New Testament, where we find the truth of the Church first and fully revealed.

As to New Testament procedure, the same principle must apply. That is to say, no Old Testament incident may support a practice intended for the New Testament economy.

The writer was astounded some time ago when he heard of an attempt to justify the practice of baptism of infants by an appeal to the fact that Moses was drawn out of the water! Another appeal was to I Corinthians 10:1, 2: "they were all baptized unto Moses." The claim was made that of course the "all" included children as well as adults! Such an appeal embodies a two-fold error. In the first place, the citation indicates Paul's application of an Old Testament incident as an illustration, not of the mode of baptism, but rather of the peril inherent in any compromise with idolatry (vs. 6-12). Apart altogether from the rightness or wrongness of the practice in question, such an appeal to an application of an Old Testament incident is again merely the adduction of an illustration—it is no evidence at all. The only admissible evidence in support of the practice would be the clear teaching of the New Testament scriptures themselves. Not only so, but those who so quote the application press the illustration out of its true measure. It is evident that the presence of children had no bearing on what was in the apostle's mind. Indeed, someone has said: "There were also sheep and oxen there, but we would not infer from that that our cattle should be baptized!"

3. Third, *the literal reality of an incident must always be kept in mind.* We must not make the mistake which has sometimes been made with regard to the Scriptures: of looking on them as if they were nothing more than an allegory. It should ever be clearly emphasized that these incidents actually happened just as they are recorded, and that our allegorizations are but the use of actual incidents as pictures or illustrations. Otherwise, a sense of un-

reality concerning the histories of Scripture may be
produced in the mind, which will easily contribute to the
confusion to which we have already referred.

4. Fourth, *it should be remembered that one application of a passage is not the only one possible.* The Psalms,
for example, may have many applications. First, there
is the Psalmist's own personal experience in his dealings
with God—experience often forgotten by us in our desire
to make other applications. Then there is the application
to the spiritual experiences of believers at the present
time. It is also evident that there is a strong prophetic
element in the Psalms. They go far beyond the Psalmist's
actual experiences, and foreshadow those of our Lord
Jesus Christ Himself, as well as the trial, regathering and
final blessing of Israel. Thus, in the illustrative use of a
figure or incident of Scripture, another may see an application quite different from the one which has impressed
itself upon my mind, and both applications will be equally
legitimate if they fulfill the purpose of illustrating the
clear teaching of the word of God.

5. Fifth, *it is not necessary to make every detail of a
type or parable mean something.* As it has been expressed: "Don't try to make a parable 'run on all fours!' "
Much of the traditional interpretation of the Lord's parables, for example, should be carefully weighed, because
of the tendency to try to make every detail stand for
something. As in the case of any illustration, the point
may center in one of two things in the parable, and the
rest may be merely the apparatus necessary to bring the
point into focus. How some have strained to make, say,
the ass, the twopence and the innkeeper of the parable of
the good Samaritan each mean something! Some such
expositions are most ingenious and most unconvincing!
The whole point of the parable is to show who is our

"neighbour" whom we are to love: our worst enemy if he be in need (Luke 10:37).

Sometime ago there appeared, in a Christian magazine, a long-drawn-out finely-detailed "exposition" of the parable of the ten virgins of Matthew 25. Much was made of the statement of the five foolish virgins (as in R. V.) that their lamps were "going out." At great length the writer laboured to prove the falling-away doctrine from this parable. The oil was the Holy Spirit. Since the virgins had had oil, which was now failing them, "the teaching" was evidently that a believer might have the Spirit (be saved) and still be finally rejected. But the whole point of the parable is simply that, when the Lord returns, He will find some professing believers prepared for His return and some unprepared. If that purpose of the parable be remembered, and if it be also remembered that the event used to illustrate the point was a common sight in the land of Palestine, one need not labour to stress some "meaning" for the "oil," for each one of the other details, remembering that these are but the apparatus of the illustration.

The student will save himself much unnecessary confusion and bewilderment by noting the general purpose of the parable, and the details which minister to that purpose and illustrate the teaching of Scripture. You are not required to make every smallest detail represent something, or you may get yourself into very deep water if you attempt this task!

6.   Sixth, *differing figures of the same object are not necessarily antagonistic.* This is another of those things which ought to be self-evident; but when it comes to the application of Scripture, it is astonishing how often common-sense is left on the shelf! I once heard a man contend that the Church could not be "the bride of Christ," because in Ephesians 2 it is called "one man," and a man

cannot be a bride! This is a conceit of which the Scripture itself seems strangely unaware, seeing that the "Lion of the tribe of Judah" appears as "a Lamb having been slain" (Rev. 5:5, 6), to give one instance of many.

Figures are but illustrations and differing figures may be used to represent different aspects of the same thing. That is why we have the two goats of Leviticus 16; one representing Christ in His atoning death; the other Christ, as bearing away sin forever from before the face of God—two aspects of the one work of Calvary. One alone was insufficient to show both. And so with the many sacrifices of the law. Many figures were needed, all referring to the same great work, for no one figure was in itself sufficient to illustrate that work in all its fulness.

Here we must let the matter rest. May the great Interpreter Himself give us understanding in all things, and impart to us the balance and wisdom we need!